(41)

blic Policy
and
Provincial
Politics

McGraw-Hill Series in Canadian Politics
Paul W. Fox, General Editor

POLITICS: CANADA, 4th Ed. Paul W. Fox
CANADIAN FOREIGN POLICY D.C. Thomson & R.F. Swanson
THE CONSTITUTIONAL PROCESS IN CANADA, 2nd Ed.
 R.I. Cheffins & R.N. Tucker
POLITICAL PARTY FINANCING IN CANADA K.Z. Paltiel
NATIONALISM IN CANADA P. Russell
POLITICAL PARTIES AND IDEOLOGIES IN CANADA
 W. Christian & C. Campbell
CANADA: A SOCIO-POLITICAL REPORT R. Manzer
PRESSURE GROUP BEHAVIOUR IN CANADIAN POLITICS
 A. Paul Pross
GOVERNMENT IN CANADA T.A. Hockin
CANADA IN QUESTION: FEDERALISM IN THE SEVENTIES,
 2nd Ed. D.V. Smiley
POLITICAL PARTIES IN CANADA C. Winn & J. McMenemy
CANADIAN POLITICS: EXERCISES IN ANALYSIS J. Jenson &
 B. Tomlin
LOCAL GOVERNMENT IN CANADA C.R. Tindal & S.N. Tindal
PUBLIC POLICY AND PROVINCIAL POLITICS M.A. Chandler &
 W.M. Chandler

Forthcoming
CANADIAN FOREIGN POLICY M.J. Tucker

Public Policy and Provincial Politics

Marsha A. Chandler
Department of Political Science
Erindale College
University of Toronto

William M. Chandler
Department of Political Science
McMaster University

McGraw-Hill Ryerson Limited

Toronto   Montreal   New York   St. Louis   San Francisco
Auckland   Beirut   Bogotá   Düsseldorf   Johannesburg
Lisbon   London   Lucerne   Madrid   Mexico   New Delhi   Panama
Paris   San Juan   São Paulo   Singapore   Sydney   Tokyo

Public Policy and Provincial Politics

0-07-082637-4

2 3 4 5 6 7 8 9 10   JD   8 7 6 5 4 3 2 1

Printed and bound in Canada

Canadian Cataloguing in Publication Data

Chandler, Marsha A., date
Public policy and provincial politics

(McGraw-Hill series in Canadian politics)

Bibliography: p.
Includes index.

ISBN 0-07-082637-4 pa.

1. Provincial governments — Canada.* 2. Policy
sciences. I. Chandler, William M., date.
II. Title.

JL198.C48   320.9'71   C79-094192-9

Contents

Foreword   vi

Preface   ix

CHAPTER 1   Introduction: the Analysis of Provincial Policy-Making   1

CHAPTER 2   The Social and Economic Environment of Provincial Public Policy   17

CHAPTER 3   Political Forces in the Provinces   38

CHAPTER 4   Structures of Policy-Making   97

CHAPTER 5   The Federal System   149

CHAPTER 6   Social Development Policies   178

CHAPTER 7   Resource Development Policies   253

CHAPTER 8   Perspectives on Provincial Policy   291

BIBLIOGRAPHY   299

INDEX   313

Foreword

Two of the areas of Canadian politics which hitherto have been neglected and are now attracting much interest are public policy and provincial government.

The great advantage of this book by Professors Marsha and William Chandler is that it brings these two domains together. The first section comprising five chapters sets the scene very clearly, describing the backdrop and structures of the ten provincial governments in Canada. The second section, composed of three chapters, then discusses the major public policies that these governments pursue.

The book therefore can be used as a unit, as a basic text, for instance, in a course focussing on provincial politics, or its two sections can be utilized separately, the first part in a course dealing with Canadian government and the second in a course concentrating on public policies.

Whatever the choice, the book has another advantage. Since it approaches every topic from the provincial perspective, it helps to right the long-standing imbalance in the study of Canadian government which has come about from the original predilection to concentrate on the federal government in Ottawa.

It is scarcely necessary to remark that paying attention to provincial governments in Canada is long overdue. Not only are the provincial governments much closer to most citizens because of their propinquity and the subjects they deal with — personal matters such as education, health, welfare, local transportation, and municipal government — but as all political science students well know, provincial governments and their creatures, the municipalities, now spend far more of the taxpayers' money than the federal government does. The major increase in recent years in the percentage of the gross national product which is spent by Canadian governments is attributable to the huge growth in provincial expenditures. In the past fifty years total spending by all Canadian governments has risen from about 15 per cent of the G.N.P. to more than 40 per cent. But while Ottawa's share of the total is now only slightly more than it was half a century ago, the provinces' proportion has more than quadrupled. Today the provinces spend about 40 cents of every tax dollar, the municipalities about 20 cents, and the federal government about 40 cents.

It is clear that the provincial governments and their municipal wards are no longer the "junior" governments in the federal system. They are the big spenders, and will continue to be for some time. They are also the big employers. In 1976 the number of provincial employees surpassed the number of federal employees and the former figure did not include municipal workers who were almost as numerous. For all these reasons a book dealing with provincial governments, and especially with their costly public policies, is timely and welcome.

Another virtue of the Chandlers' book is that it is comparative in its approach. Having done their homework thoroughly by digging into the voluminous literature and data available, the authors are able to utilize examples and evidence from all of the provinces. Although they are residents of Ontario, their work is synoptic rather than parochial. The book can be read with profit in any province in Canada.

The authors' mastery of their material is particularly evident in the first part of their book in which they describe the ingredients of provincial politics. They review the constraints and dynamics of policy changes by analyzing the social and economic environments of the provinces, the political forces at work within them, the provincial institutional structures, and the federal system itself.

Although it is risky to rate chapters in a book since the choice may reflect only personal interest, I found Chapter Three to be particularly impressive. In this chapter the authors discuss the impact of provincial parties and political systems, pressure groups, and political ideas upon the determination of public policies. Drawing together the findings from the extensive literature that now exists on these subjects, the Chandlers explain the differences in individual parties from province to province, the distinctive attitudinal patterns which prevail within the ten provinces, the kinds of party systems which are evinced, and the particular party system that characterizes each province. Altogether, I think their account is the most thorough comparison of the provincial party scenes that I have encountered. Much the same can be said of their chapter on provincial cabinets, legislatures, civil services, and administrative policy processes.

When they reach the second part of their book, the Chandlers concentrate on the major provincial public policies, dividing them into social development issues having to do with welfare, health, and education, and resource development policies dealing with natural resources, energy, agriculture, and transportation. In each case they describe the origins and development of the policy in the relevant provinces. Their work is replete with tables, graphs, and lengthy bibliographies. Every chapter is pulled together neatly with a summary or conclusion.

Their final chapter closes the circle, taking us back to the first portion of the book to assess the extent to which the factors described there affected the determination of public policies in the provinces. Their conclusions are several and too lengthy to be repeated here. The essence of them is that "there has been no single path of policy evolution and no common policy-making process." Since the provinces will continue to be key policy-makers in the future and therefore will become even more enmeshed in federal policy-making, it will be necessary for the two sets of government to engage in "project disentanglement." It also will be essential, the authors add, to devote more research and publications to provincial public policies.

The Chandlers have given us a good start in this new direction.

Erindale College
University of Toronto   Paul Fox,
April 2, 1979.   General Editor.

Preface

Although Canadian political studies have greatly expanded in the past few years, there remain important gaps in our knowledge of the Canadian political process. Provincial politics and public policy analysis, in particular, are two areas of persisting neglect. This text is intended as a first step towards the comparative analysis of public policy at the provincial level.

Until recently, understanding of provincial public policy has depended almost entirely on a wide variety of case studies. Many of these works, although excellent individual studies, have remained isolated pieces of research on an otherwise unexplored terrain. As a result, it has been difficult for students of provincial politics to generalize about policy at the provincial level. This work attempts to draw together many strands of information in order to facilitate a broader perspective on provincial politics and public policy.

In this preliminary effort to develop dimensions of provincial comparison, many significant issues have been left untouched. By opting for a broad comparison of social and resource policies, we have explicitly not attempted to treat every policy field. The politics of provincial-municipal relations, labour, and justice represent some of the more important provincial policy issue areas that have been excluded in our survey and that must await future research. As we have pursued provincial comparisons both in terms of policy patterns and policy process, it has become clear that much remains unknown about numerous aspects of provincial politics. It is perhaps inevitable that any exploratory study raises more questions than it answers, but to the extent that this study serves to stimulate further research and analysis, our original objectives will be achieved.

Numerous colleagues have provided invaluable criticism and encouragement. Among those who deserve special thanks are Michael Atkinson, George Breckenridge, William Coleman, Henry Jacek, Susan McCorquodale, Ingunn Means, Michael Stein, David Vogler, and Graham White.

We particularly want to express our gratitude to G. Bruce Doern and to Richard Simeon for their very helpful comments, many of which we have incorporated in the text. The editor of the series, Paul Fox, has provided us with guidance and advice throughout the project. Finally, we would like to thank Marlene Moore, without whose patience, competence, and good spirits we would never have completed our work. For whatever errors and omissions this book may contain, we acknowledge full responsibility.

for Alice

Chapter 1

Introduction: The Analysis of Provincial Policy-Making

The daily life of every Canadian is profoundly influenced by the actions of provincial governments. Each year provincial governments, through legislation, regulatory decisions and administrative implementation, take action covering an extraordinary scope of public concerns. These include school reorganization, hospital construction, social assistance to unemployables, road construction and maintenance, police protection, safety regulations, personal income, corporate income, gasoline, alcohol, and sales taxes. Some of these responsibilities are entirely within the jurisdiction of provincial authorities. Others are shared with Ottawa or delegated to municipal authorities. Almost every aspect of domestic policy-making involves the provinces to a significant extent. Given such breadth, it is probably not surprising to find that Canadians believe provincial governments are especially crucial public authorities. Results from the 1974 election survey show that, when asked how important levels of government are thought to be, equal numbers of Canadians rate the provinces and the federal government as most important—despite the fact that there is greater awareness of, and media exposure to, federal politics.[1]

There is in fact no dispute, either constitutionally or in terms of popular beliefs, over the critical place of the provinces. Yet until recently there has been surprisingly little attention paid to provincial politics. This situation is now changing, but there still remains little systematic exploration of provincial public policy. The central purposes of this book are to describe patterns of provincial policy and to investigate those conditions and forces which help to shape policy-making. The approach is an essentially comparative one in which there is a concern for identifying both common patterns and unique aspects of provincial politics and performance.

1

STUDYING PUBLIC POLICY

The answer to "What do governments do?" is neither simple nor obvious. Before we can consider patterns of policy development or determinants of policy we must first be able to identify those actions we call public policy.[2] The notion of "public" can refer to the activities of governmental authorities or to activities that affect the public. It certainly cannot be denied that some non-public actions, that is, those taken by private firms or individuals, can have a collective or public influence over many other people's lives.[3] We believe, however, it is most useful, given the goal of understanding provincial policy-making, to define "public" in the more general first sense of actions taken by those occupying positions of official decision-making authority.

The second definitional question is "What do we mean by policy?" The term is commonly used in numerous ways. Sometimes it refers to goals or objectives which are hoped for but not yet achieved. Think, for example, of governments which claim equal opportunity for all citizens, energy self-sufficiency, or full employment as their policies. To conceive of a policy as some objective or goal to be achieved would lead us to identify policies by what governments say they do or what they claim to be desired states of affairs. We are, however, most fundamentally interested in the actions of governments rather than in their intentions. Thus, our emphasis in the definition of policy is on actions taken and decisions carried out.

On other occasions policy has been used to mean individual decisions, as, for example, when Ontario reduced its speed limit to 100 kilometres, when Saskatchewan bought the Duval Potash Company, or when Quebec took over the construction of the Olympic stadium. In these instances the term policy is used too narrowly. Since our goal is to describe in a systematic way what it is that provincial governments do and further to assess how one province acts in comparison with another, we need a meaning for policy that will permit us to go beyond isolated and particular instances of government activity. Rarely will a single action or decision by some public authority constitute a policy by itself. The term public policy is better applied to a cluster of related activity organized around some general purpose.[4] One might, therefore, speak of health, housing, or energy policy. In each case, the reference is to those sets of governmental activities directed toward the resolution of a societal problem area.

Policies are then the outputs or products of a political system and can be thought of as patterns of goal-oriented actions. It is, however, essential to recognize the underlying complexity of this view of policy. In many instances several distinct policy actions are taken towards one common end. If the objective is, for example, improved standards of health care, means to achieve this goal might include hospital construction and expansion of the number of hospital beds, the development of public health facilities and preventive medicine programmes, or the expansion of medical education facilities and recruitment mechanisms.

Alternatively, a single output can be directed toward several goals. In some cases goals may be complementary. Tax incentives for home ownership may assist individuals in solving their housing needs while at the same time providing a stimulus for the construction industry. In other instances, different authorities may hold divergent goals. The difficulty which can result from this is demonstrated in the case of the Technical and Vocational Training Act. The government of Ontario defined the programme as part of its education policy, while the federal government viewed it in terms of manpower and the economy.[5]

POLICY SUBSTANCE

Although there are numerous ways to identify and categorize government outputs, traditional substantive categories are still the most widely used means of organizing policies.[6] In provincial politics the policy fields of health, welfare, education, transportation and communication, and natural resources account for the bulk of provincial expenditures and cover much of the range of provincial outputs. Expenditures and regulations provide indicators of two principal forms of government activity. Taken together, they furnish a general image of public activity. Since most of what governments do costs money, expenditures—the budgetary allocations for provincial programmes— provide a common yardstick for comparing policy activities. Spending figures offer one means for estimating the relative importance among policy fields. Tracing expenditures over time can reveal policy trends and changes in the priorities of policy-makers.

However, all policy activity is not represented by public spending. Much of the substance of policy involves general rules, constraints and guidelines. This facet of policy is regulation.[7] Sometimes regulations are stated in legislative bills or by orders-in-council. In other instances the power to regulate is delegated to departmental civil servants or quasi-independent boards and agencies. A few examples indicate the wide variety of concerns which may fall within provincial regulations. Quebec's Official Language Act (Bill 101) provides rules governing the use of French and English in commerce and all public functions. Ontario's Municipal Board regulates many activities of local governments including borrowing, land use, and public construction. British Columbia has restrictions on non-refillable beverage containers. Prince Edward Island restricts the amount of land that may be owned by non-residents. Municipal affairs, liquor control, and workmen's compensation are among the regulatory concerns common to all provinces.

Regulatory decisions do not directly allocate funds, nor do they necessarily cost government a great deal. They often, however, indirectly entail very significant costs or benefits for those individuals or groups affected by them. But more generally they establish rules under which interests compete for benefits. Some of the on-going issues in health care policy illustrate the utility of expenditures and regulations as policy indicators. Expenditures demonstrate the scope and growth of health policy. Prior to the late 1940s health was not a major public issue, but was primarily a matter of private and local interest. In contrast, health costs in the 1970s account for twenty-five cents of every dollar spent by the provinces. The large claim on the public sector makes health policy a significant issue in every province and in federal-provincial relations. But costs are not the only prominent health issues. Regulations within each of the shared-cost programmes are also a source of disagreement.[8] A major criticism of the Hospital and Diagnostic Services Act has been that the regulations which stipulate the qualifications for the funding of health services and facilities discourage both the use of less expensive, non-hospital, non-acute treatment alternatives and the provision of care by less expensive medical personnel. Other regulatory issues involve the administration of health care and delivery systems and the degree of public participation in health policy-making.[9]

The emphasis on substantive categories as a basis for policy comparisons reflects our principal concern for the scope of provincial policy. This preference is a function of our general objectives and does not imply any judgement that issues of policy means or distributional effects are any less significant.[10] Nor is it to suggest that these other dimensions are of no use given our objectives. Certainly the *how* of policy implementation is a central concern for any study of the institutions of policy-making. Similarly, the nature of policy impacts has an influence on the process and participants. In these regards, both are directly relevant to this work. We recognize, however, that both of these themes are so complex and so little understood—especially in the context of provincial regimes—that their full analysis must await future research.

CONSTRAINTS AND DYNAMICS OF POLICY CHANGE

Any comparison of policy will remain incomplete without consideration of the forces that shape policy outputs. Understanding depends not only on describing policy substance, but also on explaining its determinants. There exists, however, no one generally accepted theoretical model to explain policy development and to account for variations in policy across provinces. Instead, what we have is a set of factors which include the socio-economic environment, provincial political forces, federal-provincial relations, and provincial institutions. Taken together, these factors constitute "a framework which greatly restricts the alternatives [policy-makers] consider and the range of innovations they make. This framework, or set of constraints and opportunities, defines a set of problems considered to be important, a set of acceptable solutions or policy responses, a set of procedures and rules by which they will be considered."[12]

Governments as they take office are confronted with a set of laws, customs and procedures which can, at most, be modified but rarely transformed or destroyed.* They are faced with an entrenched civil service with its own values, professional standards and monopoly on administrative procedure. Bureaucracies, by their nature, tend to routinize policy initiatives and may, as Rose has noted, also create "an important inertia force maintaining policy commitments" with the consequence that a government "may add to its range of activities, but it cannot contract them".[13]

The persistence of on-going programmes and priorities is, in part, a function of the established interests of politically significant organizations (business, labour or farmers, for example) or of certain economic, social or political elites. Finally, virtually all governments, no matter what their preferred goals may be, are saddled with the problem of limited resources. All policy actions cost something—money, manpower or time—and, therefore, put strains on public revenues, systems of taxation or physical resources. Federal transfers, although an additional resource for provincial governments, have often brought with them unwelcomed constraints and responsibilities. The reluctance of the provinces to adopt universal medical insurance in the 1960s was a function of this trade-off.

---

*As the Parti Québécois government elected in 1976 illustrates, some may have as part of their policy objectives the transformation of constitutional ground rules and/or policy agendas.

Inevitably, some governments will have greater policy flexibility than others because they can operate from a stronger resource and tax base. But sooner or later all face the dilemma of limited resources. In short, policy-makers operate in a web of immediate and complex constraints on what they can do. This does not mean that there is no freedom of movement. If such constraints formed the only conditions shaping government action, policy patterns would tend to be static and little variation would be noticed. We know that this is not the case. Basic policy change is evident whether we think of the long-term evolution of various social services, or the immediate responses to the energy crisis. Within any policy area, and for any unit of decision-making, there are times of rapid, even radical, change. Think, for example, of the post-1960 era in Quebec or the post-war years in Saskatchewan. At other times policy innovation may be minimal and governments may seem oriented to consolidation or even retrenchment. The return to power of Social Credit in British Columbia (1975) and the Tories in Manitoba (1977) might both be described as efforts at consolidation following eras of NDP innovation. The other half of policy explanation must seek to explain why patterns of policy are not immutable.

Dynamics refers to the impulse or generating power whch sets a body in motion. In the context of political decision-making, it expresses the range of forces which can overcome the inertia of constraints.[14] Since in politics we are dealing not with physical forces but with human actors, the problem is one of motivation, which may range from an expectation of personal or collective gain or loss to some ideological, emotional value commitment or belief. We may then ask "What kinds of factors have this dynamic impact on governmental decisions?"

Changes in the material environment can have two divergent but equally dynamic effects. On the one hand, governments, like private firms and individuals, must have certain means—public revenues and manpower—which are extracted via taxation, public ownership, regulation or other means from existing resource bases. Alberta's public revenues based on oil royalties and taxes both free it from the constraint of provincial sales taxes and endow it with an enormous material wealth which is translatable into new policy programmes. The government of Alberta has a freedom for manoeuvre and a capacity for policy impact not realized in any other province. Where the resource base is limited, as it is in most of the Altantic region, policy-makers are more likely to be severely limited in their policy options and in their likely effect. Instead of a freedom to choose new policy initiatives, governments may often be forced into actions they would prefer not to take. This suggests the other side of policy dynamics based on material conditions. Where the threat of deprivation occurs (whether through unemployment, inflation, a lack of industrial growth, deflated farm prices or some other cause), popular demands are likely to be imposed on governments for public action to mitigate such threats. Since governments ultimately depend on popular support, the motivation for policy change is clear. In this case environmental factors imply a negative or threatening dynamic for governments compared to the positive one of "free-floating" public richesse, but in either situation there is an impetus for policy change. In the same way characteristics of the social structure—for example, material and status disparities built into the class system—may provide similar stimuli for policy change. Whatever the specific reason for demands requiring government response, this basic relationship between the rulers and the ruled defines the operating premise of responsible government. Democratic procedures are designed to allow for the possibility of public influence over policy-making. Political parties, elections and pressure groups may be seen as mediators in this relationship. They constitute, by virtue of this function, a second set of policy determinants having both constraining and dynamic potential for policy change.

Parties and elections are often seen as instruments for the principle of majority rule. We know, of course, that this is a far too simple and misleading model of policy influence. In the first place, public opinion is rarely consistent and unambiguous in its preferences. Voters are often poorly informed on major policy issues. Those who are well informed are often knowledgeable only about issues of immediate concern to them. Nor is it always the case that parties present voters with distinct policy alternatives. Parties typically seek to maximize votes to win a parliamentary majority. They can do this best by offending no one while appealing to as many as possible. Thus, moderation, brokerage between conflicting views, and fuzziness on sensitive issues is often good strategy. Finally, electoral systems may limit the likelihood that electoral results will mirror majority opinions.[15]

For all these reasons, shifts in popular policy preference are likely to have only muted effects on policy change. Parties and elections must be seen not only as translators of public opinion, but also as filters, even insulators, acting in part as constraints, against governmental responsiveness. None of this suggests, however, as is often alleged, that parties and elections are of no importance in understanding what governments do. It is to propose that the relationship between parties (either as spokesmen for ideological positions or as brokers among competing interests and opinions) and policy through competitive elections is far more complex than an idealistic view of democracy would lead us to believe.

The pluralist view of interest groups places them in a complementary position to parties as the representative of selected issue publics in the policy process. There is considerable evidence from both Canadian and comparative political research to indicate that pluralism, like majority rule, is an inaccurate model of the role of groups in policy formation. Many pressure groups enjoy privileged influence relationships in which close ties between them and state agencies operate within a patron-client relationship of elite accommodation. But, regardless of whether pluralism, elitism or some form of corporatism best describes the activities and influence of pressure groups, there is every reason to see these groups as pervasive factors—both as constraints and dynamics—in policy change.

Crucial to the study of organized interests are their links to the bureaucracy of government. Although, as noted earlier, the weight of bureaucratic impact can be argued to be heavily on the side of policy constraints, it would be erroneous to presume that bureaucratic structures have no dynamic effects. Bureaucracies represent more than red tape; they also signify the power of implementation, the importance of expertise and the regular access of powerful interests.

Finally, one can ask whether, in general, political institutions can be seen as dynamic factors in policy. Since institutions formalize the "rules of the game", their basic effect is one of structuring the modes of access, influence and conflict resolution. These determine who participates and how they participate in the policy process. But no institution or arena of decision-making is neutral.[16] Each one favours some participants and disadvantages others. Because of this, changes in institutions may signify changes in the influence relationships among policy participants and, therefore, represent a dynamic for policy change.

PROVINCE-BUILDING

Since Confederation two of the most important developments in provincial politics are the expanded scope of public policy and the differentiation and refinement of policy-making structures. The emergence of the provinces as mature and complex institutions having the strengthened "capacity to govern in the interests of regional communities"[17] is what we mean by province-building. The provinces have been significant elements in the expanded role of the state as they have come to represent an increasingly large share of total government activity. The development of provincial institutions is linked to the vast increase in the size and scope of the public sector.[18] These changes are reflected in the growth of provincial expenditures, revenues, regulatory functions and the public service. Changes in federal-provincial relations also mirror this new provincial significance.

Table 1.1: Public Expenditures, Selected Years*

	EXPENDITURES AS PERCENTAGE OF GROSS NATIONAL PRODUCT		EXPENDITURE SHARES BY LEVEL OF GOVERNMENT		
	Total Government	Provincial**	Municipal	Provincial	Federal
1926	15.7	3.2	42.0	20.2	37.8
1950	22.1	5.7	22.1	26.0	51.9
1960	29.7	7.3	24.6	24.7	50.8
1970	36.4	13.2	25.8	35.7	38.1
1976	41.5	15.0	21.0	37.3	39.7

Source: Statistics Canada, *National Income and Expenditure Accounts*, 1926-1974 and 1976, DBS
    13-531, 13-201
*Ten-year intervals are presented to demonstrate the evolution of expenditure patterns primarily in
the post-war era. The year 1976 brings this information up to date. The figures for 1926, the earliest
year for which comparable data are available, provide a longer perspective on these developments.
Expenditures for each level include transfers *received* from other governments and excludes
payments to other levels.
**Provincial Expenditures include payments to hospitals.

Expenditures

The data in Table 1.1 illustrate the magnitude of the growth of provincial
expenditures. Over the last fifty years the provinces have not only
shared in the general expansion of public budgets, they have also
increased their share of government spending. While the total public
share of GNP has more than doubled, the provincial share has increased
by more than four times. The provinces now allocate close to forty cents
of every government dollar, and if spending of municipalities, which are
subordinate to provincial authority, is added to this, the figure is almost
sixty cents. The ten provincial governments do not all spend equal
amounts on their residents. In 1974 the average expenditure per capita
was $1237. It ranged from a high of $1453 spent by Newfoundland to
$1117 per capita spent by Nova Scotia.[19]

   Expenditures on goods and services and transfers to individuals are
the principal elements of public spending. The impact of government on
the economy is reflected in spending on goods and services. Transfers,
on the other hand, represent changes in the distribution of income.[20] The
increased importance of the provinces is all the more striking when
expenditures for goods and services are isolated from the rest of the
budget. Provincial governments now account for almost 43% of total
public expenditures on goods and services. In 1955 their share was only
18.6%. The proportion spent on transfers remains roughly the same
(22.6% in 1955 and 29.4% in 1975). Ottawa still provides over 2/3 of the
transfers to individuals.[21]

Table 1.2: Public Revenues, Selected Years

	REVENUES AS PERCENTAGE OF GROSS NATIONAL PRODUCT		REVENUE SHARES BY LEVEL OF GOVERNMENT		
	Total Government	Provincial*	Municipal	Provincial	Federal
1926	16.8	3.4	39.0	20.4	44.9
1950	25.1	6.6	17.7	26.4	65.2
1960	27.9	8.7	24.2	31.0	60.8
1970	37.3	16.2	23.9	43.5	48.6
1976	38.7	18.0	21.0	46.5	48.8

Source: *Canadian Tax Foundation*, The National Finances, 1977-78, Tables 2-7, 2-8.
*Includes transfers from other governments.
**The sum of percentages for each year exceeds one hundred because transfers are included in the municipal and provincial figures.

Revenues

The changing role of the provinces is also reflected in provincial revenues and in the continuing political struggle over the distribution of revenue sources between federal and provincial governments. In the post-war era, the provincial portion of total government revenues has steadily increased while Ottawa's revenue share has undergone a gradual decline. (See Table 1.2.) In 1976, almost forty-seven cents of every dollar collected by all three levels of government went into provincial coffers. As in the case of expenditures there is a wide range among the provinces in the revenue collected per capita.[22] In 1974, the average was $1,112. Prince Edward Island led all other provinces, raising $1,357 per capita, while Saskatchewan matched its low expenditure figure with $991 per capita revenue.[23]

Regulatory Functions

Regulations are rules that limit behaviour. Economic regulations, which represent rules for the production and allocation of goods and services, constitute an important part of the growth of provincial government since 1945. The impetus for expanded regulatory action has two sources. On the one hand, economic interests have often been anxious to gain protection and assistance through the legitimacy of a public agency. On the other hand, a growing public consciousness of the sometimes drastic social consequences of unrestrained enterprise in the name of private profits has generated popular demands for public constraints on many of these same economic interests.

An additional element in the increased regulatory concerns of the provinces comes from provincial interest in participating in some spheres of federal regulatory policy. Especially in the areas of transportation and agriculture, the provinces have sought a voice in national policy-making through informal consultation as well as more formal mechanisms for representation.

Personnel

Since World War II, Canada has experienced rapid population growth. As Hodgetts and Dwivedi have noted, such an increase by itself would account for an expansion in the public bureaucracy even if services and programmes had not grown.[24] They further observe that "Growing industrialization and urbanization have brought governments into other economic arenas which in earlier *laissez-faire* days were . . . regarded as primarily private".[25] Thus, the public sector, in response to changing social and economic circumstances, has become involved in a much wider scope of responsibility. Increasing government services have naturally created the need for a larger corps of civil servants. These increases in the public service have taken place primarily at the provincial and municipal levels. From 1946 to 1971, total provincial civil service employment has increased by over 400%, whereas the federal civil service has grown by only 79% (or only in direct proportion to total population growth).[26] The quality of the provincial public service has also increased. Much of the expertise required for critical government functions is now found at the provincial level.

Intergovernmental Relations

A final indication of the increased import of the provinces is the nature of federal-provincial interaction. There have been profound changes in relations between officials, both elected and appointed, of the two levels of government.[27] Prior to the 1960s federal-provincial negotiations took place through interactions among professionals concerning specific and technical matters. From time to time there were also senior level negotiations over income tax arrangements. These technical functional interactions continue to be important. From the late fifties onward, there has been a veritable mushrooming of joint activities between Ottawa and the provinces. By 1968 an Intergovernmental Institute Report listed more than 190 on-going committees and boards that coordinated the policies of the various governments.[28] There have also been fundamental changes in executive federalism at the senior levels. Federal-provincial premiers' conferences are now held with increasing frequency; they have widened their range of issues; and they are increasingly concerned with political as opposed to administrative matters.[29] The transformations have been aptly described as going from interspecialist to intergovernmental.[30]

The changes in federal-provincial relations can be traced in part to the strenghtening of the provinces as political forces; the process of province-building has meant provincial decision-makers are no longer willing to be dictated to by the federal government. Increased demands, larger budgets and better staff have enabled provincial leaders to develop a better sense of their own power and interests with the result that they no longer simply look to Ottawa for financial support at any price.

Policy Growth

The provinces' traditional functions and jurisdictions constitute the foundation of province-building. They have a history of active involvement in creating and maintaining the conditions essential to economic growth. The provision of infrastructure, for example, roads and schools, was an important part of the provinces' earliest functions. Thus, even in the era of Macdonald's National Policy, the provinces were already playing a positive, interventionist role in economic development. Through guaranteed loans, outright grants, and favourable tax treatment all of the provinces have sought to promote their own internal economic development. Especially important for understanding the provinces' capital accumulation function are the tradition of Crown lands and the "hard frontier". Proprietary Crown lands meant that the development of land and resources required considerable public involvement. The obstacles to economic development inherent in the "hard frontier" necessitated quantities of capital and other resources that were beyond the scope of the individual. Thus, the early entrepreneurs in Canada were less "rugged individuals" than their counterparts in the United States and were more inclined to seek and/or accept assistance and partnership with the public sector. The Canadian frontier was not to be settled through individual efforts alone—it required a collective enterprise.[31] The existence of proprietary Crown lands coupled with the inability of private initiative encouraged the provinces to take an active role in their economies.

Ottawa's early economic development policies involving the railways and tariffs have often overshadowed the less grandiose activities of the provinces. But certainly, regional interests encouraged provincial governments to formulate their own policies of economic incentives for industrial growth.[32] For example, the establishment of Ontario Hydro-Electric was at the behest of business interests seeking low-cost power for industrial development. Similarly, the "manufacturing condition", an export restriction on raw materials adopted by Ontario, B.C., and Quebec was in response to demands by particular economic interests for tariff protection not provided by the federal government.[33] Defensive expansion, which refers to activities by the state in response to external threat, was also an important phenomenon at the provincial, as well as at the federal, level. Although primarily a response to foreign initiatives, defensive expansion sometimes has meant protection from threats originating in other provinces. Western fears of central Canadian financial and manufacturing interests represent one of the most recurrent manifestations of this tendency. Many of the needs and demands for state protection, subsidization, and regulation came from narrow segments of the economy. As provincial economies have developed and diversified, more interests have sought assistance. These regionally-based sectors have increasingly looked to provincial rather than federal authorities.

Social development policies, which are defined as those activities directed toward the conservation of human resources, have been the second major area for provincial policy growth. Traditionally in Canada, as in most European nations, welfare and health were considered to be private, individual concerns; in cases of extreme need any help came from charity or local government. Although education has long been a public concern, Canada's early public education meant only elementary education. Higher learning remained a prerogative of the wealthy. In the twentieth century all three areas of social policy have expanded. Public education now refers to post-secondary as well as elementary and secondary. The welfare state, characterized by public assistance through direct cash transfers and public provision of goods and services, has emerged in all industrialized societies.[34] There has been a corresponding evolution in the public's acceptance of a social responsibility for individual health and welfare. All of these developments have meant the expansion of government activity in health, welfare, and education which, according to the BNA Act, fall within provincial jurisdiction.

SUMMARY

Economically and politically the provinces have emerged as units of strength within the federal system, making them crucial focal points for the study of public policy. Provincial public policy cannot be understood without an examination of the environment, the participants, and the institutions associated with provincial politics. Chapter 2 describes some of the more basic social and economic conditions which surround provincial politics. Chapter 3 considers the role of political parties, pressure groups, and political ideas. These forces are not formally part of the structure of government or administration, but by virtue of their importance for the resolution of conflict, they help to shape policy alternatives. Chapter 4 examines the activities of provincial governments through institutions and formal participants—cabinets, legislatures and bureaucracies. Chapter 5 takes up an external but vital consideration for provincial politics by analysing the impact of the federal system.

The second half of the book describes patterns of provincial activity in the development of social and resource policies. Chapter 6 discusses the specific concerns of what can be called social development—health, social welfare and education. Chapter 7, in contrast, concentrates on issues of a more collective nature which we have termed resource development. This concept refers to those policies which are directed towards goods and resources, their use, regulation and protection. In terms of substantive areas, this involves most directly problems of natural resources, agriculture and transport.

NOTES

1. Jon Pammett, "Public Orientations to Regions and Provinces" in D. Bellamy, J. Pammett and D. Rowat, Editors; *The Provincial Political Systems*, Methuen, Toronto, 1976, p. 95. Supporting data from an earlier period are found in Mildred Schwartz, *Politics and Territory*, McGill-Queen's University Press, Montreal, 1974, pp. 216-223. We will examine public attitudes toward provincial governments in Chapter 3.
2. Richard Rose, "On the Priorities of Government: A Developmental Analysis of Public Policies" *European Journal of Political Research* 4, 1976, pp. 247-248.
3. For more on the meanings of "public" see Richard Hofferbert, *The Study of Public Policy*, Bobbs-Merrill, Indianapolis, 1975, pp. 3-5. The public impact of private decision-making is discussed by Peter Bachrach, *The Theory of Democratic Elitism*, Little, Brown, Boston, 1967 and M. Nadel, "The Hidden Dimension of Public Policy: Private Governments and the Policy-Making Process," *Journal of Politics* 37, February, 1975, pp. 2-34.
4. Our sense of policy is similar to that proposed by James E. Anderson, *Public Policy-Making*, Praeger, New York, 1975, who talks of "A purposive course of action followed by an actor or set of actors in dealing with a problem or matter of concern," p. 3. See also Charles Jones, *An Introduction to the Study of Public Policy* Prentice-Hall, Englewood Cliffs, 1970, Chapter One; and T.A. Smith, *The Comparative Policy Process*, ABC Clio, Santa Barbara, 1975, pp. 1-5.
5. Stefan Dupré, *et al., Federalism and Policy Development: The Case of Adult Occupational Training in Ontario*, University of Toronto Press, Toronto, 1973.

6. Lewis Froman, "The Categorization of Policy Contents" in Austin Ranney, Editor, *Political Science and Public Policy* Markham, Chicago, 1968, pp. 41-54.

7. Regulation or the regulatory type of output is discussed as the "other half" of government in an insightful essay by G. Bruce Doern, "The Concept of Regulation and Regulatory Reform," in G. Bruce Doern and V. Seymour Wilson, Editors, *Issues in Canadian Public Policy* Macmillan, Toronto, 1974, pp. 8-35.

8. W. Chandler and M. Chandler, "Policy Trends" in Bellamy, Pammett and Rowat, pp. 237-256.

9. For interesting discussions of some of the recent changes in health care delivery systems see Peter Aucoin, "Federal Health Care Policy," pp. 55-84 and G.R. Weller, "Health Care and Medicare Policy in Ontario," pp. 85-114 in Doern and Wilson Editors, *Issues in Canadian Public Policy* Macmillan of Canada, Toronto, 1974.

10. Richard Simeon, "Studying Public Policy," *Canadian Journal of Political Science* 9, December 1976, pp. 548-580.

11. See Theodore J. Lowi, "American Business, Public Policy: Case Studies and Political Theory," *World Politics* 16, July 1964, pp. 677-715.

12. Simeon, "Studying Political Policy", p. 555.

13. Rose, *European Journal of Political Research*, 1976, p. 262.

14. Richard Rose, "Models of Change," in Rose, Editor, *The Dynamics of Public Policy: A Comparative Analysis* Sage, London, 1976, p. 9 analyzes dynamics in terms of constraints against and pressures for policy change. We explicitly use dynamics in the context of policy change and, therefore, juxtapose constraints and dynamics.

15. Alan C. Cairns, "The Electoral System and the Party System in Canada," *Canadian Journal of Political Science*, 1, March 1968.

16. E.E. Schattschneider, *The Semi-sovereign People* Holt, Rinehart and Winston, New York, 1960.

17. Edwin Black and Alan C. Cairns, "A Different Perspective on Canadian Federalism," pp. 31-48; and David M. Cameron, "Whither Canadian Federalism? The Challenge of Regional Diversity and Maturity," pp. 304-324 in J. Peter Meekison, Editor, *Canadian Federalism: Myth or Reality*, Third edition, Methuen, Toronto, 1977.

18. For a general discussion of this growth see Richard Bird, *The Growth of Government Spending in Canada*, Canadian Tax Papers, No. 51, Canadian Tax Foundation, Toronto, 1970.

19. Statistics Canada, *Provincial Government Finance, 1974* (DBS 68-207).

20. Ontario Economic Council, *Issues and Alternatives 1977: The Process of Public Decision-Making* Toronto, 1977, p. 7.

21. Statistics Canada, *National Income and Expenditure Accounts 1926-1974, 1976* (DBS 13-531, 13-201).

22. This calculation of provincial revenues includes funds transferred conditionally and unconditionally from the federal government.

23. Statistics Canada, *Provincial Government Finance, 1973* (DBS 68-207).

24. J.E. Hodgetts and O.P. Dwivedi, *Provincial Governments as Employers,* McGill-Queen's University Press, Montreal, 1974, p. 2.

25. *Ibid.*, p. 4.

26. See W.D.K. Kernaghan, *Bureaucracy in Canadian Government,* Second Edition, Methuen, Toronto, 1973, p. 6. Growth in public personnel has not been equal in every province or for every provincial policy area. Since 1946 Saskatchewan has less than doubled its civil service, while Nova Scotia and Ontario have increased by six times their 1946 levels. (Hodgetts and Dwivedi, p. 186.)

27. For a thorough analysis of the interrelations called executive federalism see Donald V. Smiley, *Canadian in Question: Federalism in the Seventies,* Second Edition, McGraw-Hill Ryerson, Toronto, 1976, Chapter 3.

28. *Report: Intergovernmental Liaison on Fiscal and Economic Matters,* Queen's Printer, Ottawa, 1969.

29. Smiley, *op. cit.*, discusses these and other changes in this important forum, pp. 60-64. Richard Simeon, *Federal-Provincial Diplomacy, the Making of Recent Policy in Canada,* University of Toronto Press, Toronto, 1972, chapter 6.

30. Edwin Black, *Divided Loyalties* McGill-Queen's University Press, Montreal, 1975, p. 98.

31. H.V. Nelles, *The Politics of Development* Macmillan of Canada, Toronto, 1974, pp. 2-19; K. Rea and J. McLeod, Editors, *Business and Government in Canada,* Methuen, Toronto, 1976, p. 335.

32. Garth Stevenson, "Federalism and the Political Economy of the Canadian State," in Leo Panitch, Editor, *The Canadian State: Political Economy and Political Power,* University of Toronto Press, Toronto, 1977, pp. 71-100; and Alan Cairns, "Governments and Societies of Canadian Federalism" Canadian Journal of Political Science, 10, December 1977, pp. 695-726. On capital accumulation as a state function, see James O'Connor, *The Fiscal Crisis of the State,* St. Martin's New York, 1973. This aspect of the state in Canada is described in Alexander Brady, "The State and Economic Life in Canada" in Rea and McLeod, pp. 28-42.

33. Nelles, Chapter Two.

34. See Harold Wilensky, *The Welfare State and Equality,* University of California Press, Berkeley, 1975, and Gaston Rimlinger, *Welfare Policy and Industrialization in Europe, America and Russia,* Wiley, New York, 1971.

Chapter 2

The Social and Economic Environment of Provincial Public Policy

The origins of public policy can be found in the social and economic conditions which, as enduring bases of cleavage between groups or classes, are fundamental sources of conflict within each province. Characteristics of the population (for example, size, age distribution, and urbanization), the economy (wealth and industrialization) and the social structure (ethnicity and religion) act as policy determinants because they generate both demands for public action and limitations on possible policy responses. This chapter is not intended to provide a complete inventory of environmental conditions but rather to describe those socio-economic contexts which, although external to the formal political process, appear to have particular significance for government activity and patterns of policy.[1] The social factors considered here have traditionally been sources of cleavage and conflict in Canadian politics. The economic factors reflect developmental trends and have broad implications for both policy process and outcomes.

POPULATION CHARACTERISTICS

Provincial populations may be described in terms of size, concentration and growth. Table 2.1 presents some demographic differences among provinces over a ten-year period. British Columbia, Alberta and Ontario stand out as the centres of population expansion. The Atlantic provinces and Manitoba have shown limited growth in population despite considerable out-migration. Quebec grew more rapidly than these provinces, but with a net balance in migration. Saskatchewan has been stagnant in absolute population growth, partly because it has also had the highest net out-migration of any province. The figures in Table 2.1 on population

17

Table 2.1: Characteristics of Provincial Populations

	B.C.	ALTA.	SASK.	MAN.	ONT.	QUE.	N.B.	N.S.	P.E.I.	NFLD.	CAN.
POPULATION SIZE (IN THOUSANDS) JANUARY 1976	2,481	1,804	929	1,023	8,290	6,224	684	830	120	554	22,998
PERCENTAGE POPULATION GROWTH 1961-1971	34.1	22.2	0.1	7.2	23.5	14.6	6.1	7.0	6.7	14.0	18.3
NET MIGRATION RATE 1961-1971	22.3	4.2	-13.6	5.6	9.7	0.4	-8.7	-6.1	-6.4	-9.7	4.0
PERCENTAGE URBAN 1971	75.7	73.5	53.0	69.5	82.4	80.6	56.9	56.7	38.3	57.2	76.1

Source: Adapted from Economic Council of Canada, *Living Together, A Study of Regional Disparities* (Ottawa: Supply and Services, 1977), data from Statistics Canada.

flow are only for a ten-year period. But the same general pattern of net out-migration from the Atlantic provinces plus Saskatchewan and Manitoba, net in-migration for Ontario, Alberta and British Columbia and an even migratory balance for Quebec holds true with only minor deviations for the past fifty years.[2]

Migration patterns are obviously important for population growth, but they are also significant in at least two other ways. For those provinces with chronic unemployment, emigration may provide a kind of safety valve. At the same time emigration often hinders the chances for economic growth by draining from a province the younger, more productive manpower and by indirectly increasing the economically inactive or dependent proportion of the population. This part of the population includes the very young, the very old and the infirm — all of whom require some form of welfare (whether privately or publicly provided). For the prosperous and expanding provinces, immigration typically provides a needed source of labour.

Population trends may provide stimulus for policy change because they generate changes in the labour force, employment patterns and social and economic structures. Demands for public welfare, education and other public services will result from such demographic shifts.[3] Changes in the birth rate, for example, carry with them long-term implications for public education. The birth rate has been of particular political significance in Quebec. For many generations the birth rate among Québécois was by far the highest in all of North America. However, by the 1970s it had fallen dramatically to the lowest among all provinces.[4] This decline raised questions and fears about the survival of the French language and culture.

Seventy-five percent of Canada's population lives in cities, and in every province except Prince Edward Island the majority of residents is classified as urban (Table 2.1). The concentration of population into urban centres generates a host of human needs and new problems that often become the basis for collective action, because they are beyond the capacity of any individual. Urban residents often lack the self-sufficiency of those who remain in a traditional, rural setting, and they must look to government for the kinds of assistance previously available from the extended family, church, or small community. Remedies to problems of mass transportation, congestion, and pollution cannot be found without large-scale, authoritative decisions.

Along with urbanization have come demands for the extension and improvement of traditional services like sewers and garbage collection, the creation of new programmes, or the more efficient administration of older ones. Cities have spawned a variety of welfare needs requiring agencies which go beyond traditional charitable services. Similarly, the consolidation of primary and secondary education is, in part, a response to urban demands for more specialized educational facilities. The reform of urban government structures into metropolitan or regional governments must also be seen as an attempt to provide more effective decision-making and administration for large and complex urban conglomerations.

ECONOMIC DEVELOPMENT

There is a widespread recognition of the importance of economics in explaining political change. Studies in political economy provide ample evidence of the impact of economic factors on the growth of the Canadian state. Similarly, cross-national studies have shown the tendency of economic development to create pressures for the expansion of public responsibility.[5] Recent analyses of policy outputs in the American states have, moreover, argued that a syndrome of factors, including wealth, industrialization, urbanization and level of education, are more important to the evolution of policy patterns than are certain political characteristics like party competition.[6] Although dispute remains over the relative importance of economic and political factors, there can be little doubt that the emergence of a modern economic system has profound social and political consequences. These effects are likely to be associated with long-term trends in policy development rather than with particular decisions.

Industrialization

This most basic element in economic development refers to the transition from a rural economy based on hand labour to a mechanized mode of mass, factory production.[7] The extraordinary increase in productivity resulting from this change is due to a specialization of productive functions or the division of labour.[8] The typical worker is no longer the artisan who produces an entire unit but rather the assembly line worker adding one more component to a complex product. Specialization goes hand in hand with the mechanization of the productive cycle, which itself is both the product of and a stimulant for advances in technology.

The division of labour not only transforms the work place, it also forms the basis for a new class structure. The rise of an industrial working class and an urban bourgeoisie corresponds to a decline in the importance of a rural social order founded on the division between peasantry and landed aristocracy. As technology advances, the complexity of social and occupational patterns is increasingly refined, thereby maximizing the degree of social interdependence. Politically, these trends mean an increase in distinctive group interests and a growing potential for conflict as a result of incompatible interests.

The policy consequences of these changes include, first, new forms of coordination, regulation, and mechanisms for conflict resolution. There is, then, impetus for policies of structural reform to enhance the capacity for resolving issues and for controlling economic and social pressures. Second, industrialization brings new dislocations and exacerbates the impact of existing ones. The changes inherent in industrialization foster a degree of economic and social interdependence and loss of individual self-sufficiency which bring with them a need for collective action and public policy response. Those who cannot participate in the economic system because of old age, illness, injury, or unemployment can rarely protect themselves and, therefore, require help. The rise of the welfare state with its wide scope of policy concerns and its massive bureaucracy must be seen as a consequence of these basic socio-economic transformations.[9]

Early industrialization in Europe depended on the availability and proximity of coal, iron ore, and food supplies.[10] Canadian economic development, in contrast, was based on export staples derived from natural resources. The first stages of economic expansion in Canada were, therefore, primarily commercial and non-industrial in nature. Easterbrook and Aitkin, for example, tell us that,

> Throughout most of its history Canada has been an economic satellite of other more advanced nations. Its exports have been almost exclusively raw materials and foodstuffs. Its imports have been manufactured goods produced by the industries of Britain and the United States. The pace of development has been set by the rise and decline of the great staple trades: fur, fish, timber, gold, wheat, and more recently pulp and paper and the base metals.[11]

The export of primary products has remained a vital aspect of Canadian economic growth into the second half of the twentieth century.[12] The very success of the staple economy generated an impetus for economic diversification through manufacturing. In particular the expansion of wheat production in the three prairie provinces, along with the development of a trans-Canadian transportation network, which together composed the heart of Macdonald's National Policy, allowed for the growth of both a significant export and a local domestic market for Canadian manufacturing.[13]

A staple, export-based economy is necessarily subject to international economic forces. These have had both positive and negative consequences. The negative consequences are without doubt best illustrated by the disastrous repercussions of the Great Depression on the one-crop wheat economy of Saskatchewan.[14] The two world wars have had, on the other hand, rather dramatic stimulative results for the manufacturing sector. A third essentially exogenous factor for Canadian industrial growth was the development of new technology which permitted the exploitation of new energy bases, in particular, hydro-electricity and after World War II petroleum and natural gas.[15] The importance of the emergence of the manufacturing sector in Canada can hardly be over-estimated. Nevertheless, as Easterbrook and Aitkin have observed, it is essential to recall that in Canada "the development of industry has not supplanted older patterns of staple production."[16]

The most fundamental transformation in Canadian economic history was the shift from agriculture to manufacturing and services. Industrialization in Canada is a primarily twentieth century phenomenon. In 1900 most of the population still resided in rural areas and small towns. Agriculture and primary industries employed over 50 percent of the labour force. By 1971 the percentage of the population classified as rural had declined to 23.9 percent. Less than 7 percent were employed in farming and only 9 percent were still employed in the primary sector.[17] The service sector, meaning trade, finance, administration and personal services, accounts for over 50 percent of all employment.[18] Economic development occurred in waves. One surge in growth occurred during the pre-war years through to the 1920s, and the post-World War II era represented a second. The extent and the impact of economic growth was not equal for all provinces. Ontario emerged early as the industrial-urban centre of Canada. In comparison, Quebec grew more slowly and retained much of its rural character longer.

Table 2.2 compares the industrial structure of the provinces by the division of employment among the three major sectors. These figures show the relatively heavy reliance of some provinces, for example, Saskatchewan and Prince Edward Island, on primary industry and the comparative industrial preponderance of Quebec and Ontario. The provinces differ dramatically in their possibilities for staple production, economic development and prosperity. These facts are basic to understanding the constraints on provincial governments as well as to appreciating the issues and conflicts which have become the basis of provincial politics.

Although federal initiatives in economic development far outweigh other efforts, provincial governments have been and continue to be active participants in this process. In 1974-1975 the provinces spent over $1.3 billion on development activities mainly in agriculture and natural resources with some smaller expenditures in the attraction of trade and industry and tourism.[19] But only a portion of this total can properly be seen as part of an effort to stimulate depressed regions or ameliorate regional disparities. Provincial development initiatives often complement federal activities. Many of these are organized through ministries of industry and commerce and through provincial development corporations (for example, the Quebec Industrial Development Corpora-

Table 2.2: The Industrial Structure of Provinces' Share of Employment in Major Sectors of the Economy, Canada, by Province, 1970-73*

	NFLD.	P.E.I.	N.S.	N.B.	QUE.	ONT.	MAN.	SASK.	ALTA.	B.C.	CANADA
					(Percent)						
PRIMARY SECTOR	16	25	10	9	7	6	14	31	18	8	9
SECONDARY SECTOR	33	25	31	35	41	41	33	21	28	37	38
TERTIARY SECTOR	51	50	59	56	52	53	53	48	54	55	53
TOTAL	100	100	100	100	100	100	100	100	100	100	100

*The primary sector includes agriculture, forestry, fishing, and mining; the secondary sector, manufacturing, construction, transport and utilities; and the tertiary sector, community, business, and personal services, finance, trade, and government administration.

Source: Estimates by the Economic Council of Canada, *Living Together* (1977), based on data from Statistics Canada. Reproduced by permission of the Minister of Supply and Services Canada.

tion, Nova Scotia's Industrial Estates Limited, and the Manitoba Development Corporation).[20] The Cape Breton Development Corporation (DEVCO) is a federal crown corporation which, through federal-provincial cooperation, is striving to revitalize the economy of the region based on coal mining and steel production.

Wealth and Natural Resources

Because the provinces require adequate resources for public programmes, the gap between revenues and responsibilities has been a persistent problem for all provinces. Primarily through conditional grants, Ottawa has shared the cost of many provincial services. With some important exceptions, like the introduction of hospital and medical insurance in Saskatchewan, this has resulted in the federal government providing a major impetus for policy innovation. Shared-cost programmes have covered a wide range of concerns, but the most significant, in terms of policy change, have been in the fields of health and welfare. Much of the present structure of assistance for the needy, aged, sick, and unemployed began with federal initiatives. Today the predominant modes of federal assistance are no longer tied to particular programmes. Nor does the federal government retain a monopoly on policy innovation.

Perhaps the most significant aspect of wealth today is the disparity among regions. All countries have some degree of territorial economic disparity. In some cases economic development, involving the flow of capital and labour as well as the transformation from primary industry to manufacturing and services, has resulted in a gradual reduction of such regional disparities. But there is nothing inevitable about this tendency. It is also possible that the trend over time may be toward greater divergence, that is, greater inequality between units. In Canada the record is mixed. Very dramatic differences in per capita income have traditionally existed among the ten provinces. These disparities persist into the present, although they are not as great as they were a generation ago. For example, Newfoundland's per capita income was 56 percent of the Canadian average in 1956 and 69 percent in 1975. In the same years Quebec increased from 86 to 91 percent; Ontario declined from 119 to 110 percent; and British Columbia also declined from 122 to 107.[21]

The income figures found in Table 2.3 measure average family disposable income. Adjusted to take into account transfers due to differential taxation, living costs, and subsidies, they represent more precise estimates of how much wealth a typical family really has available. Compared to per capita income, these figures might be said to be more conservative estimates since the magnitude of provincial differences is reduced. But by and large the relative standing of provinces

Table 2.3: Some Provincial Differences in Wealth

	B.C.	ALTA.	SASK.	MAN.	ONT.	QUE.	N.B.	N.S.	P.E.I.	NFLD.	CAN.
AVERAGE FAMILY DISPOSABLE INCOME 1970 (CANADA = 100)	104	99	79	91	109	98	81	84	79	74	100
POVERTY — LOW INCOME FAMILIES AS % OF ALL FAMILIES 1971	12.0	17.9	27.9	19.4	11.2	17.7	24.1	23.0	34.0	33.7	15.9

Source: Adapted from Economic Council of Canada, *Living Together, A Study of Regional Disparities* (Ottawa: Supply and Services Canada, 1977), p. 46, data from Statistics Canada

is not significantly altered. It is probably not surprising to find that the highest rates of provincial poverty tend to coexist with the lowest average disposable family incomes.[22] Unemployment figures partially reinforce this pattern of inter-provincial imbalance. The Atlantic provinces have consistently manifested the highest rates of unemployment, a fact confirmed over time by Chart 2.1. British Columbia and Quebec have also tended to have above average unemployment although they have experienced relatively low or moderate levels of poverty and have remained close to the Canadian average in disposable family income. High unemployment in British Columbia, a province of relative prosperity and rapid economic growth, may be a function of dependence on the staples of forestry and metallic minerals, which are highly susceptible to fluctuations in international demand. Another possible explanation is that high wage rates in British Columbia, by encouraging in-migration, have maintained relatively high levels of unemployment.[23]

In Quebec, unemployment is typically several percentage points higher than it is in Ontario. Historically, this fact is partially explained by Quebec's high birth rate, which has produced a large pool of young job seekers. In recent times a gradual breakdown in traditional values has encouraged more women into the labour market. Reinforcing this fact is the seasonal character of many jobs in Quebec and the highly competitive nature of many of the province's labour intensive industries.[24] The prairie provinces benefit from comparative low unemployment, although two of them show low levels of disposable income. Saskatchewan comes closest to the conditions in Atlantic Canada in terms of a high incidence of poverty. It is possible that the real difference here in unemployment figures is due to the very high out-migration from Saskatchewan. High unemployment in some provinces has limited available resources and constrained policy options. Persisting disparities across provinces have also been a source of continuing dispute among them and the federal government over the desirability of economic stabilization policies.[25]

The figures presented in Tables 2.3 do not, of course, indicate anything about the problem of basic differences in the standard of living among smaller regions within each province. It is well known that areas like northern Ontario, northern New Brunswick, and the Gaspé have serious economic problems which have created pressing needs for provincial policy response.[26] While it is crucial to avoid underestimating or even overlooking the importance of such problem areas, it remains true, nevertheless, that the most politically relevant inequalities in living conditions are reflected in these inter-provincial differences. The essential policy fact is that any long-term solution to such problems must involve a degree of inter-provincial redistribution.*

*The problem of regional disparities is discussed in Chapter 5.

Unemployment Rate

CHART 2.1   Unemployment Rate, Canada (By Region), 1953-1975

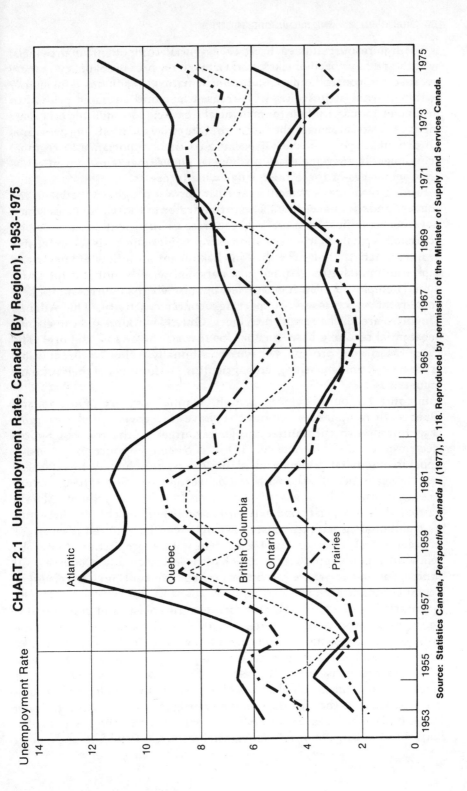

Source: Statistics Canada, *Perspective Canada II* (1977), p. 118. Reproduced by permission of the Minister of Supply and Services Canada.

Natural resources have been an essential component of provincial wealth and have been of special importance for provincial policy-makers because the control and exploitation of natural resources is primarily within provincial jurisdiction. Increases in world resource prices can mean enormous windfalls for provincial treasuries. In addition, economic interests associated with the resource sector may create strong pressures on provincial policy-makers[27] because of their importance to regional economies. In extreme cases, provincial governments may even act as representatives of these regionally-based interests.

From a resource perspective, one can draw a rough line between the "haves" and the "have-nots". The former refer to those provinces which have been the holders of varied resources of sufficient abundance and accessibility that their exploitation has provided the basis for extensive economic activity and growth. This has meant an inflow of labour and capital ultimately translatable into personal wealth, not just for those directly employed in such industries, but also via the indirect multiplier-accelerator processes of supporting economic activity. The Atlantic provinces are all "have not" provinces. Only Newfoundland can claim a substantial resource base in Labrador (hydro power and iron ore). The three Maritime provinces have traditionally relied on renewable resources — timber, fishing, and agriculture — for most of their primary industry.

In contrast, four provinces, British Columbia, Alberta, Ontario, and Quebec, fit reasonably well into the "have" category. British Columbia is endowed with substantial energy resources in the form of hydro-electric power and coal deposits. It has also been the source of extensive non-ferrous metal mining and is the leading province in forest-based enterprises, especially the pulp and paper industry. Since the discovery of vast oil and natural gas deposits from 1947 to the present, Alberta has based its prosperity and extraordinary growth on this resource plus its traditional agricultural base. Saskatchewan has limited reserves of petroleum and a monopoly of Canadian potash production. Manitoba relies on mineral production and hydro power as key resources. Of course, for all the prairie provinces, agriculture continues to represent a vital economic sector.

Ontario is well endowed with hydro-electric energy and uranium. It is an important source of iron ore, a centre for the steel industry, and a producer of various non-ferrous metals like nickel, zinc, and copper. Like British Columbia, it has an important pulp and paper industry and along with Quebec constitutes the centre for secondary manufacturing industries in Canada. Quebec has the greatest hydro-electric capacity in Canada and, as the gigantic James Bay project develops, will have even more. It also shares large iron ore deposits along the Quebec-Labrador border and in Ungava. It has substantial resources in non-ferrous metal deposits. It is also a world centre for asbestos and, like Ontario, has an important share in Canada's pulp and paper industry and various secondary manufacturing such as textiles. However, in contrast to the other resource-rich provinces, Quebec is not among the wealthiest provinces on a per capita basis. (See Table 2.3 above.) The reasons for Quebec's lag in this respect are extremely complex but include the structure of the labour force, changing demographic patterns, and the susceptibility of Quebec's primary industries to fluctuation in world markets.[28]

SOCIAL FACTORS: LANGUAGE AND RELIGION

Different economic starting points and inheritances have inevitably generated distinct political problems and responses. The heterogeneity of provincial politics is also the product of social and cultural traditions and the interaction of these with material conditions.

Some provinces, especially those of the western prairies, lacked a colonial tradition. There were no institutions, practices, or attitudes to be displaced. With the exception of resistance by native peoples, province-building took place on virgin territory, and in a kind of political vacuum. The early settlers in the prairies did not, therefore, have to integrate themselves into an existing social and political order, but instead had to establish them. Of course, there were constraints, for all settlers came from some previous political environment and had their own predispositions. Moreover, the central government predefined many political practices and adminstrative relationships in the pre-provincial era. But the fact remains that as these provinces were established and evolved during the late nineteenth and the early twentieth century, the lack of a firmly pre-established tradition of provincial and local politics made innovation and political adaptation relatively easy.

The situation was the reverse in the older, more established, regions of Canada — and most strikingly in Quebec. Here, several strains of heritage have left a deep imprint on provincial politics and have dramatically delayed political modernization.[29] That New France was the earliest colony in what became Canada is in itself probably not as important as the fact that it represented a transplant of the seventeenth-century French aristocratic, feudal system to the new world with most of its centralizing, heirarchical, and theocratic tendencies. After the Conquest by the British in 1760 and the French Revolution in 1789, French society in Quebec remained a historical remnant of the old regime in which the Church and the clergy came to play an increasingly dominant role.[30] Thus, isolation from France and exclusion from the modernizing commercial and industrial sectors, which was largely in the hands of Anglophones, meant that a distinctly traditional political order could persist in rural Quebec. An alliance of the clergy and a locally based Francophone bourgeoisie fostered the legitimacy of a regime remarkably resistant to social change.

Quebec's pre-industrial social order, in which the church continued to exert great influence over all political and social institutions and most importantly over education, persisted with little change into the modern economic era.[31] The Duplessis regime was the last stand of this order. The modernizing processes of the 1950s and 1960s brought with them profound changes in the attitudes and expectations, which deviated sharply from the traditions of the past.[32] It was in part the starkness of this contrast which created a "revolutionary" climate for the social and political transformations of the 1960s and 1970s. Thus, for Quebec in particular, secularization constituted an essential factor in political modernization.

Many of these distinctive patterns of political change must in part be accounted for by non-economic bases of cleavage. Some of the most divisive, violent, and enduring problems in Canadian politics involve social divisions based on differences in language, ethnicity, and religion. These traits often overlap and reinforce one another, creating the dynamics of complex social and political conflict crystallized in the historic tension between the two charter peoples, the French and English.*

Language divisions are imperfectly institutionalized in the federal system.[33] French speakers make up about 27 percent of the Canadian population. Eighty-four percent of Francophones live in Quebec; and the language split in this province is approximately 81 percent French, 13 percent English, and 6 percent other. French-speaking minorities are especially significant in New Brunswick (34 percent) and in Ontario (6.3 percent).** The overwhelming tendency of Francophones to live in Quebec and the fact that all other provinces (except New Brunswick) are predominantly unilingual and English might initially lead an outside observer to expect that the politics of language would take place within the federal arena or within the context of interprovincial relations. Certainly, the federal government since the 1960s, through the Royal Commission on Bilingualism and Biculturalism, the Official Languages

---

*As Table 2.4 indicates, the family origins of much of the Canadian population are neither. But the essential struggle has centred on the relationship between Francophone and Anglophone communities.

**Although Francophone Ontarians represent a relatively small percentage, this equals almost one half million people, the largest francophone group outside of Quebec.

Table 2.4: Some Provincial Differences in Ethnic, Linguistic and Religious Composition

	B.C.	ALTA.	SASK.	MAN.	ONT.	QUE.	N.B.	N.S.	P.E.I.	NFLD.	CANADA
ETHNIC GROUPS:											
BRITISH	57.9	46.8	42.1	41.9	56.8	10.6	57.6	77.5	82.7	93.8	44.6
FRENCH	4.4	5.8	6.1	8.6	9.6	79.0	37.0	10.2	13.7	3.0	28.7
OTHER	37.7	47.4	51.8	49.5	33.6	10.4	5.4	12.3	3.6	3.2	26.7
LANGUAGE MOST OFTEN SPOKEN AT HOME:											
ENGLISH	92.8	90.8	89.9	82.6	85.1	14.7	67.9	95.5	95.7	99.1	67.0
FRENCH	0.5	1.4	1.7	4.0	4.6	80.8	31.4	3.5	3.9	0.4	25.7
OTHER	6.7	7.8	8.4	13.4	10.3	4.5	0.7	1.0	0.4	0.5	7.3
RELIGION:											
CATHOLIC	19.6	26.9	30.8	27.1	35.1	87.7	52.3	36.5	45.9	36.6	47.3
PROTESTANT & OTHER	80.4	73.1	69.2	72.9	64.9	12.3	47.7	63.5	54.1	63.4	52.7

Source: Statistics Canada

Act, and a broad effort to encourage bilingualism in the federal public service, has made language policy one of its central concerns.[34] But political conflicts based on language have historically been most intense at the provincial level. Most commonly, these problems, which have been accentuated by religious divisions, have involved the rights of linguistic minorities to education in their mother tongue.

The most important provincial policy context in which divisions based on language and religion have direct impact is undoubtedly education.* Conflict between Catholic and Protestant, Francophone and Anglophone, over the right to separate schools and minority language education has played a central part in the evolution of Canadian public education. The struggle over language rights has been the single most contentious issue in Quebec politics since the Quiet Revolution. It also remains an unresolved, emotional issue in Ontario and in other provinces. The political potency of linguistic cleavages does not depend solely on questions of schooling. Such social distinctions are the source of conflict because they also correspond to systematic disparities in economic well-being and social status. Nowhere is this more obvious than in Quebec where the Anglophone minority has long constituted a distinct, isolated elite dominating, and in some cases monopolizing, key positions in industry and the professions.[35]

The influence of the Church on politics has already been alluded to in the context of Quebec where the changing balance between confessionalism and secularism has been an inseparable part of the Quiet Revolution. The political significance of religion also derives from differences among religious communities within the political order. Although in Canada there are numerous identifiable denominations or sects, the division between Catholics and Protestants has always been primordial for political conflict.[36] The struggle between these two groups for social status and political advantage is a European heritage. But in Canada this division has been intricately intertwined with the question of language. In provincial politics religion has been, and remains, important to the politics of education, to the recruitment and organization of political parties, and to the mobilization of popular support in elections.

SUMMARY

The broad impact of social and economic conditions is nowhere more apparent than in the process of province-building. For many years inadequate finances kept the provinces in a weakened and dependent

*The politics of education are explored in detail in Chapter 6 below.

state. Only as their revenue bases have been strengthened through tax arrangements, unconditional transfers, and natural resource revenues have the provinces become more autonomous and effective governments. Scarce resources remain a constraint, but provincial decision-makers are now in a better position to allocate resources according to their own priorities.

Changing socioeconomic conditions have transformed the policy relevance of the provinces' traditional jurisdictions. Control over natural resources has directly involved the provinces in two expanding and crucial issues areas — energy and environmental policy. In addition, increasing urbanization and industrialization are linked to the development and growth of those public services comprising the welfare state. This change has also brought prominence to provincial governments. One especially significant result of the increased importance of provincial responsibility has been the development of provincial bureaucracies. The increase in administrative competence has allowed provincial governments to seek further responsibilities and to deal more effectively with Ottawa in the resolution of jurisdictional disputes.

Social and economic conditions are, therefore, a vital starting point for the analysis of provincial public policy. They not only set important constraints in terms of the availability of policy resources, they also generate a set of political demands and policy options. It is essential to remember that there is no mechanism whereby these factors are automatically transformed into political factors. Social and economic circumstances should be seen as providing the potential for political divisions and policy choice. For political effects to occur, these conditions must be translated into politically significant factors via the decisional process and through political actors.[37]

NOTES

1. Important contributions to our understanding of social and economic differences across provinces and regions include Ronald Manzer, *Canada: A Socio-Political Report*, McGraw-Hill Ryerson, Toronto, 1974; Mildred A. Schwartz, *Politics and Territory: The Sociology of Regional Persistence in Canada*, Macmillan of Canada, Toronto, 1969; M.C. Urquhart and K.A.H. Buckley, Editors, *Canadian Historical Statistics* Macmillan of Canada, Toronto, 1965; Economic Council of Canada, *Living Together, A Study of Regional Disparities* Supply and Services Canada, Ottawa, 1977; Hugh Innis, Editor, *Regional Disparities* McGraw-Hill Ryerson, Toronto, 1972; and T.N. Brewis, *Regional Economic Policies in Canada* Macmillan of Canada, Toronto, 1969. On geographic factors, see C.F.J. Whebell, "Geography and

Politics in Canada: Selected Aspects," in John H. Redekop, Editor, *Approaches to Canadian Politics*, Prentice-Hall, Scarborough, 1978, pp. 3-27.

2. Economic Council of Canada, *Living Together*, op. cit., p. 174. Quebec is a partial exception to this. Although on the average there is a migratory balance, in the post-war era there have also been sharp fluctuations. The 1950s witnessed a strong in-migration, followed in the late 1960s by an exodus which, coupled with the drop in birthrate, was certainly a factor in the crisis over language and education. See Commission of Inquiry on the Position of the French Language and on Language Rights in Quebec, *Report*, Book III, p. 170.

3. For a discussion of the policy implications of these factors, see Leroy O. Stone and Claude Marceau, *Canadian Population Trends and Public Policy Through the 1980s*, McGill-Queen's University Press, Montreal, 1977. For a comparative analysis of the importance of demographic factors in shaping policy agendas, see Hugh Heclo, *Modern Social Politics in Britain and Sweden*, Yale University Press, New Haven, 1974, pp. 19-26.

4. André Bernard, *La Politique au Canada et au Québec*, les Presses de l'Université du Quebec, Montreal, 1977, p. 32.

5. Karl Deutsch, "Social Mobilization and Political Development," *American Political Science Review* 55, 3, September 1961, pp. 493-514; S.M. Lipset, *Political Man*, Doubleday-Anchor, Garden City, N.Y., 1960, Chapter 2; B. Guy Peters, "Political and Economic Effects on the Development of Social Expenditures in France, Sweden and the United Kingdom," *Midwest Journal of Political Science* 16, May 1972, pp. 225-238; B. Guy Peters, "Social Change, Political Change and Public Policy: A Test of a Model," in Richard Rose, Editor, *The Dynamics of Public Policy: A Comparative Analysis*, Sage, Beverly Hills, 1976, pp. 113-156.

6. Richard E. Dawson and James A. Robinson, "Inter-party Competition, Economic Variables and Welfare Policies in the American States," *Journal of Politics* 25, 1963, pp. 265-289; Thomas R. Dye, *Politics, Economics and the Public: Policy Outcomes in the American States*, Rand McNally, Chicago, 1966; Richard I. Hofferbert, "The Relation Between Public Policy and Some Structural and Environmental Variables in the American States," *American Political Science Review* 60, March 1966, pp. 73-82; Ira Sharkansky and Richard I. Hofferbert, "Dimensions of State Politics," *American Political Science Review* 63, 1969, pp. 867-879; Charles F. Cnudde and Donald J. McCrone, "Party Competition and Welfare Policies in the American States," *American Political Science Review* 63, 1969, pp. 858-866; Brian Fry and Richard Winters, "The Politics of Redistribution," *American Political Science Review* 64, 1970, pp. 508-522.

7. Ralf Dahrendorf, *Class and Class Conflict in Industrial Society,* Stanford University Press, Stanford, 1959, p. 40.

8. The classic elaboration of this relationship is Emile Durkheim, *The Division of Labor in Society,* trans. by George Simpson, Free Press, New York, 1964.

9. Samuel H. Beer, *Modern Political Development* Random House, New York, 1974 provides a brief but useful overview of these patterns of change.

10. W.T. Easterbrook and Hugh G.J. Aitkin, *Canadian Economic History* Macmillan of Canada, Toronto, 1956 p. 515.

11. *Ibid.*

12. For an analysis of the staple model in Canadian economic development, see the various articles in W.T. Easterbrook and M.H. Watkins, Editors, *Approaches to Canadian Economic History,* McClelland and Stewart, Toronto, 1967, Part I, pp. 1-98.

13. Easterbrook and Aitkin, *op. cit.,* pp. 476-513. See also H.G.J. Aitkin, "Defensive Expansionism: The State and Economic Growth in Canada," pp. 183-221; and V.C. Fowke, "The National Policy — Old and New," pp. 237-258 in Easterbrook and Watkins, *op. cit.* On the politics of wheat see V.C. Fowke and Donald Fowke, " Political Economy and the Canadian Wheat Grower," pp. 207-220 in Norman Ward and Duff Spafford, Editors, *Politics in Saskatchewan,* Longman Canada, Toronto, 1968.

14. On the impact of the Depression, see Easterbrook and Aitkin, *op. cit.,* pp. 492-497; S.M. Lipset, *Agrarian Socialism,* Doubleday, Garden City, N.Y. Anchor edition 1968, pp. 118-133; and David E. Smith, *Prairie Liberalism: The Liberal Party in Saskatchewan, 1905-71,* University of Toronto Press, Toronto, 1975, pp. 198-243.

15. Easterbrook and Aitkin, *op. cit.,* pp. 517-520.

16. *Ibid.,* p. 520.

17. *Canada Year Book 1976-77,* pp. 189, 395.

18. Economic Council of Canada, *Living Together,* op. cit., p. 62; Brewis, *op. cit.,* pp. 15-18.

19. Canadian Tax Foundation, *Provincial and Municipal Finances 1977,* p. 234.

20. In New Brunswick, the Robichaud government's "Program for Equal Opportunity" provided a means of equalization with both regional and ethnic effects. See Peter M. Leslie, "The Role of Political Parties in Promoting the Interests of Ethnic Minorities," *Canadian Journal of Political Science,* 2, December 1969, pp. 425-427. For case studies of other instances of provincial government involvement in economic development efforts, see Philip Mathias, *Forced Growth,* Lorimer, Toronto, 1972 and Roy E. George, *The Life and Times of Industrial Estates Limited,* Institute of Public Affairs, Dalhousie, Halifax, 1974.

21. These figures, calculated from Statistics Canada, are presented in André Bernard, *What Does Quebec Want?* Lorimer, Toronto, 1977, p. 49.
22. For contrasts based on per capita earned income see R. Ian McAllister, "Some Economic Problems of a Federal System," in Lawrence H. Officer and Lawrence B. Smith, Editors, *Issues in Canadian Economics*, McGraw-Hill Ryerson, Toronto, 1974, p. 399; and Brewis, *op. cit.*, pp. 17-24.
23. L.W. Copithorne, "Natural Resources and Regional Disparities: A Skeptical View," Economic Council of Canada (1978), pp. 5-6.
24. Bernard, *What Does Quebec Want?*, pp. 51-53.
25. Pierre Frechette, "L'économie de la Confédération: un point de vue québécois," *Canadian Public Policy* 3, 4, Autumn 1977, pp. 431-440.
26. For an analysis of regional issues and policy in one province, see Ontario Economic Council, *Northern Ontario Development: Issues and Alternatives 1976;* Government of Ontario, *Design for Development.*
27. Garth Stevenson, "Federalism and the Political Economy of the Canadian State," in Leo Panitch, Editor, *The Canadian State, Political Economy and Political Power,* University of Toronto Press, Toronto, 1977, pp. 71-100.
28. Bernard, *What Does Quebec Want?*, Chapter 2.
29. Dale Posgate and Kenneth McRoberts, *Quebec, Social Change and Political Crisis,* McClelland and Stewart, Toronto, 1976, p. 60.
30. Kenneth D. McRae, "The Structure of Canadian History," in Louis Harz, *The Founding of New Societies,* Harcourt, Brace and World, New York, 1964, pp. 219-274.
31. On the significance of the Church, see Jean-Charles Falardeau, "The Role and Importance of the Church in French Canada," pp. 342-357; and Hubert Guindon, "The Social Evolution of Quebec Reconsidered," pp. 137-161, in Marcel Rioux and Yves Martin, Editors, *French Canadian Society,* Vol. 1, McClelland and Stewart, Toronto, 1964. On the changing role of the Church in modern Quebec see Norbert Lacoste, "The Catholic Church in Quebec: Adapting to Change," in Dale Thomson, Editor, *Quebec Society and Politics: Views from the Inside,* McClelland and Stewart, Toronto, 1973 pp. 167-172; Posgate and McRoberts, *op. cit.*, pp. 54-57.
32. Posgate and McRoberts, *op. cit.*, p. 31.
33. On language cleavages generally, see Richard J. Joy, *Languages in Conflict: the Canadian Experience,* McClelland and Stewart, Toronto, 1972; Stanley Lieberson, *Language and Ethnic Relations in Canada,* Wiley, New York, 1970; John Porter, *Canadian Social Structure: A Statistical Profile,* McClelland and Stewart, Toronto, 1969, pp. 16-20, 75-86.
34. On federal language policy see *A National Understanding, the Official Languages of Canada,* Ottawa, 1977; *Report of the Royal Commission on*

Bilingualism and Biculturalism, Ottawa, 1968; V. Seymour Wilson, "Language Policy," in G. Bruce Doern and V. Seymour Wilson, Editors, *Issues in Canadian Public Policy,* Macmillan of Canada, Toronto, 1974, pp. 253-285; and D.V. Smiley, *Canada in Question: Federalism in the Seventies,* Second Edition, McGraw-Hill Ryerson, Toronto, 1976, Chapter 6.

35. John Porter, *The Vertical Mosaic,* University of Toronto Press, Toronto, 1965, pp. 73-103; Royal Commission on Bilingualism and Biculturalism, Vol. III, Ottawa, 1968, pp. 447-469; Ronald Manzer, *Canada: A Socio-Political Report,* McGraw-Hill Ryerson, Toronto, 1974, pp. 212-218; André Bernard, *What Does Quebec Want?* pp. 60-64; Dale Posgate and McRoberts, *op cit.,* pp. 35-39.

36. On religion and politics in Canada, see, for example, John Meisel, *Working Papers on Canadian Politics,* Second Enlarged Edition McGill-Queen's University Press, Montreal, 1975, Chapter 6.

37. Richard Simeon, "Regionalism and Canadian Political Institutions," in J. Peter Meekison, Editor, *Canadian Federalism: Myth or Reality?,* Third Edition, Methuen, Toronto, 1977, p. 294.

Chapter 3

Political Forces in the Provinces

Social and economic conditions take on political significance through the activities of a variety of individuals, groups, and organizations which, although not part of the formal structure of government, are important participants in the policy process. We refer to these non-official actors as political forces. In practice there is considerable overlap across differing forms of political involvement; it is nevertheless useful to distinguish among three broad types of political forces—parties, pressure groups, and political ideas.

POLITICAL PARTIES

In what ways and to what extent do political parties influence the policy outputs of provincial politics? What characteristics of parties and party systems are basic to understanding the policy process? Answers to such questions do not come easily. Nevertheless, important clues are already available in our knowledge of what political parties do. Although parties may vary in the extent and impact of their activities, they generally accomplish at least two important policy-related functions, leadership recruitment and interest aggregation.[1] Of primary significance is the fact that parties regularly determine in large part *who* will occupy formal positions of decision-making authority. In Canadian politics, as in most modern parliamentary democracies, the principle of responsible government is realized through the dependence of office holders upon the electorate through political parties. Parties are crucial to the selection of all parliamentary representatives as well as the selection of cabinet members.[2]

It is only by understanding something of the nomination of candidates and the organization of elections, both of which are largely the work of parties, that one can understand the channels of recruitment for those political leaders who come to make policy. Clearly not all of those who directly shape policy are selected by parties. Professional career public servants are for the most part selected and promoted through a quite separate process. Still, political parties play a most important role in determining who will occupy policy-making positions at the highest echelon. If we also know how social bases of support, ideologies, and policy inclinations differ among competing parties, we may be able to posit some of the policy directions of party representatives in positions of decision-making authority.

The recruitment function is reason enough for arguing that parties are essential to understanding public policy-making. However, partly because of the importance of parties for recruiting leaders through the competitive electoral process, parties also typically perform other activities which may be of equal importance to the policy process. In their efforts to win elections they must mobilize support and maintain existing loyalties. To achieve these goals parties seek to transmit public demands, to raise, present, and clarify issues which they expect to be useful to these goals.

The several successful instances of so-called "flash" protest parties reflect the clearest but certainly not the only instances of this kind of support mobilization. The unexpected and rapid rise to power by W.A.C. Bennett and the previously moribund Social Credit party in the British Columbia elections of 1952 and 1953 dramatically illustrates how by exploiting the discontent with the old parties a new political force can crystallize overnight a new base of support.[3] Where such a force also succeeds in forming a government it, of course, also results in a large scale turnover in decision-makers and has extraordinary potential for influencing policy.

Party system changes of this sort can represent a process of agenda-setting in which the alternatives open to decision-makers become structured. The defining of problems for resolution through public policy is then a process in which parties (and indirectly their supporters) may be involved on a regular basis. Such activities refer not only to the party or parties forming the government but to the role of opposition forces as well.[4] Again, as with the question of leadership recruitment, this does not mean that parties alone shape policy alternatives. Certainly other elements—interest groups, expressed public views, economic or financial constraints—may also influence what policy problems decision-makers choose to act upon or to avoid. But clearly parties by the role they play in a parliamentary democratic system will be vitally important at this stage of policy-making.

PROVINCIAL PARTIES

At first glance the most striking aspect of provincial parties is their heterogeneity. The most widely accepted generalization about provincial parties is probably that they are so different that patterns of electoral competition appear unique to each province.[5] The same party label can refer to rather dissimilar interests and policy preferences from one province to the next. Liberals and Conservatives, who thrive or at least survive in most provincial settings, differ greatly in their liberalism and conservatism. Provincial Liberals in Saskatchewan, for example, may share little in common with their cousins in Quebec or New Brunswick.[6] Liberals from British Columbia could easily be Tories were they to live in Ontario.[7] The heterogeneity among Conservatives is probably just as great. Some, by virtue of their emphasis on progressive policy issues, may have more in common with different parties in other provinces than with their Conservative counterparts.[8] Social Crediters differ noticeably even between Alberta and British Columbia.[9] Of all provincial political traditions, probably the CCF-NDP is the most internally consistent in ideology and policy directions. But even here one finds a fundamental internal difference in the rural, farming support of some provincial organizations as opposed to the trade union, industrial working class base of others.[10] The historical complexity of provincial parties has been compounded by the rise and fall of numerous other parties (which defy any common label except "protest"), such as the Progressives in Manitoba, the United Farmers in Ontario and Alberta, or in Quebec the Union Nationale and Parti Québécois.

The appearance of diversity and peculiarity of provincial parties arises not only from the contrast across provinces. It also results from the sometimes very sharp differences at provincial and federal election time between parties and party systems within the same province. The contrast is, of course, sharpest in those cases where the major federal parties are only minor parties provincially and vice versa. In British Columbia, for example, Liberals and Conservatives barely survive provincially against Social Credit and the NDP. Yet they compete actively along with the NDP in federal elections. In Saskatchewan, Conservatives have often dominated federal elections, but provincially they have, until recently, remained a marginal force. The major partisan struggle ever since the Depression has been between Liberals and the CCF-NDP. However, in the 1975 provincial election, the Progressive Conservatives enjoyed a striking resurgence gaining over 27 percent of the vote and seven seats.

Such apparent diversity of provincial parties is undoubtedly a source of some initial difficulty when we attempt to speak generally of the nature of provincial parties. There are, however, several underlying features, resulting from their common activities and functions, by which all parties including these can be compared.

Perhaps the most widely talked about feature of parties is how they come to obtain and maintain their competitive positions and strength. If we know who supports a party and why, we can have some idea of what policy positions, political beliefs, and ideologies a party is likely to espouse. This leads to questions of the size, loyalty, and characteristics of their supporters. Thus, if we can distinguish either individual parties or whole systems of parties by their social and economic antecedents, we may be in a position to convincingly describe the ideological array (or its absence) which can be associated with party systems.[12] In the case of provincial parties, there is at present an extraordinary lack of information which would permit an easy classification of provincial ideological patterns.

Because so much of the political struggle over public goods involves the interests and felt differences between broad social and economic groups, the overriding question to be asked about parties involves the social and economic bases which characterize party voters and party activists.

It has often been thought that Canadian parties are essentially middle-of-the-road, aggregating, brokerage parties.[13] There is certainly extensive evidence drawn from federal politics that the levels of class voting in Canada are quite low when compared to many other industrialized democracies.[14] We also know that the exceptional cultural, ethnic, linguistic, and religious diversity of Canada is an important part of the reason for this.[15] As we shift our focus to provincial parties, however, the same reasons for expecting such a low degree of class voting begin to recede in importance. Although the provinces vary greatly in terms of their social complexity, economic modernity, and structure of interests, no single province has the extraordinary diversity and, therefore, the potential for cross-cutting cleavages that the nation as a whole has. Provincial parties can and do adjust their appeals to a narrower and more homogeneous base of support. Indeed, this is an enduring foundation for recurrent conflict between federal and provincial parties. It is also important grounds for thinking that provincial parties may be more often associated with a particular class or group within the province and thereby articulate a relatively distinct ideology or set of policy preferences.[16]

From a different yet related perspective, some recent provincial comparisons have proposed that parties differ along a traditional-modern continuum. The basic argument behind this is that parties and party systems reflect underlying social, economic, and cultural cleavages tied to divisions and conflicts between social classes. These divisions are themselves a direct function of the stage of modernization associated with a provincial political system.[17]

There can be little doubt that provincial parties do vary greatly in their social and economic bases. Indeed, given the extraordinary social and economic diversity of the provinces (See Chapter 2 on these differences), it would be even more surprising if these systems of political conflict did not vary. It is, however, less clear that such differences can be adequately summarized in the context of a traditional-transitional-modern typology.[18]

Most of what we know about the social and economic bases of political cleavages in Canada is the result of investigation and analysis of federal parties and elections.[19] From the perspective of provincial politics, most of our understanding derives from studies of the origin and character of particular parties.[20] Systematic comparisons of cleavage patterns across provinces has received only limited attention. The broader problem is to identify within each province and compare across provinces whatever links exist between the socio-economic characteristics of the electorate and patterns of provincial partisan allegiance.[21] The 1974 election survey[22] provides a recent and reliable source of evidence for this purpose.

Tables 3.1 through 3.6 provide us with a simple breakdown in percentage figures which suggest how major social and economic groupings divide their political loyalties among the viable party alternatives in each province. Tables 3.1 and 3.2 identify two economic divisions which have been shown to be of political significance in modern, democratic societies. The comparison between white collar, blue collar, and farmers is based on individuals' actual occupations (3.1), whereas the second distinction (3.2) is based on where individuals see themselves in the social order. What these percentage figures indicate is that only in some provincial contexts do these economic divisions tell us something useful about the nature of partisan feelings. In none of the Atlantic provinces is either of these divisions helpful in explaining party preferences. On the other hand the occupational breakdown does tell us something about the politics of all other provinces except perhaps Saskatchewan. For example, blue-collar support has special meaning for NDP support in British Columbia, Alberta and Ontario. The differential is less in Saskatchewan where the dominant NDP has strong, catch-all support from all major occupational categories. In Manitoba the NDP succeeds equally well among white collar workers but loses heavily to the Conservatives among farmers. In Quebec, Liberal support (like support for the NDP in Saskatchewan) cross-cuts all occupational groups. But the P.Q. shows more strength among white collar employees, while the Créditistes have working class and rural-farmer bases.[23]

How people feel about their socio-economic status, regardless of their objective employment, generally reinforces these findings. Again, subjective class identification tells us almost nothing about political divisions in the Atlantic provinces. The one exception here is Prince Edward Island, where those who see themselves as working class or

Table 3.1:   Relationship between Occupation and Provincial Party Preference (in percentage)

	WHITE COLLAR	BLUE COLLAR	FARMERS*
BRITISH COLUMBIA			
Liberal	23%	22	
Conservative	15	9	
NDP	31	49	
Social Credit	32	20	
ALBERTA			
Liberal	23	18	7
Conservative	67	61	62
NDP	4	11	
Social Credit	6	9	31
SASKATCHEWAN			
Liberal	38	27	29
Conservative	22	14	21
NDP	41	59	50
MANITOBA			
Liberal	24	21	20
Conservative	31	33	73
NDP	45	45	7
ONTARIO			
Liberal**	47	47	39
Conservative	42	33	56
NDP	12	21	5
QUEBEC			
Liberal	66	66	67
Créditistes	7	12	25
Union Nationale	4	4	6
P.Q.	24	18	3
NEW BRUNSWICK			
Liberal	55	66	
Conservative	45	34	
NOVA SCOTIA			
Liberal	49	52	
Conservative	46	38	
NDP	5	9	

	WHITE COLLAR	BLUE COLLAR	FARMERS*
P.E.I.			
Liberal	58	67	60
Conservative	42	33	40
NEWFOUNDLAND			
Liberal	52	74	
Conservative	48	26	

* Farmers are not included as an occupational category in British Columbia, New Brunswick, Nova Scotia, or Newfoundland for lack of cases in the sample.

**

Note The 1974 survey appears to overestimate provincial Liberal party support. In Ontario, for example, the estimate is unusually high. This may be due, in part, to the timing of the survey when Liberals were leading in provincial polls and the Conservatives were at a low point in popularity.

Source: Harold Clarke, Jane Jenson, Lawrence LeDuc and Jon Pammett, *The 1974 Election Study*, Institute for Behavioural Research, York University.

(Source applies to TABLES 3.1 through 3.6.)

Table 3.2:   Relationship between Subjective Class Identification and Provincial Party Preference (in percentages)

	PERCEIVED UPPER, UPPER-MIDDLE OR MIDDLE CLASS	PERCEIVED WORKING OR LOWER CLASS
BRITISH COLUMBIA		
Liberal	21	32
Conservative	16	6
NDP	30	44
Social Credit	33	18
ALBERTA		
Liberal	23	13
Conservative	61	69
NDP	5	6
Social Credit	10	12
SASKATCHEWAN		
Liberal	39	22
Conservative	22	7
NDP	39	70
MANITOBA		
Liberal	22	24
Conservative	41	39
NDP	37	37

	PERCEIVED UPPER, UPPER-MIDDLE OR MIDDLE CLASS	PERCEIVED WORKING OR LOWER CLASS
ONTARIO		
Liberal	45	47
Conservative	43	34
NDP	12	20
QUEBEC		
Liberal	68	62
Créditiste	8	14
Union Nationale	3	6
P.Q.	21	18
NEW BRUNSWICK		
Liberal	68	63
Conservative	32	37
NOVA SCOTIA		
Liberal	55	47
Conservative	41	43
NDP	5	10
P.E.I.		
Liberal	54	72
Conservative	46	28
NEWFOUNDLAND		
Liberal	69	64
Conservative	31	36

lower class are more likely to prefer the Liberals provincially. Subjective class identification also tells us something about the politics of British Columbia, where Social Credit (and to a lesser extent the Conservatives) can claim a disproportionate share of the middle- and upper-class identifiers while the NDP finds greater support among the lower- and working-class self-labelers. In Alberta and Manitoba this distinction is not helpful. But in Saskatchewan this difference clearly captures the basic division between the NDP and their Liberal and Conservative opponents. In both Ontario and Quebec the breakdowns by subjective class largely reinforce what we already found through the comparison on occupational categories.

Economic differences furnish only part of the total picture of political cleavages. Traditional societal and cultural factors often persist and in some cases exert compelling influence on long standing political divisions. Religion is known to have had an especially enduring role to play in past and present Canadian politics—despite the fact that few major policy issues today or in the recent past have vitally affected the basic interests of the religious communities in Canada.[24] The significance of this factor varies greatly from province to province, but in most cases Conservatives do proportionally better among Protestants while Liberals are stronger among Catholics. Quebec is the major exception to this. In this overwhelmingly Catholic province, it is Protestants who demonstrate political distinctiveness by an almost unanimous support for the provincial Liberals.* The relationship between religious affiliation and New Democratic support is, in comparison, rather ambiguous. In three of the four provinces where the NDP is a major contender for power, the religious split is quite even, with Protestants providing a marginally larger share of support in British Columbia and Saskatchewan. Only in Manitoba do we observe a sharp religious division of importance to the NDP. Here 59 per cent of Catholics favour this party compared to only 28 per cent of Protestants. In both British Columbia and Alberta, Social Credit gains a greater share of Protestant support.

Table 3.3 shows that the difference between Catholics and Protestants has great partisan significance only in Manitoba, Ontario, Quebec, and New Brunswick. In Manitoba, Catholic voters opt two to one for the NDP over the Liberals. Conservative identifiers distinguish themselves by their heavily Protestant backgrounds. The same is true for Ontario Conservatives, although here Liberal but not NDP partisan preference is more common among Catholics. Quebec's anglo-Protestant minority, as we have noted, prefers the Liberals *en masse*. It is in New Brunswick where the religious-political coincidence is by far the starkest with Catholics tending strongly toward the Liberals and the Protestants toward the Conservatives.[26] Here, as in other provinces and countries, such patterns of religious division must, of course, be understood in the context of ethnic or linguistic differences as well. The confounding of ethnic divisions (especially English-French) with religion is evident in federal voting patterns, and its effects remain in provincial elections as well. But because of the greater ethnic homogeneity of most provinces, they may be easier to decipher.[27]

The results of a simple ethnic breakdown of provincial political preferences is presented in Table 3.4. For most provinces the most valuable two-way division is between those of British and non-British

---

*These data were gathered in 1974 prior to the culmination of the dispute over language rights and Bill 22. Since Protestants tend also to be Anglophone, it is likely that some of this positive sentiment toward the Liberals was eroded by the time of the 1976 election.[25]

Table 3.3:   Relationship between Religious Affiliation and Provincial Party Preference (in percentages)

	CATHOLIC	PROTESTANT*
BRITISH COLUMBIA		
Liberal	33	22
Conservative	14	15
NDP	29	33
Social Credit	24	30
ALBERTA		
Liberal	20	19
Conservative	68	65
NDP	5	2
Social Credit	7	14
SASKATCHEWAN		
Liberal	43	28
Conservative	14	23
NDP	43	49
MANITOBA		
Liberal	32	18
Conservative	9	52
NDP	59	28
ONTARIO		
Liberal	66	36
Conservative	19	51
NDP	15	13
QUEBEC		
Liberal	64	90
Créditiste	11	5
Union Nationale	4	—
P.Q.	21	5
NEW BRUNSWICK		
Liberal	79	36
Conservative	21	64
NOVA SCOTIA		
Liberal	56	50
Conservative	37	43
NDP	6	7

	CATHOLIC	PROTESTANT*
P.E.I.		
Liberal	58	69
Conservative	42	31
NEWFOUNDLAND		
Liberal	72	66
Conservative	28	34

*"Catholic" includes Roman and Ukrainian Catholics. "Protestant" includes all other demoninations but excludes Greek orthodox, non-Christian groupings, and those who gave no religious preference.

Table 3.4:   Relationship between Ethnicity* and Provincial Party Preference (in percentages)

	BRITISH	NON-BRITISH
BRITISH COLUMBIA		
Liberal	21	30
Conservative	14	10
NDP	40	31
Social Credit	25	30
ALBERTA		
Liberal	18	19
Conservative	67	61
NDP	7	5
Social Credit	8	15
SASKATCHEWAN		
Liberal	38	30
Conservative	22	16
NDP	41	55
MANITOBA		
Liberal	16	34
Conservative	53	14
NDP	31	49
ONTARIO		
Liberal	39	56
Conservative	46	30
NDP	15	14

QUEBEC	FRENCH	NON-FRENCH
Liberal	62	79
Créditiste	11	5
Union Nationale	4	3
P.Q.	23	13

	BRITISH	FRENCH
NEW BRUNSWICK		
Liberal	48	81
Conservative	52	20

NOVA SCOTIA		NON-BRITISH
Liberal	49	57
Conservative	44	36
NDP	6	7

P.E.I.		
Liberal	65	54
Conservative	35	46

NEWFOUNDLAND		
Liberal	65	60
Conservative	35	40

*Respondents were asked, "Can you tell me what ethnic or cultural group your ancestors who first came to North America belonged to?"
The dichotomization of ethnicity varies by province. All provinces west of Quebec, as well as Nova Scotia, P.E.I. and Newfoundland, are divided between British-non-British; Quebec by French-non-French; and New Brunswick by British-French.

origin. For Quebec the relevant split is between those of French or non-French origin, while New Brunswick is divided by British and French. In Manitoba the so-called ethnic communities (that is, the non-British) manifest a clear preference for the NDP and Liberals, while those of British origin lean to the Conservatives. This British-Conservative proclivity is seen as well in Ontario and New Brunswick (and less distinctly in Nova Scotia and the three westernmost provinces). The tendency of non-British voters to prefer Liberals appears in varying degrees in British Columbia, Manitoba, Ontario, New Brunswick and Nova Scotia. The strong ethnic basis of NDP support found in Manitoba is repeated only in Saskatchewan. There is a slight preference for Social Credit in B.C. and Alberta among non-British voters. But from all of these figures, it is most essential to observe the fact that whatever ethnic divisions do exist, they are sharpest in Manitoba, Ontario, Quebec, and New Brunswick, that is, precisely in the same four provinces where partisan divisions can be shown to be most sensitive to differences in religious affiliation. As Meisel and Irvine have demonstrated, religious cleavages may persist in politics because they are associated with other social divisions which remain politically salient and which are often the source of distinctive, sub-cultural patterns of political socialization.[28]

Sex has been shown to have considerable relevance for political attitudes and behaviour in many Western systems. Women often have a marked tendency to prefer conservative, and where applicable, clerical or religious political alternatives. Men are more likely to lean leftwards.[29] It would then not be extraordinary to find similar relationships in Canadian politics. When we examine the relationship between sex and provincial partisan preferences, however, we do not observe a constant relationship across all provinces. Nor are differences in provincial partisan preference according to sex particularly significant. One can observe that generally men are somewhat more likely to prefer the NDP than are women, although Saskatchewan appears to be an exception to this pattern. (See Table 3.5.) There also appears to be a slight male bias to Conservative support in several provinces.[30] The same is true for P.Q. and Créditiste support in Quebec. But through all of this, we should remember that many of these male-female percentage differences are rather small and of limited significance (Alberta, P.E.I., and B.C. are least characterized by sex-related patterns of partisanship). In only two provinces (Saskatchewan and Ontario) is the relationship statistically significant.

Age differences have often been shown to have political meaning.[31] There are two general arguments worthy of investigation in this regard. The first is that as people grow older they become more politically conservative. The second is that different generations learn distinctive sets of political values and preferences which continue to characterize each generation as it moves through the life cycle. (We should note that these two hypotheses are not totally contradictory.)

The evidence available in Table 3.6 cannot definitively answer either of these two possibilities. It can, however, shed light on whether age has partisan significance in some or all provincial contexts. For purposes of this overview, individuals have been categorized into three groups: young (35 and under), middle-aged (36 through 55), and old (56 and over).

If we think of the NDP and the Parti Québécois as the most radical or least conservative parties, we can see some evidence for the hypothesis of increasing conservatism with age. The NDP and P.Q. are relatively strongest in the 35 and under group in those provinces where they are serious contenders except Saskatchewan. This prairie province may

Table 3.5:   Relationship between Sex and Provincial Party Preference (in percentages)

	MALE	FEMALE
BRITISH COLUMBIA		
Liberal	20	28
Conservative	13	11
NDP	40	34
Social Credit	27	26
ALBERTA		
Liberal	19	18
Conservative	63	67
NDP	8	3
Social Credit	11	12
SASKATCHEWAN		
Liberal	48	18
Conservative	20	17
NDP	33	65
MANITOBA		
Liberal	14	30
Conservative	44	36
NDP	42	34
ONTARIO		
Liberal	39	52
Conservative	42	37
NDP	19	11
QUEBEC		
Liberal	62	70
Créditiste	12	9
Union Nationale	4	4
P.Q.	23	18
NEW BRUNSWICK		
Liberal	57	66
Conservative	43	34
NOVA SCOTIA		
Liberal	44	57
Conservative	46	38
NDP	10	05

	MALE	FEMALE
P.E.I.		
Liberal	63	65
Conservative	38	35
NEWFOUNDLAND		
Liberal	58	73
Conservative	42	27

Table 3.6:   Relationship between Age and Provincial Party Preference (in percentages)

	35 AND UNDER	36-55	56 AND OVER
BRITISH COLUMBIA			
Liberal	29	17	26
Conservative	10	14	13
NDP	40	34	35
Social Credit	20	35	26
ALBERTA			
Liberal	24	15	13
Conservative	64	67	65
NDP	8	6	—
Social Credit	5	13	23
SASKATCHEWAN			
Liberal	41	18	39
Conservative	17	18	22
NDP	41	64	39
MANITOBA			
Liberal	26	19	21
Conservative	23	58	39
NDP	51	19	39
ONTARIO			
Liberal	49	46	41
Conservative	31	42	50
NDP	20	12	9

	35 AND UNDER	36-55	56 AND OVER
QUEBEC			
Liberal	51	73	85
Créditiste	13	9	6
Union Nationale	2	6	7
P.Q.	34	13	2
NEW BRUNSWICK			
Liberal	68	57	61
Conservative	33	43	39
NOVA SCOTIA			
Liberal	42	59	51
Conservative	42	36	47
NDP	16	4	2
P.E.I.			
Liberal	64	86	46
Conservative	36	14	54
NEWFOUNDLAND			
Liberal	62	72	67
Conservative	38	28	33

illustrate the second, generational phenomenon; for it was here that the CCF had its first great electoral success in 1944. The popular support which brought the CCF to power then and kept it in power up until 1964 can be associated with the younger voters of the late 1940s and 1950s, that is, those who are middle-aged today. The Saskatchewan NDP retains 64 percent of this age group. Of course, where these parties are not major political contenders youth may lean toward others—as it does for the Liberals in New Brunswick and the Conservatives in Newfoundland. Table 3.6 also reflects the fact that some parties benefit disproportionately from older voters. Ontario Conservatives, Quebec Liberals, and Alberta Social Credit are the best examples. Their comparative lack of appeal among the youngest voters may be a sign of future weakness. Others have what looks like a middle-aged bulge to their base of support. Consider, for example, the strength of P.E.I.'s Liberals, Manitoba's Conservatives, or British Columbia's Social Credit. Still other parties seem to draw support in roughly equal proportions across all age groups—as do the Conservatives in Alberta and Nova Scotia, and the Liberals in Newfoundland, New Brunswick, and Ontario.

What then, in general, can be concluded about the social and economic cleavages which shape provincial party politics? The results from the 1974 survey tell us first of all that the observable patterns are of great complexity.

Some provinces like Quebec and Ontario have a multiplicity of politically sensitive social and economic cleavages. In others, notably the Atlantic provinces, it is difficult to identify any divisions which convincingly shape partisanship. From the four indicators of economic and class status, an identifiable pattern emerges which distinguishes between those provinces which are politically divided along these lines and those which tend not to be. It is, of course, not surprising to find that some fit this distinction less well than others.

From the perspective of the economic class indicators, it becomes clear that occupation and subjective class labelling overlap a great deal. These variables have partisan significance in the three largest and most industrial provinces (B.C., Ontario, and Quebec). Occupational divisions have partisan connotations in Alberta and Manitoba, while subjective class identification is significant in Saskatchewan. These variables provide no predictive properties for partisan preference in any of the Atlantic provinces. Furthermore, although we have distinguished between economic and communal-social categories, it is inaccurate to conclude that some provinces are dominated by the former type of cleavage while others are dominated by the latter. Of the four provinces where religious, ethnic-linguistic divisions are clearly identifiable, only New Brunswick is a case of partisanship being purely a function of these factors. In the other three, Quebec, Ontario, and Manitoba, economic class divisions are also of considerable importance for understanding provincial partisanship.

PROVINCIAL PARTY SYSTEMS

Party systems refer to the patterns of electoral and parliamentary competition among parties. That there is no single party system for all of Canada is now widely recognized. Each province has to some degree its own array of competing parties, no one set of which exactly mirrors the one found in federal politics.[32] But there are as yet few systematic comparisons to tell us precisely how Canadian party systems vary.[33]

Some provincial systems have always been rather simple two-party relationships. The traditional Liberal-Conservative struggle in the Atlantic provinces has gone on without serious interruption by third party forces, protest movements or the like.[34] Within the history of democratic politics, it is very rare to find such cases of party system persistence. In sharp contrast, all other provinces have in differing degrees experienced major transformations in their patterns of partisan competition. Ontario is probably most like the Atlantic provinces in the relative durability of its traditional party system. Quebec and the four western provinces share a common experience of party system transformation and complexity manifested in the frequent rise of third parties, the persistence of protest sentiments, and from time to time the demise of older parties.[35]

Parties are organizations competing with one another for the control of decision-making authority (and, therefore, for the capacity to shape the scope and direction of public policy choices). In order to comprehend the differences which may exist among party systems, it is essential to find a means of estimating the patterns of interrelationships which describe this competitive struggle. When it comes to evaluating provincial party systems not by their social bases but by their competitive interrelationships, there are several ways in which to categorize them.[36] Probably the most common is in terms of the number of competing parties or multipartism.[37] The number of parties serves, however, as only a preliminary estimate of party interrelationships. For one would want to know not only that two, three, four, or more parties occupy the electoral and parliamentary arenas but whether they do so on relatively even, competitive terms or whether one or two among them in fact so overwhelm the others that the number of parties by itself is a purely formal and misleading trait when taken in isolation. Fortunately, we have from Douglas Rae a comprehensive and efficient compilation of measures to identify such distinctions between party systems.[38] Drawing on many earlier party system analyses, Rae has encapsulated with conceptual and operational clarity the key dimensions of party competition applicable to any party system in a democratic, open regime. Because of its comprehensive quality and comparative potential, Rae's formulation provides an extremely useful tool for estimating the variation in provincial party systems. Of the several measures calculated by Rae, four appear of particular utility for sketching an overview of competitive relationships among provincial parties. These are:

1) *Bipartism.* The degree to which a system is two-party (or the degree of bipartism) can be directly estimated by the combined share of votes or seats held by the two largest parties. The Atlantic provinces have always stood as the best examples of two-party competitive systems. Their average electoral bipartism scores have been correspondingly high, for example, over 95% in Prince Edward Island and New Brunswick, and over 90% in Newfoundland and Nova Scotia. Of the other provinces, Quebec and Saskatchewan come closest to this

bipartisan pattern; while the other four (by virtue of enduring third or fourth parties) have tended away from this form of competition. Manitoba has the weakest average bipartisan tradition both electorally (72.4%) and in parliamentary partisan divisions (78.8%)

2) *Fractionalization*. If all provinces had pure two-party systems we would not need to go much beyond bipartism to establish a reasonably accurate picture of patterns of competition. But where party systems become more complex, we need more information. The measures of electoral and parliamentary fractionalization are extremely useful estimates of competitive conditions in multi-party situations. Fractionalization has a double meaning which reflects both the number of competing parties and the relative equality of their competitive positions. Fractionalization scores can vary between 0 and 1. A high score will indicate a situation in which several parties are in rather close competition (for example, a four-party contest in which each receives about 25% of the votes and seats). A perfect two-party struggle (in which each wins 50%) produces a score of .500 in the middle of the range. A low score will reflect a situation in which there is unequal competition. Where there is extreme one-party dominance, the fractionalization score will approach zero. Thus, for the Albertan landslide election of 1959, in which the Socreds won 97% of the seats, parliamentary fractionalization equalled .061.[39]

3) *One-party Dominance*. Much of provincial party politics has historically been associated with a third tendency—that of the dominance of the political scene over long periods of time (political generations) by one party. Sometimes the endurance of one party in power has been synonomous with one-man dominance in the premiership. Think, for example, of the reigns of Smallwood, W.A.C. Bennett, or Manning. But as the example of the Ontario Conservatives shows, this need not always be so. In any case, it is clear that one-party monopolies of power are very common, if not characteristic, of provincial politics.[40] It is, then, important to know how provinces have differed from one another in terms of one-party dominance. Again, relying on a measure proposed by Rae, one can calculate the proportion of votes won or seats held by the strongest party.

There are two important distinctions to be noted with respect to this concept. The first is that dominance scores will systematically differ between two-party provinces and those having three or more parties. Absolute levels of one-party dominance will be quite misleading without this qualification. Thus, all the Atlantic provinces necessarily have values of greater than 50% on this variable. But in the context of Ontario's tripartite competition, the Progressive Conservatives have been in a position of greater dominance than many of their eastern counterparts. If one looks at one-party dominance at the parliamentary rather than electoral level, the problems of interpretation are simplified by the exclusion of some of the third and fourth party phenomena through the plurality election system, the bias of which often advantages the strongest parties and disadvantages the weakest.[41] As a result the manifestations of one-party dominance are a good deal more observable in the distribution of parliamentary seats than they are in the electorate. However, third parties still retain significant representation in many provinces and continue to represent the single most important complexity in estimating how much one-party dominance really exists.

The dominance scores reported in Table 3.7 permit us to describe the relative dominance of any particular government by its competitive advantage over its opponents, so that even a party newly in power but with, say, 90% of parliamentary seats might be said to be representing a one-party dominant situation.

The second important distinction involves the alternative meaning of the term, that of endurance in power over time (as the Ontario Conservatives have experienced since 1943 and as Social Credit in Alberta did from 1935 until 1971). The scores in Table 3.7 do not reflect this temporal quality. We will, however, refer to one-party dominance in both ways, since either meaning may be of significance for the policy role of parties.

4) *Party System Instability.* Party systems, of course, are not constant in their shape. They change over time both in the number and nature of competing units as well as in the relative strengths of these units. The recent 1970-74 collapse of the Union Nationale and corresponding rise of the Parti Québécois in Quebec or the post-war decline of Conservatives and Liberals in British Columbia and Liberals in Manitoba offer useful but certainly not the only examples of party system fluctuations. Such transformations impose the need for some general measure of how much party systems change over time. Degrees of electoral and parliamentary instability can be calculated simply by taking the average amount of change in vote share or seat share of each party from one election to the next. These measures, as the others already discussed, are proposed by Rae and permit a differentiation between those party systems which are in states of flux as opposed to those which are relatively stable. What reason is there to think that the degree of flux in party systems might be related to patterns of policy? The principle of responsible government suggests that rulers will respond to the changing preferences of their popular support. Large scale voter shifts and inter-party turnover of MLAs, as reflected in the measures of instability, may reflect changes in popular demands on political leaders. If so, great change within the electorate and in the membership of

Table 3.7: Provincial Party Systems: Average Scores on Four Measures of Competitive Inter-relationships (post 1945 through 1972)*

	B.C.	ALTA.	SASK.	MAN.	ONT.	QUE.	N.B.	N.S.	P.E.I.	NFLD.
BIPARTISM										
electoral	76.9	77.4	84.9	72.4	76.0	88.1	95.8	92.6	98.4	94.4
parliamentary	90.6	94.5	97.8	78.9	89.0	95.9	100.0	97.6	100.0	97.8
FRACTIONALIZATION										
electoral	.645	.632	.610	.630	.646	.579	.529	.559	.505	.507
parliamentary	.486	.272	.419	.521	.451	.437	.414	.374	.360	.228
ONE-PARTY DOMINANCE										
electoral	44.5	51.5	47.8	40.6	44.6	48.0	51.6	50.5	53.6	61.4
parliamentary	65.1	82.9	69.1	54.8	68.6	66.4	67.3	71.8	73.8	87.0
INSTABILITY										
electoral	5.3	6.6	7.5	7.0	5.0	6.8	5.0	3.9	3.1	2.5
parliamentary	8.8	9.3	16.8	9.1	12.2	20.1	17.6	13.9	21.3	5.6

*Years included vary across provinces depending on the timing of provincial elections.

legislative bodies may presage or correlate with extensive policy innovation.[42]

Armed with these four measures—bipartism, fractionalization, one-party dominance and instability—we have the means of understanding in detail the competitive state of provincial party systems. How, then, do the ten provinces compare in terms of these competitive relationships and how have the various party systems evolved in the modern era? An examination of the provinces in terms of these dimensions will permit us to answer these questions. Information on these party systems traits is summarized in Table 3.8 and provides a useful reference point to the discussion which follows.

British Columbia

The party system of British Columbia is best thought of as a limited multi-party case, as one with a record of one-party dominance, and as one with low to moderate internal instability. The low average scores on bipartism and high electoral fractionalization demonstrate the continued importance of third and fourth parties.

British Columbia has undergone only one major party system realignment in the past thirty years. From 1941 through 1952 the province was governed by a Liberal-Conservative coalition in which the premiership was continuously held by a Liberal. The primary challenge to this governing alliance came from the CCF, which posed serious threats in 1945 and again in 1952 when it won only one seat less than its closest rival, the newly vigorous Social Credit Party. Since the coming to power of Social Credit in 1952 and the consolidation of its position in 1953, the once powerful Liberal and Conservative organizations have disintegrated and remain only minor forces. The election of 1952, a genuine four-way party battle, was a dramatic and critical turning point in the history of the province.[43] As the old parties and their coalition crumbled, the two new opposition forces quickly moved to fill the power vacuum and establish a new pattern of competitive struggle. In subsequent elections the Conservatives were to slide into virtual oblivion, leaving a three-way struggle in which the Liberals held third party status against the CCF-NDP as official opposition and Social Credit as consistent victor.[44]

In 1972 there was a short-term revival of a four party struggle resulting in a victory for the NDP with 39.6% of the vote and 38 out of fifty-five seats.* By 1975, a revived Social Credit Party under William Bennett incorporated into itself many elements from the Liberals and

*In 1972 the Liberals received 16.4% and five seats, Conservatives 12.7% and two seats and Social Credit 31.2% and ten seats.

Table 3.8: Provincial Party Systems: Comparison of Competitive Traits

	BIPARTISM	FRACTIONALIZATION	ONE-PARTY DOMINANCE	INSTABILITY
B.C.	unstable three-party	high / high	long-term (SC 1952-72)	moderate electoral / moderate parliamentary
ALBERTA	modified two-party	high electoral / low parliamentary	monopolistic long-term (SC 1935-71)	high electoral / moderate parliamentary
SASKATCHEWAN	impure two-party	high / low	long-term (CCF-NDP 1944-64)	high electoral / high parliamentary
MANITOBA	three-party	high / high	low / low	high electoral / moderate parliamentary
ONTARIO	three-party	high / moderate	long-term (PC 1943-)	moderate electoral / moderate parliamentary
QUEBEC	impure two-party	moderate / moderate	UN (1944-1960)	high electoral / high parliamentary
N.B.	pure two-party	moderate / low	low / low	moderate electoral / high parliamentary
P.E.I.	pure two-party	moderate / low	long-term Liberal advantage	low electoral / high parliamentary
N.S.	impure two-party	moderate / low	long-term Liberal advantage	low electoral / moderate parliamentary
NEWFOUNDLAND	pure two-party	moderate / low	monopolistic long-term (Liberal 1949-71)	low electoral / low parliamentary

Conservatives. This merging of forces meant that the election of that year became predominantly a two-party contest. Even though the NDP's popular support remained stable (39.2%), it was effectively deprived of its majority as a result of this party system consolidation. The victory of the NDP in 1972 now appears, with hindsight of the 1975 results, to have been not a realignment of political forces but rather a temporary deviation from an otherwise stable pattern of Social Credit governance.[45]

Alberta

The fate of Social Credit in Alberta has not been as fortunate. There the electoral realignments of the late 1960s and early 1970s have shown themselves to be enduring. The Conservatives, unlike the NDP in British Columbia, have successfully wrested electoral and governing dominance from Social Credit. They have done so in the tradition of their predecessors by winning a near monopoly of parliamentary representation. Albertan voters, it seems, prefer governing parties to operate free of serious opposition forces.[46] The 1975 election provided the Conservatives with 92% of the seats on the basis of 62.7% of the popular vote. Since 1944 the average percentage of seats for the governing party in Alberta is a remarkable 83.9%. All other provincial governments, with the exception of Newfoundland, have an average seat share ranging between about 54 and 55%.

The Albertan party system is also curious due to the fact that its average level of electoral fractionalization, although almost as high as the most fractionalized provinces (British Columbia, Ontario, and Manitoba), is matched against one of the lowest records of parliamentary fractionalization and one of the highest levels of one-party dominance in parliamentary representation.

Saskatchewan

Compared to party systems in the other western provinces, the Saskatchewan pattern of competition reflects a stronger bipartisan tradition. When viewed against eastern Canada, however, it is an impure two-party relationship. Saskatchewan is the only province in which the CCF-NDP has a record of electoral and governing supremacy. It is also the only western province in which the Liberals have continued (until recently) to be a major contender for power. Minor parties have had some limited electoral success but have gained almost no legislative representation.[47]

Since the crucial realignment of 1944 which saw the CCF first come to power after a long period of building support through the Depression and war years, Saskatchewan has experienced an era of one-party dominance in which the CCF-NDP governed from 1944 to 1964 and for all but about seven years (when the Liberals formed the government,

1964-1971) in the post-war era. This has given the province a pattern of party dominance in the temporal sense but has not meant an electoral monopoly by a single dominant party. Party competition has remained healthy in Saskatchewan—despite the consistent record of CCF-NDP electoral success.[48]

Manitoba

The Manitoban party system is notable in two important respects. First, its present, tripartite pattern of competition is quite recent. From the end of the nineteenth century up until the latter half of the Bracken era, Manitoba had a competitive party system in which the major contenders varied over time among Conservatives, Liberals, Progressives, United Farmers and Labour (later CCF).[49] But from 1940 until the early 1950s, a pattern of non-partisan provincial government emerged. This meant a form of coalition politics at the elite, cabinet level coupled with a non-competitive tendency at election time. The elections in this period were contests between a government coalition and anti-coalition forces. In 1941 the coalition included all major parties and won over 82% of the vote.[50] By 1945, the CCF constituted the most important anti-coalition force and won a third of the vote.* Throughout this period numerous seats were allocated by acclamation. For example, in 1949, sixteen of fifty-seven successful candidates won without contest. By 1953 there was a return to a more open style of party politics, resulting in a very competitive four-way struggle. Social Credit soon faded as a serious contender, and the elections of 1958 through 1969 represent a period of fairly stable three-party competition. There were, of course, substantial shifts within the electorate—most importantly the growth of the NDP electorate and the decline of the Liberals—but such realignments took place within a three-party competition.

The election of 1969 was a critical turning point because it brought the NDP to power with 38% of the vote. It was also crucial for the Liberals who fell from about 33% (in 1966) to 24% (in 1969) and from thirteen to only four seats. The election of 1973 confirmed this evolution towards a two-party system with the Liberals slipping further to 19% of the vote.[51] By 1977 the continuing decline of the provincial Liberals brought with it a further simplification of the pattern of competition as the PCs surged to over 48% of the vote with the defeated NDP retaining 38%.

Despite this recent trend, the broad picture of modern Manitoban politics, as reflected by the figures seen in Table 3.7, is one of a consistently multi-party province (i.e., the lowest bipartism scores). Consistent with this is the highest level of parliamentary frac-

*leaving aside all seats won by acclamation

tionalization and the lowest average one-party dominance scores. Manitoba is also, along with Saskatchewan, one of the two provinces with the highest rate of electoral partisan instability (although parliamentary instability has not been high). Given these figures, it is no exaggeration to view Manitoba as the most competitive of provincial party systems.

Ontario

The tripartite nature of party politics observed in Manitoba is also found in the recent history of Ontario. But Ontario does not reflect the same degree of party system transformation seen in its western neighbor. Ontario's party system is better described as showing a remarkable persistence over time. Throughout the twentieth century, with the important deviations of the UFO in 1920 and the Liberal era of Mitch Hepburn from 1934 to 1943, Ontario has been governed by the Conservative party.

Hepburn's success depended on his ability to capitalize on the widespread deprivations and consequent protest sentiment in the Depression era. But his appeal remained a highly personal one. The Ontario Liberals did not succeed in making a permanent impact on the electorate.[52] Although social and economic crisis had created great potential for political change, the end result was the renaissance of Tory hegemony following the Hepburn deviating elections and the CCF surge in 1943. One can identify no fundamental realignment of the Ontario electorate which might have ended this pattern of one-party dominance.

The party dominance scores in Table 3.7 do not, of course, record this Tory endurance. They also tend to underestimate the power of the Conservatives because of Ontario's tripartism. The three-party split necessarily produces lower party-dominance scores than in a two party situation. The relatively unchanging but high fractionalization scores are a function of this tripartism. The most significant long-term readjustment within the Ontario party system has undoubtedly been the rise of the CCF-NDP as a major opposition force. Even this development has not (as yet) dislodged either of the traditional parties from their place in provincial politics. Developments in the 1970s do, however, show important signs that Ontario's tripartism, like Manitoba's, may be in a state of flux.[53] The election of 1975 created a minority government and provided the Conservatives with their greatest challenge in over thirty years. Although both opposition parties gained votes, the election also allowed the NDP to replace the Liberals as the official opposition. The provincial contest of 1977 spared the PCs from clear defeat, gave the Liberals new hope and disappointed the NDP. The election maintained a minority government and reconfirmed Ontario's tripartite split.

Quebec

It is generally correct to think of partisan competition in Quebec as fundamentally bipartisan. The figures in Table 3.7 show this province to be more bipartisan than any of those found to the west of the Ottawa Valley. But Quebec also has some of the highest average levels of instability among both voters and parliamentary representatives. This is a reflection of the important fact that modern party politics in Quebec have been characterized by two fundamental transformations. The first of these was the displacement of the Union Nationale as the dominant party by the Liberals in the Quiet Revolution of the 1960s, a change which had immediate impact in policy as well as in the new attitudes and expectations. The second was, of course, the rise of the Parti Québécois. The PQ won 24 percent, then 30 percent of the vote in the critical elections of 1970 and 1973 before winning power in one of the most dramatic power shifts in the history of any province.[54]

The election of 1970 has properly been viewed as a realignment of political forces.[55] The rise of two minor party opposition forces (Parti Québécois and the Ralliement Créditiste which entered the provincial contest at this time) reflected a deep popular dissatisfaction with the traditional two-party competition and represented the single most striking deviation from bipartism. The realignment of 1970 was to be reinforced by 1973 as the Parti Québécois increased its share of the popular vote and became the official opposition (although it lost two seats), while the Union Nationale slipped to a new low. The steady progress of PQ popular support culminated in electoral victory in 1976 as 42 percent of the vote resulted in 71 National Assembly seats. The success of the PQ can correctly be seen as a combination of its own ability to articulate and develop the nationalism of the Quiet Revolution and the increasing unpopularity of the governing Liberals.

New Brunswick

The party system of New Brunswick has been described as traditional,[56] and as we have already seen, it has very solid roots in the long-standing ethnic and religious divisions of the province. The strength of these traditions is certainly a basic reason why minor parties have enjoyed no appreciable success here. The result of this situation is reflected in the perfect parliamentary bipartism and the near-perfect electoral bipartism of the province. The political status quo has not, however, persisted through a pattern of one-party dominance (as has been the case, for example, in Alberta). The provincial Liberals have held power more often than not, but the relationship between Conservatives and Liberals has been a competitive one is which power has frequently changed hands. In 1935 the Liberals replaced the Conservatives and governed until 1952.

The Conservatives then governed for eight years (1952-1960) and the Liberals for ten (1960-1970) before relinquishing power to Hatfield and the Conservatives once again. But vigorous competition has never led to distinctive issue positions or to ideological divisions between the two parties. As a consequence, there has never emerged an expectation that electoral politics are likely to generate policy change. Thorburn, writing in 1961, argues that, "The party system is a conservative force defending the prevailing state of affairs and working against drastic innovation".[57]

Nova Scotia

In many ways, the Nova Scotian party system appears to be only marginally different from New Brunswick's. Its tradition of bipartism is historically well established and the minimal ideological and issue difference between Liberals and Conservatives has often been noted. But, Nova Scotia does differ in two important respects. Its pattern of two-party competition has been marred by limited, sporadic success of the CCF-NDP and by the ability of this third force to secure for itself a regional stronghold in Cape Breton.[58]

The second most remarkable contrast with New Brunswick is the relative temporal dominance of the Liberals who, until 1956 when Stanfield led the Tories to victory, had governed for all but twelve of the previous one hundred years.[59] In the case of Nova Scotia it remains a question whether any fundamental realignment in the party system can be identified. J. Murray Beck has suggested 1956 as the only possible example of such a transformation in the past century.[60] Although the Conservative hold on power hardly outlasted Stanfield as Premier, the upset victory of the Tories in 1978 (who won 31 out of 52 seats on the basis of 46 percent of the popular vote) indicates that a more competitive balance may have been established.

Prince Edward Island

The province with "one of the largest governments in the world"[61] has a party system described as non-ideological with a strong lôcal bias to issues. Liberals and Conservatives alike seek to maximize a broad base of support.

As in Nova Scotia, it is hardly possible here to talk of fundamental realignments. The Liberals have governed through most of the twentieth century with interludes of Conservative victories (the last one being in 1959-1966). But none of these transfers of power can be said to have altered the nature of party competition in any fundamental way. The pattern of competition is a traditional one which, on the surface, closely resembles those in the other maritime provinces. The party system scores shown in Table 3.7 reflect this broad similarity.

As we shall see below, political attitudes and values (or provincial cultures) have more to do with maritime political differences than do party system traits.

Newfoundland

When compared to the rest of Canada, Newfoundland shares some traits in common with the Maritimes. It is today a two-party system in which third-force protest movements have had no appreciable success. But in other respects, Newfoundland stands apart from her three eastern neighbors. The province shares with Alberta the distinction of having had one of the most unbalanced, that is, one-party dominated competitive patterns.[62] This condition is reflected in both very high party dominance scores, as well as very low fractionalization scores. This tendency is sharpest in terms of parliamentary representation.

The second curious aspect of Newfoundland party politics is its extraordinarily high degree of stability (low instability scores) measured both by vote and seat shifts.[63] These figures reflect, of course, the historical reality of more than twenty years of government dominated by Joey Smallwood. The coming of the Conservatives to power via a minority government in 1971 followed by successive victories in 1972 and 1975 can be seen as the one basic political realignment in Newfoundland's post-confederation history. Whether this change means the development of a relatively balanced competitive system or a new partisan hegemony remains in doubt.

PARTY AND POLICY

It remains exceedingly difficult to specify with any precision the conditions and dynamics of partisan impact on patterns of policy. Political parties and party systems have been extensively analyzed— perhaps in greater depth and more perceptively than almost any other facet of the Canadian political scene. Party studies have tended to emphasize organizational traits, ideological traditions, and social bases of support. Many of these topics imply hypotheses about party-policy linkages, but rarely do they directly address this connection as a central research problem.

The basic controversy continues to centre on whether distinctive patterns of policy may be associated with particular parties or whether a change in party government brings with it a change in policy priorities. The two sides to this argument may be summarized briefly. The contention for a systematic correspondence between party and policy usually depends on the importance of ideology. Parties are commonly described by where they fit on a left-right continuum. Such comparisons are based on the view of parties as organizational manifestations of ideological traditions. Thus, a party system defines the relationship between competing ideologies within a given political system. Since ideologies normally include desired political goals, they carry with them direct implications for policy. A party in power might reasonably be expected to move toward the realization of its own ideology. If this expectation is true, a relationship between party and policy should be identifiable.

In Canadian politics the party-ideology model has proven remarkably difficult to evaluate because of the frequent lack of ideological clarity between the major contending forces. Liberals and Conservatives alike are often referred to as brokerage parties which seek to build broad coalitions by appealing to diverse opinions, thereby muting ideological positions. This has inclined many observers toward the hypothesis that there is no relationship between party and policy. Winn and McMenemy, for example, have recently argued that differences in partisan "style and electoral support have a negligible effect on policy".[64] However, it is probably wise to treat this negative argument with some caution, for it is doubtful that it applies equally well to federal and provincial politics. As was noted earlier with regard to the issue of class voting, there are reasons for expecting provincial politics to be more ideologically polarized and less brokerage-oriented than are federal politics.

Moreover, it is in provincial politics that the protest tradition led to the rise of ideologically distinctive parties (CCF-NDP, Social Credit, PQ, among others). Indeed, non-traditional parties with a heritage of reaction against Liberal and Conservative dominance have governed in all of the four western provinces for much of the post-war era. These facts do not, of course, repudiate the hypothesis of no partisan policy difference. They do suggest several reasons why one might expect distinctive policy differences to be associated with some parties and governments and not others.

Nor is it clear that the negative argument, even if of some validity, should apply consistently for all provinces. There is considerable evidence that distinctive provincial traditions and cleavage patterns exist. Robin, for example, has described British Columbia as "a fractured community" in which an ideological polarization between "an acquisitive individualism" and "a strong collectivism" has been institutionalized in the party system.[65] In contrast, the Nova Scotian party system is not usefully described by ideological differences. Both provincial Liberals and Conservatives "have a wide measure of support across ethnic, religious and class lines" and are "highly pragmatic and oriented to political success rather than principles".[66] The importance of ideological distinctions for British Columbian, but not for Nova Scotian, politics is instructive because it implicitly suggests very different roles for political parties in the two cases.

There is at present insufficient research based on provincial politics to convincingly resolve the dispute over party impact. There are, however, several studies which provide some hints at an answer. Two early research efforts, both of which rely on quantitative analysis of budgetary data, did not demonstrate a connection between certain party system traits and levels of provincial spending.[67] Several comments are necessary in evaluating the significance of these results. First, not all policy can be measured by budgetary figures. Decisions involving regulation, implementation, or structural reform often have only minor budgetary consequences. Even those initiating new programs may leave many financial considerations for later. In addition, those policies which are accurately reflected by budgetary indicators are also those which tend to be highly incremental in their patterns of change.[68]

Non-financial choices, on the other hand, can more easily be either/or propositions. This is important because the evidence of policy change which might demonstrate the impact of political factors would also need to manifest rather sharp, non-incremental shifts in policy direction. Finally, with regard to the limits of budgetary measures, estimates of total level of spending for given policy areas are likely to minimize the extent of possible policy change for the simple reason that by far the largest part of any policy area consists of fixed costs not amenable to short-term change.

It is also useful to note that these quantitative efforts at assessing the party-policy linkage have done so only with respect to selected aspects of party systems and political structures. It is, therefore, possible that, when more political factors are taken into account and when some of the difficulties in measuring the complexity of public policy are resolved, a more convincing solution to the party-policy connection will be possible.

Two more recent studies have reinstated political factors as partial explainers of provincial policy. Poel (1976) has looked at the question of policy diffusion. Diffusion refers to the pattern of policy adoption across units of government. Since it measures the timing of policy innovation, the concept raises questions about which parties, ideologies, or regimes are leaders or laggards in policy innovation. The findings from this study clearly support the intuition that a CCF-NDP government is more likely to be innovative than one controlled by some other party. Poel's analysis also reflects the importance of political variables such as the degree of malapportionment as a constraint on policy change and the size of the civil service as a resource for policy innovation.[69]

A second effort examining some previously unnoticed facets of the party-policy linkage involves the study of policy contagion. Normally, we think of examining the general problem of party impact by comparing the policy patterns of particular governing parties with others. But it is also possible that parties in power are in part influenced by the nature and extent of opposition forces. Where an opposition poses a serious challenge by offering a distinctive policy program, it poses a threat to the government. The latter may at times respond to this insecure situation by adopting much of the opposition's program. By doing so, it may take the wind out of the sails of an emerging challenge while at the same time resolving a policy issue. When this occurs the transfer of policy initiative may be said to be contagious.[70]

We do not as yet have enough information to say how prevalent such a phenomenon is. There are, however, several clues in the literature on provincial parties which indicate that such contagion does occur. Most of the evidence shows the CCF-NDP and, therefore, contagion from the left, to be the clearest manifestation of this tendency. Penner, for example, writing on party politics in Ontario, notes that the Conservatives led by George Drew fought and won the 1943 election on a program of sweeping social reforms at a time when the CCF was riding a strong wave of popularity. Since that time all PC governments in Ontario have understood that they "cannot allow the initiative on social reforms to pass to the NDP . . . and this problem is particularly acute when the government is a minority one with the NDP as the official opposition."[71] Signs of policy contagion have also been observed in Saskatchewan and British Columbia.[72]

The full significance of parties in the policy process cannot be understood in terms of party traits alone, for parties are often closely involved with organized interests. Because parties survive through contests for popular support, they must consistently seek to maximize and consolidate their bases of support. Thus, parties are "inclined to advocate changes that benefit their own voters and client interests and to oppose changes that leave their supporters worse off."[73] This, of course, means that some of the partisan effects on policy are a function of group representation with parties serving as access points to the policy process. But organized interests rarely, if ever, rely solely on parties as a channel for influence. Pressure groups must also be considered as political forces in their own right.

PRESSURE GROUPS

Organized interests are generally recognized as both pervasive and powerful. Given the breadth and substance of provincial government, there is every reason to presume an extensive group involvement in policy-making at this level. Not only do pressure groups articulate interests to decision-makers, they are also at times direct participants in the formulation and implementation of public policy. Yet provincial pressure groups remain a seriously understudied topic, and we know surprisingly little about their activities. This disparity between assumed significance and established knowledge should be a primary concern of students of provincial politics.

Some of the reasons for this gap in understanding stem from the difficulties inherent in studying group activity. Pressure groups are often hard to identify and compare because as a whole they are characterized by great variation in their structural traits, in their objectives, and in their impacts.[74] The defining conditions of organized interests are themselves unclear. Some are closely linked with political parties;[75] others are largely non-political in much of their normal activity. One model useful for organizing the great variation in group structures and activity is found in Pross' continuum which extends from highly institutionalized groups on one extreme to sporadic, issue-oriented groups on the other.[76] The former are defined by

> . . . organizational continuity and cohesion, commensurate human and financial resources, extensive knowledge of those sectors of government that affect them and their clients, stable memberships, concrete and immediate operational objectives that are broad enough to permit each group to bargain with government over the application of specific legislation or the achievement of particular concessions, and a willingness to put organizational imperatives ahead of any particular policy concerns.

In contrast, the latter manifest

> . . . limited organizational continuity and cohesion; minimal and often naive knowledge of government; fluid membership; a tendency to encounter difficulty in formulating and adhering to short-range objectives; a generally low regard for the organizational mechanisms they have developed for carrying out their goals; and, most important, a narrowly defined purpose, usually the resolution of one or two issues or problems, that inhibits the development of 'selective inducements' designed to broaden the group's membership base.[77]

Pross hypothesizes that, while group involvement in federal policy-making is dominated by highly institutionalized groups, provincially both issue-oriented and institutional groups are active.[78]

It is natural for issue-oriented groups to be deeply involved wherever government comes into close contact with the way people live. And since provincial governments commonly administer a wide range of social services, it is understandable that such groups should flourish at this level. Does such proximity between the people and their government mean that provincial governments are likely to be more responsive to group demands? Not necessarily, for it has also been observed that issue-oriented groups are typically weak in organization, lacking in regular access and unable to exert sustained pressure.

A second serious problem in interest group analysis is that much of the policy involvement of groups — in the form of lobbying, consultation and negotiation — goes on behind closed doors and is usually not the object of public scrutiny. These circumstances have inevitably created serious obstacles to systematic research on pressure groups, and it is consequently not surprising that much of what we do know about the role of pressure groups derives from a series of unrelated case studies of particular groups and individual policy decisions. Although many of these studies have contributed valuable insights, systematic comparative evaluation has been virtually impossible. As a result there has been almost no significant development of theory to explain the role of interest groups in the policy process.[79]

What in general can be said about the relationship between provincial politics and pressure groups? One well-established generalization, with important connotations for an appreciation of provincial politics, is that as the scope of the public sector increases, the role and influence of organized interests also increase.[80] The establishment of new services, coupled with the very complex nature of many of the policy issues associated with those services, makes government increasingly dependent on the expertise and cooperation of private interests.

A related and also widely accepted proposition is that the structure of government shapes the structure and operation of interest groups.[81] For example, group effectiveness may be influenced by the complexity and ambiguity of federal-provincial relations. Where policy-making is divided between two levels, groups must divide their own influence efforts. When it is not certain where effective decisional authority resides, the strains on group resources and the possible reduction in effectiveness are even greater.[82]

Moreover, many peak organizations in Canada are in practice loose and often uncohesive organizations due to the representation of diverse provincial sub-interests. This trait has primary significance, of course, for federal policy-making. However, this proposition might be interpreted to mean that these same organized interests as provincial groups are correspondingly stronger because they will typically lack such internal strains. Unfortunately, there exists at present no systematic comparison of provincial and federal organizations to confirm or reject this hypothesis.

Pressure group activity also reflects systemic differences in political attitudes and patterns of cleavage. Even where constitutional forms are consistent — as they are across the provinces — there is good reason to think that distinctive provincial political climates may condition the kind of legitimacy and the opportunities for influence which are central to group politics.[83] These influence opportunities are undoubtedly shaped by both socio-economic factors and partisan traditions, which, as we have already seen, can vary greatly from one province to the next.

The access of groups to decision-makers is another central theme in pressure group analysis. A lasting tradition of executive dominance in provincial politics has certainly contributed to a strong tendency on the part of most interest groups to minimize links with MLAs or legislative parties and to look to cabinets and bureaucrats as contact points.[84] On this question Presthus has provided the most comprehensive evidence to date. He confirms the general proposition of the primacy of executive access. By distinguishing several possible access targets, he is also able to show that in general civil service contacts are most common and that legislative and cabinet access occur with almost equal frequency. He further demonstrates that these patterns vary depending on the kind of interest involved.* Labour, for example, has rather weak access at the bureaucratic level and relies heavily on legislative contacts, while for business interests the pattern is reversed.[85]

Associated with the general problem of access is a model of clientelism which can be taken as one further generalization about interest groups in Canada. Several studies have observed that patron-client relationships describe many of the relationships between government and organized interests.[86] In general this refers to a pattern of influence, mutually beneficial to both sides, in which an interest group and a public agency (for example, a ministry, department, commission, or even provincial cabinet as a whole) develop a stable and regular cooperative relationship and in which the group is (usually informally) accorded special status, access, and influence. Government agencies come then to speak on behalf of this interest, which in turn lends support, information and expertise to the agency.

Nelles has provided a major historical analysis based on the relationship between Ontario provincial politics and resource, mining, and hydro industries.[87] Bucovetsky documents the ability of the Ontario mining industry to mobilize the province in opposition to the substantial mining

---

*Although the data for the Presthus study are both federal and provincial in origin (samples are drawn from Quebec, Ontario and British Columbia, as well as Ottawa), the analysis does not pursue the provincial comparison. It is, therefore, not possible to say whether such differential access patterns are consistent across provinces.

tax reforms proposed by the federal Minister of Finance following the recommendations of the Carter Commission.[88] In a similar vein, Stevenson has contended that provincial governments may come to represent the interests of regionally dominant economic groups in federal-provincial relationships.[89]

Clientelism in policy-making has not been estimated with sufficient precision to allow any convincing comparison of its relative prevalence across provinces. But there is little doubt that this mode of influence has been very common in a number of policy fields. It has led some observers to the view that certain agencies have in effect become "captured" by the very interests they are supposed to control.[90] It has, at least in part, led others to inquire into the utility of the pluralist model and the extent of elitism in Canadian politics.[91]

Much of the thinking about Canadian pressure groups has been based on pluralistic assumptions. Within the pluralist model, the public interest is seen as the changing aggregation of individual (group) benefits. This scheme also assumes that no single interest is ever so powerful as to consistently dictate policy values, and that the state acts as a neutral mediator among narrowly-based competing interests. Elite accommodation and corporatism represent two significant variants of pressure group activity. In both of these, the state-group relationship connotes a higher degree of cooperation and collaboration both among groups themselves and between political decision-makers and group leaders than is the case in the pluralist schema. Corporatism refers to a special case of accommodation in which group-state relationships become institutionalized and in which certain peak organizations gain special access and influence over those policy areas of direct concern to them.[92] Where corporatism is most developed, the state may even delegate effective decisional authority to corporatist groups.[93]

Elite accommodation is a broader and less precise model of interest group influence, describing a range of influence modes somewhere between pure pluralism and pure corporatism. It refers to a situation where the typical and crucial influence points are the links among group leaders and political elites. The prevalence of elite contacts avoids the necessity of the overt forms of group conflict more common in the pluralist model. Elite accommodation lacks the highly structured influence system of corporatism but is comparatively closed and non-competitive when set against classic pluralism. Although the evidence is far from complete, there is considerable agreement, among observers of interest group activity in Canada, that elite accommodation best describes the prevailing mode of group-state interaction.[94] Studies of provincial politics which have approached this problem are rare. Nevertheless, they tend to confirm the plausibility of the accommodative thesis.

These forms of group-state interaction are illustrated in the relationship between the provinces and the medical profession. Looking at medicare in Ontario, Tuohy demonstrates that the fee and service restrictions placed on the medical profession since the inception of medicare have arisen within the context of accommodation rather than pluralism. The College of Physicians and Surgeons, not an external agency of the state, handles the regulation of the profession. As Tuohy describes the mode of operation in accommodation, the group "prescribes and enforces rules within the context of a prevailing structure of social values."[95] Even in the cases of Quebec and Saskatchewan where greater conflict surrounded the introduction of medicare, organized medical interests were accorded a special status. The profession's approval was considered a prerequisite for the implementation of universal medical care insurance.[96]

There is little doubt that interest groups are important elements in policy-making; however, the nature and extent of that influence remains an open question. What is needed, first, is more systematic analysis of pressure group activity and, second, direct evidence of group influence within specific policy areas.

POLITICAL IDEAS

To this point, our discussion of provincial forces has concentrated on organized political activity, but some forces are not always manifested primarily or solely through parties and pressure groups. In particular, political ideas exert an influence of their own on politics and policy. Some observers even argue that ideas have a dominant role in determining basic policy choices.[97] The impact of ideas cannot be properly understood merely as an artifact of partisan or interest group organization (although it is important to recognize that many political ideas are articulated through them), but rather must be viewed as a distinct phenomenon.

The meaning of political ideas as explanations of policy can vary greatly. Those referring to specific opinions on immediate issues, political leaders, or governments may constitute short-term influences on the policy process. But ideas may also be expressed in terms of relatively stable belief systems or ideologies which represent a source of influence on the broad direction of policy change. Manzer has demonstrated the significance of "policy principles" for shaping the content and evolution of policy.[98] These principles may be usefully thought of as ideas and values which structure thinking among those political elites and interested publics most directly involved in a particular policy area. Consistent with this perspective is the concept of "social learning" which suggests a process of changing ideas and modes of perception acting as a stimulus for policy evolution.[99]

Bryden's analysis of old age pensions demonstrates the impact of the "market ethos" on policy evolution.[100] From this perspective, policy principles fall somewhere between public opinion and formalized political ideology. They constitute, in other words, the working beliefs and assumptions for policy-making participants or policy communities.

Political systems may be characterized by the presence of some dominant political belief or set of competing ideologies, by the extent of ideological polarization or consensus, or by the extent to which such beliefs are held by the mass public, by select issue publics, or by political elites. Horowitz, for example, has suggested that the complementary effect of toryism and socialism has resulted in distinctive styles of governing and patterns of public policy.[101]

Finally, we may view political ideas as ingrained orientations and feelings about the political process. Such values or cultural predispositions share with ideologies a tendency to be rather stable over time and are likely to operate as contextual constraints on political forces and decision-makers.[102] They cannot, however, be condensed into any simple left-right continuum. Nor can we assume that the same orientations toward politics prevail in all provinces.

A number of recent works have demonstrated the extent to which popular attitudes may be characterized by sectional climates of opinion.[103] Based on data from a national survey conducted after the 1965 election, Schwartz has provided a comprehensive overview of regional variations in political orientations such as levels of personal satisfaction, political awareness, cynicism, attitudes towards parties, and sense of political efficacy.[104] More recently, Simeon and Elkins have shown the extent of provincial and regional differences in political orientations.[105] Additional evidence of such differences across provinces comes from Clarke, Jenson, Le Duc, and Pammett. They show that provincial opinions differ in terms of which level of government people tend to look toward. It is not surprising that Ontario is the most federally oriented province. Somewhat unexpected is the finding of Alberta as the most provincially oriented.[106] Given the strength of Quebec nationalism one might expect this province to score highest in provincial orientation, but it is likely that the opinions of Quebec Anglophones expressed in the survey data effectively limit this tendency.[107]

This information indicates some of the range of differences we are likely to find when provincial publics are compared. But it represents only a starting point for such a comparison of regional differences in attitudes toward government and policy-making. We as yet know rather little about how people feel about politics in their own province.

Naturally, political views must be, to some extent, particular to each province. If we inquire after views of given premiers or cabinet members, or specific actions, we will find it difficult to generalize about provincial public opinion. If, on the other hand, we ask about how people see their provincial government — Are they satisfied, do they trust it, do they find it effective? — then we have grounds for saying that the public is more supportive, less trustful or more alienated in one province than in another. There are to date very few attempts to assess such similarities and differences.[108]

Fortunately, the 1974 election survey included a number of questions which permit us to identify some important characteristics of provincial public opinion. Table 3.9 gives us a brief overview of these opinion patterns from province to province. The questions which provide the basis for the percentages in Table 3.9 ask respondents to comment on how they see their role in politics generally, how they view their own state of well-being, the extent to which such conditions are the result of government action, and whether they feel they have any influence on what governments do. The substantive concerns raised by these questions allow for a description of what might best be called the standing political orientations of each provincial public. They reflect rather basic and enduring preferences and values about politics which may approximate what is often thought of as political culture.

Provincial publics appear to have quite distinctive features. British Columbia is characterized by a very high level of interest in politics. It is also the province with the highest level of both material and life satisfaction. There is an above average optimism here, but a limited inclination to explain well-being by what governments do.[109]

Three provinces, Alberta, Quebec, and New Brunswick, have publics with comparatively low levels of political interest. In New Brunswick this is coupled with exceptionally high dissatisfaction with both material and broader living conditions and a pervasive pessimism about the future. On questions of material satisfaction and future orientations, Newfoundland also ranks low. There is, however, no consistency to the Atlantic region as a whole. Public opinions in both Nova Scotia and Prince Edward Island stand in sharp contrast to New Brunswick (and to a lesser degree Newfoundland) on all attitudinal dimensions.

With the exception of the Albertans' low political interest, the prairie provinces and Ontario look quite similar on the first five issues in Table 3.9. Quebec is also consistent with these levels on questions of satisfaction and perceptions of government impact. But Quebeckers, in addition to their low overall interest in politics, represent the only provincial public in which the ratio of optimists to pessimists is greater than 1.0 (leaving aside all those who say that things are likely to be the same).* The last three items in Table 3.9 are indicators of political

---

*This optimism on the part of Quebeckers reflects a broad future orientation. As we will see below, it apparently does not imply a positive or optimistic attitude about purely political conditions in the province.

Table 3.9: Public Opinion in the Provinces: Political System Orientations

	B.C.	ALTA.	SASK.	MAN.	ONT.	QUE.	N.B.	N.S.	P.E.I.	NFLD.
POLITICAL INTEREST Percent of respondents who follow politics very closely or										
fairly closely	70.3	49.2	61.4	64.6	61.4	49.4	50.8	57.8	64.9	59.8
Not much at all	29.8	50.8	38.6	35.4	38.6	50.3	49.3	41.7	35.1	39.2
MATERIAL SATISFACTION Percent who say they are very satisfied or fairly satisfied	78.4	69.6	69.4	70.4	71.2	60.1	36.8	68.8	66.0	52.8
PERCEPTION OF GOVT IMPACT Percent who feel government has a great deal or something to do with material satisfaction	60.8	66.3	61.6	72.0	67.6	68.1	69.1	70.9	72.3	67.9
FUTURE ORIENTATION										
Optimistic	27.2	22.8	16.3	20.4	24.9	26.0	20.6	20.4	17.0	13.2
Pessimistic	33.6	38.0	24.5	31.5	28.8	24.9	45.6	26.9	27.7	35.8
(Do you think you will be better off, worse off, same in next 3 to 4 years?)										

TABLE 3.9 (CONT. . . .)

	B.C.	ALTA.	SASK.	MAN.	ONT.	QUE.	N.B.	N.S.	P.E.I.	NFLD.
LIFE SATISFACTION										
Percent who are very or fairly satisfied	88.0	86.9	79.6	87.1	86.8	82.2	42.6	81.8	87.2	75.4
Percent who agree that government does not care what people think.										
Strongly agree	41.7	57.4	46.2	61.0	50.3	63.9	68.2	52.8	52.0	61.2
Agree										
Percent who say politics is so complicated, a person cannot understand what is going on:										
Strongly agree	55.9	74.7	71.1	84.7	62.5	63.3	78.8	57.4	64.0	85.7
Agree										
Percent believing they do not have any say in what the government does.										
Strongly agree	37.0	50.6	57.7	66.1	45.7	66.5	47.0	44.8	66.0	67.3
Agree										

efficacy, that is, the feeling that one can have some influence on public decisions and that governments are to some extent responsive to citizen demands. The question of whether governments care what ordinary people think reflects degrees of cynicism about the political process. In this case agreement with the statement indicates a high degree. New Brunswick clearly has the most cynical public, followed by Quebec, Newfoundland and Manitoba with above average cynicism. British Columbia defines the other extreme (only 41.7% agreeing).

The remaining two questions refer more directly to an individual's perceived ability to comprehend and influence public events. Public opinion in Ontario and Quebec is least likely to see politics as too complicated to understand. Newfoundland and, perhaps surprisingly, Manitoba reflect the highest levels of feeling that politics is too complicated. The feeling that one cannot have any say in (influence on) what government does is most widespread in Newfoundland, Quebec, Manitoba, and Prince Edward Island. Again British Columbia is the province where people are least likely to express this sense of powerlessness.

Although the pattern is less than perfect, the overriding impression one gains from this evidence is one of distinctive attitudinal patterns within provinces. British Columbia and New Brunswick stand out as polar extremes on a number of dimensions. The political climate on the west coast is one of high optimism, satisfaction interest, and a relatively high sense of efficacy. New Brunswick's dominant political feelings seem to be those of pessimism, dissatisfaction, and low political interest but moderate sense of efficacy. The sharp differences on these attitudinal dimensions between this province and her maritime neighbors suggests that we have here distinctive provincial climates of opinion which do not necessarily characterize a whole region and which cannot be entirely explained by common economic problems.[110]

When we turn from political attitudes to political actions, there is also considerable variation from province to province. Table 3.10 provides percentage figures on the extent of political participation in each province. The seven questions on participation refer to distinctive forms of participation. Despite this, we can note a broad difference between those types of political activity which are personal, that is, undertaken by individuals, and those activities which occur in some regularized group context. Reading newspapers, talking about politics with others, and trying to convince someone else of your position are examples of the former. Working in the community, attending meetings, and contacting officials all require a person to interact with some formalized group or institution. This distinction, although crude, is useful because it seems to tell us something about differences in participation across provinces.

From Tables 3.10 and 3.11 we can observe, for example, that in

Table 3.10: Provincial Political Participation

	B.C.	ALTA.	SASK.	MAN.	ONT.	QUE.	N.B.	N.S.	P.E.I.	NFLD.
Percent who read about provincial politics in newspapers, often or sometimes	85.8	70.1	73.1	69.5	73.3	61.9	57.6	75.9	84.0	57.2
Percent who discuss provincial politics with others: Often or Sometimes	75.6	56.3	59.6	62.7	60.8	61.9	57.6	63.2	54.0	51.0
Percent who try to convince friends to vote same way: Often or Sometimes	26.8	18.4	23.1	13.6	20.6	25.5	13.7	32.1	16.0	16.3
Percent who work with others in community to solve local problem: Often or Sometimes	18.1	26.4	43.3	15.3	18.6	17.3	27.3	36.7	34.0	22.4
Percent who attend political meeting or rally: Often or Sometimes	19.7	19.5	21.1	20.3	13.6	24.3	25.7	29.9	36.0	26.5

TABLE 3.10 (CONT. . . .)

	B.C.	ALTA.	SASK.	MAN.	ONT.	QUE.	N.B.	N.S.	P.E.I.	NFLD.
Percent who contact public officials or politicians: Often or Sometimes	14.9	10.3	17.3	13.6	14.8	15.2	13.6	22.9	24.0	—
Percent who often or sometimes work for provincial party or candidate	7.9	8.0	19.2	8.5	8.4	12.9	10.6	17.2	20.0	8.1
Percent who often or sometimes put political sticker on car, put up a sign or the like	14.9	10.3	17.3	13.6	16.3	7.9	12.1	27.5	12.0	42.9

Table 3.11: Provincial Political Participation: Rank Scores* and Composite Score

FORM OF PARTICIPATION	B.C.	ALTA.	SASK.	MAN.	ONT.	QUE.	N.B.	N.S.	P.E.I.	NFLD.
Reading about provincial politics	10	5	6	4	7	3	2	8	9	1
Discussing provincial politics with others	10	3	5	8	6	7	4	9	2	1
Trying to convince friends to vote same way	9	5	7	1	6	8	2	10	3	4
Working with others in community	3	6	10	1	4	2	7	9	8	5
Attending political meetings, rallies	3	2	5	4	1	6	7	9	10	8
Contacting public officials or politicians	6	2	8	4	5	7	7	9	10	1
Working for provincial party or candidate	1	2	9	5	4	7	6	8	10	3
Putting up a sign, sticker on car	6	2	8	5	7	1	4	9	3	10
Composite Score	6.0	3.4	7.3	4.0	5.0	5.1	4.5	8.9	6.9	4.1

*Provinces are ranked on each item by the percentage of respondents reporting that they often or sometimes participate. The province with the highest percentage has

British Columbia, a province with an above average participant tendency, it is the non-group-related forms of participation which account for this political activism. The same tendency applies to Ontario, although here participation in general is not above average.* The reverse seems true for Prince Edward Island, also a highly participant province. Here it is the group- or institution-related actions which comprise the typical forms of provincial participation. The same tendency in favour of such group-oriented involvement appears as well (but less sharply) in New Brunswick and Newfoundland. This distinction between types of participation tells us little or nothing about Nova Scotia (where all forms of political action are high), Quebec, or Saskatchewan.

Besides information on specific types of political participation, a perspective on how provinces compare in terms of overall patterns of participation could indicate a broader style of politics. One means of estimating degrees of participatory politics is to rank each province against all the others on each form of participation. If, for each type of participation, we accord to the province with the highest level of participation a maximum score of 10, to the second a score of 9 and so on down to the lowest a score of 1, we then have a rank ordering on each question. If we also assume that a total image of participation can be seen as an additive combination of such traits, then we can sum these scores and calculate an average provincial participation score. This simple ranking and averaging is presented in Table 3.11. From this evidence four provinces stand out by their high overall level of activity. In the west, Saskatchewan and British Columbia can be said to be participant provinces—in comparison with their two neighbors, Alberta and Manitoba, which manifest the two lowest overall rankings among all ten provinces.[111] In the east, it is Nova Scotia which stands apart from all other provinces by an extraordinary level of all forms of participation. Prince Edward Island follows as the second most politically active province.[112] Perhaps surprisingly the central provinces do not reflect extremes of participation at all. It is rather in the "peripheries" that the most interesting variations in provincial political participation are to be found.

SUMMARY

Parties, pressure groups and political ideas define much of the framework within which decision-makers must operate. The policy impact of these forces is largely indirect and because of this also

---

*If we were to average only the four "individual" types of participation, Ontario's average score would be 6.5.

difficult to assess. Their significance, moreover, cannot be expressed in terms of policy outputs alone, for political forces most immediately affect policy-making participants, as well as patterns of conflict and interaction which constitute the usual processes through which policies develop. The impact of political forces cannot be fully understood without a careful examination of the formal structures of provincial governments.

NOTES

1. The comparative literature on the nature and functions of political parties is varied and rich. Major works include Robert Dahl, Editor, *Political Oppositions in Western Democracies*, Yale, University Press, New Haven, 1966; Maurice Duverger, *Political Parties*, Wiley, New York, 1954; Leon Epstein, *Political Parties in Western Democracies*, Praeger, New York, 1967; V.O. Key, Jr., *Political Parties and Pressure Groups*, Fifth Edition, Crowell, New York, 1964; Joseph LaPalombara and Myron Weiner, Editors, *Political Parties and Political Development*, Princeton University Press, Princeton, 1966; S.M. Lipset and Stein Rokkan, *Party Systems and Voter Alignments*, Free Press, New York, 1967.

2. There are, of course, a number of non-party constraints — especially the need for regional and group representation — which shape cabinet appointments within parties. On the selection of cabinet members, see: W.A. Matheson, *The Prime Minister and the Cabinet*, Methuen, Toronto, 1976, chapters 2, 3; Fred Schindeler, "The Prime Minister and the Cabinet: History and Development," in T.A. Hockin, Editor, *Apex of Power*, Second Edition, Prentice-Hall, Scarborough, 1977, pp. 22-47; J.R. Mallory, *The Structure of Canadian Government*, Macmillan of Canada, Toronto, 1971, pp. 80-85; Fred Schindeler, *Responsible Government in Ontario*, University of Toronto Press, Toronto, 1969, pp. 32-42.

3. On the rise of Social Credit in British Columbia see Martin Robin, *Pillars of Profit, the Company Province 1934-1972*, McClelland and Stewart, Toronto, 1973, chapters 5 and 6; Paddy Sherman, *Bennett*, McClelland and Stewart, Toronto, 1966; David Elkins, "Politics Makes Strange Bedfellows: the B.C. Party System in the 1952 and 1953 Provincial Elections," *B.C. Studies*, no. 30, Summer, 1976, pp. 3-26. Third party or protest movements based on the successful mobilization of substantial new bases of electoral support are common to the history of several provinces. The rise of the CCF in

Saskatchewan, Social Credit in Alberta, the Progressives and later the NDP in Manitoba, the Créditistes and the Parti Québécois in Quebec all illustrate this phenomenon. See Maurice Pinard, *The Rise of a Third Party, A Study in Crisis Politics,* Enlarged Edition, McGill-Queen's University Press, Montreal, 1975; Walter Young, *Democracy and Discontent: Progressivism, Socialism and Social Credit in the Canadian West,* Ryerson, Toronto, 1969, S.M. Lipset, *Agrarian Socialism,* Anchor Books Edition, Doubleday, Garden City, N.Y., 1968; C.B. McPherson, *Democracy in Alberta: Social Credit and the Party System,* Second Edition, University of Toronto Press, Toronto, 1962; W.L. Morton, *The Progressive Party in Canada,* University of Toronto Press, Toronto, 1950; Michael Stein, *The Dynamics of Right-Wing Protest: A Political Analysis of Social Credit in Quebec,* University of Toronto Press, Toronto, 1973.

4. Lawrence LeDuc, Jr. and Walter L. White, "The Role of Opposition in a One-Party Dominant System: the Case of Ontario," *Canadian Journal of Political Science* 7, March, 1974, pp. 86-100; William M. Chandler, "Canadian Socialism and Policy Impact: Contagion from the Left?" *Canadian Journal of Political Science* 10, December 1977, pp. 755-780.

5. J. Murray Beck, "Elections," in David J. Bellamy, Jon. H. Pammett and Donald C. Rowat, Editors, *The Provincial Political Systems, Comparative Essays,* Methuen, Toronto, 1976, p. 177; John Wilson, "The Canadian Political Cultures: Towards a Redefinition of the Nature of the Canadian Political System," *Canadian Journal of Political Science* 7, September 1974, pp. 438-483.

6. On the variations among provincial liberals see Escott M. Reid, "The Saskatchewan Liberal Machine Before 1929," in Hugh Thorburn, Editor, *Party Politics in Canada,* Third Edition, Prentice-Hall of Canada, Scarborough, 1972, pp. 23-34; David E. Smith, *Prairie Liberalism: The Liberal Party in Saskatchewan 1905-1971,* University of Toronto Press, Toronto, 1975; John Wilson, "The Decline of the Liberal Party in Manitoba Politics," *Journal of Canadian Studies* 10, 1975, pp. 24-41; John Wilson and David Hoffman, "The Liberal Party in Contemporary Ontario Politics," *Canadian Journal of Political Science* 3, June 1970, pp. 177-204; Vincent Lemieux, "Quebec: 'Heaven is Blue and Hell is Red'," in Martin Robin, Editor, *Canadian Provincial Politics,* Prentice-Hall of Canada, Scarborough, 1972, pp. 262-289.

7. Robin, *Pillars of Profit, passim.* W. Christian and C. Campbell, *Political Parties and Ideologies in Canada: Liberals, Conservatives, Socialists, Nationalists,* McGraw-Hill Ryerson, Toronto, 1974, pp. 33-75.

8. Christian and Campbell, *ibid.,* pp. 76-115; Jonathan Manthorpe, *The*

Power and the Tories: Ontario Politics — 1943 to the Present, Macmillan of Canada, Toronto, 1974; Edwin R. Black, "Federal Strains in a Canadian Party," *Dalhousie Review* 45, 1965, pp. 307-323.

9. Robin, *Pillars of Profit*, pp. 128-137; Macpherson, *Democracy in Alberta*; John Irving, *The Social Credit Movement in Alberta*; University of Toronto Press, Toronto, 1959.

10. Major works on the CCF-NDP include S.M. Lipset, *Agrarian Socialism*; Walter Young, *The Anatomy of a Party: The National CCF, 1932-1961*, University of Toronto Press, Toronto, 1969; L. Zakuta, *A Protest Movement Becalmed: A Study of Change in the C.C.F.*, University of Toronto Press, Toronto, 1964; Gerald L. Caplan, *The Dilemma of Canadian Socialism: The CCF in Ontario*, McClelland and Stewart, Toronto, 1973; Desmond Morton, *NDP: The Dream of Power*, A.M. Hakkert, Toronto, 1974; and Ivan Avakumovic, *Socialism in Canada, A Study of the CCF-NDP in Federal and Provincial Politics*, McClelland and Stewart, Toronto, 1978.

11. On federal-provincial partisan differences see Harold D. Clarke, Jane Jenson, Lawrence LeDuc and Jon H. Pammett, "Partisanship and Party Images: the Canadian Federal System," paper presented at the Annual Meeting of the Canadian Political Science Association, Quebec City, May 1976; Donald Smiley, *Canada in Question: Federalism in the Seventies*, Second Edition, McGraw-Hill Ryerson, Toronto, 1976, chapter 4; George Perlin and Patti Peppin, "Variation in Party Support in Federal and Provincial Elections," *Canadian Journal of Political Science* 4, 1971, pp. 280-286; Wilson and Hoffman, *Canadian Journal of Political Science*, 3, 1970, pp. 171-204.

12. Giovanni Sartori, "European Political Parties: the Case of Polarized Pluralism" in Joseph LaPalombara and Myron Weiner, Editors, *Political Parties and Political Development*, Princeton University Press, Princeton, 1966, pp. 137-176, is an example of party systems analysis which formulates such an ideological array as an explanation of the impact of party systems on the workings of governing institutions.

13. Paul Fox, "Politics and Parties in Canada" in Paul Fox, Editor, *Politics: Canada*, Fourth Edition, McGraw-Hill Ryerson, Toronto, 1977, pp. 253-256.

14. The class basis of Canadian party politics has been explored in considerable depth at the federal level but less fully within provinces. The bulk of the evidence drawn from federal election and survey analyses shows comparatively low partisan division along class lines. Important analyses include: Robert Alford, *Party and Society*, Rand McNally, Chicago, 1963, pp. 250-286; Robert Alford, "The Social Bases of Political Cleavage in the 1962 Election" in John Meisel, Editor, *Papers on the 1962 Election*, University of Toronto

Press, Toronto, 1965, pp. 203-234; John C. Courtney, *Voting in Canada*, Prentice-Hall of Canada, Scarborough, 1967 includes federal and provincial analyses; John Meisel, *Working Papers on Canadian Politics*, Second Edition, McGill-Queen's University Press, Montreal, 1975; John Meisel, *Cleavages, Parties and Values in Canada*, Sage, London, 1974; Peter Regenstreif, *The Diefenbaker Interlude: Parties and Voting in Canada*, Longman Canada, Toronto, 1965, pp. 84-106; Peter Regenstreif, "Some Aspects of National Party Support in Canada," *Canadian Journal of Economics and Political Science* 29, February, 1963, pp. 59-74; Mildred A. Schwartz, "Canadian Voting Behavior," in Richard Rose, Editor, *Electoral Behavior: A Comparative Handbook*, Free Press, New York, 1974, pp. 543-618; Mildred A. Schwartz, *Politics and Territory*, McGill-Queen's University Press, Montreal, 1974; Mildred A. Schwartz, *Public Opinion and Canadian Identity*, University of California Press, Berkeley, California, 1967, pp. 172-186. For alternative views of class voting, see John Wilson, "Politics and Social Class in Canada: The Case of Waterloo South," *Canadian Journal of Political Science* 1, September, 1968, pp. 288-309 and N.H. Chi, "Class Voting in Canadian Politics," in O.M. Kruhlak et al., *The Canadian Political Process*, Holt, Rinehart, and Winston of Canada, Toronto, 1970, pp. 226-247; and N.H. Chi, "Class Cleavage," in Conrad Winn and John McMenemy, Editors, *Political Parties in Canada*, McGraw-Hill Ryerson, Toronto, 1976, pp. 89-113.

15. On these cleavage patterns, see J.A. Laponce, "Ethnicity, Religion, and Politics in Canada: A Comparative Analysis of Survey and Census Data," in Mattei Dogan and Stein Rokkan, Editors, *Social Ecology*, MIT Press, Boston, 1969, pp. 187-216; Meisel pp. 253-274; Meisel (1974), Schwartz (1974); Mildred Schwartz, *Politics and Territory*; William P. Irvine, "Explaining the Religious Basis of the Canadian Partisan Identity: Success on the Third Try," *Canadian Journal of Political Science* 7, September, 1974, pp. 560-563.

16. Frederick Engelmann and Mildred Schwartz, *Canadian Political Parties: Origin, Character, Impact*, Prentice-Hall of Canada, Scarborough, 1975, have suggested some reasons for thinking that there may be a stronger ideological/class basis to some provincial party systems than to the federal party system, pp. 186-199.

17. This developmental view is explicitly formulated by John Wilson in the context of comparing Canadian political cultures. Wilson distinguishes between political cultures identified by modernity of party systems and posits a threefold typology: "Underdeveloped," including the four Atlantic provinces, "Transitional," which applies to Quebec, Ontario, Manitoba, and British Columbia, and "Developed," Alberta and Saskatchewan (pp. 457-474). Jane Jenson has also discussed provincial parties within the same developmental

perspective but has relied on survey data to analyze these differences. Her findings provide further substantiation of the variation across provinces in the traditional, transitional or modern bases of party politics; John Wilson, *op. cit.*, pp. 438-483; Jane Jenson, "Party Systems" in David Bellamy, Jon. H. Pammett and Donald C. Rowat, Editors, *The Provincial Political Systems*, Methuen, Toronto, 1976, pp. 118-131. See also J. Murray Beck (1976), pp. 177-196.

18. Jenson, *op. cit.*, pp. 124-125. The complexities of the linkage between social change and party system development, the crystallization of traditional cleavages, and the consequent impurity of the class conflict model of partisan support have been discussed at length by S.M. Lipset and Stein Rokkan (1967), pp. 1-64; and by Richard Rose and Derek Urwin, "Social Cohesion, Political Parties and Strains in Regimes," *Comparative Political Studies* 2, 1, April, 1969, pp. 7-67.

19. Meisel (1975) Working Papers; Meisel *Cleavages, Parties* (1974); Regenstreif *Diefenbaker Interlude* (1965); Alford *Party and Society* (1963); Schwartz, *Politics and Territory*; Schwartz, "Canadian Electoral Behaviour" (1975); Engelmann and Schwartz, pp. 186-208; David Elkins, "The Perceived Structure of Canadian Party Systems," *Canadian Journal of Political Science* 7, September, 1974, pp. 502-524.

20. Many of the most valuable sources of this category are historical case studies of the rise of protest movements. The best known works of this sort are footnoted above (#3). Also of interest is Graham White, "One Party Dominance and Third Parties: the Pinard Theory Reconsidered," *Canadian Journal of Political Science* 6, 1973, pp. 399-421.

21. Jenson represents the most recent comprehensive effort to identify these connections. Schwartz, *Politics and Territory* also provides some comparative assessment of regional political patterns.

22. The 1974 national election study was made available by the Institute for Behavioural Research, York University. The data were originally collected by Harold Clarke, Jane Jenson, Lawrence LeDuc, and Jon Pammett. Neither the Institute for Behavioural Research nor the original collectors of the data bear any responsibility for the analyses or interpretation presented here.

23. For a detailed analysis of the bases of PQ support see Richard Hamilton and Maurice Pinard, "The Bases of Parti Québécois Support in Recent Quebec Elections," *Canadian Journal of Political Science* 9, 1, March 1976, pp. 3-26.

24. On the importance of the religious factor in Canadian politics see, for example, John Meisel (1975), pp. 253-284; John Meisel (1974); J.A. Laponce, "Ethnicity, Religion and Politics in Canada."

25. See also Hamilton and Pinard. *op. cit.*

26. The 1974 data on Newfoundland do not demonstrate a clear religious basis to provincial partisanship despite a long-standing sectarian cleavage. On this, see S.J.R. Noel, *Politics in Newfoundland*, University of Toronto Press, Toronto, 1971, pp. 21-25, 278-283; Susan McCorquodale, "Newfoundland: The Only Living Father's Realm," in Robin, *op. cit.*, pp. 134-152.

27. Meisel (1975), pp. 258-261 for a useful treatment of this using federal data.

28. Meisel (1975), pp. 258-274. William P. Irvine, 1974, pp. 560-563.

29. Federally, see Meisel (1975), op. cit., appendix Tables I, II and pp. 12, 84-88, Schwartz in Rose (ed.), "Canadian Voting Behaviour". There are several comparative studies showing associations between partisan support and male-female categorizations. The tendency has been strongest in Italian politics where the church-going, female population has been a bulwark of Christian Democratic support in the post-war era. On this see Dogan, in Lipset and Rokkan, *op. cit.*, pp. 159-167; Raphael Zariski, *Italy, the Politics of Uneven Development*, Dryden, Hinsdale, Illinois, 1974, p. 105.

30. It should be noted that these tendencies in *provincial* partisan preference found in the 1974 survey are at variance with the *federal* results reported by John Meisel (1975), *op. cit.*, p. 12.

31. Important studies which demonstrate partisan differences by age group include: Butler and Stokes, pp. 33-66, 122-175, 135-147; Dogan, pp. 165-167; Meisel (1975), pp. 11-12; Schwartz (1974), pp. 597-599; Regenstreif, *The Diefenbaker Interlude*, pp. 85-89.

32. David Elkins notes that, despite this awareness, many observers continue to work within a left-right model of party positions. He demonstrates that federally there is a consistent view of the ideological left-right positioning of the NDP, Conservatives and Liberals, but some confusion over the place of Social Credit and the Créditistes, p. 510. His evidence also indicates regional differences in perceptions of the left-right placing of parties, pp. 518-519, 522.

33. An important exception is Wilson (1974), *op. cit.*

34. Beck (1976), pp. 177-182. See also the chapters on the Atlantic provinces (P.J. Fitzpatrick on N.B., Susan McCorquodale on Newfoundland, J.M. Beck on Nova Scotia and Frank McKinnon on Prince Edward Island) in Martin Robin, Editor, *Canadian Provincial Politics* (1978)

35. Pinard (1975). See also the chapters on the western and central provinces in Robin (1978).

36. Duverger, *Political Parties* (1954); Lipset and Rokkan, *Party Systems and Voter Alignments* (1966); Dahl, *Political Oppositions;* LaPalombara and Weiner, *Political Parties and Political Development;* Douglas Rae, *The Analysis of Political Cleavages*, Yale University Press, New Haven, 1970.

37. Two-party and multi-party situations are analyzed at length in Duverger (1954); Giovanni Sartori, "European Political Parties: the Case of Polarized Pluralism," in LaPalombara and Weiner, pp. 137-176; Epstein (1967), pp. 46-76.

38. Douglas Rae, *The Political Consequences of Electoral Laws*, Yale University Press, New Haven, 1967.

39. The calculating formula for fractionalization scores from Rae, p. 56 is F = 1.

40. On one-party dominance, see Pinard (1975); LeDuc and White (1974); Macpherson (1953); Irving (1959); G. White (1973); John T. McLeod, "Explanations of Our Party System" in Fox (1970), pp. 215-222.

41. It is essential to note that third parties are not necessarily disadvantaged by the electoral system. Where their support is regionally concentrated such parties are less likely to be penalized in this way. This is so because they can remain the dominant party locally or regionally while obtaining only minor party status provincially or federally. The disadvantage for minor parties is, however, very real wherever their support is geographically diffuse. See Alan C. Cairns, "The Electoral System and the Party System in Canada, 1921-1965," *Canadian Journal of Political Science* March 1968, pp. 55-80.

42. For a related study, see Benjamin Ginsberg, "Elections and Public Policy," *American Political Science Review* 70, 1, March 1976, pp. 41-49.

43. David Elkins, "Politics Makes Strange Bedfellows: the B.C. Party System in 1952 and 1953 Provincial Elections," *B.C. Studies*, 30, Summer, 1976, pp. 3-26; Henry F. Angus, "The British Columbia Election of 1952," *Canadian Journal of Economics and Political Science* 18, 1952, p. 518-525.

44. General discussions of B.C. party politics are found in Robin, *Pillars of Profit;* Sherman, *Bennett;* Daniel J. Koenig and Trevor B. Proverbs, "Class, Regional and Institutional Sources of Party Support Within British Columbia," *B.C Studies*, 29, Spring, 1976, pp. 19-28.

45. On the 1972 election, see Daniel Koenig, et al., "The Year That British Columbia Went N.D.P.: N.D.P. Voter Support Pre and Post-1972," *B.C. Studies* 24, Winter 1974-75, pp. 65-86.

46. On one-party dominance in Alberta, see Macpherson, *Democracy in Alberta;* Beck (1976), pp. 186-87; J.A. Long and F.Q. Quo, "Alberta: One-Party Dominance" in Robin (1972), pp. 1-26.

47. General sources on Saskatchewan party politics include Norman Ward and Duff Spafford, Editors, *Politics in Saskatchewan*, Longman Canada, Toronto, 1968; David E. Smith, *Prairie Liberalism, The Liberal Party in Saskatchewan 1905-71*, University of Toronto Press, Toronto, 1975; Lipset, *Agrarian Socialism*.

48. John C. Courtney and David E. Smith, "Saskatchewan: Parties in a Politically Competitive Province," in Robin, ed., *Canadian Provincial Politics*, pp. 290-318.
49. Beck (1976), p. 185.
50. Nelson Wiseman, "The C.C.F. and the Manitoba 'Non-partisan' Government of 1940," *Canadian Historical Review* 59, 1973, pp. 173-195.
51. John Wilson, "The Decline of the Liberal Party in Manitoba Politics," *op. cit.*
52. Dennis H. Wrong, "Ontario Elections, 1934-1955: A Preliminary Survey of Voting," *Canadian Journal of Economics and Political Science* 23, August, 1957, pp. 395-403.
53. David Hoffman and John Wilson, "Ontario: A Three-Party System in Transition," in Robin, pp. 198-239.
54. Vincent Lemieux, Marcel Gilbert and André Blais, *Une élection de réalignment*, Editions du Jour, Montreal, 1970; Vincent Lemieux, *Le quotient politique vrai, le vote provinciale et fédérale au québec*, Laval, Quebec, 1973; Daniel Latouche, Guy Lord and Jean-Guy Vaillencourt, Editors, *Le Processus électoral provinciale de 1970 et 1973*, Hurtubise HMH, Montreal, 1976; Vincent Lemieux, ed., *Quatre élections provinciales au Québec, 1956-1966*, Laval, Québec, 1969; Jane Jenson and Peter Regenstreif, "Some Dimensions of Partisan Choice in Quebec, 1969," *Canadian Journal of Political Science* 3, 2, June, 1970, pp. 308-317; Maurice Pinard, "The Ongoing Political Realignments in Quebec," in Thomson, *Quebec Society and Politics*, pp. 119-138; Hamilton and Pinard, pp. 3-26; Herbert F. Quinn, *The Union Nationale, A Study in Quebec Nationalism*, University of Toronto Press, Toronto, 1963; and John Saywell, *The Rise of the Parti Québécois 1967-1976*, University of Toronto Press, Toronto, 1977.
55. Lemieux *et al.* (1970).
56. Hugh Thorburn, *Politics in New Brunswick*, University of Toronto Press, Toronto, 1961, pp. 83-84; P.J. Fitzpatrick, "New Brunswick: the Politics of Pragmation" in Robin, *op. cit.*, pp. 116-133.
57. Thorburn, p. 114.
58. J. Murray Beck, *The Government of Nova Scotia*, University of Toronto Press, Toronto, 1957, pp. 168-169; J. Murray Beck, "The Party System in Nova Scotia: Tradition and Conservatism" in Robin, pp. 176-179. Minor parties had their greatest success in Nova Scotia in the provincial election of 1920, when United Farmers plus the Independent Labour Party combined to capture 32.3 percent of the vote and thirteen seats. Reinforced by a national popular surge in the latter years of World War II, the CCF managed to win 13.5 percent in 1945, after which it suffered gradual decline. In the 1970s, the NDP has shown signs of revival with 7.0 percent (2 seats)

in 1970 and 13.0 percent (3 seats) in 1974, and 14.5 percent (4 seats) in 1978. But the NDP has not made any dramatic breakthroughs outside of its traditional mining and industrial areas of Cape Breton.

59. Beck (1957), p. 157.
60. Beck (1972), p. 185.
61. Frank MacKinnon, "Prince Edward Island: Big Engine, Little Body" in Robin, Second Edition, *op. cit.*, p. 222. The only substantial work on Prince Edward Island remains Frank MacKinnon, *The Government of Prince Edward Island*, University of Toronto Press, Toronto, 1951; on parties see pp. 242-258.
62. Susan McCorquodale, "Newfoundland: The Only Living Father's Realm" in Robin, *op. cit.*, p. 148. See also S.J.R. Noel, *Politics in Newfoundland*, University of Toronto Press, Toronto, 1971.
63. This is a measure of average partisan instability, not the instability of individual legislators. As McCorquodale notes, the turnover of members of the House of Assembly has been high, p. 152.
64. Conrad Winn and John McMenemy, *Political Parties in Canada* McGraw-Hill Ryerson, Toronto, 1976, p. 1.
65. "British Columbia, the Company Province" in Robin, Third Edition, pp. 35, 39.
66. J. Murray Beck, "Nova Scotia, Tradition and Conservatism" in Robin, *ibid.*, p. 201.
67. David Falcone and William Mishler, "Canadian Provincial Legislatures and System Outputs: A Diachronic Analysis of the Determinants of Health Policy," paper presented at the Annual Meeting of the Southern Political Science Association (November 1974); and Dale H. Poel, "Canadian Provincial and American State Policy: A Qualitative Explication of an Empirical Difference," paper presented at the Annual Meeting of the Canadian Political Science Association, Montreal (1972).
68. Richard Rose, "Models of Change" in Richard Rose (ed.), *The Dynamics of Public Policy: A Comparative Analysis*, Sage, London, 1976, p. 22.
69. Dale H. Poel, "The Diffusion of Legislation among the Canadian Provinces, a Statistical Analysis," *Canadian Journal of Political Science* 9, 4, December, 1976, pp. 620-625. See also Donald E. Blake, "LIP and Partisanship: An Analysis of the Local Initiatives Program," Canadian Public Policy 2, 1, Winter, 1976, pp. 17-32.
70. William M. Chandler, *op. cit.*
71. Norman Penner, "Ontario, the Dominant Province" in Robin, 3rd edition, pp. 214-215.
72. S.M. Lipset, *Agrarian Socialism*, pp. 269-281; Martin Robin, *Pillars of Profit*, pp. 50-62.

73. Rose, *op. cit.*, p. 25.
74. A. Paul Pross, "Pressure Groups" in David J. Bellamy, Jon H. Pammett and Donald C. Rowat, Editors, *The Provincial Political Systems, Comparative Essays*, Methuen, Toronto, 1976, p. 132; Mildred A. Schwartz, "The Group Basis of Politics" in John H. Redekop (ed.), *Approaches to Canadian Politics*, Prentice-Hall of Canada, Scarborough, 1978, p. 325.
75. On party-group linkages see Frederick C. Engelmann and Mildred A. Schwartz, *Canadian Political Parties: Origin, Character, Impact*, Prentice-Hall of Canada, Scarborough, 1975, Chapter 7. On organized labour in particular see Martin Robin, *Radial Politics and Canadian Labour, 1880-1930*, Industrial Relations Centre, Queen's University, Kingston, 1968; Gad Horowitz, *Canadian Labour in Politics*, University of Toronto Press, Toronto, 1968; and David Kwavnick, *Organized Labour and Pressure Politics, the Canadian Labour Congress, 1956-1968*, McGill-Queen's University Press, Montreal, 1972.
76. A. Paul Pross, "Pressure Groups: Adaptive Instruments of Political Communication" in Pross (ed.), *Pressure Group Behaviour in Canadian Politics*, McGraw-Hill Ryerson, Toronto, 1975, pp. 1-27.
77. Pross (1976), *op. cit.*, p. 133.
78. *Ibid.*, pp. 133-136.
79. Important exceptions are the major works of Robert Presthus, *Elite Accommodation in Canadian Politics*, Macmillan of Canada, Toronto, 1973 and *Elites in the Policy Process*, Cambridge University Press, London, 1974.
80. The general argument has been formulated by Harry Eckstein, *Pressure Group Politics*, Stanford University Press, Stanford, 1960, Chapter 1; and Samuel H. Beer, *British Politics in the Collectivist Age*, Knopf, New York, 1966, Chapter 12. With reference to provincial politics, see Pross (1976), *op. cit.*, pp. 134, 142.
81. Schwartz, *op. cit.*, pp. 332-340; Richard Simeon, "Regionalism and Canadian Political Institutions" in J. Peter Meekison (ed.), *Canadian Federalism: Myth or Reality*, Third Edition, Methuen, Toronto, 1977, p. 301; and Kwavnick, *op. cit.*
82. Helen Jones Dawson, "National Pressure Groups and the Federal Government" in Pross (ed.), *Pressure Group Behaviour*, op. cit. p. 30.
83. Pross (1976), *op. cit.*, p. 132.
84. Schwartz, *op. cit.*, pp. 329-332. Federal access is treated in Dawson, *op. cit.*, pp. 27-58.
85. *Elite Accommodation*, op. cit., pp. 152-154.
86. S.J.R. Noel, "Leadership and Clientelism" in Bellamy, Pammett and Rowat (eds.), *op. cit.*, pp. 197-213.
87. H.V. Nelles, *The Politics of Development: Forests, Mines and Hydro Electric Power in Ontario 1849-1941*, Macmillan of Canada, Toronto, 1974.

88. "The Mining Industry and the Great Tax Reform Debate" in Pross (ed.), *Pressure Group Behaviour*, op.cit., pp. 89-114.

89. "Federalism and the Political Economy of the Canadian State" in Leo Panitch, Editor, *The Canadian State, Political Economy and Political Power*, University of Toronto Press, Toronto, 1977, pp. 71-100.

90. Michael J. Trebilcock, "Winners and Losers in the Modern Regulatory State" in K.J. Rae and J.T. McLeod, Editors, *Business and Government in Canada, Selected Readings*, Second Edition, Methuen, Toronto, 1976, pp. 362-378.

91. Rea and McLeod write of the "drift toward corporatism" in their *Business and Government in Canada*, ibid., pp. 334-345. For a commentary on this model see Philippe C. Schmitter, "Still the Century of Corporatism?" *Review of Politics* 36, January 1974, pp. 85-131; and *Comparative Political Studies* 10, April 1977, special issue on corporatism.

92. Phillippe Schmitter, "Modes of Interest Intermediation and Models of Societal Change in Western Europe," pp. 7-38, and Leo Panitch, "The Development of Corporatism in Liberal Democracies," pp. 61-90, *Comparative Political Studies* 10, April 1977.

93. Gerhard Lehmbruch, "Liberal Corporatism and Party Government," *ibid.*, pp. 91-126.

94. Presthus, *Elite Accommodation*, op. cit. There has been extensive debate on the applicability of the consociational model to Canadian politics. Consociationalism may be seen as a special form of elite accommodation, usually occurring in systems characterized by severe social fragmentation, usually along ethnic-linguistic and religious cleavages. In these cases accommodation among political elites from the various social segments provides a mechanism for compromise and moderation in an otherwise highly explosive and centrifugal social structure. See Kenneth McRae, Editor, *Consociational Democracy, Political Accommodation in Segmented Societies*, McClelland and Stewart, Toronto, 1974, especially the essays by Lijphart, Lorwin, McRae, and Noel.

95. Carolyn Tuohy, "Pluralism and Corporatism in Ontario Medical Politics" in K.J. Rea and J.T. McLeod, *op. cit.*, p. 397.

96. Malcolm G. Taylor, "Quebec Medicare: Policy Formulation in Conflict and Crisis," *Canadian Public Administration*, 15, (September 1972) p. 230.

97. Anthony King, "Ideas, Institutions and the Policies of Governments: A Comparative Analysis," Parts I-III, *British Journal of Political Science* 3, 1973, pp. 291-313, 409-423; Gaston Rimlinger, *Welfare Policy and Industrialization in Europe, America and Russia*, Wiley, New York, 1971.

98. Ronald Manzer, "Public Policies in Canada: A Developmental

Perspective," paper presented to the Annual Meeting of the Canadian Political Science Association, Edmonton (June 1975).

99. Hugh Heclo, *Modern Social Politics in Britain and Sweden*, Yale University Press, New Haven, chapter 6.

100. Kenneth Bryden, *Old Age Pensions and Policy-Making in Canada*, McGill-Queen's University Press, Montreal, 1974, pp. 19-24, 183-187.

101. Gad Horowitz, "Conservatism, Liberalism and Socialism in Canada: An Interpretation," *Canadian Journal of Economics and Political Science* 32, 2, May 1966, pp. 144-171.

102. Richard Simeon, "Studying Public Policy," *Canadian Journal of Political Science* 9, 4, December 1976, pp. 570-573.

103. Mildred A. Schwartz, *Public Opinion and Canadian Identity*, University of California Press, Berkeley, 1967, pp. 156-8; Mildred A. Schwartz, *Politics and Territory*, McGill-Queen's University Press, Montreal, 1974. See also Donald E. Blake, "The Measurement of Regionalism in Canadian Voting Patterns," *Canadian Journal of Political Science* 5, March, 1972, pp. 55-81. Richard Simeon and David J. Elkins, "Regional Political Culture in Canada," *Canadian Journal of Political Science* 7, September, 1974, pp. 397-437; John Wilson, "The Canadian Political Cultures: Toward a Redefinition of the Nature of the Canadian Political System," *Canadian Journal of Political Science* 7, September, 1974, pp. 438-483.

104. *Politics and Territory*, passim.

105. Simeon and Elkins, *op. cit.*

106. Harold Clarke *et al.*, "Partisanship and Party Images in the Canadian Federal System," paper presented at the Annual Meeting of the Canadian Political Science Association, Quebec City (May, 1976), pp. 4-6.

107. On the increase in the perceived importance of provincial politics in Quebec, see Leon Dion, *Quebec, the Unfinished Revolutioon* McGill-Queen's University Press, Montreal, pp. 31-51.

108. Jon. H. Pammett, "Public Orientation to Regions and Provinces," in David J. Bellamy, Jon H. Pammett and Donald C. Rowat, Editors, *The Provincial Political Systems, Comparative Essays*, Methuen, Toronto, 1976, pp. 86-99 is an important exception. Like the data reported here, Pammett's work is based on findings from the 1974 Election survey.

109. The findings of Simeon and Elkins based on 1965 and 1968 data generally substantiate these findings. They write, "British Columbia stands out as the province with the highest levels of trust and efficacy and the greatest degree of psychological involvement in politics," p. 415.

110. Prince Edward Island might be thought remarkable for its high level of political interest, its highest perception of government impact,

its high life satisfaction and its low feeling of government being too complicated. Frank MacKinnon's discussion (Robin *op. cit.*) of the closeness and preponderance of political life in this smallest province helps to explain these attitudinal patterns.

111. This provincial ranking produces results which are partially consistent with those of Simeon and Elkins. They distinguish between two polar types — provinces with high levels of efficacy trust and involvement or "citizen societies," which include B.C., Manitoba, Ontario and anglophone Quebec versus those tending to have low levels on these orientations or "disaffected societies," which include Atlantic Canada and francophone Quebec. In between but closer to the first group are Saskatchewan and Alberta.

It is essential to recall that the two estimates are not based on the same indicators, nor are the data taken from the same time period. Our ranking is based solely on reported political participation at the provincial level. Simeon and Elkins base their comparison on general attitudes which do not specify level of government, pp. 404-415.

112. Useful insights on why this pattern tends to prevail in Atlantic Canada are found in the analyses of MacKinnon, Beck, Fitzpatrick, and McCorquodale in Robin, *op. cit.*

Chapter 4

Structures of Policy-Making

Formal institutions represent a complex, regularized process made up of patterns of activity through which conflicts are structured and controlled in order to make public choices. These processes are authoritative or universally binding because they normally hold a monopoly of coercive power and because they benefit from a diffuse legitimacy. Although political institutions are the usual transmission lines between social conflict and government action, they provide no instant or simple route by which assertions of power automatically become policy. Institutions are never neutral; the procedures and ground-rules which they incorporate help to determine which options form a government's policy agenda and who the effective policy-makers are.[1] By excluding some participants and including others, by defining access points and influence opportunities, institutional arrangements may reflect effective power relationships and influence likely policy outcomes. They must, therefore, be viewed as among the most pervasive constraints and dynamics on both the style of policy-making and the substance of policy change.[2]

As the scope of government broadens and becomes increasingly complex, there is a corresponding tendency for the differentiation and specialization of decision-making and administrative structures. The significance of new forms of decision-making, whether the establishment of new ministries, the creation of a complex cabinet structure, the reform of parliamentary procedures or the granting of authority to some regulatory agency, cannot be understood simply as efforts to improve the efficiency, effectiveness or rationality of public decisions. Such institutional modification must also be viewed as part of the dynamics of policy change.

Political structures develop, persist, or decay in response to changing value systems, socio-economic cleavages, and interests. The policy impact of structures is correspondingly a function of interaction with these conditions and is therefore difficult to estimate. Much of the evidence on such relationships comes from cross-national studies because these permit comparisons of very basic institutional differences, for instance, the contrast between federal and unitary or parliamentary and separation-of-powers systems.

Within a common heritage of parliamentary-cabinet government, all provinces have undergone substantial institutional maturation through the process of province-building. This has meant, above all, an expansion in the capacity of provincial systems to respond to and resolve social and economic issues. This structural evolution applies to all three core elements of provincial parliamentary regimes: the cabinet, the bureaucracy, and the legislature.

THE CHANGING CABINET

Canadian provincial governments are among the inheritors of the British tradition which places the cabinet in the centre of the policy process by granting it responsibility for the formulation, coordination, and implementation of policy. Another tradition of British origin, responsible government, defines the essential political position of cabinets. They are accountable to the legislature and cannot govern without its confidence. Individually and collectively, ministers are responsible for the execution of public policy. The cabinet is the crucial link between the legislative and executive branches.[4]

From 1867 until the Second World War provincial cabinets could best be described as small informal groupings operating in an unstructured environment that reflected the personality of a particular premier rather than any enduring set of operational procedures.[5] For the most part individual ministers dealt with their own departments, showing little concern for policy coordination or integration. Provincial cabinets conformed to descriptions of the early phase of federal cabinet development: there was ". . . no agenda, no secretariat, no official present at meetings to record what went on, and no minutes of decisions taken and no system to communicate the decisions to the departments responsible to implement them."[6]

Increased demands for public goods and services, greater willingness to respond to these demands, and more complex interrelationships among policy areas have led to structural and operational changes in federal and provincial cabinets. Besides increases in size, cabinets have adopted a number of reforms to facilitate their policy-making function (or to improve their policy-making capability).

Cabinet Growth

One of the most obvious developments has been the expanding size of provincial cabinets. The first cabinet in Ontario numbered five, in Nova Scotia four and in Quebec and Alberta seven. As cabinet functions were added, there was often a tendency to enlarge the responsibility of

Table 4.1: Changing Size of Cabinets

PROVINCE	NUMBER OF MINISTERS	
	(1955)	(1976)
BRITISH COLUMBIA	10	15
ALBERTA	11	24
SASKATCHEWAN	14	17
MANITOBA	10	17
ONTARIO	19	26
QUEBEC	16	26
NEW BRUNSWICK	11	17
NOVA SCOTIA	8	17
PRINCE EDWARD ISLAND	8	10
NEWFOUNDLAND	12	17
MEAN	11.9	18.6

Source: *Canadian Parliamentary Guide*, 1955, 1976.

existing departments rather than to create new cabinet positions. However, as provincial governments took on more and more activities, cabinets also expanded (See Table 4.1). On average in 1955 they constituted twenty-three percent of the legislative assembly. By 1976 the cabinet average size had jumped to 18.6 with the smallest having ten members (Prince Edward Island), and the largest having twenty-six (Ontario and Quebec), with the average cabinet consisting of twenty-nine percent of the legislature.

There have been two important results of the increase in size. First, informal procedures and decision-making by the entire group have become less effective and, second, increased size has made the cabinet more powerful *vis à vis* the legislature and the caucus.

> Other things being equal, the greater the proportion of the House or the party taken up by the cabinet, the easier it will be for it to dominate proceedings. . . . With a large number of cabinet positions to be allotted, aspiring politicians are inclined to be rather tractable. And if a majority of the caucus holds cabinet positions as is sometimes the case in provincial parliaments then the role of the Government backbenchers in controlling the cabinet is greatly diminished.[7]

Since World War II the provinces have clearly shown a preference for a large number of small departments. Often this has entailed giving individual ministers multiple responsibilities rather than necessarily increasing the size of the cabinet. The smaller provinces have tended to make greatest use of this procedure. In 1976 the most extreme case was Prince Edward Island, where eight out of ten ministers held double departmental responsibilities. Three ministers in Nova Scotia and two in New Brunswick held multiple departmental responsibilities.

Hodgetts and Dwivedi have pointed out that there are positive as well as negative implications for organizing of provincial responsibilities into a large number of departments.[8] On the one hand, small portfolios are more manageable. They facilitate clearer lines of ministerial responsibility and more coherent programme development. Small departments also tend to be more responsive to client demands. On the other hand, there are also some negative consequences. Multiplicity maximizes the problem of coordination and a large number of small departments may also lead to the duplication of service personnel. Small specialized departments may be more susceptible to the influence of powerful pressure groups as well as more vulnerable to structural reorganization.

The growing range of cabinet portfolios is a good indicator of the expanding provincial state.[9] Early cabinets reflected the limited functions of provincial governments. The Nova Scotia cabinet at the time of confederation contained departments for Finance, Attorney General, Public Works and Mines, and Provincial Secretary. The Executive Councils[10] of Quebec and Ontario, provided for in the BNA Act, sec. 63, were made up of Attorney General, Provincial Secretary, Treasurer, Commission of Crown Lands, and Commission of Agriculture and Public Works. Quebec also had a Speaker of the Legislative Council and Solicitor General in its cabinet. A Department of Education was created in Ontario in 1876. In 1873 Quebec also instituted a Department of Education which was, however, abolished in 1875 and replaced by a non-cabinet level Superintendent of Education.[11] In 1905 the first cabinet in Alberta contained Departments of Attorney General, Public Works, Treasury, Agriculture, Provincial Secretary, Executive Council, and Education.

The departments that have been added to provincial cabinets illustrate the nature of expanding provincial responsibilities.[12] Each province has portfolios for health, social welfare, labour, economic development, transportation, and municipal affairs. Each also has at least one department for those natural resources which are pertinent to its economy, e.g., Fisheries in Nova Scotia and Newfoundland, Lands and Forests in Quebec and British Columbia. The most recent addition to all provincial cabinets is a Department of Environment. Intergovernmental Affairs has departmental status in Ontario, Alberta, Manitoba, and Quebec, and given the ever increasing importance of federal-provincial relations, it is likely to be adopted in other provinces.

Generally, the establishment of ministries has been quite similar federally and provincially. The major differences, such as provincial departments of municipal affairs and education and federal departments of defense and external affairs, reflect the differing constitutional responsibilities of the two levels of government. Matters of concern to specific provinces are reflected in unique departments. Quebec is the only province with a department for immigration and a separate communication department. Manitoba, Saskatchewan, Ontario, and Alberta have departments devoted solely to Northern Affairs.

The creation of a new department is an important policy decision for several reasons. First, the new portfolio is an indication of government concern and willingness to take on new policy responsibilities. Second, the new department is a focal point for the growth of public activity. Its bureaucracy sees its interests advanced by departmental expansion, while it also becomes a regular point of access for pressure groups seeking new public involvements in defense of their interests.

Taken by itself, increased size is not an adequate solution to the problem of managing expanding provincial responsibilities.[13] In order to increase their policy-making capacity the provinces have all, to some extent, adopted four major cabinet reforms: the creation of standing committees, an increase in staff assistance, establishment of horizontal portfolios, and techniques for systematic policy evaluation and choice.

Cabinet Committees

The use of cabinet committees was one of the first reforms in cabinet decision-making. Committees facilitate policy-making in two ways. First, they allow for specialization and more detailed consideration of policy than is possible before the full cabinet. Second, they permit the examination of issues that straddle departments or that no individual minister wants to tackle. By involving several departments, committees also promote coordination across policy fields.

It was not until the Trudeau reforms that standing committees became an integral part of the federal policy process.[14] Three crucial elements of the federal committee system—a top level Priorities and Planning Committee, Treasury Board, and operational policy committees, have to some degree been incorporated into provincial cabinet systems. Coordination, priority setting, and long-range planning are the jobs of the Priorities and Planning Committee which is chaired by the Prime Minister. The Treasury Board, the other major broad-range committee, now handles all financial and management aspects of policy and operations committees focus on specific issue areas.

Ontario is one of the provinces to have gone the furthest in cabinet committee reform. The Committee on Government Productivity established by the Robarts government in 1969 recommended a total restructuring of Ontario's cabinet system. Up until that time, the cabinet operated with a Treasury Board and a series of *ad hoc* committees to deal with specific, usually short-run, problems. For example, the Drainage Committee, made up of ministers from departments that had drainage programmes, was constituted to revise old legislation and to develop a new statute. Other *ad hoc* committees were created to coordinate on-going multi-departmental programmes. Prior to the establishment of the Department of Transportation, a committee coordinated all highway safety programmes.[15]

The COGP recommendations, adopted in 1971, created a standing committee system aimed at "transforming informal uncoordinated personal activities leading to policy decisions into a formal policy process."[16] Two coordinating committees were created—the Management Board and the Policy and Priorities Board and three policy committees corresponding to the policy fields of social development, resource development, and justice were established. These policy committees were made up of cabinet members whose ministries related to the policy field. Each policy committee is chaired by a provincial secretary, who is a minister with no line (functional) responsibilities, except to chair the committee's work. Also created was a kind of "super-ministry"—Treasury, Economic, and Inter-Governmental Affairs (TEIGA), which is more comparable to a policy field than to a departmental ministry. TEIGA serves to coordinate economic and financial policy as well as intergovernmental relations (federal, provincial and municipal). TEIGA's superior status is evident by the fact that it has the largest secretariat of any of the other cabinet committees, and that departmental policy proposals must go through TEIGA as well as the Treasury and Policy-Priorities Boards.

Starting in the mid-60's, several other provinces began to study and to consider cabinet reform. Newfoundland's Committee on Government Administration and Productivity recommended one of the most thorough restructurings of a cabinet. Under the premiership of Joey Smallwood, the cabinet had functioned on a personal and rather informal basis in which decisions were made by one person—the Premier. The structure of the cabinet did not facilitate extended policy examinations or interpretation. Although there were some *ad hoc* committees, all policy proposals came directly to the full cabinet. Similarly, the Treasury Board, created in 1952, did not begin to function until the 1960s. The Smallwood cabinet essentially served as a sounding board for his ideas and to legitimate his decisions.

Under the recommendations of the Committee on Government Administration and Productivity the cabinet was to operate through five standing committees—Policy/Planning, Treasury Board, and three operational policy committees.[17] Since its institutionalization in 1973, the committee system has been modified. There are now only two operational committees and their decisions go to full cabinet rather than to a coordinating committee. In his analysis of the Newfoundland cabinet, Johnson reports that both the bureaucrats and politicians who have worked within the new structures have been pleased with the changes. The civil servants felt that they were in a better position to offer advice, and the politicians felt they were in a better position to utilize that advice.[18]

The other Atlantic provinces have adopted more modest cabinet committee systems. New Brunswick, Nova Scotia, and Prince Edward Island all have Treasury Boards, and New Brunswick and P.E.I. also have coordinating Planning and Priorities Committees. None of the three have standing policy committees. New Brunswick is the only one that has undertaken a formal restructuring of its cabinet.

In Quebec as of 1975 the cabinet had a Treasury Board and five standing policy committees. The whole cabinet, rather than a central committee, functioned as the coordinator of policy. When the Parti Québécois came to power at the end of 1976, it instituted a Priorities Committee to coordinate policy and new policy committees, which have thus far played a significant role in policy-formulation.

The cabinet structures of the western provinces are quite varied. Based on its "Operation Productivity," an internal study, Manitoba was the first province to establish a planning-priorities committee. However, in 1973 the NDP government abolished this committee in its belief that planning and coordination are so important they require the input of the entire Cabinet. The Treasury Board and policy committee instituted by the former P.C. government were retained and two new policy standing committees were added. Manitoba's gradual approach to cabinet reform has been contrasted with Ontario's more comprehensive approach. In Manitoba there was no single complete and detailed blueprint for change comparable to Ontario's Committee for Government Productivity reports. Manitoba's reform process has been more incremental than that in Ontario, with policy committees added as they have been deemed necessary.[19]

As in so many other areas, the CCF in Saskatchewan was an innovator in cabinet reform. In 1945 it established the Economic Advisory and Planning Board to act as coordinator and to facilitate long-range policy planning. The Board initiated several changes in the operation of the cabinet, one of the most important being the creation of the Bureau of the Budget to centralize the functions of budgeting and administrative management.[20] The Planning Board and many of its innovations were abolished by the Liberal government in 1964. However, a similar board was resurrected when the NDP returned to power in 1971.

Alberta's present committee system, adopted in 1972, consists of a central coordinating committee as well as policy committees. Treasury Board functions are performed by the Committee on Finance, Priorities and Coordination. During the twenty years of Social Credit Government, British Columbia's cabinet was run on an informal personalized basis with little organization and staff. The NDP government, which came to power in 1972, did little to alter the cabinet's traditional structure. As Tennant explains, one major change that did take place was that the NDP Premier did not provide centralized leadership as had the Social Credit leader. Thus, the NDP, while adopting the traditional cabinet format, "discarded the one feasible means of attaining coordination."[21] When it returned to power in 1975 the Social Credit government instituted a committee on Planning and Priorities, a strengthened Treasury Board, and several substantive operational committees.

The provinces' efforts to facilitate more rational policy-making have followed rather similar lines. They have moved toward greater coordination by Treasury Boards and planning/priorities committees and increased division of labour through the use of standing policy committees. Treasury Boards that coordinate budgetary appropriations are the most common cabinet structure. Central coordinating committees have had more mixed reception. In a small cabinet like Newfoundland's which has only two policy committees, a central coordinating committee does not seem necessary, since half the cabinet has examined each proposal before it goes to full cabinet.[22] In several of the larger provinces, coordinating committees have proven more useful. At the federal level a planning/priorities committee evoked the fear of a "super cabinet" or inner circle. Because geographical representation is an important function of the federal government a smaller committee grouping endangers that function. For provincial cabinets, representation has not been so important, and therefore smaller, coordinating committees are less threatening.

Secretariats

In order for cabinet committees to be useful parts of the policy process they need to be backed up by support staffs, for without adequate research and information services the committees cannot perform their requisite functions. The provision of support staff is a relatively recent phenomenon which represents one more response to the increasingly complex world with which the cabinet must deal. In the provinces there has been a vast improvement in cabinet secretariat facilities. In most provinces the original secretary to cabinet was a cabinet minister (usually provincial secretary). Prince Edward Island was the only province to permit an individual from outside the cabinet to act as secretary. Similar to events at the federal level, the blossoming of provincial secretariats has followed the development of the cabinet committee system. As cabinet decision-making procedures have become more formal and more specialized, there has emerged an obvious need for technical support staff. The days of temporary staff assistance from the premier's office are past, as secretariats have been recognized as necessary for the success of the new policy-making structures. When the Economic Advisory and Planning Board was created in Saskatchewan in 1945, the Clerk of the Legislative Council served as the cabinet secretary for the CCF government. One of the earliest changes brought about by the Planning Board was the establishment of a formal Cabinet Secretariat.[23]

In the 1960s, when the other provinces began to revamp their cabinet systems, they also developed secretariats to service the new arrangements. Generally, the more elaborate the committee structure, the more developed the secretariat. Cabinet secretariats have been a second major response to increased cabinet responsibilities. The secretariats

> . . . have come to occupy a more and more important place in the policy-making picture. . . . Recommendations from departmental officials are no longer accepted almost routinely by Ministers who lack the expertise to question them effectively. Instead these recommendations are subjected to analysis and evaluation by committees of Ministers who together have a much broader perspective than an individual Minister and who can call on independent staff support in assessing department arguments.[24]

Besides providing an alternative source of information to the departmental bureaucracies, cabinet secretariats are also important to policy integration. George Szablowski, writing with reference to Ontario, argues that much of the coordinating of vertical departments is dependent on good staffing of the secretariat.[25] Most new policy proposals go first to the secretariat of the Planning/Priorities Committee and at that point the proposals are considered in the context of overall cabinet priorities.

Horizontal Portfolios

A third aspect of provincial cabinets' efforts to create a policy machinery better able to cope with complex societal problems has been the establishment of new horizontal coordinating portfolios. Horizontal portfolios and policy ministers (or secretaries as they are called in Ontario) are an attempt to integrate policy *within* a single broad area, whereas Planning/Priorities and Treasury Board committees focus on coordination among policy areas.

Horizontal portfolios have their origins in two types of cabinet concerns, the addition of relatively broad, new issues to the policy agenda and the consolidation of responsibilities across existing departments. Some horizontal ministries emerge from a combination of these two pressures, for example, the creation of ministries of environment, intergovernmental relations, human resources, and energy.

The most thorough-going movement toward horizontal structures has been in Ontario and Quebec. Among the major recommendations of the Ontario Committee on Government Productivity was the establishment of policy fields. Social Development, Justice, and Resource Development encompass most of the cabinet ministries. Each field and its corresponding cabinet committee is chaired by a Provincial Secretary or Policy Minister. Like the federal Ministers of State, policy ministers have no operating responsibilities; instead, their duties are solely in the areas of policy advice, formulation, and coordination. Essentially, they were to be the thinkers while departmental ministers were, in the main, the doers. Perhaps the most important of the Ontario horizontal structures is the Treasury, Economic Intergovernmental Affairs Ministry (TEIGA). It is a single ministry acting as a fourth policy field and as a coordinating committee. TEIGA's wide-ranging substantive responsibilities include fiscal and economic policies as well as intergovernmental relations.

Although several horizontal agencies, including Natural Resources and Environment, existed before the PQ came to power, the Lévesque government has created four important planning ministries that are similar to the policy fields in Ontario. The Quebec Ministries of Cultural Development, Social Development, Economic Development, and Regionalism are new structures whose role is to coordinate policy and to develop priorities within a broad subject area.

Horizontal portfolios are part of the provincial and federal governments' efforts to broaden the bases of decision-making. At a minimum, horizontal portfolios try to create a wider decisional scope. However, in Ottawa and in Ontario and Quebec the concept has meant more than a mere aggregation of vertical units. Rather, the new horizontal structures represent a qualitatively different approach to ministerial functions. The basis for the new ministries was research and formulation as opposed to implementation. In recommending the creation of the policy secretaries, the Committee on Government Productivity explicity called for a separation of policy-making and administration.[26]

Compared to cabinet committees and increased support staffs, the efforts to facilitate decision-making via horizontal portfolios have not been very successful. Szablowski and Doern agree that the attempts to separate policy and operations have been somewhat unrealistic. Operational departments are "reluctant to be relegated to the status of mere cogs in the wheel."[27] Research and analytical roles have not been an adequate power base. The result has been that policy ministers with no operational responsibilities have no power.[28]

Rational Policy Techniques

The fourth response to the pressure of cabinet overload has been the development of policy planning and systematic evaluation techniques. As in the case of the other reforms, the provinces have not moved uniformly to adopt any single technique. Although there are, of course, important differences, Planning, Programming and Budgeting (PPBS), Management by Objective, Cost/Benefit Analysis, and Programme Management Information Systems have a common objective, to set up a systematic process for decision-making. In order to utilize any of the rational policy techniques policy-makers must be able to make their objectives explicit and to measure and weigh the consequences of alternative courses of action.[29]

When Ottawa introduced PPBS in the late 60s most of the provinces expressed interest in the possible application of Planning, Programming and Budgeting. Despite their initial enthusiasm, the provinces have been quite cautious in adopting rational policy techniques. Two fundamental aspects of PPBS have proven especially difficult to implement. The cabinet must produce a detailed and specific listing of priorities, and data must be collected and measures developed for evaluating programme effectiveness.[30]

Ontario and Quebec, the provinces with the largest budgets, are the only ones to have made any thorough efforts to utilize PPBS. Although there was some interest in the 60s, it was not until 1971 that Ontario incorporated some of the key components of PPBS. Adoption of rational policy techniques was linked to the recommendations for structural cabinet reform of the Committee on Government Productivity (COGP). As part of its general effort in the late '60s to centralize decision-making, Quebec considered adopting PPBS,[31] and by 1973 it had begun to implement a system directly relating proposed expenditures to policy goals.

Under the Economic Advisory and Planning Board in Saskatchewan, procedures for systematic budgetary review and programme evaluation were instituted in the late 1940s! Throughout the 1950s Saskatchewan contined to use systematic policy techniques, and the Treasury Board emerged as the crucial instrument for rational formulation of policy.[32] Although these reforms were abolished by the subsequent Liberal government, when the NDP returned to power it implemented a "Programme-based Management Information System." Similar to PPBS, the Saskatchewan system permits decision-makers in the cabinet to compare and evaluate programmes in terms of costs and objectives.[33]

The days of informal decision-making are past; federal rational policy-making innovations are slowly being adapted to the more circumscribed needs of the provinces. Lack of personnel and other resources has made it difficult for provincial governments to improve their decision-making procedures. In fact, several provinces are really too small to utilize complex PPBS techniques.[34] However, it must be recognized that all provinces now accept the necessity of forward planning.

The common problems confronting provincial cabinets have produced a variety of reforms which generally have centralized decision-making. The changes toward more rational and efficient policy-making have made the process longer, more demanding, and more technical.[35] The emphasis on information and expertise could be the basis for enhancement of the role of the bureaucracy because it is the main source of information. There is even competition among departments for technical experts and information resources. However, new and/or strengthened secretariats have become important alternatives to the traditional departmental sources.

Efforts to expand the policy-making capability of the cabinet have tended to broaden the arena of conflict within Priorities/Planning and Treasury Board committees. The interrelationships among policy choices are made more explicit, and new proposals must compete and be justified across policy areas. In addition to employing a more comprehensive framework, cabinet policy-making is also more concerned with policy effectiveness. This means a greater awareness of the constraints and limitations posed by the environment and an increased sensitivity to the provincial implications of actions by the federal government.

BUREAUCRACY

Once described as the "missing link," the role of the public service is now widely recognized by students of both comparative and Canadian politics as a consistently important influence on policy development.[36] Similarly, Lipset, in *Agrarian Socialism*, contends that:

> It is impossible to understand the operation of a government simply by analyzing the goals of politicians in power and the non-governmental pressures on them. The members of the civil service constitute one of the major houses of government with the power to initiate, amend and veto actions proposed by other branches. The goals and values of the civil service are often as important a part of the total complex of forces responsible for state policy as those of the ruling political party.[37]

Traditionally, politics and administration have been viewed as separable activities in which politicians engage in conflict resolution and policy-making, while leaving administrators to handle the routine implementation of those decisions. This simple dichotomy fails to accurately portray the policy process. Politics and administration are two elements of a seamless web in which both are central participants in the overall process of policy development.[38] Not only does the bureaucracy play a prominent role in initiation and formulation of policy alternatives, it is also formally involved in decision-making in two ways. Through the instrument of delegated legislation, authority is transferred by the legislature to various administrative agencies[39] which are granted the power to make specific and detailed regulations in keeping with the principles of the legislation. Secondly, the bureaucracy is involved in rule-making in the actual execution of laws. The discretionary powers inherent in any administrative situation mean that in any given application of a general law the civil servant is making the rules for the individual or firm involved.

The Changing Public Service[40]

The development of a professional, highly skilled bureaucracy has been an essential component in province-building, for an efficient administrative machinery is a precondition for the expansion of the policy-making capacity of any political regime.[41] As noted in Chapter II, economic and social development have expanded the scope of the public sector. The jump in the number of provincial personnel can be explained in part by the fact that much of this growth has occurred in those areas under provincial jurisdiction, namely, health, social welfare, and education. Consequently, it is the expansion of traditional departments that accounts for most of the growth. As Hodgetts and Dwivedi observe, this pattern of bureaucratic expansion ". . . is not so much related to the assumption of new functions but to the provision of a higher level of service for health and hospitals, police and protection, education, highways, public works and public welfare."[42] In the post-war period from 1946 through to 1971 the number of provincial public servants within governmental departments increased from 38,370 to 209,760, representing a phenomenal growth of over 400 percent, while federal public service employment increased by only 80 percent.[43]

The largest number of provincial employees work within executive departments, but, because expanding economic regulation and the growth of public ownership have tended to take place outside the departmental structure,[44] there has been a corresponding increase in public employment among non-departmental provincial employees who work on regulatory boards and commissions or in public enterprises such as Ontario Hydro and Alberta telephone.

Personnel Management

Formerly, recruitment into the public service was based on patronage in which partisan and personal ties were the principal prerequisites for government jobs. The establishment of independent civil service commissions represented early efforts at reform through the promotion of a merit system. It was not until 1917 that British Columbia became the first province to follow Ottawa's lead in creating such a commission. Other provinces then followed suit, with Ontario, Manitoba, and Alberta in 1918, Saskatchewan in 1930, Nova Scotia in 1935, Quebec and New Brunswick in 1943, Newfoundland in 1953, and Prince Edward Island in 1962. These attempts at reform had the unanticipated result of bringing into the open an inherent contradiction in governmental personnel administration.

The desire to eliminate patronage and to provide uniform conditions of employment across the public service has led to efforts to establish neutral central agencies with authority for personnel decisions, yet the control of manpower is necessarily a part of the overall policy functions of the political executive. Hodgetts describes the results of this dilemma:

> The Civil Service Commission has been left with two roles which, in contemporary times, appear to have become increasingly incompatible. On the one hand it has been assigned personnel management functions which make it an integral part of the executive team largely responsible for service-wide conditions of employment that help to unify the public service. On the other hand, viewed in its traditional role as an independent agent, the commission is expected to serve as guarantor to parliament that the exercise of managerial prerogatives by the executive does no violence to the merit principle.[45]

Provincially, this ambivalence often resulted in Civil Service Commissions that were neither guarantors of the merit system nor effective personnel administrators for the government. The original four Commissions (in British Columbia, Ontario, Manitoba, and Alberta) were single member bodies with no tenure. This deprived them of any effective degree of independence and meant that provincial commissions were unprepared to act as serious checks on the spoils system.[46] In 1959 Alberta became the first province to transfer the personnel responsibilities of the Civil Service Commission to an admittedly political agency—the Office of the Premier. Later, in the '60s, Ontario and Quebec established cabinet level Departments of Civil Service to act on behalf of the executive in handling personnel matters. [Ontario's Department was abolished in 1972 and personnel was once again placed under the Civil Service Commission.] The other provinces transferred many of the important responsibilities of the Civil Service Commissions to their Treasury Boards.

Although all provinces have formalized procedures for recruiting public servants, it is more likely the need for technically skilled workers and the rise of collective bargaining procedures that account for the decline in patronage rather than any specific institutional reform.[47] Since the 1960s provincial personnel administration has emphasized the development of effective personnel management rather than the control of patronage.

Two patterns of personnel management have emerged in the provinces. In New Brunswick, Manitoba, Newfoundland, Quebec, and Ontario, personnel functions are divided between a political agency such as the Treasury Board or, in the case of Quebec, a line department, and an independent Civil Service Commission. This functional division is similar to the federal model and means that the Civil Service Commission retains the control-oriented functions of staffing and classification, while a political agency acts as the employer of the Civil Service in collective bargaining as well as supervising other personnel functions.

The second pattern continues the integrated role of the Civil Service Commission. In British Columbia, Alberta, Saskatchewan, Prince Edward Island, and Nova Scotia, the Civil or Public Service Commission has retained its role of personnel manager. Not only does it continue to preside over most aspects of manpower management, it also acts as the employer agent in collective bargaining (except in Prince Edward Island, where the Treasury Board carries out that role). In one survey of provincial personnel administration, it has been contended that the second pattern is inherently unsatisfactory and those provinces with integrated personnel management have begun to move closer to the model of functional separation, that is, shifting some personnel management functions to a central political agency.[48]

Policy Influence

The importance of the bureaucracy for policy-making is based on both its relationship with formal institutional actors, namely cabinet, and its informal ties with organized interest groups. Many pressure groups, like bureaucracies, are organized on the basis of functional specialization by policy areas. Thus, agencies of government come to be in regular and ongoing control with interested and selective publics. In many cases close clientele relationships emerge between civil servants and interest groups. Such ties are beneficial to both sides: groups desire favourable policy decisions, while public servants in their roles of policy-making and administration often need the expertise, information, cooperation, and political support of groups.

In his major study of Canadian interest groups within both federal and provincial politics, Presthus has argued that the bureaucracy is a prime target for pressure group activity[49] because of the number and breadth of policy issues within its general competence. The wide discretionary powers exercised by public servants permit them to initiate helpful policies as well as provide sympathetic implementation. Not all groups are equally successful in establishing direct contacts with government, nor ought one to assume that all government agencies are equally receptive to clientistic arrangements. Nevertheless, the exchanges of information and support in return for access and influence reflect a pervasive pattern of group-bureaucracy interaction which is regular and continuous.[50]

The importance of pressure groups should not overshadow the fact that ultimately it is the political masters to whom the public service must be most responsive. Elected officials remain at the apex of the departmental structure and,

> . . . the political criterion is to the public service what the profit criterion is to industry—the thread which runs through the decision-making process, and the standard against which these decisions must ultimately be weighed. That is not to say that every action must be calculated for political advantage of the party in power any more than every action in business must be calculated to maximize profit. Short run disadvantages must sometimes be borne and there are many actions whose political consequences are too remote to affect decisions significantly. But in the long-run top management of the public service must on balance redound to the credit of the party in power and in the short-run, actions which may produce adverse political consequences must be avoided as much as possible.[51]

Cabinets (and legislatures) must normally rely on public servants for much of what they do because the bureaucracy has several resources which politicians lack. Most of the stages in policy-making require a consideration of possible options. Choice must ultimately depend on a calculation of the need, the cost, and the likely impact of alternative solutions. All of these require information, much of which is technical, and an awareness of procedural and legal hurdles in the implementation of a given alternative. The bureaucracy is made of a staff of experts, many by virtue of the permanence of their positions having many years of experience dealing with similar problems. Thus, on most technical issues a minister's first resource will be his own civil service. But as has already been noted, bureaucrats often have a degree of support, deriving most importantly from their close ties to influential pressure groups, which can be used as a resource in those aspects of policy-making which involve essentially non-technical, that is, political options. For all these reasons—information, tenure of position and political support—public servants are in a position to exert a regular and pervasive influence on the workings of government.

For the most part the department is the key structural arena for administrative involvement in decision-making. The definitions of the problem as well as the policy alternatives tend to occur within the confines of the department responsible for implementation. Although there have been efforts to bridge departmental boundaries, departmentalism is still the most prevalent mode of policy-making.[52] Even within a single hierarchically structured department, it is difficult to look upon the public service as a like-minded monolith. Gow describes the department as a "coalition of adverse elements held together by the Minister and Deputy Minister."[53] In some cases the only unifying internal factor is shared professional values.

The ever-increasing complexity of policy and the ubiquitous role of the bureaucracy has led many observers to agree with Mallory's contention that the "centre of gravity" in decision-making has shifted from the politicians to the public service.[54] Not only is it a key access point for pressure group demands, it also provides its own inputs in its efforts to maintain the influence of the department and of those within it. As the major source of information and expertise within government, the bureaucracy possesses an indispensable resource. Occasionally a cabinet may go beyond the public service monopoly and may call upon additional sources of information from task forces, royal commissions, and executive secretariats, but these opportunities are limited and do not represent a consistent alternative to bureaucratic expertise. In those provinces characterized by long periods of one-party dominance the bureaucracy occupies an especially crucial position; the careers and perspectives of the ministers and civil servants gradually become more intertwined. Quite often the bureaucracy becomes the major source of policy innovation because there is no party competition to generate new policy ideas.[55]

A counter-hypothesis (based mainly on federal experience), challenging the view of the primacy of bureaucratic influence, suggests that many of the reforms of the '60s and '70s, including cabinet reform and increased staffing, have brought about a diminution in the role of the bureaucracy. As the influence of departmental policy-making is reduced through the availability of alternative sources of information, and as there is increasing emphasis on horizontal and comprehensive planning, the cabinet is better able to assert itself over the bureaucracy.[56] However, the case for a strengthened political executive more effectively in command of its administrative machine can be easily overstated. Information and specialization remain crucial resources, and departmental civil servants continue to monopolize this expertise. Aucoin, for example, concludes that although structural reforms have strengthened the position of the cabinet, "in many policy fields, especially those out of the public limelight, departmental programmes remain much the way departments want them."[57] The policy impact of the bureaucracy is greatest when there is limited participation, limited visibility, and when it is defending the status quo. As the scope of conflict broadens, generating more interest and including more participants, the role of the bureaucracy diminishes, because in the expanded arena policy questions are often ones of priorities rather than feasibility.

Given the resources of the bureaucracy, it is perhaps understandable that a new government might be uneasy with public servants who had worked so long under another regime. Any new minister finds himself in an incredibly difficult situation—confronted with a vast department with a myriad of ongoing programmes of which he has little information and even less experience. For this reason neophyte ministers are exceptionally dependent on the assistance of the more experienced, and more expert, bureaucracy. As Lipset has observed, this was precisely the dilemma confronting the CCF when it came to power. In this case the new Douglas government chose not to replace experienced civil servants but sought to control them. The CCF no doubt paid a price for bureaucratic expertise, for the civil service was able to exert a restraining influence over important facets of policy change.[58]

The idea of the bureaucracy as an obstacle to change is widely accepted, but represents only one side of the policy role of the public service. Bureaucracy also contributes to the growth of the public sector and the development of policy innovations. Much of the impetus for growth is a function of bureaucratic empire-building or attempts to maintain and increase the strength of a department.[59] There is also evidence that a competent and respected bureaucracy is an important element in public acceptance of costly social programmes.[60]

In addition to its positive role in the expansion of government, bureaucracy is also associated with policy innovation. The size of the public service has been found to be an important factor in explaining provincial adoption of specific policy reforms.[61] Because most policy development is essentially the result of efforts to correct previous policies and to adapt them to changing social conditions, the bureaucracy has been consistently important in policy formation.[62]

THE LEGISLATURE

The legislature is not generally considered to be a dominant force in the policy process. It has been described as a "policy refinery" with the primary role of legitimizing and ratifying cabinet decisions.[63] Executive dominance of the policy process is, if anything, even more prevalent at the provincial level. Shorter sessions, fewer backbench resources, greater ideological convergence, and a tendency towards one-party dominance and weak oppositions have traditionally combined to make provincial legislatures extremely pliable in the face of cabinet dictates.

The recognition that provincial legislatures are not directly involved in day-to-day decision-making should not, however, obscure their indirect contributions to policy-making. Legislative links with both the cabinet and bureaucracy constitute a complex system of interaction and influence.[64] The operations of provincial legislatures help to focus public attention on the actions (or inactions) of the government and help to create the public agenda for future actions. Through the performance of the functions of law-making, surveillance, and representation the provincial parliaments can have an impact on policy.

Former Upper Houses

When we look at provincial legislatures today, our focus is on the lower house or the legislative assembly (National Assembly in Quebec, Provincial Parliament in Ontario, and House of Assembly in Newfoundland). Historically, however, there have been two other elements that together with the Assembly constituted the legislature—an Upper House and Lieutenant-Governor. In the post-Confederation era five provinces (Quebec, Nova Scotia, New Brunswick, Prince Edward Island, and Manitoba) had bicameral legislatures. In all five cases legislation had to pass both houses. Except for Prince Edward Island, membership was decided by appointment, not by election. Partly because of their undemocratic quality, these upper houses gradually fell into disuse and were abolished. By 1928, when Nova Scotia dismantled its Legislative Council, Quebec remained the only province with a second house. The Union Nationale government abolished this one remaining Legislative Council in 1968. The main reasons for the demise of provincial upper chambers were that they were seen as too costly, and that they were havens for partisan appointments.[65]

The Lieutenant Governor is the representative of the Crown as well as a federal officer. Appointed by the Governor-General in Council, the Lieutenant-Governor has several responsibilities which directly affect the legislature. These include the power to open, prorogue and dissolve the legislature; to assent, withhold assent or reserve provincial legislation; to approve orders in council, to consent to the submission of all money bills, and to exercise formal executive powers.[66]

Today the Lieutenant-Governor's role is largely symbolic and ceremonial. In spite of an impressive list of duties, he does not significantly influence the policy process. As the provinces have developed politically, the Lieutenant-Governor's main function has been to ratify the decisions of the cabinet and legislature rather than to serve as a significant source of authority.

The Structure of Legislative Assemblies

Like the House of Commons in Ottawa, provincial assemblies are derived from the Westminster model. All parliaments in this tradition are founded on the principles of responsible and representative government. The former principle provides that no government may rule without the confidence of the legislature. The latter affirms the legitimacy of free elections which guarantee the popular basis of government. Formally, governments can be overturned by a vote of the assembly (which is itself dependent on public confidence), but it is today widely recognized that the rise of disciplined parties has made remote the possibility of legislatures choosing new governments between elections.[67] Thus, the crucial meaning of responsibility involves the link between governments and their publics.

Provincial parliaments operate on a smaller scale than the House of Commons. The size ranges from the 32-member Prince Edward Island House to 110 in Quebec and 125 in Ontario (compared with 282 in Ottawa—see Table 4.2). As of 1974 each federal MP represented approximately 80,000 people. Ontario has the largest provincial ratio, with each MPP standing for 67,000 people, and Prince Edward Island has the smallest, with each MPP standing for 3,800 people. (See Table 4.2.)

The provincial legislatures vary not only in size and representative ratios, they also differ in terms of degree of professionalism—the extent to which politics is a full-time occupation. Two indicators of legislative professionalism are salary and number of days in session.[68] The data in Table 4.2 show that in many provinces being an MLA is a part-time job. Most provincial assemblies sit only for a couple of months, and salary has certainly tended to be commensurate with the part-time schedule. There is some evidence that the role of the MLA is evolving into a full-time occupation. In Ontario from 1867 up until 1964 the average number of days in session was 45.5; since 1969 the sittings per session have not been below 100.[69] In some of the smaller provinces there is other evidence of change. In New Brunswick MLAs work increasingly on a full-time basis, not because of expanded sittings, but because legislative committees use the time when the House is not in session to meet and to hold hearings.

Increased professionalization is another aspect of the maturation of provincial political institutions. This has resulted, not unexpectedly, in heightened concern over the role of the legislature in the policy process. Several provinces have initiated studies and later adopted reforms to facilitate the legislature in its three main functions of law-making, surveillance, and representation. Through the improved performance of these functions, the legislature can expand its role in policy-making.

Table 4.2: Comparisons of Legislative Assemblies (1978)

PROVINCE	SIZE OF LEGIS- LATURE	NUMBER OF PEOPLE REPRE- SENTED PER MLA	SALARY + ALLOWANCE $	AVERAGE SITTING DAYS (1969-1974)
BRITISH COLUMBIA	55	45,600	24,000	57
ALBERTA	75	24,800	12,469 + 6,234	64
SASKATCHEWAN	61	15,500	18,110	
MANITOBA	57	18,100	15,300	86
ONTARIO	125	67,100	19,242 + 7,500	113
QUEBEC	110	57,100	27,800 + 7,000	92
NEW BRUNSWICK	58	11,900	11,088 + 3,696	48
NOVA SCOTIA	48	18,100	9,600 + 4,800	50
P.E.I.	32	3,800	10,500	31
NEWFOUNDLAND	51	10,900	15,500	85
HOUSE OF COMMONS FEDERAL GOVERNMENT	282	80,000	28,600 + 12,700*	155

Source: *Canadian Parliamentary Guide 1978.*
  * 1979

Law-Making

The Legislative Assembly debates broad issues and narrow details, proposes amendments to the government's submissions, but, most importantly, it processes bills into law. However, it is questionable whether one should view the job of provincial legislatures as primarily law-making, for as Jackson and Atkinson have observed federally, the legislative function is much more one of passing than of making laws.[70] In order to perform the law-making function effectively the legislature must make efficient use of its time and provide avenues of meaningful participation for its members. Toward these ends most provinces have a time limit on members' speeches. (Saskatchewan, Prince Edward Island, and Ontario are exceptions.) The duration of debates on the throne speech, on the budget, and on department estimates is limited in Newfoundland, Ontario, British Columbia, Quebec, and Saskatchewan. The most significant measure to emerge from legislative efforts to reform the use of time is the legislative committee system. Committees not only take some of the workload off the floor of the House, they also provide an arena for more detailed consideration of proposed legislation and estimates. With regard to legislative committees in Ottawa, it has been concluded that as a forum for informed discussion and a source of expertise, committees can be useful mechanisms for countervailing executive power.[71] Committees can provide for the effective utilization of backbenchers because they offer a place for members to pursue policy interests and improve the quality of legislation without posing a threat to the government. In some cases committees offer opposition parties an opportunity for cooperative inputs in which opposition members stress accommodation rather than confrontation.[72] Generally, it can be said that the expansion of the role of committees in the legislative process will not only permit inputs by MLAs, but will also provide a greater opportunity for pressure groups to participate more directly and publicly on issues before the legislature. Pre-legislative hearings, which are information-seeking meetings on issues that have not yet been decided by cabinet, are another method by which committees can help to expand policy inputs.[73] In short, committees give members a better chance to develop policy ideas and an opportunity to express those ideas.

To what extent have the provinces set up effective legislative committees? In most provinces the committee stage of legislation means sending the bill to the Committee of the Whole (a committee of the entire House with less stringent rules of procedure). Just as there have been many variations among the provinces in their other institutions, there has been no single pattern in the use of legislative committees. A 1973 survey of committee activity in all ten provinces showed that only three—Ontario, Quebec, and New Brunswick—had active standing committees.[74] In the early 1970s both Ontario and Quebec reformed their committee systems to provide for smaller committees and to permit members to concentrate on one or two committees. Ontario reduced the number of standing committees from 18 to 7 and the size of the committees was dropped from approximately 44 to an average of 18 members. Although the committees in Ontario have been organized into more suitable work units, they have not yet become very effective because of their narrow focus and dependence on government willingness to process bills through them. Most legislation does not go to a standing committee after second reading.

It is Ontario's smaller, better-staffed, ad hoc select committees that have become useful elements in the policy process. Select committees, which meet when the legislature is not sitting and investigate specific areas of public concern, provide more vital outlets for backbencher policy interests than do standing committees.[75]

Quebec's reformed committee system is the most successful among all the provinces. Quebec has 14 standing committees with a membership of about 12 on each. In contrast to Ontario, where the government decides whether or not to refer a bill to committee, in Quebec all bills as well as estimates go to standing committees. The committees become the major arena for detailed analysis of a bill and the committee debate is not repeated once more on the floor of the House. Assessments of Quebec's reorganized committees suggest that the reforms have benefitted all participants in the process. The government gains by having improved legislation and by allowing committees to defuse political issues. The opposition is given a greater chance to influence policy, and even the public benefits from increased openness and communication.[76]

Surveillance

The job of examining and criticizing the actions of the government through calls for information and justification is primarily a task for opposition parties. The main components of this "watch-dog" role are *checking* the government's integrity, *prodding* the government to act, *probing* for information, and *reinterpreting* government performance.[77]

Performance of surveillance has been hindered in the provinces by weak oppositions and in a few cases by coalition government. Manitoba and British Columbia both experienced a period of government by coalition during the 1940s. There are no recent examples of this phenomenon, but long periods of one-party dominance have created opposition parties with little chance to recruit good talent and little information and experience with which to challenge the government. Coalition governments are even more insidious in this respect since there is often no viable opposition at all.

The question period is the most visible means of surveillance. In all provinces oral questions may be asked of ministers. In most provinces there is provision for a daily question period limited to less than an hour. Floor debate, another opportunity for the opposition, has often tended to be more of an occasion for public posturing than for systematic criticism of the government.[78] A third opportunity for criticism by the opposition comes from the assembly's control of the purse, for the legislature must authorize all spending. Nine provinces have retained the Committee of Supply (a committee of the whole) to consider estimates. Several have, however, provided for some division of labour in the review of the estimates. For example, Alberta uses subcommittees of the Committee on Supply. Ontario sometimes permits the standing committees to review estimates in their subject area. Quebec is the only province to have followed Ottawa's lead and has abolished the Committee of Supply. Quebec's standing committees are responsible for reviewing the estimates.

The post audit of government expenditures by provincial Public Account Committees is an additional opportunity for surveillance.[79] The Public Accounts Committee's purpose is to check on government expenditures: "to see if money is being spent properly and if the public is getting value for the money spent".[80] Thus, the role of the PAC goes beyond guarding against fraud and waste. Its work can lead it into an increasingly policy-oriented evaluation of programme effectiveness. Some provincial PACs are more potent forces than others. Much depends on their independence and commitment. Based on a number of measures of effectiveness, Ontario, Manitoba, and Saskatchewan's PAC have been rated as highly effective. But in Newfoundland, Prince Edward Island, Alberta, and British Columbia, PACs were found to be rather weak instruments of oversight.[81]

A final area of surveillance that has direct policy implications concerns delegated legislation. Due to limited time and expertise, all of the provincial legislatures have on many occasions delegated their law-making authority to boards and commissions. As the extent of delegation has increased (the Committee on Government Productivity has estimated there are over 300 boards and commissions based on delegated authority in Ontario), legislatures have sought some control over delegated legislation. In Manitoba, Saskatchewan, Alberta, and Ontario, Committees on Regulation have been established. In Quebec the standing committees are permitted to review regulations in their area. None of these arrangements has proved as yet to be very successful in returning effective control over regulatory policy to the legislature.

Representation

The third legislative function relevant to policy-making is representation. Legislatures are arenas for the formal expression of public views and preferences. This is accomplished through the organization of disciplined parliamentary parties which structure the debates and divisions between government and opposition. These mechanisms, coupled with a system of competitive elections, provide the primary modes of political representation. Despite the central importance of partisan divisions, MLAs are in the first instance representatives of local constituencies. For many members the constituency is the defining characteristic of their job. Constituency service is viewed by most MLAs as their proper role, and many spend the bulk of their time on activities directed toward the constituency.[82] The MLAs' established communication with the riding is the major link between the people and the government, and members are the most likely avenue for expressing the day-to-day needs of constituents. Ministers have come to expect private members to have their ears to the ground. The member is a channel for the communication of diffuse moods as well as for specific demands. In some provinces—Nova Scotia, for example—recommendations to increase backbenchers' resources are based on a desire to further facilitate their representational role. In contrast, the Ontario recommendations had the objective of augmenting law-making functions of MLAs.[83]

Representation also occurs at the group level. Opposition parties, in their efforts to criticize the government, are likely to articulate interests that have been unorganized and have gone unrepresented.[84]

The role of provincial legislatures in the policy process is, on the surface, rather limited and very much overshadowed by the cabinet. However, the legislature can serve as a constraint as well as an impetus for change. Through criticism (sometimes obstruction) the legislature limits the discretion of the executive; alternatively, by calling attention to societal conditions and policy problems, it can compel the government to take action.

POLICY PROCESSES

There is a natural tendency to think of governments responding to one policy problem at a time. Case studies of individual decisions sometimes encourage this perspective by isolating for analysis only those events directly associated with the decision in question. Unfortunately, the reality of the political process is far more complex. At any given moment political decision-makers are normally engaged in a number of policy issues which span a variety of policy fields. Moreover, any particular policy problem is likely to be dealt with through several different routines and stages. Because of this, policy-making can best be understood as the simultaneous operation of multiple policy processes in which politicians and bureaucrats alike are constantly under the pressures of limited time, information, and resources as they respond to demands and seek to resolve conflict.[85] Given the intricate network of institutional and personal connections which compose the structures of government, a policy process can most generally be defined as a pattern of interaction involving various institutions of government and non-governmental actors which produce the instruments of policy (for example, expenditures, regulations, and symbolic gestures) through which values are ultimately allocated. In most facets of policy-making, even though the prime participants and basic interactions (executive-bureaucratic relationships) are known, there are few pre-established routines which fully describe the nature of the decisional process. Provision of support for the unemployed and aged, consolidation of school districts, expansion of bilingual education, encouragement of energy conservation, or opting out of federal shared-cost programmes all illustrate changing arenas of conflict, bargaining, and decision-making in which the constraints and dynamics on public choice may be variable and sometimes unpredictable.

To understand the diversity of such policy-making, it is essential to have some analytical frameworks for organizing and making comparable otherwise disparate bits of information about the policy process. One useful framework is developmental in character and suggests a set of essential stages or functions in policy formation. Every policy process is made up of at least four activities: identification, formulation, selection, and implementation.[86] These stages of activity can be distinguished analytically, although they are by no means always separate operations. Problem identification is part of the larger concept of setting the public agenda through the selection of certain problems as the basis for public action. The process starts with the perception by individuals who are directly or indirectly affected that certain human needs require public action. Once these demands are acknowledged by decision-makers, problem-identification has occurred. However, it is certainly erroneous to assume that the identification stage must be a grassroots expression of public opinion to which policy-makers eventually respond. Clearly most issue identification does not require a massive public awareness. For example, where intense but small issue publics are involved or where organized and influential groups are active, the inclusion of an issue on the policy agenda may occur with little or no public concern. Additionally, in some situations issue identification may be deliberately generated by public authorities or by powerful economic or social groups.

Once a problem is identified, courses of action are formulated to deal with it. Despite the executive dominance which characterizes provincial policy-making, there is no one method of formulation. In some cases, options may develop primarily through routine interaction among experts in the bureaucracy and from pressure groups. Royal Commissions and task forces have also been important sources of policy. For example, the recommendations of the Bryne Commission for reform of provincial-municipal relations were accepted, virtually as a package, by the New Brunswick government.[87] In other cases cabinet members or other political leaders may play a substantial part in the shaping of policy alternatives.

Once the political agenda is set and options are articulated, the subsequent and crucial step in the policy process is selection. The essential quality of this phase is found in the decisions which approve, reject or modify patterns of policy. Policy selection may be intertwined with formulation,[88] for options are often created with an eye to winning the approval of decision-makers. Although the critical decision point may sometimes be obscured, the function of policy selection must always occur.

Selection is by no means the end of the policy process. Decisions authorize certain actions to be taken, funds to be spent, or rules to be enforced. These policy choices must also be carried out, making implementation an integral stage in any policy process. The implementation of some policy choices may be immediate, such as lowering the minimum voting age or changing provincial speed limits. Others may be implemented only gradually on a case-by-case basis. What is perhaps most important to understand about this administrative stage is the fact that the meaning and effect of governmental decisions may be sharply altered and even contradicted by the way they are carried out. Implementation raises the important problem of authority. The ease and speed of implementation will result, in part, from the legitimacy of the process and the officials who operate it and, in part, from the degree to which those affected by a policy accept and support it. Although it should be evident that the policy process does not always fit into a neat series of distinct steps, the concepts of identification, formulation, selection, and implementation can serve as sign posts for analysis of any particular process.

A second perspective on policy-making focuses on the methods of decision-makers. Disjointed incrementalism and rational decision-making constitute two fundamentally opposed models of the ways governments define and handle issues.[89] The former suggests that because policy-makers have only partial information and a limited analytical capacity, they operate within a narrow range of alternatives. In this context the policy-making process is of necessity made up of a disjointed series of piecemeal decisions, and policy development only occurs through gradual and limited changes. The rationalist model is, in comparison, a more comprehensive approach to problem solving. (Its critics argue that it is also less realistic.) Ideally, decision-makers achieve rationality through a broad evaluation of all viable alternatives and their consequences.

Mixed scanning represents a middle position between these two views and posits that in certain policy areas perceived to be of particular significance, decision-makers are inclined to spend the time and energy necessary for a thorough evaluation of a broad range of alternatives in order to define policy principles and establish priorities. Where this is not the case, policy-making consists of small-scale incremental decisions.[90]

Another approach to the study of the policy process rests on the proposition that the preceived impact of policy determines the mode of policy-making.[91] According to Lowi, three kinds of policies, distributive, regulatory, and redistributive, generate identifiable policy processes differentiated by scope of participation, degree of conflict, and the nature of interaction.[92] For example, distributive policies (patronage, public works) correspond to a process in which the number of participants is limited, the degree of conflict is low, and the typical forms of interaction are "log-rolling" and mutual non-interference. In contrast, redistributive policies (e.g., social welfare) are more conflictual, the circle of participation is broader, and interests are sufficiently incompatible that trade-offs and compromise are precluded by overt competition and struggle for benefits.

At any one time, provincial decision-makers are involved in several processes. Some are made up of established routines in which the timing, the roles of participants, and the nature of interaction are predictable. Two of these, budgeting and regulation, are particularly significant by virtue of the fact that they normally span every major substantive policy field.

The Expenditure-Budgetary Process

The allocation of public funds is often viewed as the single most important component of provincial policy-making. The annual budget which details the planned expenditures for the coming fiscal year (which in all provinces now runs from April 1 to March 31), is not just an indication of the policy directions desired by the government, it is also a reflection of its efforts to resolve conflicts among competing elements in the political system.

All major institutional participants in policy-making see the budget as a crucial and functional document. For the legislature, the power of the purse is potentially its strongest means for controlling the executive. For the bureaucracy, the budget defines the parameters of its work. For the cabinet, the budget is not only a plan for future operations, it is also an instrument for policy-making.[93] Each year the legislative passage of the main estimates is the culmination of the series of activities called the expenditure-budgetary process. Although the details of budgetary procedures in the provinces may vary, ". . . the essence of all of them is a process of tough bargaining between the Treasury/Management Board Staff and the programme departments and agencies."[94]

The development of public budgeting in Canada has, in the main, entailed a change in the relative emphasis given to three budgetary purposes.[95] Governments have sought to use the annual budget as a vehicle for controlling the bureaucracy, for better management and planning, and for policy choice. The trend has meant a shift away from the narrow focus of control toward more wide-range conceptions of management, planning, and policy choice.

Control Budgeting

For most of their history the provinces used the budget exclusively for purposes of control of the bureaucracy. Despite important shifts toward long-range planning, the budgetary process continues to reflect this control orientation. Traditionally, departments and agencies prepare their annual requests with no formal procedures for future planning. Indeed, there is no place in the estimates for such consideration. Although new programmes do come up, the submission for each department is made on the incremental basis of "What I have I need,"[96] which, in practice, means that the current year's spending is the minimal base for next year's requests. Within departments the estimates preparation is totally separate from policy-making. Under conventional budgeting the submissions from each department are expressed in terms of input costs (salaries, equipment, and the like). There is no explicit linkage of these costs to either specific programmes or general objectives. Thus, neither the legislature nor the Treasury Board is in a position to evaluate submissions on the basis of desired activities or functional priorities.

Under traditional methods the total estimates are essentially an aggregation of departmental requests within the limitation of expected revenues. Budgeting in this fashion is a bottom-up process with little policy direction imposed by central control agencies. Bringing the estimates back into line with available resources is generally accomplished by the rather indiscriminate method of across-the-board cuts rather than priority based departmental reductions. The absence of an overall plan allows for a greater probability of end-runs, that is, efforts by individual ministers to get around Treasury Board decisions by going to full cabinet. This often enables influential ministers to shelter favoured programmes and/or departments from the knife of the central agency.

The usual major budgetary function of the central agency is to check the legality of expenditures and the efficiency of agency heads. This means that the Department of Finance or Treasury Board tends to get involved in the oversight of department administration rather than in the implementation of government priorities and the coordination of departmental programmes. The presentation of the budget to the legislature is also based on input costs rather than on programmes or government goals.

Budgetary Change

The Report of the Royal Commission on Governmental Organization (The Glassco Commission) marked the beginning of the transformation of the budget away from a negative control purpose toward its use for better management and eventually for planning and policy choice. Although directed primarily at federal practices, the questions raised by the Commission were an important impetus for change in the provinces by creating a climate for questioning and reforming the budgetary process.

The Glassco Commission was highly critical of traditional control-oriented budgeting and especially of the role played by the central control agency, the Treasury Board.[97] It recommended that the Treasury Board leave administrative details to the programme departments and agencies in order to concentrate on the tasks of planning and co-ordination. To facilitate this oversight role of Treasury Board, the Commission called for estimates to be based on programme rather than inputs, which would give decision-makers a more useful picture of proposed expenditures. The Glassco Commission paved the way for the introduction of PPBS and the other rational policy techniques discussed earlier in this chapter. The provinces' moves to adopt PPBS brought about major transformations of their budgetary structures and processes.

Because planning systems make objectives explicit and weigh programme consequences, budgets may become vechicles for policy choice. In contrast to traditional budgetary methods, where expenditure decisions have only the most tenuous relation to policy goals, planning and other rational policy-making techniques attempt to make budgeting an integral part of the policy process. PPBS is composed of the following elements that link inputs to outputs and permit decision-makers to see the implications of budgetary choices:

   (i) the setting of specific objectives;
  (ii) the systematic analysis to clarify objectives and to assess alternative ways of meeting them.
 (iii) the framing of budgetary proposals in terms of programmes directed toward the achievement of the objectives.
 (iv) the projection of the costs of these programmes a number of years in the future.
  (v) the formulation of plans of achievement year by year for each programme.
 (vi) an information system for each programme to supply data for the monitoring of achievement of programme goals and to supply data for the reassessment of the programme objectives and the appropriateness of the programme itself.[98]

As we have seen, PBBS has proved to be quite difficult to implement, due to obstacles to the determination, reconciliation, and weighing of objectives. There are also problems for departments in developing programmes to achieve goals and for Treasury Board in the evaluation of the effectiveness of programmes. Where it has been implemented, PPBS has had some positive results. In Ontario there is now greater consideration of alternative programmes, the economic, social and political implications of policies are given more attention, new programmes are scrutinized in the context of total allocation, and there is some, albeit limited, ongoing programme review by Management Board.[99] Quebec, besides making efforts toward a more complete and informative presentation of budgetary information, has also sought to develop performance indicators to permit more systematic programme evaluation.[100] PPBS has not, however, turned out to be a panacea for budgetary problems. In fact, its implementation has generated a host of new problems with only a limited amelioration of the old ones.

The Mixed Budget

Current provincial budgeting contains elements of both traditional control and modern planning and programming systems. Although all provinces have become interested in forward planning and have sought to make their programmes consonant with established priorities, none has moved to fully adopt PPB systems.[101] Even in Quebec and Ontario, which have gone the furthest in the direction of rational budgeting, where the estimates framework has been modified to a programme basis, the budget still remains primarily a process in which existing programmes are fit to priorities.

The impact of PPB techniques can be easily overestimated, for much of the shift toward rational budgeting is a result of structural reforms in cabinet. Each province has strengthened its Treasury Board or comparable financial control agency. Increased staff assistance has enabled central agencies to carry out a more systematic review of programme proposals and their implications. In addition to the strengthening of the management function, provincial planning has also been increased and has typically been manifested at the cabinet rather than at the departmental level. Provincial cabinets have instituted Planning/ Priorities Committees to provide the Treasury Board with a set of priorities for programme evaluation. Also, cabinet policy or functional committees facilitate goal-related programme initiation and policy review.

Newfoundland provides a good example of the mixed process. Cabinet reform has enabled more forward planning and consideration of the implications of proposed programmes. Nevertheless, the budget is still best described as control-oriented and traditional. Established in 1972, Newfoundland's Committee on Government Administration and Productivity, following Ontario's Committee on Government Productivity, recommended a complete restructuring of cabinet. Its recommendations included establishing a planning/priorities committee, three policy subcommittees, and a greatly increased support staff for Treasury Board and the new committees. Under the new system, the Planning/ Priorities Committee develops policy guidelines for the Treasury Board. Departmental submissions are examined by Treasury Board as well as the relevant policy committee secretariat. Standard objects of expenditure are still used for the estimates, and control remains an important consideration. But now, the process has built-in programmatic consideration of departmental submissions. The budget can no longer be described as a simple aggregation of departmental requests, for there is much more policy direction provided by the centre (cabinet).

British Columbia is the last province to have changed the nature of its budgetary process. As noted earlier, throughout the reign of W.A.C. Bennett (1952-1972), the cabinet was a very simple structure revolving around the Premier. There was no planning or division of labour through committees and no assistance via support staffs. The NDP government of 1972-75 changed neither the cabinet nor budgetary structure. Individual ministers could exercise initiative in their departments, but there was no overall planning or control agency. The situation, aptly described by Tennant as "unaided politicians in an unaided cabinet," had by 1974 generated a budgetary crisis in which the balanced budget of the past disappeared as provincial expenditures far exceeded revenues. In response to these difficulties, Premier Barrett appointed a Planning Advisor to the Cabinet. This was no more effective than weak Treasury Boards previously tried in the other provinces had been. Like these impotent central agencies, the Planning Advisor lacked the strong support of the Premier and Cabinet and had little staff assistance. He was, therefore, unable to exercise control over the departments and agencies. With the return to power of Social Credit in 1975 and in reaction to this situation, Premier William Bennett has tried to bring British Columbia up-to-date in budgetary reform by establishing a Treasury Board. Moreover, the cabinet now has a planning and priorities committee, policy committees, and support staff assistance.

The dominant trend in provincial budgeting is fairly clear. In the last decade there has been a gradual evolution away from purely control purposes. With the exception of Saskatchewan, which was far ahead of any other government, the provinces have been affected by the budgetary changes occurring at the federal level. If nothing else, wide ranging federal-provincial interactions make it necessary for the provinces to try to keep up with the technology of the federal bureaucracy. Even more importantly, the provinces have come to recognize that the budget is a crucial part of policy-making and a valuable instrument for planning and policy choice.

The Regulatory Process

Budgets reflect those actions of the state involving the provision of goods and services and transfer payments from one part of the population to another. Although they are commonly used to reflect the scope of government, it is important to be aware of the budget's limitations as an indicator of public policy.[102] On the one hand, due to the inclusion of uncontrollable expenditures, the budget is an over-estimation of public decision-making. The funding of uncontrollables is part of the "givens" of the budgetary process and is external to the annual decision-making process. Such fixed costs are based on continuing statutes and, therefore, are not subject to parliamentary control (short of revoking the statute). On the other hand, the budget is an underestimation of state activities because it excludes two significant aspects of public decision-making, regulation and public ownership.

Regulation, which has aptly been called the "missing half" of public policy, involves intervention in the economy and society through the formulation and application of general rules.[103] Conflict in the regulatory arena is often over the rules and procedures which define the conditions of bargaining and communication and which also ultimately influence the allocation of benefits or the question of "who gets what". Such rules, enforceable by the legitimate sanctions of the state, typically affect the conditions and means by which goods and services are produced and made available to the public. Although this definition emphasizes the regulation of economic relationships, it is important to recognize that the concept of regulation more generally refers to rules governing all aspects of behaviour, for example, civil rights and the criminal code.

The regulatory function may be carried out by a number of units which include: (i) independently established regulatory structures (called variously commissions, agencies, boards, or institutes), the members of which are ordinarily appointed by the Lieutenant Governor-in-Council, having decisional autonomy although remaining formally responsible to a Minister or the legislature as a whole, (ii) producer groups which have been delegated the power to regulate themselves (professions like medicine as well as some agricultural producer groups are good examples of this) or (iii) regular cabinet departments. Although all three perform regulatory functions, it is the first type, statutory quasi-independent agencies with delegated responsibility in the public interest, that we usually think of as regulatory agencies.[104] Since 1945 there has been a remarkable expansion of such agencies in both provincial and federal politics. The sporadic nature of their development coupled with a lack of uniformity in their nomenclature has made it extremely difficult to make an accurate assessment of exactly which agencies have been developed in which provinces and what they are empowered to do. Generally, it is useful to think of these agencies as public institutions to which has been delegated through legislation the authority to regulate some area of economic or social activity.

There exists no standard or modal form for regulatory agencies.[105] They differ widely in how much discretion they have, in methods of personnel selection, and in their basis of financing. Perhaps the most significant dimension on which agencies may be compared is the extent to which they legislate as opposed to adjudicate. The degree of discretion exercised by agencies is a function of the specificity of the legislation; the more general the legislation, the more that is left for the agency to fill in. A legislative directive that grants an agency the authority to defend the public interest creates a very wide range of discretion for that agency and in fact often transforms it into the effective policy-maker. In some instances, however, an agency may work under a tightly constructed statute in which it retains a predominantly judicial function through the applications of policy rules to specific cases.

Today there are provincial regulations for almost every area of human activity, including the arts, civil service, consumer credit, conservation, insurance, labour, liquor control, agricultural marketing, public utilities, and health. An inventory prepared for the Canadian Consumer Council estimated that each province has at least fifty regulatory boards and commissions.[106] Typical agencies found in all provinces include agricultural marketing boards for almost every major agricultural commodity (for example, poultry, eggs, beef, pork, milk, tobacco, and grains). In 1956 there were about thirty of these boards; today there are over one hundred, almost all of which have been established under provincial authority. The specific powers of marketing boards may vary, but they are commonly authorized to control the number of producers, the volume of production, pricing systems, and collective bargaining.[107]

There are numerous provincial agencies involved in natural resource use and energy supply.[108] Besides the hydro power commissions that operate in all provinces, several provinces (Alberta, Saskatchewan, Manitoba, Ontario, and Newfoundland) also have energy and environmental boards. The functions of these boards vary a good deal across provinces. In Alberta and Saskatchewan they are primarily involved in the regulation of oil and gas production; in other provinces they are largely restricted to matters of energy distribution (for example, pipeline systems) or environmental standards. Agencies concerned with water resources and supply are found in most provinces. Another type of energy-related regulation is seen in public utilities commissions. As of 1971 seven provinces had a public utilities board or commission generally empowered to regulate the provision and rates of utilities services. In a number of cases, for example, British Columbia and Nova Scotia, such agencies also regulate a variety of other activities (cemeteries, motor carriers, salvage yards).

Transportation and telecommunications represent another set of agencies which deal with intra-provincial trucking, inter-city busing, telephone and telecommunication rates and the like.[109] Most provinces have a highway traffic or transportation board. (Manitoba alone also has a taxi-cab board.) However, the federal Canadian Transport Commission plays a crucial role due to the interprovincial implications of most of the regulatory issues in this policy area.

A number of other agencies concern themselves with the regulation of specific sectors of the economy. Securities commissions, for example, exist in all provinces outside of the Atlantic region. Marketing boards are, of course, primarily concerned with this form of regulation. In addition to these sectoral concerns there are also a variety of provincial development corporations and advisory councils having influence over broader economic issues.

All provinces have a regulatory interest in issues affecting labour. All have workmen's compensation boards. Most have some mix of labour relations, mediation, arbitration or industrial relations boards. Employment policy is also regulated via civil service commissions in all ten provinces and by human rights commissions. Ombudsman functions are now institutionalized in British Columbia, Alberta, Manitoba, Ontario, Quebec (Public Protector), New Brunswick, and Newfoundland (Parliamentary Commissioner).

All of the boards mentioned are statutory agencies to which the provincial legislature has transferred authority. The main reasons for delegating legislative power are to permit the appropriate application of general rules to specific cases and to bring technical expertise to bear on rule-making. The legislature's limited time and information are thus the rationale for delegation. The independence of these agencies, which have an "arm's length" relation with the minister and cabinet, is predicated on the need to insulate regulatory decision-making from partisan political forces. The appeal of placing regulation outside regular departmental channels is also due to the administrative advantage of greater flexibility in personnel, finances, and programme development.[110]

Regulation can be said to be rule-making backed up by the coercive powers of the state. It is essentially a negative or limiting function in that it generally prohibits freedom of action by the individual, firm or industry. In comparison, expenditures and exhortation represent positive incentives to elicit certain behaviours either through subsidization or more symbolic encouragement. Although the latter two methods undoubtedly influence the allocation and distribution of resources, regulation is potentially a more potent policy instrument because it demands compliance. There is a range of coercive measures available to government and regulation is at the high end of the scale.

Why do governments formulate rules that interfere with the functioning of the market? Regulatory action may be a response to the internal problems of an industry or sector of the economy.[111] In pursuit of essentially internal objectives, actions tend to be corrective in nature. In this case, the aim is to bring prevailing market conditions into a more perfectly competitive arrangement. So, for example, the presence of a monopoly means that normal, competitive forces are not working to efficiently allocate resources. State regulation of the monopoly is an effort to compensate for the absence of competitive forces and to ensure that the consumer will get as much for his money as is economically possible. In the context of endogenous objectives, regulation is applied when the market is imperfect. The thrust of such regulations is neutral, that is, they are aimed at correcting market distortions and in this way at increasing the general welfare rather than the well-being of any particular group, region, or industry. The second basis for regulation involves responses to difficulties originating outside of the particular economic sector in question. In this case the origin and the objectives of regulation may be referred to as exogenous. This means that the regulated sector may be used as an instrument for achieving broader policy goals which might include economic development, social equity, and regional growth. In these cases regulation is not considered corrective or neutral; it is promotional. The object is to alter the rate or pattern of development of a particular sector in order to facilitate the achievement of other policy goals.[112]

Public Ownership

One other policy instrument which may be seen as a special, albeit extreme, form of regulatory activity is found in those enterprises providing public goods and services which are owned and operated within the public sector. Public ownership supplants the private sector, and because of this it differs from most expenditure and regulatory activities, which normally operate in conjunction with private interests. In some cases, for example the Syncrude project and Sidbec, government enterprise may exist alongside private firms. In other instances like the public utilities—gas, electricity, and telephone—the public enterprise constitutes a monopoly. The earliest examples of public corporations can be seen in municipal operation of water, gas, and electric utilities.

One might suppose that most initiatives toward public ownership are the consequence of socialist ideologies and, therefore, the product of CCF-NDP governments. Certainly, this party has traditionally had a stronger commitment to direct public control than any other. Moreover, one can find instances, such as the Saskatchewan potash case, where an NDP government has nationalized private firms. But other parties have also established public corporations or been involved in a variety of joint public-private undertakings. It is at best risky to presume a close fit between ideology, party in power, and the pattern of policy as far as public ownership is concerned.

The oldest provincial example of public ownership, Ontario Hydro, established in 1906, remains one of the most important examples of public enterprise.[113] In 1919 Nova Scotia and Manitoba followed Ontario's lead and established provincial corporations for electric power. By the 1960s, as the Bennett government in British Columbia took over British Columbia Electric and the Lesage government in Quebec established Hydro Quebec, all provinces had moved into provincial ownership of electric power systems as one means of encouraging industrial development. Today all of the provinces have experimented with some form of public ownership.[114]

Regulatory Issues

Unlike the budgetary process where the paramount policy trend has been to move away from control towards policy planning, in regulation there has been no such clear line of development. The changes in regulatory policy-making can best be viewed as attempts to resolve the three persistent issues of economic effectiveness, representation, and accountability.

Economic Effectiveness. Regulation implies an interference with existing market forces. At times the purpose of the intervention is to bring about a more efficient and rational allocation of resources; at other times it is to facilitate a "different" (e.g., more equitable or more redistributive) allocation of resources. Regulation must thus be evaluated from the perspective of both goals. First, does regulation engender a more efficient and rational allocation of resources? Most economists believe the answer is no. In fact, the general criticism of regulation is that, if anything, its impact is quite the opposite. Regulatory policy is thought to:

a) distort competition
b) distort the allocation of resources within the industry
c) raise prices
d) protect inefficient operations and hamper innovation
e) create administrative delays and high costs.[115]

Beyond the criticism that regulations have not brought about a more perfectly competitive market situation, it is also contended that regulation is an ineffective means of securing other goals such as regional development.[116] Direct subsidies are posed as more efficient ways of achieving desired social and economic goals.

Representation of the Public Interest. There are two seemingly paradoxical facts which strike the observer of regulatory policy-making in the provinces. The first is that such institutions are pervasive. They are involved in virtually every major area of provincial policy. The Ontario Committee on Government Productivity has estimated that there are over three hundred public or quasi-public agencies in that province alone and that such organizations account for some 40 percent of all government employees in Ontario.[117] The second is that regulatory agencies remain very poorly understood. There is massive public ignorance of what they are and what they do. Perhaps more surprising is the general lack of precise information about and interest in regulatory agencies on the part of otherwise well informed political observers.[118] No doubt an important reason for this neglect is found in the independence which agencies are granted to execute their functions. This necessarily results in limited scrutiny from cabinet and the legislature and, therefore, minimal public accountability.

There is, however, a growing recognition of the importance of these agencies. This stems in part from doubts about how well the public interest, which such agencies have been designed to defend, has been served. It is well-known that some agencies become "captured" by the very interests they are supposed to control. The agency is seen to both represent and regulate its sector clientele. Regulators are often dependent on producer groups for information, expertise, and even personnel. This can result in a closed clientistic network of regulation in which non-producer interests (consumers) may find the costs and opportunities of participation to be extremely restrictive.[119] A number of studies carried out under the auspices of the Canadian Consumer Council have explored in detail the problems of access to and accountability of various regulatory agencies. The captive agency thesis is supported by the lack of consumer representatives on most boards and commissions and by the closed nature of the process. Regulatory decision-making provides little or no opportunity for external consumer participation. Doern has described this system as the professional model in contrast to the democratically open model.[120] The professional model contains a small number of like-minded participants whose relationships are characterized by mutual trust and low conflict. The democratically open model provides for a wider scope of participation which may permit greater conflict and confrontation. In Manitoba, Saskatchewan, and Ontario, efforts to include consumer representatives on boards and agencies are beginning to move regulation toward this second model.

Regulation, like all state activity, is supposed to serve the public welfare. Sometimes the impetus for the establishment of regulatory boards has been public dissatisfaction with prices and services, and in many of the enabling statutes, the public interest is cited as the basis for regulatory decisions. The dilemma, of course, is to find a workable definition of the public interest. Whose interests constitute the public's? Do policies in the public interest mean lower prices, better service, regional economic development or more capital formation?

Although it is important to have other than producer views represented, and on a short-run basis public interest representation is a crucial reform, consumer participation ought not to be viewed as a panacea for regulatory problems. Even if consumer advocates were on every board and commission, there would still not necessarily be any more policy coordination or promulgation of regulations that would be part of a coherent governmental policy. Essentially the system would still be that of a parcelling out of authority in which individual regulatory concerns would exercise power in their own narrow spheres.[121]

Accountability. A third issue in regulatory policy concerns the political accountability (or lack of it) of regulatory agencies. To what extent are independent regulatory agencies antithetical to the concept of responsible government? The independence of the agency is predicated on an effort to ensure impartiality and objectivity in economic intervention. And certainly in terms of its judicial function (applying rules to specific cases), objectivity is critical. However, adjudicative functions may give regulatory bodies a powerful defense against political intervention, even when such intervention is both desirable and necessary. That is, through its legislative or rule-making function the agency is in fact resolving political issues, a condition which makes normal channels of political accountability necessary.[122]

The necessity for accountability is related to another issue—the question of how much discretionary authority should be delegated by the legislature. Wide-discretionary powers make weak accountability an even greater problem. Firm policy guidelines are important in assuring that the agency applies well-defined rules to particular instances instead of making policy by giving substance to fuzzy legislation and directives. The thrust for reform of the regulatory process is the demand for greater accountability and less discretion through more integrated and coherent provincial policy and executive leadership. Trebilcock has nicely described the problem as one of overregulation and undergovernment.

Comparing the Two Processes

Although budgeting involves some regulation and regulations entail some expenditure, regulatory arenas stand in sharp contrast to the structures of expenditure policy-making. The budgetary process is visibly political and highly centralized, with its own set of participants. The annual budget is a regular focus of conflict and bargaining as agencies and departments strive to defend and increase their resources while central agencies endeavor to impose government priorities and budgetary constraint. Each year the government must receive from the Legislative Assembly authorization for its proposed expenditures. These expenditures constitute a perspective of the priorities of government and must be defined as such. Because the expenditure budget is an announcement of government objectives, it is a frankly political statement and is subject to scrutiny and criticism by the opposition. To some extent the implications of budgetary decisions are clear and winners and losers are apparent.

Regulatory decisions do not directly allocate public funds and are rarely the object of immediate control by Cabinet or one of its committees. By their very diversity and specificity, regulatory actions require multiple agencies and a degree of autonomy from central control. As extra-departmental agencies limit participants, control conflict, and insulate decisions from partisan forces, they commonly take on a quasi-judicial style and often are imbued with a non-political aura.

It is now widely understood that regulation involves much more than a purely technical, administrative task and that it may directly affect the allocation of values and, therefore, constitutes an important arena of political decision-making.[123] But the conflictual and redistributive quality tends to be much less obvious than in the expenditure sphere. The regulatory process also can be distinguished by its lack of centralization and hierarchy. Well in advance of the fiscal year, the budgetary process begins. The various programme submissions go up the departmental ladder to be submitted to the Treasury Board. The Board Secretariat acts as a coordinating, central control agency that brings requests into line with established government priorities. There is no Treasury Board or functional equivalent for regulatory policy. Each source of regulations (cabinet, department, and agency) makes its own regulations within the context of its individual substantive sphere. Not only are the regulations uncoordinated with each other, there is no central board to make sure that they are at least in line with established government policies.[124] Four provinces (Alberta, Saskatchewan, Manitoba, and Ontario) have legislative committees to scrutinize all regulations promulgated within the province but their job is really to watch for illegalities rather than inconsistent policies.

Federal-provincial cooperation is more difficult in the regulatory arena than the expenditure arena. Where spending issues are concerned, constitutional difficulties can often be minimized or avoided. Since costs can be divided and differences split, such issues are conducive to compromise. But in the case of regulation, it is more difficult to compromise over the substance of rules and their implementation. The constitutional division of powers creates a greater obstacle for regulatory cooperation than it does in the case of expenditures.

A final difference between the two processes is in the nature of the participants. In the budgetary process the regular departments, Treasury Board, Planning and Priorities Committee, full cabinet and legislature each play a part. In regulatory policy-making, agencies outside the departmental structure are the main decision-makers. They are not directly tied to Ministers. Often they may be more closely affiliated with the regulated sector. No central agencies are involved although the cabinet may, in some cases, have the power to override agency decisions. Beyond the legislative scrutiny committees, there is no involvement of the legislature in regulation except in its initial delegation of authority and the degree of discretion left to the agency.

CONCLUSIONS

Provincial political institutions and the multiple processes which operate within them represent primary factors in policy formation. Not only do they serve as channels of influence for social, economic, and political forces, they also have their own independent effect on outputs. This does not mean that institutions by themselves provide an accurate or complete basis for understanding why governments develop distinctive patterns of policy. As we have already seen, environmental and political factors are prominent in the genesis and evolution of policy options and shape the setting in which decision-makers must operate. Furthermore, provinces are not autonomous political units; they exist within a federal structure and operate within an elaborate array of federal-provincial relationships that impinge on almost every area of policy.

NOTES

1. E.E. Schattschneider, *The Semi-sovereign People*, Holt, Rinehart, and Winston, New York, 1960.
2. Two studies comparing Canada with other systems indicate significant institutional effects. See Lennart Lundqvist, "Do Political Structures Matter in Environmental Politics," *Canadian Public Administration*, 17 Spring, 1974, pp. 119-141 and Christopher Leman, "Patterns of Policy Development: Social Security in the United States and Canada," *Public Policy*, 25:2 Spring, 1977, pp. 261-291.
3. Richard Simeon, "Studying Public Policy," *Canadian Journal of Political Science* 9, December, 1976, p. 574; Arnold Heidenheimer, "The Politics of Public Education, Health and Welfare in the U.S.A. and Western Europe," *British Journal of Political Science* 3, July, 1973, pp. 315-340.
4. See J.P. Mackintosh, *The British Cabinet*, Second Edition, Stevens, London, 1968, and Sir Ivor Jennings, *Cabinet Government* Third Edition, Cambridge University Press, Cambridge, 1959. For general discussion of the Canadian cabinet government, largely at the federal level, see W.A. Matheson, *Prime Minister and Cabinet*, Methuen, Toronto, 1976 and R.M. Punnett, *The Prime Minister in Canadian Government and Politics* Macmillan, Toronto, 1977. See also K. Bryden, "Cabinets," in

D. Bellamy *et al.*, *The Provincial Political Systems* Methuen, Toronto, 1976, pp. 310-322.

5. For a description of the early provincial cabinets see J. Murray Beck, *The Government of Nova Scotia*, University of Toronto Press, Toronto, 1957; Fred Schindeler, *Responsible Government in Ontario*, University of Toronto Press, Toronto, 1969; and M. Donnelly, *The Government of Manitoba*, University of Toronto Press, Toronto, 1963.

6. Gordon Robertson, "The Changing Role of the Privy Council Office," *Canadian Public Administration*, 14, Winter, 1971, p. 489.

7. Schindeler, *op. cit.*, pp. 31-32.

8. "Administration and Personnel" in Bellamy *et al.*, *op. cit.*, p. 345.

9. Richard Rose, "On the Priorities of Government: A Developmental Analysis of Public Policies," *European Journal of Political Research* 4, September, 1976, pp. 247-289.

10. The makeup of the Executive Council is the same as that of cabinet. Executive Council is the formal statutory designation.

11. Education remained in the hands of the Church until 1964 when a cabinet level Department of Education was re-established.

12. For a complete listing of each provincial cabinet see the current Parliamentary Guide. For an up-to-date listing of the members of each cabinet see *Corpus Administrative Index*, Toronto, 1978.

13. Richard Simeon, "The Overload Thesis and Canadian Government," *Canadian Public Policy* 2, Fall, 1976, pp. 541-552.

14. On the development of federal cabinet committees see G.B. Doern, "The Development of Policy Organizations in the Executive Arena" in G.B. Doern and P. Aucoin, *The Structures of Policy-Making in Canada*, Macmillan, of Canada, Toronto, 1971, pp. 39-78.

15. These examples are from Schindeler, *op. cit.*, p. 84.

16. See George Szablowski, "Policy-Making and Cabinet" in Donald MacDonald, Editor, *Government and Politics of Ontario*, Macmillan of Canada, Toronto, 1975, pp. 114-134; J. Fleck, "Restructuring the Ontario Government," *Canadian Public Administration* 16, 1973, pp. 56-72; and K. Bryden, "Executive and Legislature in Ontario: A Case Study in Governmental Reform," *Canadian Public Administration* 18, 1975, pp. 235-252.

17. Newfoundland Committee on Government Administration and Productivity, *Report*, St. John's, 1972.

18. Ross Johnson, "Cabinet Decision-Making: Taking Issues out of Politics?" paper presented at the Canadian Political Science Association Meetings, Quebec City, 1976.

19. Bryden, "Cabinets," *op. cit.* See also D. Jarvis, "Cabinet: Organization" in D. Rowat, Editor, *Provincial Government and Politics: Comparative Essays*, Carleton University, Ottawa, 1972.

20. M. Brownstone, "The Douglas-Lloyd Governments: Innovation and Bureaucratic Response" in L. LaPierre, Editor, *Essays on the Left* McClelland and Stewart, Toronto, 1971, pp. 65-80.
21. "The N.D.P. Government of British Columbia: Unaided Politicians in an Unaided Cabinet," *Canadian Public Policy* 3, Fall 1977, p. 492.
22. Johnson, *op. cit.*
23. George Cadbury, "Planning in Saskatchewan" in L. LaPierre, *op. cit.*, pp. 51-64.
24. Bryden, "Cabinets," p. 322. See also J. Deutsch, "Governments and their Advisors," *Canadian Public Administration* 16, Spring, 1973, pp. 25-34.
25. *Op. cit.*, p. 129.
26. Ontario Committee on Government Productivity, *Report #9*, Toronto, 1973, p. 15.
27. Szablowski, *op. cit.*, p. 124. See also J.R. Mallory, "Restructuring the Government of Ontario: A Comment," *Canadian Public Administration* 16, Spring, 1973, pp. 69-72.
28. G.B. Doern, "Horizontal and Vertical Portfolios in Government" in G.B. Doern and S. Wilson, Editors, *Issues in Canadian Public Policy* Macmillan of Canada, Toronto, 1974 p. 331.
29. Economic Council of Canada, *Design for Decision-Making, 8th Annual Review*, Ottawa, 1971, p. 35. For a criticism of several of the rational policy techniques see Douglas Hartle, "Techniques and Processes of Administration," *Canadian Public Administration* 19, Spring, 1976, pp. 21-33.
30. A.W. Johnson, "PPB and Decision-Making in the Government of Canada, *Cost and Management* 45, March-April 1971, p. 13.
31. Jacques Benjamin, "La Rationalisation des choix Budgetaires: les cas quebecois et Canadien," *CJPS* 5, September, 1972, pp. 348-364. See also D. Bedard, "La Notion de Programme et son application au environnement du Quebec," *L'Actualité Economique*, Av.-Jn. 1973, pp. 202-210.
32. A.W. Johnson, "The Treasury Board in Saskatchewan," Proceedings of the Conference of the Institute for Public Administration in Canada, 1955.
33. D.M. Wallace, "Budget Reform in Saskatchewan: A New Approach to Program-Based Management," *Canadian Public Administration* 17, Winter, 1974, pp. 586-599; V. Fowke, "PPB for the Provinces," *Canadian Public Administration* 12, Spring, 1969, p. 592.
34. R.M. Burns, "Budgeting and Finance" in Bellamy, *et al.*, Editors, *Comparative Provincial Political Systems*, Methuen, Toronto, 1976, p. 327.
35. G. Szablowski, "The Optimal Policy-Making System: Implications for the Canadian Political Process" in T. Hockin,

Editor, *Apex of Power*, Second Edition, Prentice-Hall, of Canada, Scarborough, pp. 197-210.

36. B. Guy Peters, "Social Change, Political Change and Public Policy: A Test of a Model" in R. Rose, Editor, *The Dynamics of Public Policy* Sage Publications, Beverly Hills, 1976, pp. 113-156; H. Heclo, *Modern Social Politics in Britain and Sweden*, Yale University Press, New Haven, 1974; and Doern and Aucoin, *op. cit.*, p. 102.

37. Anchor Books, New York, 1950, p. 304.

38. Two good general sources on the bureaucracy in Canada are J.E. Hodgetts, *The Canadian Public Service*, University of Toronto Press, Toronto, 1973, and W.D.K. Kernaghan, *Public Administration in Canada, Selected Readings*, Third Edition, Methuen, Toronto, 1977.

39. See J.R. Mallory, "Delegated Legislation in Canada: Recent Changes in Machinery," J.E. Hodgetts and D.C. Corbett, Editors, *Canadian Public Administration*, Macmillan of Canada, Toronto, 1960, pp. 504-514. For a case study of delegated legislation within the provinces see Gerard Veilleux, "The Ontario Labour Relations Board and the Quebec Rental Commission," *CPA* 7, Spring, 1964, pp. 45-62.

40. Much of this section is drawn from the excellent study of provincial civil servants by J. Hodgetts and O.P. Dwivedi, *Provincial Governments as Employers*, McGill-Queen's University Press, Montreal, 1974. See also Saul Frankel, *Staff Relations in the Civil Service, The Canadian Experience*, McGill-Queen's University Press, Montreal, 1962.

41. Peters, *op. cit.*, p. 117; and S. Huntington, *Political Order in Changing Societies*, Yale University Press, New Haven, 1968.

42. Hodgetts and Dwivedi, *Provincial Governments as Employers*, p. 11.

43. Hodgetts and Dwivedi, *op. cit.*, p. 190. In 1951 there were 3.6 provincial employees for every thousand persons; by 1971 there were 9.7 employees per thousand of population.

44. On the extradepartmental growth of regulatory boards see Taylor Cole, *The Canadian Bureaucracy, 1939-47*, Duke University Press, Durham, 1949; and Peter Silcox, "The Proliferation of Boards and Commissions" in T. Lloyd and J.T. McLeod, *Agenda 1970: Proposals for a Creative Politics*, University of Toronto Press, Toronto, 1968.

45. *The Canadian Public Services*, p. 264.

46. Cole, *op. cit.*, p. 190.

47. Hodgetts and Dwivedi, *op. cit.*, p. 33.

48. R.H. Dowdell, "Public Personnel Administration" in Kernahan, *op. cit.*, pp. 208-226.

49. Robert Presthus, *Elite Accommodation in Canadian Politics*, Macmillan, of Canada, Toronto, Chapter 8.

50. See David Hoffman, "Interacting with Government: The General Public and Interest Groups" in MacDonald, *op. cit.*,

pp. 271-293; Paul Pross, "Pressure Groups" in Bellamy *et al.*, *op. cit.*, pp. 132-146; J.E. Anderson, "Pressure Groups and the Canadian Bureaucracy" in Kernaghan, *op. cit.*, pp. 292-301; and S. Noel, "Leadership and Clientelism" in Bellamy, *et al.*, *op. cit.*, pp. 197-213.

51. Dowdell, *op. cit.*, p. 213.
52. Peter Aucoin, "Pressure Groups and Recent Changes in the Policy-Making Process" in A.P. Pross, *op. cit.* Erecting horizontal links among departments is one of three key reforms of the policy process suggested by Malcolm Rowan, "A Conceptual Framework for Government Policy-Making," *CPA* 13, Fall, 1970, p. 280.
53. D. Gow, *The Progress of Budgetary Reform in the Government of Canada*, Special Study #17, Economic Council of Canada, Ottawa, 1973, p. 39.
54. J.R. Mallory, *The Structure of Canadian Government*, Macmillan, of Canada, Toronto, p. 111. For other discussions of the relationship between Ministers and Civil Servants see M. Lamontagne, "The Influence of the Politician," *CPA* 11, Autumn, 1968; The Honourable Darcy McKeough, "Relations of Ministers and Civil Servants," *CPA* 12, Spring, 1969, pp. 1-8; J.E. Hodgetts, "The Civil Service and Policy Formation," *CJEPS* 23, November, 1957, pp. 467-479; J. Deutsch, *op. cit.*; A. Blakeney, "The Relationship between Provincial Ministers and their Deputy Ministers," *CPA* 15, Spring, 1972, pp. 42-45; and W.D.G. Kernaghan, "Policies, Policy and Public Servants" in Kernaghan, *op. cit.*, pp. 248-263.
55. Doern and Aucoin, *op. cit.*, p. 101.
56. Wm. Matheson, "The Cabinet and the Canadian Bureaucracy" in Kerhaghan (ed.), *op. cit.*, pp. 264-272. See also Paul Pross, "Canadian Pressure Groups in the '70s: their role and relations with the Public Service," *CPA* 18, Spring, 1975, pp. 121-135 for an assessment of these changes.
57. Richard Schultz, "Prime Ministerial Government Central Agencies and Operating Departments: Towards a More Realistic Analysis" in Hockin, *Apex of Power*, *op. cit.*, pp. 229-236. See also Aucoin, "Pressure Groups and Recent Changes," *op. cit.*, p. 182.
58. Lipset, *op. cit.*, p. 317.
59. For discussions of the behaviour of the bureaucracy see Anthony Downs, *Inside Bureaucracy*, Little Brown, Boston, 1966, Wm. Niskanen, *Bureaucracy and Representative Government*, Aldine, Chicago, 1971, and Douglas Hartle, *A Theory of the Expenditure Budgetary Process*, University of Toronto Press, Toronto, 1976, pp. 73-75.
60. Heidenheimer, *op. cit.*, pp. 324-326.
61. Dale Poel, "The Diffusion of Legislation Among Canadian

Provinces: A Statistical Analysis," *CJPS* 9, December, 1976, pp. 605-626.

62. Heclo, *op. cit.*, pp. 301-322.

63. R. VanLoon and R. Whittington, *The Canadian Political System*, Second Edition, McGraw-Hill Ryerson, Toronto, 1976, p. 416.

64. This model is proposed by R. Jackson and M. Atkinson, *The Canadian Legislative System*, Macmillan, of Canada, Toronto, 1974, p. 19. It is a conceptualization that treats the legislature and executive as a part of a single merged system rather than as isolated entities.

65. See, for example, Donnelly, *op. cit.*, p. 72. See also G.W. Kitchin, "The Abolition of Upper Chambers" in Rowat, *op. cit.*, pp. 305-330.

66. See John Saywell, *The Offices of Lieutenant-Governor*, University of Toronto Press, Toronto, 1957; Frank MacKinnon, *The Crown in Canada*, Glenbow Alberta Institute, Calgary, 1976.

67. Denis Smith, "President and Parliament: The Transformation of Parliamentary Government in Canada" in Paul Fox, Editor, *Politics: Canada*, Fourth Edition, McGraw-Hill Ryerson, Toronto, 1977, pp. 426-430.

68. For studies that use these as indicators of professionalism see Poel, *op. cit.* and D. Falcone and Wm. Mishler, "Legislative Determinants of Provincial Health Policy in Canada, *Journal of Politics* 39, August, 1977, pp. 345-367.

69. For the earlier period see Schindeler, *op. cit.*; for the latter see Michael Atkinson, *Backbench Participation in Legislative Policy-Making: A Test of the Ambition Hypothesis*, unpublished Ph.D. Dissertation, Carleton University, 1978.

70. Jackson and Atkinson, *op. cit.*, p. 38.

71. J.R. Mallory and B.A. Smith, "The Legislative Role of Parliamentary Committees in Canada: The Case of the Journal Committee on the Public Service Bills," *CPA* 15, Spring, 1972, pp. 1-23.

72. Lawrence LeDuc and W. White, "Opposition and One-Party Dominance," *CJPS* 7, March, 1974, pp. 86-100.

73. Pre-legislative hearings are the major reform advocated by J.A. Lovink, "Parliamentary Reform and Governmental Effectiveness in Canada, *CPA* 16, Spring, 1973, pp. 35-54.

74. P. Clutterbuck, "Reforms in Organization and Procedure" in Rowat (ed), *op. cit.*, pp. 317-341. See also P. Landry, "Legislatures" in Bellamy, *et al.* (eds.), *op. cit.*, pp. 266-292; Donald MacDonald, "Modernizing the Legislature" in MacDonald, *op. cit.*, pp. 93-113; and Ken Bryden, "Executive and Legislature in Ontario," *CPA* 18, Summer, 1975.

75. MacDonald, *op. cit.*, p. 105. Ontario Commission on the Legislature, *Fourth Report*, Toronto, 1975, p. 14.

76. J.N. Lavoie, "New Standing Orders for the National Assembly of Quebec," *The Parliamentarian* (1969), and Alex McLeod,

Reform of the Standing Committees of the Quebec National Assembly: A Preliminary Assessment," *CJPS* 8, March, 1975, pp. 22-39.

77. T. Hockin, "Adversary Politics and the Functions of the Canadian House of Commons," Orest Kruhlak *et al.*, *The Canadian Political Process: a Reader*, Revised Edition, Holt, Rinehart and Winston, Toronto, 1973, p. 377.

78. See H. Thorburn, *Politics in New Brunswick*, University of Toronto Press, Toronto, 1961, C.E.S. Franks, "The Legislatures and Responsible Government" in N. Ward and D. Spafford, Editors, *Politics in Saskatchewan*, Longman Canada, Don Mills, 1968; and F. Mackinnon, *The Government of Prince Edward Island* University of Toronto, Press, Toronto, 1951.

79. See Simon McInnes, "Improving Legislative Surveillance of Provincial Public Expenditures: The Performance of the Public Accounts Committees and Auditors General," *CPA* 20, Spring, 1977, pp. 36-86, for an up-to-date and comprehensive comparison of the PPAC and the role of the Provincial Auditors General. For an in-depth study of Saskatchewan's PAC, see C.G.S. Franks, "The Saskatchewan Public Accounts Committee," *CPA* 9, September, 1966, pp. 348-366 and for Ontario see Schindeler, *op. cit.*, pp. 250-257.

80. McInnes, *op. cit.*, p. 56.

81. *Ibid.*, p. 65.

82. LeDuc and White, *op. cit.*, and Harold Clarke *et al.*, "Constituency Service Among Canadian Provincial Legislators," *CJPS* 8, December, 1975, pp. 520-543.

83. Atkinson, *op. cit.*

84. Hockin, "Adversary Politics," *op. cit.*, p. 376.

85. C. B. Doern and P. Aucoin, *The Structures of Policy-Making*, Second Edition, Macmillan of Canada, Toronto, 1979, introduction.

86. This discussion is drawn from James Anderson, *Public Policy-Making*, Praeger Publishers, New York, 1975, and Charles Jones, *An Introduction to the Study of Public Policy*, Second Edition, Duxbury Press, North Scituate, Mass., 1977. For a more detailed analysis of policy stages see Richard Rose, "Comparing Public Policy: An Overview," *European Journal of Political Research* 1, 1973, pp. 67-94.

87. Ralph Krueger, "The Provincial-Municipal Government Revolution in New Brunswick," *CPA* 13, Spring, 1970, pp. 51-99.

88. M. W. Bucovetsky, "The Mining Industry and the Great Tax Reform Debate" in P. Pross, Editor, *Pressure Group Behaviour in Canadian Politics*, McGraw-Hill Ryerson, Toronto, 1975, pp. 87-115. This analysis of tax reform for extractive industries is an important illustration of the merging of policy stages. The 1969 Benson White Paper included the government proposals

for tax reform. Formulation and selection became inter-
meshed as Commons Committee Hearings produced a long
line of witnesses in opposition to the proposals. Bucovetsky
ably demonstrates formulation did not end with the cabinet's
white paper decision.

89. These models are described in David Braybrooke and C.
Lindblom, *A Strategy of Decision,* Free Press, New York, 1963;
Charles Lindblom, "The Science of Muddling Through," *Public
Administration Review* 19, Spring, 1959, pp. 79-88; and Yehezkel
Dror, *Public Policy-Making Re-examined,* Chandler, San Francisco,
1968.

90. Amitai Etzioni, "Mixed Scanning: A 'Third' Approach to
Decision-Making," *Public Administration Review* 27, December,
1967, pp. 385-392. See Kenneth Bryden, *Old Age Pensions and
Policy-Making in Canada,* McGill-Queens, University Press,
Montreal, 1974, for an analysis that illustrates policy
development as a mix of major innovative leaps and incremental changes.

91. Theodore Lowi, "American Business Public Policy: Case
Studies and Political Theory," *World Politics* 26, July, 1964,
pp. 677-715. Lowi later divided policy structures into four
categories. See "Decision-Making vs. Policy-Making. Toward
an Antidote for Technocracy," *Public Administration Review* 30,
May/June 1970, pp. 134-325. For other policy categorizations
that emphasize process differences see E. Redford, *Democracy
in the Administrative State,* Oxford University Press, New York,
1969, Chapters IV and V; J. Heinz and R. Salisbury, "A Theory
of Policy Analysis and Some Preliminary Applications," in I.
Sharkansky, *Policy Analysis in Political Science* Markham, Chicago,
1970; Lewis Froman, "The Categorization of Policy
Contents," Robert Salisbury, The Analysis of Public Policy: A
Search for Theories and Roles" both in Austin Ranney,
Editor, *Political Science and Public Policy* Markham, Chicago,
1968; and Marsha Chandler *et al.,* "Policy Analysis and the
Search for Theory," *American Politics Quarterly* 2, January, 1974,
pp. 107-118.

92. For applications of Lowi's typologies to Canadian politics see
G. B. Doern and S. Wilson, "Introduction" and Robert Best,
"Youth Policy" both in G. B. Doern and S. Wilson, Editors,
Issues in Canadian Public Policy, Macmillan, of Canada, Toronto,
1974; and John Shiry, "Distributive and Regulatory Policy in
Ontario: A Test of Lowi's Arenas of Power Schema," paper
presented at Canadian Political Science Association Meetings,
Quebec City, 1976.

93. J. C. Strick, *Canadian Public Finance,* Holt, Rinehart and Winston,
Toronto, 1973, p. 27.

94. Bryden, "Executive and Legislature in Ontario," *op. cit.,* p. 321.

95. Gow, *op. cit.* See also Robert Vaison, "Public Budgeting and Financial Management: The State of the Art," *Canadian Chartered Accountant* 101, July, 1972, pp. 22-26 and J. C. Strick, "Recent Developments in Canadian Financial Administration," *Public Administration* 48, Spring, 1970, pp. 69-85.

96. D. S. Campbell, "Planning, Programming and Budgeting in the Ontario Government," *Cost and Management* 49, July-August, 1975, pp. 6-13.

97. For a brief description of the Glassco Commission proposals see W. L. White and J. C. Strick, *Policy, Politics and the Treasury Board in Canadian Government,* Science Research Associates, Don Mills, 1970. For criticisms of these proposals see *CPA,* 1962.

98. Treasury Board, *Planning, Programming and Budgeting Guide* Queen's Printer, Ottawa, 1969, p. 8. There are several useful discussions of PBBS in Canada. See, for example, G. B. Doern, "The Development and Objectives of the PPB Approach" in Doern and Aucoin, *op. cit.,* pp. 87-106; H. Balls, "Planning, Programming and Budgeting in Canada," *Public Administration* 48, Autumn, 1970, pp. 289-305.

99. Campbell, *op. cit.*

100. Conseil du Trésor, *Le Système de Budget par programmes et son application au Gouvernement du Québec,* Gouvernement du Québec, 1972; Benjamin, *op. cit.*

101. See Burns, "Budgeting and Finance," *op. cit.*

102. There are numerous discussions of appropriate indicators of state activity. See Richard Bird, *Growth of Government Spending in Canada,* Canadian Tax Foundation, Toronto, 1970; Rose, *op. cit.;* Ontario Economic Council, *Issues and Alternatives 1977: The Process of Public Decision-Making,* Toronto, 1977, pp. 5-6.

103. For useful discussions of regulation see G. B. Doern, "The Concept of Regulation and Regulatory Reform" in Doern and Wilson (eds.), *op. cit.,* pp. 8-35. G. J. Stigler, "An Economic Theory of Regulation," *Bell Journal of Economics and Management Science* 2, 1971, pp. 3-21; and G. B. Doern, Editor, *The Regulatory Process in Canada* Macmillan of Canada, Toronto, 1978.

104. On regulatory units as distinct from the regulatory function see G. B. Doern, *The Regulatory Process in Canada,* Macmillan of Canada, Toronto, 1978, chapter 1; Regulatory agencies are discussed in G. B. Doern, *et al.,* "The Structure and Behaviour of Canadian Regulatory Boards and Commissions: Multidisciplinary Perspectives," *CPA* 18, Summer, 1975, pp. 189-215; and Richard Schultz, "Regulatory Agencies and the Canadian Political System" in Kernaghan (ed.), *op. cit.,* pp. 333-343.

105. *Committee on Government Productivity, Report Number Nine,* Toronto, 1973, pp. 29-53. On degrees of responsibility to governments

see Silcox, *op. cit.* A useful description of the scope and variation in regulatory activity in one province is Peter Silcox, "The ABC's of Ontario: Provincial Agencies, Boards and Commissions" in MacDonald (ed.), *op. cit.,* pp. 135-152.

106. K. Rubin, *Inventory of Provincial Regulatory Agencies in Canada* Canadian Consumer Council, Ottawa, 1971, includes a comprehensive listing of the most important provincial regulatory agencies. This source provides a basic reference for the regulatory examples cited here. On provincial regulation, for example of utilities, see B. G. Reschanthaler, "The Performance of Selected Independent Regulatory Commissions in Alberta, Saskatchewan and Manitoba," Canadian Consumer Council, Ottawa, 1972, and Ontario Economic Council, *Issues and Alternatives 1978 Government Regulation,* Toronto, 1978.

107. Until the federal Farm Products Marketing Act of 1972 the only important exception to this was the Canadian Wheat Board, established in 1935. Since this Act, other national agencies have emerged, for example, the Canadian Egg Marketing Agency in 1973. For more detail on marketing boards see Canada, Department of Agriculture, *Marketing Boards in Canada,* annual report, Ottawa, Information Canada. See also Federal Task Force on Agriculture, *Canadian Agriculture in the Seventies,* Queen's Printer, Ottawa, 1970 pp. 311-314.

108. See Reschanthaler, pp. 10-48 and 146-190; W. T. Stanbury, "The B. C. Utility Commissioners and their Work," Canadian Consumer Council, Ottawa, 1973; John Erkkila and John Palmer, "The Role of the Consumer in Affecting the Decisions of the Hydro-Electric Power Commission in Ontario," Canadian Consumer Council, Ottawa, 1973.

109. Studies of provincial transport and communication regulation include B. G. Reschanthaler, *op. cit.,* 1972, pp. 181-194; John Palmer, "Taxation by Regulation? The Experience of Ontario Trucking Regulation," Canadian Consumer Council, Ottawa, 1972; John Palmer, "A Further Analysis of Provincial Trucking Regulation," *Bell Journal of Economics and Management Service* 4, Autumn, 1973, pp. 655-664; K. W. Studnicki-Gizbert, "The Administration of Transport Policy: The Regulatory Problems," *Canadian Public Administration* 18, Winter, 1975, reprinted in K. J. Rea and J. T. McLeod, Editors, *Business and Government in Canada,* Second Edition, Methuen, Toronto, 1976, pp. 259-270; Department of Communications, *History of Regulation and Current Regulatory Setting,* Information Canada, Ottawa, 1971.

110. *Committee on Government Productivity Report Number Nine,* Toronto, 1973, pp. 37-38.

111. See R. Poser, "The Social Cost of Monopoly and Regulation," *Journal of Political Economy* 83, 1975, pp. 807-827; and K. W. Studnicki-Gizbert, "The Administration of Transport Policy: the Regulatory Problems" in Rea and McLeod (eds.), *op. cit.*, pp. 259-270.
112. See W. G. Waters, "Public Policy and Transport Regulations: An Economic Perspective" in K. Ruppenthal and Wm. Stanbury, Editors, *Regulation, Competition and the Public Interest*, Centre for Transportation Studies, Vancouver, 1976, pp. 9-38.
113. See M. V. Nelles, *The Politics of Development*, Macmillan of Canada, Toronto, 1974; A. Brady, "The Ontario Hydro-Electric Power Commission," *CJEPS* 2, 1936; J. E. Hodgetts, "The Public Corporation in Canada" in W. G. Friedman and J. F. Gardner, Editors, *Government Enterprise: A Comparative Study*, Columbia University Press, New York, 1970, pp. 201-226. J. H. Dales, *Hydroelectricity: Quebec 1808-1940*, Harvard University Press, Cambridge, 1957.
114. Some of these efforts can be rated successful, others much less so. In the latter category is New Brunswick's ill-fated involvement with the Bricklin Automobile. See M. A. Fredericks with Allan Chambers, *Bricklin*, Brunswick Press, Fredericton, 1977. See also P. Mathias, *Forced Growth*, James Lorimer, Toronto, 1971.
115. Studnicki-Gizbert, "The Administration of Transport . . .," *op. cit.*, p. 266.
116. See for example, N. Bonsor, *Transportation Rates and Economic Development in Northern Ontario*, Ontario Economic Council, Toronto, 1977, and Posner, *op. cit.*
117. *Report Number Nine, op. cit.*, pp. 29, 37. A study of federal statutes has found some 14,885 powers pertaining to regulatory activities. Philip Anisman, *A Catalogue of Discretionary Powers in the Revised Statutes of Canada 1970*, Information Canada, Ottawa, 1975.
118. C. Lloyd Brown-John, "Defining Regulatory Agencies for Analytical Purposes," *Canadian Public Administration* 19, 1976, pp. 140-157, explores the difficulties in constructing a comprehensive and accurate overview of regulatory policy-making.
119. Canadian Consumer Council, *Report on the Consumer Interest in Regulatory Boards and Agencies*, Ottawa, 1973, pp. 5-31. A valuable discussion of these problems is in Michael J. Trebilcock, "Winners and Losers in the Modern Regulatory State: Must the Consumer Always Lose?" *Osgoode Hall Law Journal* 13, December, 1975; Wm. Stanbury, *Business Interests and the Reform of Canadian Competition Policy, 1971-75*, Carswell/Methuen, Toronto, 1977; and G. J. Stigler and M. F. Cohen,

Can Regulatory Agencies Protect Consumers? American Enterprise Institute, Washington, 1971.

120. G. B. Doern, Regulatory Processes and Jurisdictional Issues in the Regulation of Hazardous Products in Canada, Background Study #41 Science Council of Canada, Ottawa, 1977.

121. Trebilcock, op. cit.

122. See Schultz, "Regulatory Agencies and the Canadian Political System," op. cit., and J. W. Langford, "The National Transportation System: Restructuring for Effective Regulation," in Ruppenthal and Stanbury (eds.), op. cit., pp. 93-107.

123. On the political nature of regulation see L. Jaffe, "The Illusion of Ideal Administration," Harvard Law Review (1973); J. Q. Wilson, "The Dead Hand of Regulation," The Public Interest, 25, Fall, 1971, pp. 39-58 and Richard Schultz, "Regulatory Agencies and the Canadian Political System" in Kernaghan, op.cit., pp. 333-343.

124. There is provision for ex post review of regulatory decisions by Cabinet for many agencies, for example, the Ontario Municipal Board and the Ontario Highway Transport Board.

Chapter 5

The Federal System

A federal system is defined as

> that form of political system (of a nation state) in which the values, institutions, and patterns of political action operate to give autonomous expression to both the national political system and political culture, and to regional political subsystems and subcultures (defined primarily by ethnic-linguistic factors). The autonomy of each of these systems and subsystems is counterbalanced by a mutual interdependence.[1]

Within the Canadian federal system there are three levels of government—national,* provincial, and municipal; the policies of any single level cannot be fully understood without reference to the workings of the rest of the system. This chapter is concerned with federal-provincial relationships and their implications for provincial policy.

The tension between autonomy and interdependence has been a persistent theme in the evolution of the federal system.[2] Each government is accorded its own constitutional jurisdiction in which it has independent law-making authority. In the Canadian federal system the autonomy of each government is accentuated by specific regional interests and distinct political cleavages. In short, there are eleven unique political systems; yet in almost every sphere, there is a tremendous overlap in responsibilities. With a few exceptions no policy field is in the exclusive jurisdiction of any one government. For example, transportation is primarily a federal responsibility, but provinces regulate trucking and own railroad and airline companies, while municipalities often own and operate their own surface transit systems. Interdependence goes beyond shared responsibilities; even where there is no specific overlap, provincial and federal policies often have ramifications for each other.[3] It is clear, for example, that Ottawa's fiscal and tariff policies have had profound implications for provincial economic prosperity. Similarly, the actions of a single province can have important effects on Ottawa and on other provinces. In 1970 when the Quebec Egg Marketing Board (FEDCO) established quotas for out-of-province eggs, the other egg producing provinces acted to defend their

*usually referred to as the federal government.

149

interests and passed similar restrictions. The provincial "chicken and egg war" was an important impetus for the passage of federal legislation establishing a national marketing board.[4] Even policies not aimed outside the province, such as pollution control or education, often have external implications.

The jurisdictions established in the British North America Act in 1867 gave the Dominion government control over defence, trade, and other national concerns. Set out in Section 91, the powers granted to Ottawa included a list of some twenty-nine specifically enumerated powers as well as a more general grant to "make laws for the peace, order, and good government of Canada". The provincial powers, stated for the most part in Section 92, were enumerated as sixteen specific areas of jurisdiction. These powers included what were believed to be essentially minor and/or local matters, for example public welfare, as well as those activities in the social and cultural spheres. However, among them were the powers over "property and civil rights", and "matters of a local or private nature" which were to become the bases for expanded provincial policy-making.

Immigration and agriculture were the only two powers originally given to both federal and provincial governments. A third concurrent power was established by amendment in 1951 which gave Ottawa authority in the provincial jurisdiction of old age pensions. There is little doubt that the British North America Act was intended to create a political system dominated by Ottawa. Federal supremacy was guaranteed in concurrent powers, in its role as guardian of the education rights of minorities, and by its right to appoint Lieutenant-Governors to supervise provincial governments and even to disallow provincial legislation.[5] Most importantly, Ottawa was given the bulk of governing powers as well as the financial resources to carry them out. The "peace, order, and good government" clause was an important cornerstone of superior federal power.

The division of power in the British North America Act soon ceased to be an accurate description of the jurisdiction of Ottawa and the provinces. Decisions of the Judicial Committee of the Privy Council fundamentally affected the original centralist distribution of authority. In 1896 the decision in the *Local Prohibition Case*[6] struck at a key element of federal power. The "peace, order, and good government" clause was rendered subordinate to the enumerated powers in Sections 91 and 92. This meant that the enumerated power to make laws respecting property and civil rights within the province" took precedence over the residual powers of Parliament. In fact, the property and civil rights clause became the real grant of residual powers. In the 1920s the "peace, order, and good government" clause was relegated to the status of an emergency power.[7]

Federal authorities tried to recoup their lost dominance by going back to one of the enumerated powers in Section 91—"the regulation of trade and commerce". However, the Judicial Committee once again sided with the provinces: the federal power to regulate trade and commerce was interpreted to mean the regulation of international and interprovincial trade to facilitate some other federal function. Federal regulations could not be used to interfere with the provinces' right to regulate trade within the provinces.[8]

As the provinces became more equal partners within the federal system, a series of federal-provincial arrangements developed that brought about close contact and collaboration between the two levels.[9] In the 1940s and 1950s joint programmes and activities were established across a wide range of policy areas. The cooperative form of federalism[10] exemplified by shared-cost programmes gave rise to legitimate provincial concerns about the erosion of their autonomy.

Starting in the 1960s the provinces began to reassert control over their finances. For example, tax collection agreements freed the provinces from federal determination of tax revenues; tax abatements increased the provincial share of public revenues and unconditional grants replaced conditional ones as the major vehicle for reducing provincial inequalities.[11] Despite these measures, the continued growth of government responsibilities at all levels increased the degree of federal-provincial interdependence. In new policy areas such as regulation of cable television, where jurisdiction is ambiguous, both levels have claimed authority. In other areas where jurisdictional boundaries are established, the growth of government has led to the intervention of one level of government into the affairs of the other, for example, federal entry into urban affairs or provincial attempts to develop counter-cyclical fiscal policies. Superimposed on these developments has been the fundamental conundrum of the status of the Canadian constitution.

There have been repeated attempts to patriate the constitution, to find an acceptable formula for amendment, and to redefine the basic jurisdictional divisions of Canadian federalism. Some of these efforts have produced partial solutions, but as a whole they have fallen far short of any consensual, comprehensive redefinitions of Canadian federalism.[12] The Parti Québécois victory in November 1976 reopened many of these questions and of course expanded the debate on constitutional options to include the most basic question of separation or survival. The PQ argues that reform of the present constitutional order is not possible because the gap between what Quebec wants and what the rest of Canada views as acceptable is simply too great. In these circumstances a fundamental redefinition of the relations between Quebec and Canada on the basis of the principle, "sovereignty-association" is both necessary and desirable.[13]

FEDERAL-PROVINCIAL ARENAS

One result of the simultaneous growth of autonomy and inter-dependence is the increased scope of the federal-provincial arena. Federal-provincial negotiations range over a vast number of issues which include constitutional amendment procedures, occupation of tax fields, as well as deliberations over lesser matters such as the Young Voyageur Programme. At Confederation there were no constitutional provisions for intergovernmental negotiations. There was a Secretary of State for the Provinces, but this position was abolished some six years later. The creation of devices and procedures for adjustment between the federal and provincial levels became necessary as the scope of government expanded and as the provinces became more viable political units. As both levels took on new policy functions there was a need for procedures both to manage conflict and to co-ordinate the greater federal-provincial interdependence. In 1906 Dominion-Provincial Premiers' Conferences were instituted as a forum for discussing specific issues of current importance. By 1935 it was agreed by the Dominion and Provincial Premiers that more institutionalized modes of cooperation were needed. A few years later the Royal Commission on Dominion-Provincial Relations (Rowell-Sirois) also recommended establishing regular means of cooperation.[14] But not until 1955 was a continuing body established to deal with federal-provincial relations.[15] The Continuing Committee on Fiscal and Economic Matters was created to act as a secretariat to the Federal-Provincial Conference and has been an important element in bringing about fiscal and programme cooperation between Ottawa and the provinces.

> The committee members agree on facts, clarify problems, discuss memoranda submitted by members, but make no independent decisions, take no votes, exercise no executive powers as a committee, do not lobby as a body and do not bind their principles in any way.[16]

There have been other efforts to regularize federal-provincial relations, most importantly the establishment of the Committee of Ministers of Finance and Provincial Treasurers in 1959, and the Tax Structure Committee in 1964. Four provinces (Ontario, Alberta, Manitoba, and Quebec) have cabinet level positions for Intergovernmental Relations. In Ottawa there is a standing committee of cabinet on federal-provincial relations and as of 1977 a Minister of State for Intergovernmental Relations.[17]

The past twenty years have seen a tremendous increase in the number of federal-provincial committees. In 1957 the number of committees was estimated to be about sixty-four, by 1965 the figure had doubled, and by 1968 the *Intergovernmental Liaison on Fiscal and Economic Matters* listed almost two hundred committees or joint boards.[18] The proliferation of these committees is at the very least an indication of the increasing range of federal-provincial interdependence. Claude Morin has argued that the number of federal-provincial conferences increases with Ottawa's desire to intervene in matters under provincial jurisdiction.[19] Intergovernmental consultations are more common in some policy areas than in others. One study has found that over one-third of federal-provincial negotiations concern natural resources and primary industry. About one-fifth of all consultations have been in the spheres of health and welfare. Transportation and communication, an area that used to account for over ten percent of intergovernmental meetings, by 1967 was the subject of only one percent of the meetings.[20]

Federal-provincial committees span a wide range of interactions. They range from the highly publicized and structured First Ministers' meetings to the informal, ad hoc, and unheralded workings of specialized civil servants from both levels. The First Ministers' Meetings must be seen primarily as meetings among politicians. Fighting Ottawa has generally been rewarding for provincial leaders, and many of the pronouncements of the participants are directed as much toward the folks back home as to conference colleagues. Most of the broad changes in federal-provincial relations have been reflected in the First Ministers' Conferences. Over time they have become more visible and publicized (although they are not always open to the press), and the scope of issues has also increased. Topics for discussion now go beyond matters of taxation to questions ranging from constitutional review to foreign investment. More effective staffs in many of the provinces and in Ottawa have maximized the capacity of these meetings to serve as significant arenas for conflict resolution and policy development.[21]

First Ministers' meetings evoke an image of sovereign units meeting to negotiate. Because they are often highly politicized, they receive the bulk of public and media attention. Alongside these Premiers' meetings are the more numerous officials' meetings which are run as work sessions dominated by like-minded professionals seeking technical solutions to specific problems. The agendas are narrower in scope and the interactions less political than is the case for the Premiers. Not surprisingly, these consultations are less visible and of less interest to the public.

Eleven governments, each coping with its own economic conditions, social and ideological goals, and political interests, are the major participants in intergovernmental bargaining. However, since 1960 there have been several efforts by the provinces to develop structured lines of interprovincial communication.[22] Annual meetings of provincial premiers have become a forum for expressing shared policy concerns, and regular meetings at the ministerial and sub-ministerial levels provide opportunities for specific forms of interprovincial cooperation. Common regional interests are the basis for some of the most significant interprovincial activity. The maritime and the western provinces have developed their own distinct approaches to interprovincial cooperation. The three maritime provinces, sometimes joined by Newfoundland, have built up a system that focuses on the discussion and coordination of provincial policy-making.[23] In contrast, the western provinces, through the formulation of common positions, have attempted to maximize their influence on those federal policies having special importance for the region.[24]

Federal-provincial relations have constituted a unique policy setting that is separate from federal or provincial politics. The political forces most prevalent at either the federal or provincial level are often not particularly important in this arena. Political party lines are not a common source of cleavage,[25] nor are pressure groups very effective.[26] The unique set of political forces which make up this arena are typically based on the long-standing interests of the provinces. It is the pursuit of these interests by provincial leaders, not partisanship, which determines relationships between Ottawa and the provinces.[27] Smiley comments on the political forces at work in federal-provincial relations.

> Both the permanent and occasional cleavages in this context are on axes other than partisan ones: between "have" and "have-not" provinces; between governments which put an urgent priority on bilingual and bicultural matters and those which do not; between Quebec and the other jurisdictions; between the heartland of Ontario and Quebec and the peripheral provinces.[28]

The Federal-provincial arena must be seen as a unique mode of policy-making. The participants are governments and the proceedings take place behind closed doors, where the role of opposition forces is excluded and the normal parliamentary mechanisms are by-passed.[29] This arena has evolved into a forum for elite decision-making relatively insulated from the normally constraining divisions of Canadian society.

Much of the variation in the outcomes of federal-provincial negotiations depends on the nature of the issue as well as the particular needs and resources of the participants. When they have shared goals and mutual interests, provincial autonomy can be a source of policy initiative and interdependence an impetus for compromise.[30] But when shared goals and interests are lacking, autonomy can mean separate, even conflicting, positions and interdependence can mean hopeless policy entanglement.[31] In any event, the results are always a crucial part of the framework of provincial policy-making—nowhere is this more apparent than in the significance of the fiscal arrangements negotiated every five years by Ottawa and the provinces.

FISCAL RELATIONS

The fiscal network is the key component of federal-provincial relations and reflects the distribution of power within a federal system.[32] Intergovernmental fiscal arrangements have undergone a number of fundamental changes, from their origins in the BNA Act. At Confederation Ottawa was given what were, at the time, the more important governmental functions and the revenue capacity to deal with these functions. In contrast, the jurisdiction of the provinces was limited and their revenue sources restricted. Provincial revenues come from three sources: direct taxes, federal transfers, and non-tax revenues. In 1974, taxes constituted 57 percent of provincial revenues, while federal transfers and non-tax revenues made up 23 and 20 percent respectively.[33]

Taxes

The British North America Act permits each province to levy direct taxes within its territory. Direct taxes are taxes paid by the user rather than by persons who will pass on the cost. For example, personal income tax is a direct tax, whereas a customs tax is indirect because it is expected the cost will be passed on by the importer.

The provinces entered the field of taxation slowly.[34] By 1900 only British Columbia and Prince Edward Island had levied a personal income tax. Although urbanization and increased development created new pressures on provincial budgets, it was not until after the Depression that most provinces began to move into the personal and corporate tax fields. By 1940 all nine provinces, plus the federal government, levied their own corporate income taxes and seven provinces (plus Ottawa) had their own personal income tax. Alberta, Saskatchewan, and Quebec were the first provinces to introduce retail sales taxes in 1936, 1937, and 1940 respectively. All in all taxpayers across Canada were confronted with a confusing array of overlapping and multiple taxes and procedures.

The Depression, which generated new social needs and at the same time reduced public revenues, exacerbated the provinces' fiscal difficulties. Subsequently the Rowell-Sirois Commission was constituted to investigate the division of revenue and expenditure responsibilities between the provinces and Ottawa. It recommended that the provinces give up the right to tax personal income, corporate income, and inheritances and that the federal government provide National Adjustment Grants to the poorer provinces. Although the provinces rejected the Commission's proposals to relinquish their tax fields, the Wartime Tax Agreements of 1941 created uniformity across Canada by *temporarily* centralizing the taxation system. The provinces gave up their taxing powers over individual and corporate incomes, and in return the federal government made rental payments to each province.

After the war the agreements of 1947 and 1952 continued the rental arrangements.[35] The 1952 Federal-Provincial Tax Arrangements contained an important provision for additional compensation for the 'have-not' provinces by guaranteeing them a fixed rental payment, regardless of their low tax yields. The 1957 Arrangement formalized the concept of compensation for the poorer provinces. Under the equalization programme, rental payments to each province were to be based on the tax yield of the *two* wealthiest provinces. Thus, the poorer provinces received an unconditional equalization grant to bring their tax yield payments up to the level of the wealthiest provinces.

The 1962 Tax-Sharing Agreements abolished the rental system. Under the new arrangements the federal government partially withdrew from the personal and corporate income tax fields in order to provide tax room for the provinces in these areas. Initially, the federal government reduced its income tax by 16 percent (the reduction would increase to 20 percent in the five-year period) and reduced federal corporate taxes by 9 percent. Ottawa was willing to collect the provincially-imposed taxes as long as the provincial tax base (income subject to taxes) was the same as that for the federal taxes.

In response to new pressures for autonomy generated by Quebec's Quiet Revolution, in 1965 the federal government agreed to substitute income tax abatement points for its contributions to specified shared-cost programmes. The Established Programmes (Interim Arrangements) Act permitted the provinces to opt out of joint activities without financial penalty. Quebec has been the only province to exercise this option.[36] A year later, also at the urging of Quebec, the federal government shifted the funding of post-secondary education from conditional grants to universities and colleges to tax abatements and cash payments to the provinces. As a result of this change, all provinces were to receive an abatement of 4.35 points of personal income tax and one point of corporate income tax.

The 1967 and 1972 tax agreements extended and modified the existing arrangements and continued to enlarge the equalization system. The 1977 Fiscal Arrangements and Established Programmes Financing Act represented a significant departure from previous agreements by providing 13.5 personal income tax and one corporate tax point as well as cash payments in place of federal participation in hospital and medical insurance and post-secondary education. The federal government by reducing its taxes has left room for the provinces to raise theirs as they take responsibility for the continuation of the established programmes.

Since the post-war rental agreements, the trend has been away from the integration of federal and provincial tax systems. Little evidence remains of the tax uniformity once sought by Ottawa. Due to its opting-out of several federal-provincial programmes over 50 percent of the income taxes in Quebec stay in the province. In 1977 provincial personal income tax expressed as a percentage of the federal rate ranged from 38.5 percent in Alberta to 58.5 percent in Saskatchewan. Corporate income taxes ranged from 10 percent in Prince Edward Island to 15 percent in Manitoba and British Columbia.

Despite the efforts toward greater independence in taxation, Ottawa still has a large impact on provincial tax systems because of their identical tax bases. Once federal abatement ended in 1972 and provincial taxes were no longer simply a proportion of federal taxes, Ottawa agreed to continue to collect the provincial income taxes as long as the tax bases remained the same as the federal. Nine provinces agreed; Quebec continued to collect its own taxes. Although Ottawa decides which elements are subject to personal and corporate taxation, provincial governments have often been active participants in Parliament's consideration of changes in the tax base.[37] More recently, Ottawa has been willing to accept *some* provincial variations in the uniform tax base. For instance, Ontario and Manitoba have their own property tax credits and several provinces have low-income tax relief and high-income tax surcharges.

Federal Transfers

In addition to the agreements regarding shared tax fields, the federal and provincial governments are interrelated through transfer payments which account for over one-fifth of total provincial revenues. There are three ways the federal government transfers resources to the provincial level—unconditional grants, conditional grants, and special tax abatements.*

Transfers not earmarked for any specific expenditure function are called unconditional grants or general purpose transfers. In 1976 such payments to the provinces totalled $3,234.9 million.[38] The statutory subsidies originally provided for in Section 118 of the B.N.A. Act were the first unconditional grants to the provinces. Although specified as in "full settlement of all future demands on Canada" statutory subsidies have been augmented and revised to meet special regional and/or provincial needs. These subsidies constitute less than one percent of overall federal transfers.

*These tax abatements are discussed under the Tax System above.

Table 5.1: Federal Grants as Sources of Provincial Revenues — 1974

PROVINCE	EQUALIZATION PAYMENTS AS A % OF PROVINCIAL REVENUES	CONDITIONAL GRANTS AS A % OF PROVINCIAL REVENUES
Newfoundland	26.7%	23.4%
Prince Edward Island	26.9	24.9
Nova Scotia	24.4	18.9
New Brunswick	21.7	21.4
Quebec	11.1	11.6
Ontario	0	16.3
Manitoba	10.9	18.4
Saskatchewan	9.1	14.3
Alberta	0	10.5
British Columbia	0	15.3

Source: Statistics Canada, *Provincial Government Finance 1974*, DBS 68-207.

Table 5.2: Average Percent of Provincial Policy Expenditures Derived from Conditional Federal Transfers

YEAR	HEALTH	WELFARE	EDUCATION	TRANSPORTATION AND COMMUNICATION	NATURAL RESOURCES AND PRIMARY INDUSTRY
1940	1.9%	33.0%	9.0%	0.1%	0.8%
1945	2.8	44.1	8.7	0.6	3.0
1950	11.8	48.9	3.2	4.9	3.7
1955	14.8	23.0	2.1	7.2	5.7
1960	35.2	36.0	7.7	10.1	8.6
1965	36.0	37.5	9.5	13.8	13.4
1970	36.9	41.2	13.5	12.5	16.1
1973	38.0	40.1	12.0	12.4	15.2

Source: Statistics Canada, *Provincial Government Finance, 1940-1973*, DBS 68-207.

Most unconditional grants come under the equalization programme and represent a major federal remedy to the problem of regional economic disparities. The object is to increase the revenues of the poorer provinces so that they may provide certain levels of service without an undue tax burden on their residents. The provinces are free, however, to allocate the payments in any way they choose. All provinces except Ontario, British Columbia, and Alberta have tax yields below the national average and, therefore, qualify for equalization payments. Table 5.1 shows clearly that equalization benefits constitute a significant portion of provincial revenues.

Shared-cost grants or specific-purpose transfers are conditional grants made by the federal government toward the cost of a particular programme. In accepting the payments the recipient government is obliged to spend the funds for the designated programme. Conditional grants are directed toward providing, or raising the level and/or quality of, a specific provincial activity. In 1976 Ottawa's contribution to shared-cost programmes equalled $4,045 million.[39] About twelve cents out of every dollar spent by the provinces comes from federal funds earmarked for specific purposes.

As provincial functions have become more important and more costly, the federal government has used its spending powers to enter into matters within the legislative domain of the provinces. Although Parliament does not pass programmatic legislation in creating grants-in-aid, it provides for federal-provincial arrangements and authorizes the budgetary allocation. Each participating province must pass the implementing legislation which sets up the programmes directly affecting its residents. For example, the federal Medical Care Act provided that Ottawa pay one-half of the national average per capita costs of insured medical services in all provinces having insurance plans meeting federal requirements. Ottawa required the coverage to be universal, comprehensive, and portable, and that the plan be administered by a public authority. Within these guidelines each province is free to set up its own plan.

Generally, federal cost-sharing funds are granted on a matching basis, which means that eligibility depends on a province committing a certain amount of its own funds—usually 50 percent. Conditional grant payments generally do not take regional disparities into account. Under most shared-cost arrangements rich and poor provinces receive the same degree of help, with some important exceptions. In these cases, especially Medical Care Insurance, federal payments are based in part on national average costs with Ottawa assuming a greater proportion of the expenses of the lower (below average) cost provinces.[40]

Although conditional grants are available in almost every area of provincial activity, the grants are not evenly distributed across the range of provincial expenditures, making some fields more heavily subsidized than others. Table 5.2 illustrates the extent of federal transfers for expenditures in the five major provincial policy areas. The figures represent the *average* portion of provincial spending in each area that comes from conditional grants. For example, in 1970 Ottawa provided, on the average, about 41 percent of provincial gross expenditures on social welfare.

It is apparent in Table 5.2 that there are wide differences in the extent of federal fiscal involvement in provincial policies. Each of these areas will be discussed at length in Chapters 6 and 7. We might note here, however, differing federal involvement in the areas of greatest provincial expenditure. With the growth of the welfare state in Canada, the national government (as in other federal regimes) has sought to establish national minimum standards for health and social services through large-scale federal spending. In contrast, although education is the major expenditure area of the provinces, federal assistance has been consistently quite low and has been confined to the relatively narrow spheres of universities, vocational training, and the education of native peoples. Education is one area within provincial jurisdiction that has been closely guarded because of its significance for local and regional identity. Moreover, emotion-laden linguistic and religious conflicts are often involved in educational issues, making any federal efforts toward uniformity both difficult and politically unrewarding.

Non-Tax Revenues

The final category of provincial revenues consists of the residual, non-tax revenues. The main sources here are natural resources, licenses and permits, liquor board profits, and sales of provincial goods and services. A recent addition to non-tax revenues has been lottery proceeds.[41] On the average, non-tax revenues account for one fifth of total provincial budgets. Some mineral-rich provinces like Alberta derive almost 45 percent of their revenues from non-tax sources, whereas for Prince Edward Island the figure is 15 percent.

Natural resource charges are the most lucrative of these revenues. Every province taxes the profits, acreage and/or assessed value of minerals within its boundaries. Natural resource revenues are also derived from the rental and royalties from minerals produced from the land. In 1974, to benefit from sky-rocketing energy prices, Alberta, Saskatchewan, and British Columbia instituted "super royalties" which are surcharges in addition to the base royalty when the price of a natural resource rises above its set level. Of the three categories, non-tax revenues have been least subject to influence from the federal system. However, as natural resources policy is increasingly the object of federal as well as provincial concern, corresponding revenue decisions will also become more subject to intergovernmental negotiations.

A Note on Regulation

The regulatory function is a second important component of federal-provincial relations. Unlike fiscal arrangements, which have reflected the changing role of the provinces, the regulatory process has not kept pace with transformation in the federal system.[42] In particular the interdependence of governments resulting in part from province-building has not been mirrored in regulatory matters. This has meant that the expanded scope of the public sector has generated increased regulatory conflict. As with fiscal policies, regulatory conflicts arise from jurisdictional issues and from the impact of these policies on other governments. However, unlike fiscal policy, no effective mechanism has emerged for handling intergovernmental regulatory disputes. Furthermore, much regulation is formulated through agencies not directly accountable to governments, making many of the normal channels for intergovernmental communication of little use in resolving regulatory conflict.

SOURCES OF CONFLICT IN FISCAL RELATIONS

Many of the developments in intergovernmental fiscal relations result from two problems common to federal regimes: the inadequacy of provincial revenues in light of their expanding responsibilities and the economic disparities among regions. These problems and efforts to resolve them demonstrate the ways in which the federal system can create restraints for provincial decision makers.[35]

The Revenue/Responsibility Imbalance

It was not until after the Depression that the revenue/responsibility imbalance in the federal system was recognised as a significant political problem. For the provinces, where increased demands for those services within their jurisdiction—education, health, and social welfare—had not been accompanied by a comparable expansion of provincial revenues, the situation was acute. One way of meeting the financial needs of the provinces was through the tax-rental agreements described above. This method was especially pleasing to Ottawa because it provided funds for the provinces while allowing the federal government to centralize control over taxation. In 1945 Ottawa proposed to continue the centralization of the tax system as well as to assume some of the provinces' responsibilities in the field of social policy. The concentration of taxation and expenditure powers were central to the federal government's post-war economic goals of full employment and economic growth. Although the provinces' incomes from tax rental were insufficient to meet their expanded fiscal needs, they rejected Ottawa's attempts to make wholesale changes in the division of powers and limited subsequent efforts to deal with the revenues/responsibilities imbalance to piecemeal changes.

Through shared-cost programmes (conditional grants), the federal government used its spending powers to augment provincial resources while increasing its involvement in traditionally provincial jurisdictions. These intrusions into the provinces' legislative domain were justified on a number of grounds. Many of the functions within provincial jurisdiction, especially social welfare, were seen as national concerns subject to national action. Shared-cost programmes permitted concerted action by federal and provincial governments toward the achievement of national goals. Also, these joint programmes enabled the establishment of national minimum standards of service. Provision of supported services would no longer depend on the wealth of the province. It was envisaged that through shared-cost programmes every Canadian would be guaranteed certain basic services.[44] By permitting Ottawa to contribute to the provision of services falling within provincial jurisdiction, shared-cost grants appeared to be the means for stable, yet flexible, adaptation to new conditions facing Canada and the welfare state could be achieved without major constitutional amendment.

Federal participation in provincial responsibilities continued in full force during the 1950s. It was not until the 1960s that provincial leaders began to challenge Ottawa and its policy instrument, conditional grants. Events in Quebec were certainly the most crucial factor in halting the march toward greater centralization. With the death of Duplessis, traditional, negative nationalism in Quebec was replaced by a more vigorous, interventionist state. Turning away from the anti-statism of the past generated new demands for government activity. Years earlier, increased demands in other provinces paved the way for federal intrusion through shared-cost programmes. In Quebec, however, demands for a larger public sector were coupled with a challenge to Ottawa's power in provincial jurisdictions.[45] During the 1960s Quebec forced several important policy changes in Ottawa. In addition to the fiscal reforms already discussed, a Quebec Pension Plan was established separate from the Canada Pension Plan. All of these decisions represented a weakening of the constraining influence of conditional grants. Tax abatements for post-secondary education and opting out can be seen as part of the trend toward using unconditional funds as the federal contribution to provincial programmes. The formulation of the Canada and Quebec

Pension Plans represents both an instance of important provincial inputs into federal-provincial programmes, and the attainment of a national social goal through a decentralized programme.

Quebec's demand for a return of responsibilities to the provinces was based on a recognition of the importance of social and economic factors on cultural survival. While demanding greater autonomy, Quebec, like the other provinces, needed increased revenues. It sought more unconditional grants and larger federal tax abatements. Led by protests from the Lesage government in Quebec, other provincial premiers voiced their discontent with conditional forms of federal assistance.[46] The grants were not seen as windfalls, but as restraints.[47] Nor was it merely the provision of federal matching funds for specified programmes that was objectionable. The provinces also took issue with the way Ottawa acted unilaterally without consulting the provinces when initiating and abolishing shared-cost programmes. The Quebec Royal Commission of Inquiry on Constitutional Problems (the "Tremblay Commission") had earlier described provincial feelings of subordination.

> A vast network has been spread which binds the provinces to the central government and which, to a certain extent, provides them with the financial means of discharging their legislative functions and always at the discretion and on the terms of the wealthy and powerful donor.[48]

The progression of province-building has increased provincial displeasure with the system of conditional grants. The expanded functions of provincial governments have led to more competent bureaucracies and provinces need no longer defer to federal expertise.[49] Their new interest in long-range planning makes them distrustful of the uncertainties associated with unilateral action by Ottawa.

Although Quebec eventually came to argue for a special status rather than a return of the constitutional rights of all provinces, the other provinces certainly shared and continue to share Quebec's grievances against shared-cost programmes. Conditional transfers were an unwelcome constraint on provincial decision-makers. According to the provinces, shared-cost programmes distort provincial priorities and interfere with provincial structures, and unilateral and arbitrary actions by Ottawa often leave participating provinces to carry difficult financial burdens.[50] Their restrictive impact is increased by the fact that the grants must usually be matched by provincial funds. Therefore, although shared-cost grants account for twenty percent of provincial revenues they put constraints on forty percent of provincial budgets.[51] Given that conditional funds must be spent on a specified function, they effectively structure provincial priorities. Edwin Black contends:

> If conditional grants did not significantly affect the independence of a provincial cabinet on at least some of its policy choices, the grant programme would have failed its basic rationale. The whole point of a conditional grant is to persuade the recipient government to take decisions they would not adopt in the absence of the grant programme.[52]

Smiley argues further that the grants distort policy-making in two ways. One, provincial functions receiving support are extended at the expense of unaided functions. Two, federally-aided activities are insulated from political control because, once established, they are in the hands of networks of specialists rather than political leaders directly accountable to the people.[53]

Economic studies cast additional light on the policy-impact of conditional grants. In an examination of Ontario's budget it was found that shared-cost programmes in health and social welfare did not produce any significant re-allocation of provincial resources. There was no evidence that Ontario diverted resources away from some functions in the budget to other federally-aided policy areas. But these findings cannot be generalized to poorer provinces. In a "low-income, high-tax province, the introduction of a programme such as Medicare could cause significant substitution (distortion) effects on a government's actual expenditure."[54]

Another analysis of all the major expenditure categories for the ten provinces concluded that conditional grants served to stimulate provincial expenditure, whereas unconditional grants resulted in a reduction of tax burden rather than increased spending and/or services.[55] A third study comparing the impact of federal grants on the budgets of Ontario and New Brunswick concluded that poorer provinces are more likely to use unconditional grants to reduce tax burdens.[56]

Since the late fifties provincial revenues have accounted for a steadily rising proportion of total government revenues. Rising federal transfers based on equalization grants and shared-cost health programmes explain much of the relative growth in provincial revenues. In 1975 almost 25 percent of provincial revenues came from federal transfers. Although their magnitude makes these transfers significant to the provinces, it is the nature of the transfer programmes that has been of specific relevance to policy-makers.

Using conditional grants as a means of solving the provinces' revenue imbalance had tended to aggravate the problem of federal-provincial policy overlap. Provinces have found these grants to be unduly restrictive, for, when money is tied to a specific programme, it is difficult for provincial decision-makers to pass up the additional revenues even if they are not interested in the programme. In some cases the grants not only biased provincial spending toward certain programmes, they also affected the substantive nature of the programme when only certain programme costs are eligible for federal matching. From the federal point of view, participation in a programme such as Hospital Insurance left Ottawa in the unenviable position of having an open-ended (unlimited) commitment to pay for half the costs of a programme over which it had virtually no control.

The provinces' concern over the erosion of their autonomy coupled with Ottawa's desire to extricate itself from open-ended contributions to provincial activities has resulted in a pruning away of conditional grants as the main mode of federal transfers. Since the late sixties no new significant cost-sharing programmes have been proposed, and in 1973 a 15 percent ceiling was imposed on the growth of federal payments to post-secondary education. In 1976 a similar limitation was imposed on the annual growth rate of federal payments to medicare. The 1977 Fiscal Arrangements and Established Programmes Financing Act brought an end to the most expensive shared-cost programmes, and Ottawa now uses tax abatements and cash payments as its contribution to hospital and medical insurance and post-secondary education. Ottawa has also proposed to replace conditional grants in social welfare with a per capita, unconditional block grant. These changes in the major shared-cost programmes appear to mark the end of the era of conditional grants. Federal assistance in the form of unconditional transfers and larger portions of shared tax fields should reduce the conflict generated by Ottawa's intrusion in provincial legislative areas.

The federal withdrawal from shared-cost programmes was clearly a way to avoid further blame for escalating costs in open-ended and increasingly expensive areas. Furthermore, because the federal contribution is no longer tied to programme costs, any new increases will become the concern of the provinces who will have to face them through new revenues, shifting funds from other areas, or cutbacks in services. The conversion of conditional to unconditional grants cannot be interpreted to mean greater policy autonomy for the provinces since they have inherited the full burden of these increasingly expensive responsibilities.[57]

Regional Disparities

The equalization of provincial resources is a second important problem for Canadian federalism. There is no disagreement that there are vast regional economic disparities; geographic, economic and political factors have combined to make some provinces even less able than others to meet increased demands for services. Arrangements which provide increased tax room for the provinces to levy their own taxes may provide more revenues to the provinces, but they do little to mitigate inequalities.

At Confederation, statutory subsidies to the provinces were based on a uniform per capita rate. New Brunswick and Nova Scotia, however, also received special additional grants. As each new province joined Confederation its extraordinary needs were met by a "special" grant. Conditional grants were also conceived in part as a way to compensate for inequalities in provincial capabilities. As we have described, the grants were envisaged as assistance from the federal government to make certain services available to all Canadians.

The Rowell-Sirois Commission, concerned with the inequalities among the members of the federal system, was critical of the conditional grants programmes. It recommended other ways to deal with provincial inequalities. First, a system of National Adjustment Grants to provide unconditional payments to the provinces in order to equalize provincial financial resources. These grants were to give poorer provinces the capacity to provide average levels of services without extra tax burdens. In addition, emergency grants were to be available if a province encountered some special temporary economic setback. Secondly, the Commission proposed the centralization of unemployment relief, as a means of lifting a heavy financial burden from the provinces, while at the same time creating a single national level of relief.

As we know, the Rowell-Sirois proposals were not accepted by the provinces. Directly contrary to the Commission's recommendations, conditional grants became Ottawa's main instrument for bringing financial relief. The equalization impact of conditional grants has been subject to many criticisms: (i) conditional grants do not take into account relative fiscal capacities or needs of the provinces or their peculiar problems; (ii) poorer provinces expand the aided service at the expense of other functions, thus further increasing the disparities in those latter services; (iii) providing across-the-board assistance may generally upgrade the levels of service while maintaining vast differences among provinces; (iv) the autonomy that is left to provinces in the implementation of the cost-sharing programme undermines the notion of a single nation-wide standard.[58]

Further adjustments of regional disparities have been handled in much the same way as the problem of revenue imbalances; that is, through the transfer of resources from Ottawa rather than by federal assumption of provincial responsibilities. Thus, it was the Rowell-Sirois Commission's idea of unconditional subsidies to the poorer provinces that has gradually been incorporated into federal-provincial relations as the major vehicle for fiscal adjustment.[59] The Rowell-Sirois Commission had proposed that adjustment grants be based on fiscal need. However, the 1957 Tax-sharing Agreement, while explicitly recognising the need to assist low-income provinces, based equalization on fiscal capacity. Each province received an unconditional grant bringing its tax revenues from personal, corporate, and succession duties up to the average yield of the two richest provinces. This meant that the agreement did not take into account differences in provincial needs or costs of service.[60] Fiscal need has not been built into subsequent transfer arrangements. The trend has been to increase the number of income sources (from three in 1957 to twenty-nine in 1977) when comparing and equalizing provincial revenue yields.[61]

Equalization payments, which form a significant portion of the revenues of have-not provinces, expand the choices open to provincial decision-makers: the grants may stimulate provincial expenditures or lower provincial tax burdens. When provincial per capita expenditures are compared, the range of spending is seen to be relatively narrow. In 1974-1975 no province's spending differed by more than 15 percent from the provincial average per capita spending of $1,268. Equalization grants permit poorer provinces to provide a normal range of services without resorting to extraordinary tax burdens.

Further reductions in regional disparities have occurred as a consequence of federal conditional and unconditional grant programmes. Because residents of rich provinces pay more federal taxes than those in poor provinces, and because federal payments are not correspondingly greater to rich provinces (in the cases of unemployment relief and the Canada Assistance Plan they are lower), the overall impact of these federal programmes is redistributive. According to a study done for the Ontario Economic Council, "the equalizing effect of shared-cost, individual transfer, and unemployment insurance programmes . . . is about as important as that of the equalization programme in the Atlantic region, Quebec, and Manitoba, somewhat more important in Saskatchewan."[62]

Federal efforts to ameliorate regional disparities have also taken the form of financial incentives to private industry. Today these are coordinated under the Department of Regional Economic Expansion (DREE), although some of the specific programmes pre-date the establishment of the Department in 1969. Under the Regional Development Incentives Act, DREE designates areas to which assistance is to be directed.* Since 1974 a series of General Development Agreements (GDA's) have been signed with nine provinces.** Each GDA is typically implemented through a series of more specific, project- and industry-oriented subsidiary agreements.[63] These are gradually replacing the

*Designated areas include the four Atlantic provinces, Manitoba, Saskatchewan, Quebec (excepting the Montreal-Hull corridor), and Northern Ontario.
**Prince Edward Island has a fifteen-year Comprehensive Development Plan with the federal government.

older (pre-1969) federal-provincial programmes such as ARDA (Agricultural and Rural Development Act).[64] Federal regional assistance may be directed toward private firms, primarily in the form of industrial incentives; or it may consist of public sector action for the development of infrastructure, such as highways. Over the first five years of DREE, total spending was over one and a half billion dollars.[65] There is little consensus on the success of this development strategy. Controversy ranges from debates over whether any such public initiative can be effective to the specific performance of DREE to date. The overriding objective of this approach was to stimulate employment in exceptionally depressed regions. However, it is questionable whether unemployment in depressed areas has decreased. One study has argued that DREE incentives have tended to encourage capital expenditure much more than labour expenditure.[66] It is also uncertain whether many of the enterprises stimulated might have occurred in any case or whether such new activity has forced some existing firms out of business.[67]

Federal programmes that transfer resources to the poorer provinces have undoubtedly enhanced the policy options of the have-not provinces. There remains the question, however, of whether these programmes go far enough. Given the commitment to reducing regional disparities, there are serious gaps in efforts so far. For example, the scope of provincial equality could be expanded in the following ways:

1. equalization of the range and quality of public services
2. equalization of tax rates
3. equalization of economic opportunities
4. equalization of prices in the private sector.[68]

It must be pointed out that equalization and provincial autonomy may, at times, be conflicting goals. Analyzing regional economic development, Careless cautions:

> ... the federal methods used for reducing regional disparities have led to such an emasculation of self-determination in the poorer provinces that it may well be that these political regimes will not have the tools and revenues ... available to pursue an independent cultural or social policy through economic decisions even if they should wish to do so.[69]

Equalization pursued through the institutionalization of a single uniform national service or through conditional grants obviously detracts from the autonomy of provinces. Even unconditional grants and tax abatements, while not directly involving Ottawa in provincial jurisdictions, still make the provinces dependent, to some extent, on federal decisions over which they have very little control.[70]

THE IMPACT OF FEDERALISM

The question of the impact on provincial policy can be approached on three levels: First and most general, to what extent does federalism affect the nature of conflict? Second, what are its effects on the range of choice available to decision-makers? And third, what is its influence on specific policy outcomes? Federalism is a major determinant of the structure of conflict in the Canadian political system because it institutionalizes a most significant political dimension—the territorial cleavage. The importance of the cleavage is reinforced both by regional social forces that look to the provincial rather than national government and by provincial political leaders who generate support by emphasizing their differences with Ottawa. The many issues that are subject to federal-provincial negotiations are cast in terms of regional interests, for example, redistribution of wealth to meet social needs perceived as regional disparities rather than inequalities among individuals or classes. Moreover, the policy debates that arise often tend to be over structure—How will costs be split?—rather than substance—What is to be done?[71]

The most visible way in which the federal system has affected the scope of provincial policy has been through conditional grants. In the 1950s federal control via the tax system was exchanged for domination via expenditures.[72] During the fifties and sixties many joint programmes were proposed by Ottawa as a means of assisting the provinces in meeting their constitutional responsibilities. It was virtually impossible for a province to refuse to participate in such programmes. Even for Quebec it was often too costly to refuse to join.[73] Through the initiation of social and health services on a national level, the federal government was an important policy catalyst and diffuser. Services and programmes that had begun in one province were dramatically made available in all ten. Fifty-cent dollars made any shared-cost programme too attractive to pass by. Provincial reactions were, however, not always appreciative of the federal policy role. "Distorter of provincial priorities" and "destroyer of provincial autonomy" were some of the less positive assessments of the federal actions. Besides federal effects on the broad direction and scope of provincial policy, there is also evidence of impact on the internal workings of the provincially legislated programmes. The designation of provincial health services eligible for federal cost sharing provides an example of this impact. Similarly categoric social welfare programmes involved Ottawa in the determination of who qualified for social assistance.

Federal transfers, both conditional and unconditional, have had another, less anticipated, effect on the scope of provincial policy. The many new programmes and infusion of funds were a crucial part of province-building. More confident provincial governments with stronger bureaucracies began to assert themselves and to do so effectively. Thus, the overall impact of the transfers may have been to contribute to the growth of provincial autonomy and to the expansion of their range of policy-making.

Since the Second World War much of the impact of federalism has been on the scope and substance of social policies. The entanglement of federal and provincial jurisdictions occurred mainly as a result of Ottawa's using its financial powers to enter into provincial policy fields. However, it appears that now the major arena for federal-provincial conflict is economic policy and that the instruments are regulatory as well as fiscal powers. As in most federal nations, the central government has traditionally monopolized economic policy. Counter-cyclical policies concerning stabilization, unemployment, and inflation, have generally been the result of unilateral action by Ottawa. From the late 1950s the failure of federal economic policies, coupled with the developing sense of regional interests and provincial efficacy, led Quebec and other provinces to assert their right to make economic policy. In the "Battle of the Balance Sheets," Quebec argued that it loses more than it gains from Confederation. As the Western and Atlantic provinces have claimed at other times, Quebec contended that federal policies designed to benefit other parts of the country had a depressing effect on its own economic performance.[74] As a result of such grievances, independent provincial fiscal policies (traditionally thought to be ineffective or even counter-productive) have begun to gain new support.[75] In the 1970s the four largest provinces have all implemented their own "explicitly counter-cyclical policies."[76] Even those smaller provinces that do not wish to make their own economic policies join in the consensus that the provinces ought to have inputs into Ottawa's decision-making so that national policies would recognize varying regional needs.

Federal-provincial entanglement in the economic sphere is a result of pressures from Ottawa as well as from the provinces. In its efforts to deal with economic problems of stabilization and growth, the federal government has intruded into provincial jurisdictions. A striking example of this occurred in April 1978 when the Federal Minister of Finance, Jean Chrétien, proposed a reduction in provincial sales tax as a means of stimulating the economy. Although the provinces were to be reimbursed by Ottawa for their lost revenues, this clearly represented an infringement of jurisdiction.

The size of provincial and municipal governments makes them significant economic forces in their own right. Whatever policy actions they take are likely, along with similar federal initiatives, to affect economic growth or stabilization. Because of this, economic management policies must be seen as legitimate concerns for all three levels of government. There are two major obstacles to the coordination of economic policy among the three levels of government. One is the persisting failure to establish any regular procedures or mechanisms through which such coordination must occur. The second is the more fundamental difficulty that economic interests may sharply diverge among the eleven governments. This became evident in the 1978 economic summit meeting of first ministers which, although called to discuss concrete, medium-term economic objectives, could only find consensus on vague long-term goals and immediate, specific projects. Although it may be possible to clarify responsibilities, the basic conflict resulting from different needs among Ottawa and the provinces makes economic policy an especially sensitive area of federal-provincial relations.

Regardless of one's assessment of who benefits from the federal system and of whether federal actions have brought about better provincial policies, there is agreement that the federal system generates a complex set of constraints and dynamics on provincial politics. Besides directly affecting the policy choices open to provincial decision-makers, it also helps to shape the socioeconomic environment and the political forces within the provinces. The examination of specific policy areas in the discussions which follow permits some further and more detailed analysis of these effects.

NOTES

1. Michael Stein, "Federal Political Systems and Federal Societies," *World Politics* 20, July, 1968, p. 731.
2. See Richard Simeon, "The Federal-Provincial Decision Making Process," Ontario Economic Council, *Issues and Alternatives 1977: Intergovernmental Relations,* Toronto, 1977, pp. 25-29.
3. Donald V. Smiley, "Federal-Provincial Conflict in Canada," *PUBLIUS* 4, Summer, 1974, pp. 7-24 discusses this problem of "extra-jurisdictional externalities".
4. See Grace Skogstad, "The Farm Products Marketing Agencies Act and The Food Policy Debate: Case Studies of Agriculture Policy." Paper presented at Canadian Political Science Association Meetings, 1978.
5. On the use of the power of disallowance, see J. R. Mallory, *Social Credit and the Federal Power in Canada,* University of Toronto, Toronto 1953.
6. Attorney-General for Ontario v. Attorney General for Canada (1896), A.C. 348. There are many good discussions of the impact of

the Judicial Committee. See for example Alan Cairns, "The Judicial Committee and its Critics," in *Canadian Journal of Political Science* 4, September, 1971, pp. 301-345; and G. P. Brown, *The Judicial Committee and the B.N.A. Act*, University of Toronto Press, Toronto, 1967.

7. Fort Frances Pulp and Power Co., Ltd. v. Manitoba Inc. Press Co., Ltd. (1923), 3 DLR 629.

8. For an analysis of the cases involved in the limited construction of the trade and commerce clause see Bora Laskin, *Canadian Constitutional Law*, Fourth Edition, Carswell, Toronto, 1975, pp. 300-314.

9. This notion of coordinate federalism is one of five conceptualizations of the federal state described by Edwin Black in *Divided Loyalties*, McGill-Queen's Press, Montreal, 1974, pp. 113-148.

10. See Anthony Birch, *Federalism, Finance and Social Legislation in Canada, Australia and the United States*, Clarendon Press, Oxford, 1955.

11. Black, *op. cit.*, p. 143.

12. See Richard Simeon, "Current Constitutional Issues" in Ontario Economic Council, *op. cit.*, pp. 9-29 and D. V. Smiley, *Canada in Question: Federalism in the Seventies*, Second Edition, McGraw-Hill Ryerson, Toronto, 1976, Chaps. 1, 2.

13. For a review of the positions of the chief antagonists, see John Trent "Common Ground and Disputed Territory," in Richard Simeon, Editor, *Must Canada Fail*, McGill-Queens, Montreal, 1978, pp. 131-151.

14. Royal Commission on Dominion-Provincial Relations, *Report*, King's Printer, Ottawa, 1940, Book I, p. 255.

15. Up to that time a section in the Department of Finance handled these matters.

16. A. R. Kear, "Cooperative Federalism: A Study of the Federal-Provincial Continuing Committee on Fiscal and Economic Matters," in *Canadian Public Administration* 6, March, 1963, p. 46.

17. The importance of this post is reflected in the Prime Minister's choice of one of his closest associates, Marc Lalonde, to fill the position.

18. See Edgar Gallant, "The Machinery of Federal-Provincial Relations," in P. Meekison, Editor, *Canadian Federalism: Myth or Reality?*, Third Edition, Methuen, Toronto, 1977, pp. 254-264, and *Report: Intergovernmental Liaison on Fiscal and Economic Matters*, Queen's Printer, Ottawa, 1969.

19. *Quebec vs. Ottawa: the Struggle for Self-government 1960-1972*, University of Toronto Press, Toronto, 1976, p. 105.

20. Gerard Veilleux, *Les Relations Intergouvernementales au Canada 1867-1967*, Université du Quebec, Montréal, 1971, p. 90.

21. Smiley, *Canada in Question*, pp. 60-71.

22. Richard Leach, "Inter-Provincial Cooperation" in Bellamy *et al.*

Comparative Provincial Political Systems, Methuen, Toronto, 1976, pp. 381-394 and J. H. Aitchison "Inter-Provincial Cooperation in Canada," J. H. Aitchison, Editor, *The Political Process in Canada*, University of Toronto Press, Toronto, 1963.

23. See A. A. Lomas, "The Council of Maritime Premiers Report and Evaluation After Five Years," *CPA* 20 Spring, 1977, pp. 188-200, Guy Henson, *Interprovincial Relations in the Maritime Provinces*, Maritime Union Study, Toronto, 1970, and R. M. Leach, *Inter-Provincial Relations in the Maritime Provinces* Maritime Union Study: Fredericton, 1970.

24. For example, in preparation for the Western Economic Opportunities Conference in 1973, the Western Premiers developed and presented to Ottawa four joint papers in the following areas: Agriculture, Economic and Industrial Development, Regional Financial Institutions, and Transportation. See M. Westmacott and P. Dore, "Intergovernmental Cooperation in Western Canada: the Western Economic Opportunities Conference" in Meekison, *op cit.*, pp. 340-352; W. J. Blackman, "A Western Perspective on the Economics of Confederation," *Canadian Public Policy* 3, Autumn, 1977, pp. 414-430 and Gerry Gartner "A Review of Cooperation among the Western Provinces," *CPA* 20, Spring 1977, pp. 174-187.

25. Smiley, *Canada in Question*, pp. 83-104.

26. Richard Simeon, *Federal-Provincial Diplomacy*, University of Toronto Press, Toronto, 1972; see also Glyn Berry, "The Oil Lobby and the Energy Crisis," in *Canadian Public Administration*, 17 Winter, 1974.

27. The dispute between Ottawa and the east coast provinces over fishing the 200-mile limit typifies the non-partisan nature of federal-provincial politics. The provinces want to take immediate advantage of the new fishing limits and they want Ottawa to fund a ship construction programme to help the Atlantic fishermen, whereas Ottawa favours a more gradual and planned approach to the new fishing and it wants further study of the necessity of the construction programme. *Globe and Mail*, 1 September 1977, p. 1B.

28. Smiley, *Canada in Question*, pp. 109-110.

29. Simeon, *Federal-Provincial Diplomacy*, Chaps. 11 and 12. See also T. Courchene, "The New Fiscal Arrangements and the Economics of Federalism," paper presented at Options Canada Conference, University of Toronto, 1977.

30. Christopher Leman, "Patterns of Policy Development: Social Security in the U.S. and Canada," *Public Policy* 25, Spring, 1977 pp. 261-291. See also Rand Dyck "The Canada Assistance Plan; the ultimate in Cooperative Federalism," *Canadian Public Administration* 19, Winter, 1976 pp. 587-602.

31. Simeon, *Federal Provincial Diplomacy*.

32. For an analysis that uses fiscal transfers as indicators of decentraliza-

tion see R. Bastien, "La Structure fiscale du federalism Canadien: 1945-1973" in *Canadian Public Administration* 17, Spring, 1974, pp. 96-118.

33. Canadian Tax Foundation, *Provincial and Municipal Finances 1975,* Toronto, 1975, p. 62.

34. For a description of the early taxation procedures in the provinces see A. M. Moore and J. H. Perry, *The Financing of Canadian Federation,* Canadian Tax Foundation, Toronto, 1953, pp. 1-16.

35. For good summaries of the post war agreements see A. M. Moore, J. H. Perry and D. Beach, *The Financing of Canadian Federalism: the First Hundred Years,* Canadian Tax Foundation, Toronto, 1966, and Canadian Tax Foundation, *The National Finances 1977-78,* Toronto, 1978, Chap. 10.

36. S. Dupre, "Contracting Out: A Funny Thing Happened on the Way to the Centennial," in *Report of the Proceedings of the Eighteenth Annual Tax Conference,* Canadian Tax Foundation, Toronto, 1965; and George Carter, *Canadian Conditional Grants Since World War II,* Canadian Tax Foundation, Toronto, 1971, Chapter 5.

37. See, for example, M. Bucovetsky, "The Mining Industry and the Great Tax Reform Debate" in A.P. Pross (ed.), *Pressure Group Behaviour in Canada,* McGraw-Hill Ryerson, Toronto, 1975, pp. 89-114.

38. Canadian Tax Foundation, *National Finances 1976-1977,* Toronto, 1977, p. 146.

39. *National Finances,* p. 146.

40. See Table 6.1 in Chapter 6 for the variation in federal medical insurance contributions.

41. For a discussion of lotteries and their impacts in Canada see J. A. Johnson, "An Economic Analysis of Lotteries," in *Canadian Tax Journal,* 24 Nov.-Dec., 1976, pp. 639-651.

42. Richard Schultz, "The Regulatory Process and Federal-Provincial Relations" in G. B. Doern, Editor, *The Regulatory Process in Canada,* MacMillan, Toronto, 1978 pp. 128-146. See also W. Lederman, "Telecommunications and the Federal Constitution of Canada," in H. E. English, *Telecommunications for Canada: An Interface of Business and Government,* Methuen, Toronto, 1973, and Richard Schultz, "Intergovernmental Cooperation, Regulatory Agencies, and Transportation Regulation in Canada: the Case of Part III of the National Transportation Act," in *Canadian Public Administration* 19, Summer, 1976, pp. 205-206.

43. For discussion on these problems with special reference to economic policy see R. Phidd and G. B. Doern, *The Politics and Management of Canadian Economic Policy,* Macmillan of Canada, Toronto, 1978, pp. 492-507.

44. See Donald Smiley, *Conditional Grants and Canadian Federation,* Canadian Tax Foundation, Toronto, 1962, pp. 25-26; George Carter, *Canadian*

Conditional Grants Since World War II, Canadian Tax Foundation, Toronto, 1971; and G. Young "Federal-Provincial Grants and Equalization" in Ontario Economic Council, *Issues and Alterations 1977: Intergovernmental Relations*, Toronto, 1977, pp. 39-54.

45. Donald Smiley, *The Canadian Political Nationality*, Methuen, Toronto, 1967, p. 54. For discussions of the changes in Quebec society see D. Posgate and K. McRoberts, *Quebec: Social Change and Political Crisis*, McClelland and Stewart, Toronto, 1976; Dale Thomson, *Quebec Society and Politics: Views from the Inside*, McClelland and Stewart, Toronto, 1973, and Henry Milner, *Politics in the New Quebec*, McClelland & Stewart, Toronto, 1978.

46. Statements of Provincial Premiers, *Proceedings of the Plenary Federal-Provincial Conference, 1960* Queen's Printer, Ottawa, 1960.

47. Black, *op. cit.*, p. 82.

48. *Report of the Royal Commission of Inquiry on Constitutional Problems*, Vol. II, p. 214, as quoted in A. Brady, "Quebec and Canadian Federalism," in P. Meekison, Editor, *op. cit.*, p. 413.

49. Paul Fox, "Regionalism and Confederation" in Ontario Advisory Committee on Confederation, *The Confederation Challenge*, Queen's Printer, Toronto, 1970.

50. The Honourable W. D. McKeough, *Supplementary Actions to the 1975 Ontario Budget*, Queen's Printer, Toronto, 1975, pp. 2-3.

51. Black, *op cit.*, pp. 82-83.

52. *Ibid.*, p. 81.

53. D. V. Smiley, *Conditional Grants and Canadian Federalism*, pp. 44-60. For other criticisms of conditional grants see Geoffrey Young, *op. cit.*, pp. 40-41.

54. J. Strick, "Conditional Grants and Provincial Government Budgeting" in *Canadian Public Administration* 14, Summer, 1971, pp. 234.

55. J. Maley, "The Impact of Federal Grants on Provincial Budgets: Canada," Ph. D. Thesis, University of Rochester, 1971.

56. H. M. Hardy, "Some Aspects of Federal Grants in Canada" in *Canadian Tax Journal* 22, May-June, 1974, pp. 285-294.

57. See Courchene, *op cit.*, and George Carter, "Financing Health and Post-Secondary Education: A New and Complex Fiscal Arrangement," *Canadian Tax Journal* 25, Sept.-Oct., 1977, pp. 534-550.

58. Smiley, *Conditional Grants and Canadian Federalism*, pp. 57-58. See, however, G. Carter, "Financing Post-Secondary Education Under the Federal-Provincial Fiscal Arrangements Act: An Appraisal" in *Canadian Tax Journal* 24, September-October, 1976, pp. 505-522.

59. The seeds of equalization are found in the 1952 Agreement which guaranteed minimum tax yield payments to the provinces.

60. D. Clark, *Fiscal Need and Revenue Equalization Grants*, Canadian Tax Foundation, 1969, and Eric Hanson, *Fiscal Needs of the Canadian Provinces*, Canadian Tax Foundation, Toronto, 1961.

61. For the list of current revenue sources used to calculate equalization see David Perry, "The Federal-Provincial Fiscal Arrangements Introduction 1977," in *Canadian Tax Journal* 25, July-August, 1977, p. 431.

62. Young, *op. cit.*, p. 51.

63. For a brief summary of these agreements see *Provincial and Municipal Finances 1977*, Canadian Tax Foundation, Toronto, 1977, pp. 237-241.

64. On regional policy initiatives prior to the establishment of DREE, see T. N. Brewis, *Regional Economic Policies in Canada*, MacMillan of Canada, Toronto, 1969, pp. 95-192 and Hugh Whalen "Public Policy and Regional Development: the Experience of the Atlantic Provinces" in A. Rotstein, Editor, *The Prospect of Change: Proposals for Canada's Future*, McGraw-Hill, 1965, pp. 133-142.

65. Economic Council of Canada, *Living Together: A Study of Regional Disparities*, Ottawa, 1978, pp. 150-151.

66. Robert S. Woodward, "The Effectiveness of DREE's New Location Subsidies," *Canadian Public Policy* 1, Spring, 1975, pp. 217-230.

67. On some of these issues, see Dan Usher, "Some Questions About the Regional Development Incentives Act," *Canadian Public Policy* 1, Autumn, 1975, pp. 557-575; *Living Together, op. cit.* Chapter 8; W. J. Gillespie and R. Kerr, "The Impact of Federal Regional Expansion Policies on the Distribution of Income in Canada," Economic Council of Canada, Discussion Paper 85, 1977.

68. Smiley, *Canada in Question*, pp. 152-153. For other criticisms of the equalization programme, see A.M. Moore, "Income Security and Federal Finance," *Canadian Public Policy* 1, Fall, 1975, pp. 473-479.

69. *Initiative and Response: The Adaptation of Canadian Federalism to Regional Economic Development*, McGill-Queen's University Press, Montreal, 1977, p. 216.

70. It has also been suggested that the equalization formula may affect the tax policies of the provinces. That is, they have more of an incentive to tax in those areas which will result in an increase in their equalization grants. See T. J. Courchene and D. A. Beavis, "Federal Provincial Tax Equalization: An Evaluation," *Canadian Journal of Economics*, November, 1973 pp. 483-502.

71. This discussion of the impact of federalism on the structure of conflict is taken from R. Simeon, "Regionalism and Canadian Political Institutions," *Queens Quarterly* 82, Winter, 1975 pp. 499-511.

72. Careless, *op. cit.*, p. 36.

73. This was especially apparent in the consideration of medical care insurance. See Malcolm Taylor, "Quebec Medicare: Policy Formulation in Conflict and Crisis," in *Canadian Public Administration*, 15 September, 1972, pp. 211-250.

74. See Peter Leslie and Richard Simeon, "The Battle of the Balance Sheets" in R. Simeon, Editor, *Must Canada Fail?* pp. 243-258 and

Andrew Johnson "Canada and Quebec. The Implications of Economic Stress on Intergovernmental Relations," paper presented at the Western Political Science Association Meetings, March, 1978.

75. The negative view is presented in R. Burns, "The Operation of Fiscal and Economic Policy" in G. B. Doern and S. Wilson, Editors, *Issues in Canadian Public Policy*, MacMillan, Toronto, 1977, pp. 286-309, and *Report of the Royal Commission on Taxation* (Carter Commission), Queen's Printer, Ottawa, 1966, Vol. 2, pp. 91-102. For more positive assessments of such policy in Ontario see C. L. Barber, *The Theory of Fiscal Policy as applied to a Province. A Study Prepared for the Ontario Committee on Taxation* Queen's Printer, Toronto, 1967; Thomas Wilson, "The Province and Stabilization Policy" in Ontario Economic Council, *Issues and Alternatives 1977: Intergovernmental Relations* pp. 123-136. Two Toronto economists have put forward an analysis of independent fiscal policies in all provinces. See Arthur Donner and Fred Lazar, "Cost of Decentralizing Canada Could be High," *Globe and Mail*, January 29, 1977.

76. See T. A. Wilson and G. V. Jump, "Economic Effects of Provincial Fiscal Policies, 1975-76," *Canadian Tax Journal* 23, May-June 1975, pp. 257-262.

Chapter 6

Social Development Policies

AN OVERVIEW OF POLICY TRENDS

The public sector has evolved through a combination of incremental shifts and substantial innovations in which the broad outlines of policy have been transformed and the choice of policy instruments has changed. In the preceding chapters our task has been to describe the structures, processes and contexts of provincial policies with a view to explaining what factors influence policy. Now our focus shifts to the content of policy development, by which we mean the scope and methods that characterize the activities of provincial governments. Specific developments within each of the policy fields are discussed in this chapter and in the next. In each field the evolution of policy is analysed by looking at the conflicts and issues in the policy arena and the particular forces that have acted as the dynamics of policy development.

No analysis is likely to encompass all facets of provincial policy. Our focus is on social policy, which includes welfare, health, and education, and on resource development policy, which includes transportation, natural resources, and agriculture. Certainly, it must be acknowledged that there are other significant areas of provincial policy, but social and resource development are of interest because they constitute the major problem areas of provincial politics and account for the bulk of provincial spending.

In the decades following the Second World War, the provincial public sector has undergone a vast transformation. As we have noted in Chapter 1, the most striking aspect has been the changing size of provincial budgets. They have risen from 5.7 percent of the GNP in 1950 to 15 percent in 1976. In that time the provincial share of total government expenditures has gone from about one fifth to more than one third. Changes in the level of provincial expenditures are evidence of province-building, while changes in the pattern of spending reflect new provincial priorities.

Table 6.1: Provincial Policy Expenditures

PERCENT OF PROVINCIAL BUDGETS

	TRANSPORTATION AND COMMUNICATION	HEALTH	SOCIAL WELFARE	EDUCATION	NATURAL RESOURCES AND PRIMARY INDUSTRY
1950	22.4%	16.7	16.7	16.5	6.0
1975	8.5%	25.2	13.8	23.3	5.0

Source: *Provincial Government Finance, 1950, 1975* DBS 68-207

Table 6.1 illustrates the transformations in provincial spending between 1950 and 1975. Transportation in the 1940s and 1950s was a crucial element in Canadian economic growth. As the transportation system developed, public spending in this area was destined to decline, while at the same time demands for health, education, and social assistance services became important competitors for public funds. Although it was the largest expenditure category in 1950, the field of transportation and communication has dropped to less than ten percent of provincial budgets. Regulation is now a key instrument in transportation policy-making. It is in the regulatory arena that the conflicts arising from intergovernmental relations, from concerns with the environment, and over allocation of scarce natural resources are brought to bear on policy-making.

Natural resources and primary industry continue to make up a relatively small portion of provincial budgets. Despite its small share of the budget, resource development and related issues have become more significant as public awareness of limited resources has increased. The growing perception of scarcity has increased the interest and, consequently, the degree of conflict in this policy sphere.

The largest increases have been in health and education, which now account for almost one-half of provincial expenditures. In social welfare, the third field associated with the growth of the modern welfare state, provincial spending has dropped slightly; but this should not be taken to reflect a corresponding decline of interest in social welfare. Today the provinces and municipalities fund about one quarter of all welfare expenditures. The federal government is the principal provider of welfare support through programmes which include family allowance, unemployment insurance, and old-age security. Despite their secondary expenditure role, the provinces are very much concerned with social welfare through regulatory and administrative policy-making.

The emergence of the welfare state in the century after Confederation represents an enormous transformation in social policy. In Canada, as in other western nations, the rise of the welfare state is primarily a result of the social and political changes which have accompanied economic development. These conditions produced both the wealth that made large-scale social policies possible and the personal vulnerabilities and dislocations that made such policies necessary.[1]

Public assistance was originally directed only towards the destitute in the lowest stratum of society. Gradually, however, the concept of need has been broadened to include the principle that anyone is liable to need assistance at some time. This idea views individual needs as the results of universal risks that apply to a cross-section of the population, and it is against these risks that government provides a minimum standard of existence, a floor below which no one is allowed to sink, as a right of every citizen.[2] The welfare state means in essence public action to meet basic human needs and offers the guarantee of collective social care to all citizens.

Although the welfare state can include a wide range of public activity, three areas of policy—welfare, health, and education—form the core elements. There are, of course, conceptual and empirical linkages among these three areas. Nonetheless, there is ample evidence that each sphere has had its own unique pattern of development.[3] We shall, therefore, consider social welfare, health, and education as distinct policy arenas.

SOCIAL WELFARE

Social welfare refers to the system of benefits provided by governments to relieve poverty and to permit individuals to meet their essential subsistence needs.[4] Although these benefits constitute a range of services, including unemployment insurance, day care, work training, and family counselling, the term "social welfare" is often used primarily with reference to one central feature of welfare policy—income maintenance. Heclo points out:

> The heart of the last century's revolution in social policy is the change from punitive and disqualifying poor law approaches to a new conception of guaranteed social rights of citizenship. Throughout this period it is the question of cash payments for income loss that has unfolded the basic change from public aid as a matter of sufferance to public aid as a matter of right.[5]

The analysis presented here will concentrate on provincial efforts directed toward providing cash payments for those unable to support themselves.

An Overview

At the time of Confederation, relief for the destitute was essentially a matter for private charity or, in some cases, a concern of local authorities. There was, however, no serious expectation of government aid for the poor. The limited reference to social welfare in the British North America Act places it within provincial jurisdiction; among the legislative powers granted to the provisions in Section 92 are ". . . the establishment, maintenance, and management of hospitals, asylums, charities, and eleemosynary institutions in and for the province" and ". . . generally all matters of a merely local or private nature in the province" (subsections 7 and 16). As reflected in the B.N.A. Act, public assistance meant responsibility for certain custodial institutions rather than the provision of aid to individuals in need. Social assistance was directed toward relieving the community of pauperism rather than providing help for the individual.

Municipal governments and voluntary welfare organizations provided what limited assistance was available when family resources had been exhausted. The fact that little provision was made for the poor did not mean that such people did not exist; for disease, disability, and unemployment provided a steady stream of individuals unable to support themselves. As the municipalities spent more and more on welfare and yet were unable to provide reasonable assistance, demands arose for the provinces to take on the welfare function. The provinces responded slowly with supervisory regulations, administrative assistance, and financial grants to municipal and voluntary private organizations.[6] As the provinces were faced with the rising costs of relief, they in turn looked to the federal government.

It was not until the Depression that social welfare began to be recognized as an important and widespread problem requiring effective government action. The magnitude of the economic crisis made it impossible to argue that the unemployed were personally responsible for their situation. The Depression vastly increased the number of Canadians seeking social assistance. In British Columbia, for example, almost one quarter of the population was receiving public support by 1933.[7] Since the municipalities were obviously unable to handle the demands for assistance, Ottawa came forth with a series of temporary work projects and ad hoc direct relief measures. These programmes, which were funded by all three levels of government, were terminated as the Depression abated.

Between 1937 and 1943 two major governmental inquiries, the Royal Commission on Dominion-Provincial Relations (Rowell-Sirois) and the House of Commons Advisory Committee on Post-War Reconstruction (The Marsh Report) examined the social welfare "system." Both concluded that existing arrangements were inadequate, that there was a need for substantial increases in the social assistance available to Canadians, and that Ottawa as well as the provinces would have to assume greater responsibilities in the field of social welfare. It was not until the end of the war that the federal government, fearing a drastic downturn in the economy, proposed new and expanded social assistance programmes. The provision of wide-scale social assistance was one of the key components of federal plans for economic and social reconstruction.[8] Acceptance of the Keynesian principle of governmental demand management for economic stability led to the expectation that increased social benefits would bolster aggregate demand. Public spending on the welfare state was thus believed to be necessary for the survival and growth of the economic system.[9]

The ensuing thirty-five years saw the creation of a vast range of assistance programmes. Ottawa established programmes in the areas of unemployment insurance, family allowance, and universal old age security, and participated in a number of shared-cost programmes for relief to specific groups. But for the most part, the provinces and municipalities continued to bear the major responsibility for welfare. Today, social welfare very much reflects the divisions of power in the federal system. All three levels of government are involved in the provision of benefits, and each province has its own welfare system.

Social assistance has evolved from an essentially private and some-times local concern to a public responsibility that claims resources from municipal, provincial, and federal governments. Almost one quarter of all governmental expenditures are devoted to social welfare, as seen in Table 6.2. In 1973 the provinces and municipalities spent close to three billion dollars in social assistance. As the public sector has expanded the scope of this policy area, public beliefs about welfare have undergone a corresponding transformation. In 1874 the *Toronto Globe* warned that ". . . it is true mercy to say that it would be better that a few individuals should die of starvation than that a pauper class should be raised up."[10] The poor were seen as the stigmatized recipients of public charity. Today there is no serious question of the necessity of governmental assistance to the needy. As Richard Titmuss has aptly stated: "We no longer believe that the social costs of change should lie where they fall."[11] Even though welfare is now built into our expectations of governmental activities, it still is a source of political conflict. Whether the goal is to guarantee a minimum standard of living or to equalize the distribution of income, welfare policy contains an element of redistribution, and conflict may arise whenever the resources of some are used to provide benefits for others.

The evolution of welfare policy is, however, more than a series of responses to the demands of the poor. It must also be understood as a part of policies directed toward economic stability and management. In

Table 6.2: Government Spending* on Social Welfare 1933-1973

	ALL LEVELS OF GOVERNMENT		PROVINCIAL & MUNICIPAL GOVERNMENTS		
YEAR	EXPENDITURES ($ MILLION)	% OF TOTAL EXPENDITURES	EXPENDITURES ($ MILLION)	% OF TOTAL EXPENDITURES	% OF ALL GOVT. WELFARE SPENDING
1933	133	14.0%	88	16.9%	66.0%
1945	307	5.4	57	7.8	18.6
1950	638	15.4	161	9.9	25.2
1955	1,020	14.5	167	6.1	16.4
1960	1,629	15.1	301	6.1	24.5
1965	2,385	14.9	512	6.5	21.5
1970	5,808	18.5	1,720	8.7	29.6
1973	10,540	22.4	2,992	10.6	28.4

Source: M. C. Urquhart and K. Buckley (eds.), *Historical Statistics of Canada* (Macmillan, Toronto, 1965) and Statistics Canada, *Consolidated Government Finance* (DBS 68-202). Reproduced by permission of the Minister of Supply and Services Canada.

*Excluding transfers

this context, business interests have often supported welfare initiatives.[12] In Canada, much of the redistributive conflict has centred on regional disparities in which the goal of national minimum standards of service have been pursued through the equalization of provincial revenues. Moreover, these conflicts have often been structured by federal-provincial relations as is evident in the creation of the Canada and Quebec Pension Plans.[13] Two kinds of issues, the methods of assistance and the structure of assistance programmes, have been primary focuses of controversy.

Methods of Assistance

Income maintenance policy is made up of several cash transfer programmes. Some individuals receive payments because their incomes are below a means-test standard, others receive benefits because they have made previous contributions, and others because they are members of a population that is entitled to an income supplement. Although there are many seemingly different programmes, they may all be summarized into categories corresponding to three principles of assistance: relief, insurance, and universality.[14]

Relief was the basis of the earliest kinds of assistance, and it is still the basis for most provincial and municipal programmes. Under the concept of relief, the needy who qualify (generally based on a means or needs test) are given assistance. This approach to welfare requires the individual to be able to demonstrate his personal need for assistance, and public support is conditional on the existence of certain criteria that explain why the individual is prevented from coping with his needs, for example, age, inability to work, or absence of family breadwinners. Mother's Allowance, which provided aid to mothers who had dependent children and who passed a means test, was one of the first major provincial programmes based on the principle of relief.

Relief programmes financed by general revenues have an explicitly redistributive quality and are often the basis for conflict. Maximizing benefits to the poor and controlling welfare costs are two fundamentally inconsistent goals. Even though relief may be broadly considered as a right of citizenship, when there are strong pressures for budgetary restraint, a common policy response may be to decrease the number of recipients by toughening the criteria for eligibility.

Provincial welfare has tended to be centred on the notion of relief. In the 1970s almost two thirds of provincial welfare expenses were for relief programmes. Relief coverage is generally quite broad and deals with most cases of severe need. However, benefits are not guaranteed, that is, each recipient must be *judged* needy according to criteria set by provincial and/or local administrators. As we shall see, this leads to problems of equity in the system.

2 *Public insurance* programmes are predicated on protecting people from the risks of income loss due to disability, sickness, unemployment and/or death. Under the *insurance* principle assistance is based not on rights or citizenship but on contractual obligations by which previous contributions earn one the right to later benefits. In fact, it is well documented that public insurance schemes for unemployment, social security, and the like are not self-supporting and must depend on taxes and transfers.[15] However, the contributory principle of insurance payments removes much of the social stigma associated with simple relief programmes. Partly because of this it also reduces the potential for such policies to be controversial by minimizing the public perception that they are simple "give away" subsidies to some and, therefore, deprivations to others.

Public Insurance differs from private insurance in several ways: (1) it is often compulsory; (2) public premiums are not based on risk; (3) it is not self-supporting; and (4) it covers a wider range of risk than the private sector is likely to insure.[16] The provinces' first experience with assistance based on the insurance principle was in the area of workmen's compensation—insurance against industrial injury. Workmen's Compensation was established first in Ontario in 1914.[17] Five other provinces (Nova Scotia, British Columbia, Alberta, New Brunswick, and Manitoba) implemented similar programmes by 1920.

Universality is the third approach to income maintenance. In this case social assistance takes the form of a demogrant for everyone in the target population (*e.g.*, those over sixty-five or families with children under eighteen), regardless of personal need. Under a universal programme ". . . people are entitled to receive certain welfare benefits, not because they are destitute [as in relief] and not because they have contributed [as in insurance], but simply because they are citizens and are entitled to an adequate standard of welfare."[18] As with insurance, universal assistance is directed toward a cross-section of the population rather than one stratum. The major demogrants that exist today come from Ottawa. In 1977 the Family Allowance programme provided each family $23.89 per month for each child under eighteen and Old Age Security provided $143.46 per month for all people over sixty-five. On the provincial level, however, universal plans, which tend to be both expensive and inefficient ways of aiding those most in need, have not been frequent policy choices. One of the few examples of provincial programmes based on universality was the Quebec School Allowance of 1961 which provided a small subsidy to all families with children between the ages of sixteen and seventeen, still attending school.[19]

Structure of Assistance

There are two important policy concerns in considering the structure of welfare: first, the impact of the federal government, and second, variations among provincial welfare systems. Although welfare is essentially a matter for provincial jurisdiction, Ottawa has played an active role in the provision of public assistance since the Second World War.

Federal responsibilities in social welfare have developed through jurisdictional changes based on constitutional amendment and through the use of its spending power to provide conditional grants for social programmes. Amendments to the B.N.A. Act in 1940, 1951, and 1964 gave Ottawa responsibility for unemployment insurance, old age benefits, and supplementary survivor benefits. Family Allowance, the first universal assistance programme in Canada, was based on the federal government's right to make payments directly to individuals, and was, therefore, established without constitutional amendment.

The most contentious vehicle for federal participation has been the conditional grant. Ottawa has extended its jurisdiction by providing funds to the provisions for selected welfare programmes. The Old Age Pensions Act of 1927 was the first shared-cost programme in the welfare sphere. Under the programme Ottawa paid fifty percent of the cost of means-tested pensions. (This was subsequently increased to seventy-five percent.) By 1933 all the provinces took part in the programme. After the federal government instituted its own Old Age Security Act which provided pensions for all individuals over the age of seventy, the provinces still shared the cost of old-age assistance to the needy (*i.e.*, those between sixty-five and sixty-nine, who qualified under a means test).

In the fifties Ottawa expanded its role in social assistance by providing more categoric relief. The 1956 Federal Unemployment Assistance Act instituted a shared-cost programme for assistance to the needy unemployed. Similar assistance programmes were instituted for the elderly, blind, and disabled. These shared-cost programmes did not, however, solve the provinces' administrative and financial problems.

At first the provinces appeared to accept sharing their social welfare responsibilities. However, by 1956 the Tremblay Commission forcefully stated Quebec's objections to Ottawa's entry into this area of provincial jurisdiction.[20] Because of its bearing on cultural autonomy, social policy continues to be especially significant to Quebec governments. Subsequent to Quebec's initiatives, social welfare responsibilities became an important issue in federal provincial relations, and greater communication between Ottawa and the provinces on federal welfare involvement has developed.

In 1966, in close consultation with the provinces, Ottawa enacted the Canada Assistance Plan. As described by the Senate Report on Poverty, the plan ". . . was a new way of spreading welfare assistance money around, a fiscal device to take some of the burden off the provincial treasuries."[21] The C.A.P. represented a major federal effort to co-ordinate assistance to the needy. It remains, nevertheless, more of a shopping list than a package because it offers the provinces a number of shared-cost opportunities which are only as integrated as the provinces want to make them. Each province may opt for partial or total participation in the Plan. Only four (Quebec, Alberta, Saskatchewan, and Ontario) have taken up the aid to the blind option and seven (Newfoundland, Prince Edward Island, Nova Scotia, Quebec, Ontario, Saskatchewan, and Alberta) the disability option.

The C.A.P. has not brought about uniform welfare standards. Ottawa leaves the basic decisions over size of benefits and eligibility of recipients to each province. The main federal role is to share benefits and administrative costs. In order for a province's programmes to qualify for federal assistance, Ottawa sets three criteria: (1) benefits must be based on need; (2) there may be no provincial residence requirements;[22] and (3) an appeal mechanism must be available for those declared ineligible for provincial benefits. The C.A.P. must be viewed primarily as a cost-sharing mechanism rather than as a plan that has brought well-defined uniform welfare benefits to Canadians. A major impact of the plan has been the broadening of the definition of the needy. Any provincial assistance based on need (as opposed to the means criterion) is eligible for federal funding. By defining need without regard to cause, the Plan opens the way for provinces to deal with needs beyond the usual established categories.

In the 1970s issues of both jurisdiction and substance have been the focus of federal-provincial relations. In the constitutional review process that culminated at the Victoria Conference in 1971 social welfare responsibilities were one of the key problem areas. Although the "Victoria Charter" proposals did appear to increase provincial control over social welfare, they were seen by Quebec to be inadequate[23] and were one of the reasons given for its rejection of the Charter. The criticisms of public assistance programmes contained in the 1971 Special Senate Committee Report on Poverty and a general desire to limit costs have provided impetus for a comprehensive reappraisal of welfare policies. The 1973 publication of the federal *Working Paper on Social Security in Canada* served as a starting point for the Social Security Review carried out by the Federal-Provincial Conference of Welfare Ministers. Over a period of two years the Review was able to achieve a consensus that a guaranteed income system should be established across Canada.[23] Subsequently, however, it was not possible to get agreement on the implementation and financing of such a system. Only the New Democratic Governments of Manitoba and Saskatchewan were willing to commit themselves to implementing a guaranteed income system.

The only legislation (Bill C-57) which emerged from the Review did not concern income maintenance programmes, but instead was directed toward reform of social services. Introduced in June 1977, the Social Services Bill provided for two significant changes in Ottawa's contribution to provincial social service programmes. First, the range of federal cost-sharing was to be extended to include more at-home services for the aged and handicapped and to provide some social services, such as children's services, rehabilitation, and crisis intervention, on a more universal basis, and second, a "user-pay" formula was to be introduced for some programmes. Ottawa would pay fifty percent of the costs and depending on income the user would pay a portion of the costs and the provinces would pay the rest. These proposals, based on a wider view of social services, were subsequently withdrawn by the federal Minister of Health and Welfare, Marc Lalonde. In its stead he proposed a block grant system of federal contributions through which each province would receive an unconditional grant on a per capita basis. The block financing system goes a long way to restoring welfare jurisdiction to the provinces. There are, however, many unresolved questions. How much will each province receive? To what extent is equalization built into the grant? To what extent will Ottawa share the rising costs of programmes? The most vocal criticism of the block financing plan has come from private social agencies. Associations for the retarded and the disabled fear that the provinces, when given financial control, may not continue all their social service programmes.[25] At this point it is impossible to predict what changes, if any, the provinces will make when they gain control of social services funds.

Although Ottawa has played an important part in the provision of social assistance, welfare must still be viewed as a predominantly provincial policy area, which means among other things, variations across the provinces. There are ten different welfare systems across Canada. Each province has retained authority over the three fundamental welfare issues: (1) What programmes will be established? (2) Who will be eligible for the programmes? (3) How much help will individuals receive?

Comparing Provincial Welfare

Operating in the midst of both pressures from Ottawa and policy examples from other provinces, each provincial political system has dealt in its own way with the issues of welfare assistance. The provincial variations that exist today are not new. In 1940 British Columbia spent $12.44 per capita on public health and welfare while New

Brunswick spent $4.40.[26] The overall differences in provincial welfare assistance can be analyzed as variations in two categories: eligibility and benefits.

Because most provincial/municipal welfare falls within the assistance category of relief, the determination of eligibility is an especially important aspect of welfare systems. In 1973 11.4 percent of all families were considered low income by Statistics Canada.[27] As one might expect, these poor families were not distributed evenly across Canada. Twenty-three percent of the families in Newfoundland are below the low income line, while in Ontario the corresponding figure is nine percent, in Saskatchewan seventeen percent, and in British Columbia, the lowest proportion of all, just under eight percent. In order to compare provincial welfare systems by eligibility, we have determined the percentage of the provincial population receiving welfare and the percentage of the provincial population with incomes below established poverty lines.[28] By comparing the estimated needy with the actual recipients of welfare, it is possible to make some inferences about provincial eligibility standards. The eligibility ratio in Table 6.3 (Column A) is the proportion of families with incomes below a selected poverty line who actually receive provincial assistance. The provinces of Newfoundland and British Columbia give assistance to more than half of those defined as poor, whereas the provinces of Saskatchewan and Prince Edward Island are much less generous. The number of families below the poverty line who do not receive provincial assistance is a partial indicator of the substantial size of the working poor in Canada. Income supplementation for the working poor is an issue we will take up later in the chapter.

A second comparative consideration is the size of benefits. As of 1974 a family of four on maximum social assistance in British Columbia received $4320, whereas in New Brunswick the same family received only $3780 (Table 6.3, Column B). When the levels of benefits are compared with poverty line standards, we find no province provides benefits near the poverty levels. The poverty lines for a family of four, as estimated by the C.C.S.D. and Statistics Canada, are, respectively, $6358 and $5826,[29] whereas the highest benefits for that family are $4320 (see Chart 6.1).

Variations in provincial welfare are even greater if municipal differences are taken into consideration. Newfoundland, Prince Edward Island, and New Brunswick have assumed all responsibility for welfare. The other provinces continue to place some responsibility at the municipal level. For example, in Ontario, Manitoba, and Nova Scotia municipalities provide short-term assistance to those in need due to temporary misfortunes such as illness or unemployment. The provinces generally provide partial subsidies to the municipalities for the costs

Table 6.3: Comparing Provincial Welfare

PROVINCE	ELIGIBILITY RATIO (PROPORTION OF LOW INCOME FAMILIES RECEIVING SOCIAL ASSISTANCE)*	ANNUAL BENEFITS INCLUDING FAMILY ALLOWANCES FOR A FAMILY OF 4 (1974)**
NEWFOUNDLAND	54.7	$4080
PRINCE EDWARD ISLAND	28.4	4068
NOVA SCOTIA	37.1	3834
NEW BRUNSWICK	46.1	3780
QUEBEC	n.a.	4224
ONTARIO	40.0	4200
MANITOBA	47.4	3831
SASKATCHEWAN	26.7	4140
ALBERTA	37.8	3936
BRITISH COLUMBIA	50.6	4320

*Source: Based on data from 1973. Statistics Canada, *Income Distribution by Size in Canada*, DBS 13-207, and *Canada Yearbook 1976*.
**Source: Federal-Provincial Working Party on Income Maintenance, *Background Paper on Income Support and Supplementation*, February 1975. Table 5

of such assistance. In Saskatchewan and British Columbia the munici-palities contribute two percent and ten percent respectively to the total cost of provincially administered social welfare.

The history of each province's welfare system reflects, in part, the socio-economic conditions of that province, as well as some important characteristics of its political culture and party systems. The western provinces have generally been in the forefront of welfare reform. They were, for example, leaders in creating their own Mothers' Allowance Programmes and were the first to join the federal cost-sharing programmes for Old Age Pensions. As Cassidy stated in 1945, British Columbia was "if not the first, then the most generous" in the provision of social assistance.[30] Table 6.3 indicates that this assessment still holds true into the 1970s.

There are several reasons which may account for the more vigorous development of social welfare policy in the western provinces. As some of the evidence seen in Chapter 3 illustrates, the reformist impulse of protest movements and their impact on political parties has been a vital component of western provincial politics. Protest parties are by their nature less tied to the *status quo* than are the traditionally centrist Liberals and Conservatives, and are more willing to push for new social options. The very existence of protest parties may have stimulated the traditional parties themselves toward innovation.[31]

CHART 6.1 Provincial Social Assistance* for a Family of Four and Selected Income Standard Measures — 1974

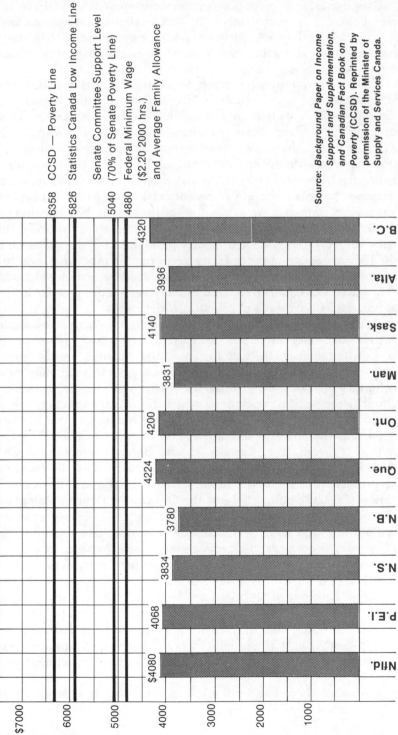

6358 CCSD — Poverty Line

5826 Statistics Canada Low Income Line

5040 Senate Committee Support Level (70% of Senate Poverty Line)

4880 Federal Minimum Wage ($2.20 2000 hrs.) and Average Family Allowance

B.C.	4320
Alta.	3936
Sask.	4140
Man.	3831
Ont.	4200
Que.	4224
N.B.	3780
N.S.	3834
P.E.I.	4068
Nfld.	$4080

$7000
6000
5000
4000
3000
2000
1000

Source: *Background Paper on Income Support and Supplementation, and Canadian Fact Book on Poverty* (CCSD). Reprinted by permission of the Minister of Supply and Services Canada.

Other sources of variation in the development of welfare systems may be found in the provinces' distinctive climates of opinion and their historical traditions. As Bryden points out, in order for the policy process to begin, public opinion must be *beyond the point* of considering such assistance sacrilege.[33]

The western provinces were to a large extent founded through state-sponsored immigration, public support for the construction of the railroad and the necessity of public assistance for scattered farming communities. Given these patterns of state involvement, it is not surprising that there was a widespread acceptance of collective social responsibility. Moreover, traditions of local political autonomy have generally been weaker in the West than in Ontario, Quebec, or the Atlantic Provinces because of recent settlement patterns coupled with large-scale immigration of diverse groups. This has encouraged the public to look to provincial authorities rather than to local-municipal ones for policy solutions to social problems. By way of contrast, in the East it was common for many years for the municipal level to serve as the sole public source of primitive social assistance. In addition, voluntary associations have traditionally been more popular in the East as an alternative means of meeting social needs.

The development of welfare policy in Ontario illustrates a distinctive pattern of policy evolution at variance with that observed in the western provinces. Instead of an initial reliance on the provincial government, Ontario welfare was based primarily on municipal and voluntary institutions. Unlike the eastern provinces, however, the Ontario government responded when the welfare function proved too great for the municipalities and private groups. Ontario has been an important leader in the administration of social welfare. The Ontario Act for Prevention of Cruelty to and Better Protection of Children (1893) has been described as a welfare landmark. It established a system of protection and aid for minors that was adopted throughout the nation.[33] Equally influential was the Ontario Workmen's Compensation Act in 1914. This legislation, establishing an insurance scheme with compulsory and employer funding and an independent board to administer the programme, was a model for other provinces.

Ontario has been similar to the western provinces in its early creation of Mothers' Allowance (1920) and adoption of shared cost Old Age Pensions (1929). Perhaps because of its wealth and superior staff capabilities, Ontario has always been prepared to develop programmes in order to avail itself of funds from federal-provincial shared-cost plans.[34] The province has also been a leader in administrative reforms and was the first in 1931 to establish a Department of Public Welfare.

In Quebec there has been a greater and longer reliance on private charity than in any other province. In 1921, when public money was made available under the Public Charities Act, it was channeled to the needy through private charitable institutions, primarily the Church. In comparison, Ontario's Public Charities Act some fifty years earlier (1874), also provided public funds for private institutions performing welfare functions. However, unlike the Quebec legislation, the Ontario Act provided for provincial supervision of the private institutions. In Quebec social measures were for the most part regarded as outside the scope of government. Anything left to provincial initiative and funding was left undone. The notions prevalent at Confederation carried over for many years—welfare was thought to be essentially a Church matter.[35] Ramsay Cook has argued that even as the grip of the Church was weakened, the development of public social services remained atrophied as a consequence of provincial desires for autonomy. Bread-and-butter issues of welfare have often taken a back seat to the more emotional and symbolic issues of nationalism.[36]

Even before the Quiet Revolution Quebec was the most active critic of the federal role in social welfare. Successive governments in Quebec have viewed control over social policy as a crucial element for the maintenance of cultural and ethnic identity. Opting out of the Canada Assistance Plan has given Quebec the flexibility and resources to pursue its own welfare programme. The Commission of Inquiry on Health and Welfare Services in Quebec (Castonguay-Nepveu Commission) provided a thoughtful basis for policy change and resulted in the 1971 Bill 65, which represents a pioneering effort in Canada to create an integrated pattern of provincial social and health services.[37]

The Atlantic provinces have historically presented a pitiful picture for the needy. Grim poor laws and reliance on local responsibility were the main modes of "assistance." Mothers' Allowance, adopted in Manitoba in 1916, did not come to Nova Scotia until 1930 and to New Brunswick until 1943. The poverty of the region made it difficult for the provinces even to carry the usual fifty percent burden necessary to participate in federal shared-cost schemes. Old Age Pensions were not adopted until Ottawa paid seventy-five percent of the costs.

Without exception the poorer eastern provinces have lagged behind the rest of the country in the provision of social assistance. Their municipalities received little supervision or assistance from provincial governments,[38] and in many localities the more costly and less desirable mode of institutional relief has been the only assistance available. Years after the other provinces had reasonably functioning welfare programmes, those of the Atlantic provinces were underdeveloped and in some cases entirely lacking. The non-ideological and patronage-based political traditions of the Atlantic provinces[39] have certainly minimized the prospects of major policy innovations in the field of welfare.

Reinforcing this have been public fears of the high costs of social welfare and a common belief that such matters are the proper function of local authorities.

The weak fiscal resource base of the Atlantic provinces has been strained even further by the larger number of potential welfare recipients (17.9 percent of the families in the Atlantic provinces fall below the poverty line), and by the matching requirement in most shared-cost programmes. This means that those have-not provinces with greater needs are unlikely to have the funds necessary to participate in the federal programme. Non-participation, of course, disadvantages residents of these provinces because their federal taxes go to pay for services which are not available to them.

Welfare Today

What kinds of programmes are currently available to Canadians needing income assistance? First, there are federal programmes: Family Allowance, Unemployment Insurance, and Old Age Pensions, which are available nation-wide. If, however, an individual's needs are beyond, or do not fit, the provisions of these programmes, then he must turn to the province and/or municipality. We will use the welfare system of Ontario to illustrate current provincial social assistance.[40]

Welfare in Ontario still bears some of the marks of the initial reliance on local assistance. Although the municipalities have more responsibility for welfare than those in most other provinces, today the bulk of administrative and budgetary welfare responsibilities rests with the province (and Ottawa). There are two major assistance programmes: General Welfare Assistance and Family Benefits. Some individuals may be eligible under both, but each programme is targeted toward different sets of needs. As is the case in Newfoundland, Nova Scotia, Manitoba, and Alberta, Ontario deals separately with short- and long-term needs.

The General Welfare Assistance Act of 1958 provides for short-term relief to the needy unemployed. The locally-administered assistance comes as weekly or monthly allowances. Ottawa pays fifty percent, the provinces thirty, and municipalities twenty percent. The province sets minimum general welfare assistance rates, while supplementary payments are left to the discretion of the municipality. The municipalities also can make available additional aid such as dental or optical services. The province will share the cost of the municipal supplements.

The other major welfare programme in Ontario was created under the Family Benefits Act of 1966. Established as part of the Canada Assistance Plan, Family Benefits replaced the various separate categorical programmes for unemployables (the blind, disabled, and dependent children). Administered by the province, Family Benefits provide long-term assistance for those who qualify. In other words, there is a means test

CHART 6.2 The Structure of Welfare in Ontario

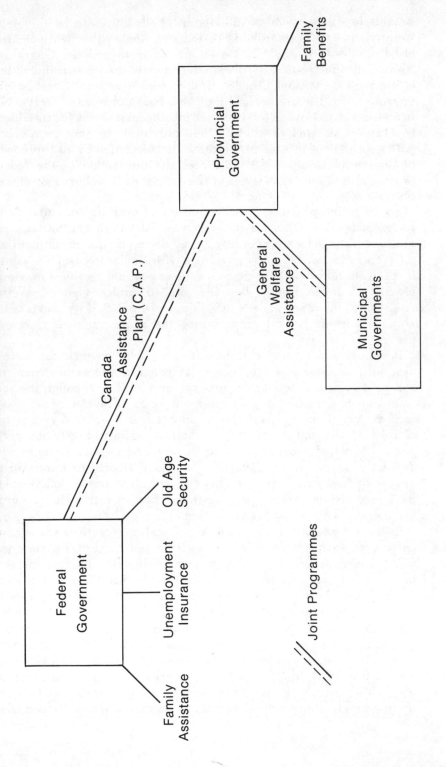

as well as a determination of categorical eligibility. To be eligible for Family Benefits, a person must be either a single parent with children, blind, disabled, or aged. In 1974 Ontario instituted the Guaranteed Annual Income System (GAINS) which established a guaranteed level of income for the blind, disabled, and persons over sixty-five. Six other provinces (British Columbia, Manitoba, Saskatchewan, Alberta, New Brunswick, and Nova Scotia) provide income guarantees for the elderly. In Ontario, as well as in the other provinces, income maintenance policy consists of diverse programmes implemented by all three levels of government. Chart 6.2 illustrates the interaction of the federal, provincial, and municipal levels in the provision of welfare assistance in Ontario.

As in other provinces, the provision of welfare in Ontario is a hodge-podge of assistance programmes. Although the various programmes do provide wide coverage, they also result in some unjustifiable differences in assistance to individuals with similar needs. For example, in 1975 an individual with no other income would receive a maximum of $2280 under Family Benefits, $1740 under General Welfare Assistance and $2880 under OAS, GIS, and GAINS. If we also take into account various federal programmes the range in benefits is even greater.[41]

Provision for income maintenance in each province can best be described as a piecemeal collection of programmes rather than as a coherent system. The maze of programmes built up through the years is as much a result of political realities as of social needs. Social welfare programmes have been adopted in "politically digestible chunks."[42] Although an integrated system of welfare has obvious merits, narrow, isolated programmes and incremental welfare changes allow decision-makers greater flexibility. In their efforts to minimize the degree of conflict inherent in this redistributive arena, policy-makers have focussed on narrow, programmatic changes rather than on broad questions of equity and redistribution.

Even if understandable from a political perspective, the uneven patchwork character of provincial welfare assistance has some unfortunate consequences. Through variations in eligibility and benefits, some of the needy are left with inadequate assistance. The fact that the Canada Assistance Plan matches provincial welfare spending does not necessarily help the situation. The poor provinces are still less able than the rich to meet the welfare needs of their citizens. Inequities in eligibility and benefits are further exacerbated by the discretionary role of the municipalities in some provinces. As in the case of the poorer provinces, local areas with the greatest number of needy are least able to bear the costs of reasonable welfare assistance. There is no horizontal equity among provincial welfare systems. Individuals in different provinces, who are equally poor, do not receive the same amount of assistance. Moreover, as we have noted, even within a single province, individual needs are treated differently, depending on the reason for poverty.

Another major deficiency in the present situation is the treatment of the working poor, those who work but do not earn an income adequate for their basic needs. The working poor, who are estimated to constitute fifty percent of Canada's poor, are generally not eligible for welfare assistance although their wages may be less than the amount available through social assistance.[43] The recognition that the earnings of many in low-paying jobs may not be adequate for family support has led to efforts to broaden the welfare system to accommodate the working poor. A related issue of long standing is the problem of work incentives for those receiving social assistance. Low-level earnings exemptions and/or high tax-back rates (sometimes as high as a dollar reduction in benefits for every dollar earned) provide little incentive for an individual to take a low-paying job and receive less income when employed than when on welfare. The present welfare system penalizes those in low-paying jobs and offers little incentive to move people from public assistance to low-paying employment.

The administration of public assistance is a long-standing problem area. The 1971 Senate Poverty Report makes many of the same criticisms that Henry Cassidy did in his study of the evolution of provincial welfare prior to 1945. The administration of provincial welfare is often ineffective, costly, unresponsive, and inhumane.[44] In the seventies two provinces, British Columbia and Quebec, have tried in different ways to reorganize administrative systems. In Quebec a new pattern of welfare delivery has been attempted. The essence of the plan is integration through local Community Service Centres and uniformity through the Health and Social Service Council and Social Service Centres. In British Columbia the reform based on the 1974 Community Resources Board Act focussed on decentralization and community responsiveness.[45]

Throughout the 1970s recommendations for reform of Canadian welfare have come from many sources: *The Special Senate Committee Report on Poverty, The Real Poverty Report, The Castonguay-Nepveu Commission Report*, the federal *Working Paper on Social Security* and the Canadian Council on Social Development's *Social Security in Canada*.[46] The studies are unanimous in their recommendation for a guaranteed income for all unemployables and income supplements for the working poor. A negative income tax plan in which families with income below a certain level (depending on family size) would be entitled to income subsidies is the most commonly suggested method for providing income support (for unemployables) and income supplementation (for the working poor).[47] The most recent study by the Working Party on Income Maintenance, *Income Support and Supplementation*, a part of the federal-provincial Social Security Review, indicated in 1975 wide support among the provinces and Ottawa for some general guaranteed income programme.[48] But by 1978 there was still no agreement by the provinces and Ottawa or any unilateral efforts to implement this acclaimed reform.

The continued failure of decision-makers to act on the recommendations by welfare specialists is due to several factors, including prohibitive costs, negative public opinion, and federal-provincial conflict. In rejecting Ottawa's proposals for a guaranteed income plan, provincial decision-makers clearly indicated that their already strained budgets could not bear the additional burden. Moreover, assistance based on guaranteed income does not benefit from the same public acceptance as social insurance schemes. Finally, many reform proposals either fail to deal with the sensitive issue of welfare jurisdiction, or simply assume that Ottawa will bear the financial responsibility. However, when these substantive proposals become policy options, they often are submerged by these questions.

Although there have been some marginal improvements in individual provincial systems, for the present, however, we must refer to the conclusion of the Senate Committee on Poverty.

> The report is critical of the welfare system. It presents a dismal, dreary picture of life as it is lived by those unfortunate enough to be dependent on government assistance for survival . . . . Despite our good intentions and substantial expenditures, the welfare system has failed to achieve its social and humanitarian goals.[49]

This system annually costs Canadians eleven billion dollars! We can expect welfare reform to be a high priority issue for politicians and for experts alike.

HEALTH POLICY

Epidemics provided the major stimulus for the first stage of provincial health policy. During the early part of the nineteenth century outbreaks of cholera, smallpox, and typhus precipitated the development of temporary public boards. In 1849 the united provinces of Upper and Lower Canada went so far as to establish a Central Board of Public Health to be mobilized whenever there was an outbreak of contagious disease. Local health boards along with some medical services for the indigent sick and for the scattered farming populations in the West constituted the bulk of early public activities in health.[50]

Constitutionally, health has long been regarded as a provincial concern, albeit one of low priority. Robert Kohn sums up the early attitudes: "Health problems were not thought of as matters of sufficient permanent concern of government at any level to mention them or health specifically when the BNA Act was drafted".[51] In its few health-related references, the BNA Act assigned to Ottawa responsibility for quarantine and marine hospitals, Indian, Eskimo, military and immigrant health matters, and food and drug control (Section 91, Subsections 11, 24, 25). The provinces were given exclusive power in matters dealing with "the establishment and maintenance and management of hospitals, asylums, charities and eleemosynary institutions in and for the province other than marine hospitals". (Section 92, Subsection 7) and "generally all matters of a merely local or private nature in the province". (Section 92, Subsection 16).

As with social welfare at the time of Confederation, health was believed to be a personal, family matter. Illness was normally treated at home; only those who had no alternative went to local custodial institutions (hospitals) operated by religious orders and voluntary groups. The early public health services that did emerge were directed toward those community problems beyond the scope of any individual. By 1909 all nine provinces had passed legislation establishing permanent public health boards. The municipalities were required to appoint medical officers and sanitary inspectors to local health boards. Local health board activities were directed, with varying success, toward the control of disease, environmental sanitation, and medical aid to the poor.

Today the provinces support and administer the financing of medical and hospital insurance and have primary responsibility for community health services. Provincial health functions now include hospital services, preventive health services, communicable disease control, treatment of tuberculosis and mental illness, and the rehabilitation of the chronically ill and disabled.[52] The scope of provincial health activities is reflected in the fact that in the 1970s health costs account for over one quarter of provincial budgets. In five provinces (N.S., Ontario, Manitoba, Saskatchewan, and B.C.) health is the single largest category of expenditures. In the other five provinces health is second only to education.[53]

The guarantee of a minimum standard of health services is now accepted as a basic right and has been achieved through the removal of financial barriers to health care. Universal, comprehensive health care is a central pillar of the welfare state. Health has evolved from a private, and in some instances, local concern in which the public had only the most limited expectations of government action into a policy sphere in which there is a national commitment to meeting the health needs of all Canadians.[54]

Table 6.4: Net Public Expenditures on Health*

YEAR	MUNICIPAL		PROVINCIAL		FEDERAL	
	EXPENDITURES (IN MILLIONS) $	PERCENT OF TOTAL HEALTH SPENDING %	EXPENDITURES $	PERCENT OF TOTAL HEALTH SPENDING %	EXPENDITURES $	PERCENT OF TOTAL HEALTH SPENDING %
1945	21	30.8	42	61.7	5	7.3%
1950	40	17	158	68	34	14
1955	65	17	246	66	57	15
1960	66	7.8	508	60	267	31
1965	73	4.6	1070	68	426	27
1970	119	3.4	2254	66	1036	30.3
1973	109.8	2	3563	65	1789	31

*Excluding Transfers — intergovernmental grants for health are entered for the donor government. i.e. federal transfers to the provinces are in the federal column.
Source: (1945-1960) M.C. Urquhart and K.C. Buckley, *Historical Statistics of Canada*, (Macmillan, Toronto, 1965). pp. 206-211.
(1965-1973) *Canadian Year Book 1975* (Information Canada, 1976). Reprinted by permission of the Minister of Supply and Services Canada.

Chart 6.3: Three Stages of Provincial Health Policy

CRITERIA	COMMUNITY DISEASE CONTROL	PUBLIC INSURANCE	COMMUNITY HEALTH CENTRES
1. Extent of public/private	Sharp division	Merging due mainly to financial arrangements	Fused
2. Main unit of health care delivery	1. doctor & 2. hospital	1. hospital 2. doctor	Community Health Centres
3. Governmental level of operational responsibility	Municipal	Provincial	Provincial with decentralization to region
4. Government that is impetus for change	Provincial	Federal	Provincial with decentralization to region
5. Relationship between medical profession and the state	Self-regulation by profession	Some regulation of price and volume of medical services	Regulation of allocation of health functions, as well as costs and volume

Resulting from initiatives at all levels of government, public sector involvement in health has changed in three crucial respects. The responsibility for health care has steadily shifted away from the individual and towards government. The public provision of health services has moved from local to provincial and federal levels and, finally, the medical profession has become subject to increasing regulation. Table 6.4 illustrates, in part, the changes in public involvement in health care. While the provinces continue to pay the major portion of health costs, Ottawa has replaced the municipalities in providing almost one-third of public funds for health care. Total public sector spending on health care as a proportion of the Gross National Product has risen from 3.1% in 1967 (pre-medicare) to over 5% in 1973.[55]

The evolution of provincial health policy can be traced over three separate stages, community disease control, public insurance, and community health centres. These terms are short-hand labels to suggest the dominant policy pattern in governmental health care services. Each phase of development may be described and compared with the others in terms of five criteria:

(a) the extent of public vs. private health services
(b) the main governmental unit of health care delivery
(c) the level of government that has primary operational responsibility
(d) the level of government that provides the main impetus for change
(e) the relationship between the medical profession and the state.[56]

Chart 6.3 briefly illustrates differences among the three phases. There are two important provisos to this schematic depiction of health policy. First, there is in reality considerable overlap between stages. For example, during the first stage, public insurance had already begun in some provinces. Second, the provinces have not moved uniformly from one stage to the next. Some provinces have been leaders in the evolution of health policies; others have always lagged behind. The three stages represent a simplified distinction in order to trace the development of health policy. As will be clear in the discussion of each phase, the real world of health policy has not been quite so neat.

Phase 1: Community Disease Control

In this early stage health was of limited importance in the public sector. The distinguishing characteristic is that public action was taken, in the main, to protect the community. For example local authorities slowly became involved in matters of sanitation, safe water supply, and disease control. There were also some isolated instances of public services for individual problems (immunizations and infant care). However, typically there was a sharp distinction between individual, private health care and community/public health matters. The doctor and, to some extent, the hospital constituted the main units in the delivery of individual health care. Most governmental services came from the municipal level with innovations and reform coming from the provincial government. Finally, because the medical profession was permitted to regulate itself and to control most public health policies,[57] the policy of the period has been characterized as one of benign neglect.[58]

During this phase there was a wide range of variation among provincial policies. It is in the western provinces that one observes the first efforts to provide government health services to individuals who were neither indigent nor suffering from a specific disease. The early acceptance of public involvement in health was based on the fact that the province was the only agency capable of bringing health services to the scattered agricultural population. Even if individuals could afford private services, it was difficult to get individual medical personnel to service the areas. Agriculture and health became linked because of the farming population. In 1883 Manitoba established a Department of Agriculture, Immigration, Statistics and Health. Even before Saskatchewan and Alberta became provinces, public health services were provided to the territory by the federal Department of Agriculture.

Unlike the eastern hospitals, which were predominantly financed by religious and voluntary philanthropic organizations and received provincial and/or municipal assistance for the care of indigents, the western hospitals received more general public funding.[59] The Union Hospital Districts first established in Saskatchewan in 1916 permitted municipalities to join together to erect and maintain hospitals. These publicly supported hospital plans were then broadened when Saskatchewan and Alberta enacted the first programmes for municipally sponsored hospital prepayment plans. Groups of municipalities could form Union Hospital Districts which not only built and maintained hospitals, but also provided hospital care for all their residents. The costs were met by local taxes and provincial grants. By 1942 eighty-eight municipalities took part in these hospitals' insurance plans.[60]

Another important prairie innovation was the "Municipal Doctor System" which began unofficially in 1914. As a result of the difficulty which the rural municipalities had in attracting and keeping physicians, Saskatchewan in 1916 authorized municipalities to levy taxes to pay doctors a salary. This salary constituted prepayment for residents' medical care. Alberta (1926) and Manitoba (1921) also permitted municipal doctor plans, but it was in Saskatchewan that the idea really took hold. By 1948 there were close to two hundred functioning municipal doctor agreements.[61]

In the interwar years the provinces began to show a concern for the administration of health services. Starting with New Brunswick in 1918, each province created a cabinet department for health.[62] Health functions remained divided between provincial and municipal governments. But based on variations in the degree of decentralization, three distinct provincial patterns of responsibility began to emerge.[63] The Maritimes and Quebec moved toward the centralization of public health policy. (Their welfare services remained, nevertheless, with local authorities.) This was accomplished through the creation of regions, districts, or county health units[64] which assumed many of the tasks carried out by the municipalities in Ontario and the West. In comparison with the piece-meal organization of welfare relief, public health became well organized. In the case of Quebec, the Church was much more deeply involved in welfare than in health services. The Church's role in health centred on sharing responsibility for institutionalized care. It had virtually no role in the provision of public health services.[65]

The most serious limitation on the development of health services in all of eastern Canada remained the problem of inadequate financing. In

1941 New Brunswick's public health expenditure (excluding mental health and tuberculosis) was 34¢ per capita; in 1943 Nova Scotia's was 80¢ per capita, while the generally accepted pre-war standard level for adequate public health services was $2-2.50 per capita.[66]

In Ontario the municipalities had more responsibilities than those in the East and more autonomy than those in the West. The established tradition of municipal government and strong voluntary agencies resulted in the provincial department primarily providing supervision and financial aid. Through a rather *ad hoc* series of grant programmes which lacked any systematic sharing of expenses, the province provided funds for many municipal activities.

Public health in the prairies and British Columbia depended on both the provincial and local levels. The fact that the western provinces never developed a municipal system as strong as Ontario's meant that municipalities never played as great a role, and in all the western provinces the provincial governments supervised the work of the localities. In many rural districts the provinces directly provided public health services.

The relationship between the medical profession and provincial governments reflected the limited public sector involvement in health matters. Weller describes this public health stage as an era of "benign neglect" because of the virtually total delegation of state authority to the medical profession. The College of Physicians and Surgeons was the licensing and regulatory body in each province. In some the role of the medical profession went even further. For example, in 1934, the province of Ontario reached an agreement with the Ontario Medical Association to provide medical services to those on relief. The programme was financed by the province and municipalities but administered totally by the OMA.

Prior to the introduction of hospital insurance in Saskatchewan in 1946, provincial health policies reflected the traditional notion of public health—services directed toward the protection of the community rather than any single individual. Gradually this perception underwent a transformation, and interest in health care began to reflect the general thrust of the welfare state. Ill health came to be viewed as one of the universal risks against which government should provide protection. Like other facilities, such as safe water and roads, personal health care services were to be available without regard to income. Governmental concerns spilled over into the individual sphere in several ways. One was the financing of services to individuals for the treatment of specific diseases such as tuberculosis, cancer, venereal diseases and mental illness. A second involved provincial payment for the personal health services of specific groups. The most widespread case of organized provincial activity in this regard was the provision of hospital and/or medical services for the indigent.[67] In 1931, B.C. was the first to institute a provincial programme of medical care for the poor, and in 1935, Ontario was the first province to require the municipalities to provide such services.

In various provinces other groups had publicly sponsored personal health services. Alberta's Maternity Act of 1944 instituted free hospital care for expectant mothers and their newborn. The Union Hospital and Municipal Doctor Plans discussed above brought public personal care to all the residents of participating municipalities. The 1946 Public Medical Care Act in Saskatchewan enabled municipalities to join together to provide tax-supported medical services in health regions, although the Swift Current Health Region was the only region in Saskatchewan to adopt this form of publicly supported medical care.

By the late 1950s the traditionally limited scope of community public health was no longer an accurate model for describing the pattern of policy. The public-private distinction was being blurred and the individual was no longer solely responsible for his own health care. Many of the provinces were taking over health responsibilities from the municipalities, and Ottawa was beginning to enter the health arena. The medical profession continued to regulate itself, but changes were coming. The private medical market[68] concept was giving way to modifications that developed into the insurance phase of health policy.

Phase 2: Public Insurance

In the span of one hundred years the role of the province had been transformed from that of sporadic fighter of epidemics to provider of myriad health services. During the 1950s and 1960s the personal and public health domains became irreversibly interwoven. The provinces, rather than the municipalities, became the main suppliers of health services and the federal government took on the previous provincial role of innovator. In the ten years between the adoption of hospital insurance and medical insurance, the hospital began to overshadow the physician as the major unit in health care delivery, but the individual doctor-patient relationship was still important. The essential difference was that the individual, market economy model had given way to what Weller describes as a "subsidized entrepreneurial model" in which . . . "although health resources were still viewed as primarily a consumption good (available to individuals in their private capacities) they were seen to be so inequitably distributed that some public policy was needed to bring about greater equity".[69]

National hospital insurance and medical insurance are landmarks in the transformation of provincial health policy. It was Ottawa's entry into the field that eventually brought universal health insurance to all provinces. Although B.C. and Saskatchewan had their own public hospital insurance, they were most eager for Ottawa to share the costs. Pressure for federal action also came from the Frost government in Ontario. At the Federal-Provincial Conference in 1955, Ottawa announced its decision to go ahead with national hospital insurance. The Hospital Insurance and Diagnostic Services Act (HIDS), passed by Parliament in 1957 and by 1961 adopted in all the provinces, marks the realization of the insurance phase. Several factors paved the way for the introduction of universal hospital insurance, the most important being: (i) the success of existing provincial plans in Saskatchewan, British Columbia, Newfoundland, and Alberta, (ii) the widespread enrolment in private Blue Cross plans in other provinces, and (iii) the reduction in the shortage of hospital facilities.[70]

Successful Provincial Plans. Interest in provincial hospital insurance can be traced back at least as far as 1919. In that year a British Columbia Royal Commission recommended the adoption of health insurance. A second B.C. Royal Commission established in 1929 recommended a similar course. The legislation that finally passed the British Columbia legislature in 1936 provided for insurance to cover doctor and hospital services. However, strong opposition by the medical profession persuaded the Patullo government to postpone indefinitely the implementation of the plan. In 1948 the province finally adopted and implemented a hospital insurance programme.[71] In Alberta a committee of inquiry in 1934 recommended the development of province-wide, locally administered health insurance. The legislature passed a comprehensive health insurance plan, but it was not proclaimed. Similar bills were passed in 1942 and in 1946. Finally in 1949 a provincial-municipal insurance plan was implemented which was based on the existing municipal hospital plans rather than the recommended comprehensive provincial insurance plan.

Although there were earlier studies and legislation in other provinces, it was in Saskatchewan in 1946 that the first provincially sponsored universal hospital insurance plan was established. The Regina Manifesto (1933) had stated the CCF's commitment to universal health care, and within two years of coming to power the CCF passed the Saskatchewan Hospitalization Act (1946). The importance of health policy for the Douglas government was underscored by the Premier's taking on the duties of Minister of Health until 1949.[72]

Prior to the federal act in 1957, the only publicly supported hospital insurance plan that existed outside the western provinces was the Cottage Hospital and Medical Care Plan in Newfoundland. Instituted in 1935 by the Commission government, the Plan provided hospital and medical care for those in isolated outports.

Widespread Voluntary Health Insurance. One of the earliest forms of non-governmental hospital insurance was hospital-sponsored prepayment plans. Miners, lumbermen, and other occupational groups took out what amounted to a service contract with a hospital. Later, these contracts were also available to unaffiliated individuals. By 1934 hospital-sponsored prepayment plans were operating in six provinces.

In addition to the residents of the four provinces with their own insurance plans, many Canadians had private, voluntary hospital insurance. They were covered by an assortment of plans such as Blue Cross, cooperative insurance, and commercial insurance. The coverage and costs varied among provinces, companies, and individuals. In spite of the inconsistencies it was clear Canadians wanted hospital insurance. Blue Cross, which started in Winnipeg in 1939, had by 1957 enrolled almost half of the population of Manitoba. Throughout the forties it spread to Ontario, Quebec, the Maritimes, B.C., and Alberta, attracting large numbers of people who sought some security from catastrophic hospital bills.[73]

Increased Facilities. Leaving aside the provisions for national health insurance contained in the federal post-war Green Book reforms (1945), Ottawa's first significant legislation in the health arena came in 1948 in the form of the National Health Grants Programme.[74] The grants were available for many ongoing provincial activities such as public health, as well as for new provincial projects such as hospital construction. Grants for hospital construction made up one third of the programme.

Ottawa believed these grants were the necessary groundwork for a national health insurance system. From 1948 until the Hospital Construction Grant was terminated in March 1970, hospital capacity was expanded by 130,000 beds, bringing the total number of 198,000 in 1970.[75] The federal construction grants also helped to fund nurses' and interns' residences, public health laboratories, and community health centres. The National Health Grants Programme paved the way to hospital insurance. It helped to create the facilities necessary to meet the demands of a universal hospitalization scheme. However, these modern, technologically advanced hospitals led to a rapid rise in hospital costs making it even more difficult for individuals to afford the costs of hospitalization.

The Hospital Insurance and Diagnostic Services Act. The Hospital Insurance and Diagnostic Services Act brought hospital insurance to Canadians in every province. By 1961, 99% of the Canadian population as covered by provincial public hospital insurance plans. The HIDS Act is a good reflection of the nature of the federal system. In light of the constitutional responsibilities of the provinces, each province developed an insurance plan with its own particular administrative structure and system of revenues. In order to create certain uniform services, federal funding was made contingent on four federally established criteria. The provincial plans had to be universal, comprehensive, portable, and administered by a non-profit agency.

Federal payments to each province are based on a formula of 25% national average per capita costs and 25% of the provinces' average per capita costs multiplied by the insured population within the province. Thus, to some extent, there is a slight equalization factor built in because the lower cost provinces (those below the national average) receive more than 50% federal funding. It is worth noting that this limited equalization is based on costs, not fiscal need. Table 6.5 shows the range in federal funding. Quebec is the only province to have opted out of HIDS. Under the Established Programmes Act (Interim Arrangements) Quebec received fourteen points of federal income tax in lieu of 50% of health costs.

Although the federal government sought both to guarantee a national minimum standard of health care and to determine which services would be eligible for cost-sharing, the HIDS Act permits important inter-provincial differences. Certain facilities, such as tuberculosis sanatoriums, mental institutions, and nursing homes for custodial care, are not defined as hospitals and are not subject to federal funding. If a province wants to include any of these facilities under its public insurance plan, it is responsible for the entire cost. For example, British Columbia insures home renal dialysis, Saskatchewan insures services in Community Health and Social Centres and Ontario, Manitoba, and Alberta insure nursing home care. Federally excluded services may form a significant segment of health costs. In 1975 the Treasurer of Ontario complained that in his province one quarter of health expenditures goes toward excluded services.

Each province determines the method of financing its share of hospital insurance costs. Most rely on general revenues alone. Ontario, Alberta, and B.C. supplement general revenues with premiums, while British Columbia and Alberta employ patient (user) charges. Table 6.5 summarizes these patterns of provincial financing.

Ottawa, for its part, was careful not to appear to pose a threat to the existing structure of health care. The individual doctor-patient relationship was preserved and the prevailing pattern of hospital ownership was retained so that 90 percent of Canadian hospitals are still governed by voluntary bodies rather than by a governmental agency. The HIDS Act planned to make existing health care more accessible by eliminating the financial pressures on the individual. There was no attempt to change the existing system except in respect to who pays the bill.

Table 6.5: Provincial Hospital and Medical Insurance

	DATE OF ENTRY HIDS	DATE OF ENTRY MEDICARE	METHOD OF FINANCING HOSPITAL INSURANCE	FEDERAL SHARE OF HIDS COSTS (1973-74)	FEDERAL SHARE OF MEDICARE COSTS (1973-74)
NEWFOUNDLAND	1958	1969	General Revenues	57.6%	81.5%
P.E.I.	1959	1970	General Revenues	59.8	74.3
NOVA SCOTIA	1959	1969	General Revenues	54.6	63.0
NEW BRUNSWICK	1959	1971	General Revenues	51.3	75.7
QUEBEC	1961	1970	General Revenues	48.1*	50.8
ONTARIO	1959	1969	G.R. & Premiums	49.4	44.8
MANITOBA	1958	1969	General Revenues	53.1	58.7
SASKATCHEWAN	1958	1968	General Revenues	53.1	60.0
ALBERTA	1958	1969	G.R., Premiums & User Charges	50.1	56.3
BRITISH COLUMBIA	1958	1968	G.R., Premiums & User Charges	52.9	44.3

*This is a tax rebate under opting out arrangements.
Source: S. Andreopoulos (ed.) *National Health Insurance: Can We Learn From Canada?* (Wiley, New York, 1975). Tables 1, 2 and 13.

Medical Care Insurance. The development of insurance for medical, as opposed to hospital, services has been far more contentious because the former was perceived as a threat to both the traditional medical market economy model and the doctor-patient relationship.[76] As with hospital services, prepayment for medical services had scattered beginnings. Perhaps the most important forerunner was the Municipal Doctor Plan. In 1914 the municipality of Sarnia used taxes to pay doctors providing medical services to its residents. The same plan was, as we have already seen, institutionalized by the Saskatchewan legislature two years later.

Many of the royal commissions and committees of inquiry mentioned earlier considered and recommended medical as well as hospital insurance. But, prior to the implementation of provincially sponsored medical insurance in Saskatchewan in 1962, only two groups, other than welfare recipients in some provinces, were covered by public medical insurance—the residents of the Swift Current Health Region in Saskatchewan and children under sixteen years in Newfoundland.

In 1961, in spite of strong opposition from the medical profession, the Saskatchewan CCF government passed the Medical Care Insurance Act, instituting universal, compulsory health insurance. The new law was scheduled to become effective July 1, 1962, but a doctors' strike (the first in North America) postponed its implementation until July 23rd.[77]

Alberta instituted a government-regulated but privately owned medical insurance scheme in 1963. The province set the standard service contract and regulated the rates which private companies could charge, and the government subsidized those individuals who could not afford the premiums. About fifty percent of the population was insured under the Alberta plan.

With the exception of Newfoundland's Cottage Hospital and Medical Care Plan, no province east of the Ottawa Valley gave serious consideration to public medical insurance before it was introduced by the federal government in 1965. At the federal level, however, there had been a great deal of interest in medical insurance. In 1919, the platform of the Liberal Party endorsed universal health insurance. In 1928 the House of Commons Standing Committee on Industrial and International Relations received a report on insurance against unemployment, sickness, and disability. At the Federal-Provincial Conference on Reconstruction in 1945, Ottawa proposed a federal-provincial health insurance plan. At that time, the provinces were unable to agree on the all-important federal tax centralization proposals and also rejected the health plan. It was not until the successful introduction of hospital insurance that medical care insurance once again became a serious option.

In response to party and consumer demands for action a Royal Commission on Health Services was appointed in 1961. The medical profession and the insurance industry, both of whom favoured a limited federal plan "to supplement not supplant" existing insurance arrangements, welcomed the establishment of the Hall Commission. They believed the Commission would put an end to radical schemes and that it would add its stamp of approval to a marginal modification of the status quo. In fact, the Hall Commission brought forth a stinging criticism of the existing situation and forcefully urged universal and compulsory national medical care insurance. The Report recommended that Ottawa help finance insurance plans administered by the provinces.[78] The Canadian Medical Association and insurance companies waged a grand battle to alter several aspects of the proposed medical care legislation, especially the compulsory requirement. Nonetheless, the Medical Care Insurance Act was passed in 1966. By 1971 every province had joined this arrangement. (See Table 6.5 for dates of entry.)

The Medical Care Insurance Act. The Medicare Act is similar to HIDS in that each province created its own plan subject to the four federally set criteria: universal, compulsory, portable, and operated on a non-profit basis by a public agency. If the province's plan met these requirements, Ottawa paid fifty percent of its shareable costs. This federal share was based on fifty percent of the national average costs. If a province's costs were below the national average, Ottawa's contribution constituted more than fifty percent. In Table 6.4 it can be seen that for five provinces Ottawa pays at least 60 percent of the medical care programmes. The highest contribution is 81.5 percent in Newfoundland. Because the entire federal contribution is based on the national average, the equalization impact is greater for medical care contributions than Hospital Insurance, where only half of the federal contribution is based on national costs.

Each province determines how it will raise its own part of medical care costs. Most use general revenues. Copayment or deterrent fees in which the patient pays a nominal sum for each visit was tried by the Liberal government in Saskatchewan from 1968 to 1971. When the NDP returned to power the province abandoned the practice because it was demonstrated that fees deterred the poor from seeking medical services but did not alter the overall volume of demands for health care.[79]

The Medicare Plan left to the provinces much the same control over the scheme as they had over hospital insurance. However, Medicare created a significant rupture in federal-provincial relations. Few provinces saw the necessity for being forced into such a programme at that time. Ontario's strong opposition was based on the contention that it already had a smoothly operating private system. The Robarts government resented being obliged to divert funds to pay for the new public plan. Quebec's opposition to the federal plan stemmed primarily from the belief that health insurance was an integral part of social services and therefore a provincial function.[80] The imposition by Ottawa of a two percent Social Development tax to fund the health programme exacerbated the provinces' displeasure. Even if a province did not join the Plan, its residents still had to pay for medicare through this national tax. In addition, this special tax was not part of the basic tax of which the provinces receive a share.

The federal medicare plan received a more hostile reception from the provinces than the hospital plan had almost ten years earlier. The hospital insurance programme had been developed in close consultation with the provinces and, at that time, they were eager for federal financial assistance in bringing about this much needed service. Perhaps both because the provinces felt there was little need for public medical insurance and because they now realized the enormity of the expenses involved, by 1966 the provinces were very reluctant for Ottawa to initiate a new massive programme in the health sphere. Nonetheless, by January 1, 1971, all ten provinces had entered the medicare programme.

Perhaps the most striking aspect of the insurance phase of provincial policy has been the tremendous increase in health costs. Since the inception of HIDS in 1957, average provincial spending on health has gone from 15% of the budget to 25% in 1974. In their efforts to control costs without reducing services or limiting access, the provinces have moved toward regulating the medical profession. For example, Ontario has pursued avenues which put limits on the discretion of the medical practitioners. It has sought to control the *price* of medical services through negotiated fixed fees for service[81] and it has sought to control the *volume* of medical services by establishing a Medical Review Committee to investigate physicians whose billings are out of line with others in their specialty.

It is important to understand the extent to which insurance has altered the health system. Certainly removing financial barriers to health services means that no longer would cost make adequate health care prohibitive to the less well-off. However, studies confirm that the non-economic barriers remain and although all classes have increased their utilization of health care facilities, there is still a positive relationship between socio-economic status and utilization of the health system.[82] The insurance phase did not in and of itself alter the structure of the health care delivery system; the medical profession retained primary control over the production and distribution of health care.[83] But once government began to pay the bills and permit unlimited access, the portents for change were apparent.

Phase 3: Community Health Centres

Although public hospital and medical service insurance plans have made great advances toward the goal of providing quality health care to all Canadians, provincial governments are now trying to cope with two formidable problems—cost and structure. The most obvious difficulty facing provincial governments is spiralling health costs. In 1974 close to 25 cents of every provincial budget dollar was spent on health. Despite the infusion of vast amounts of money it has become increasingly evident that provincial health care delivery systems are not equally available to all Canadians and that they have failed to be responsive to community needs.[84] In the efforts to solve the problems of the insurance stage, provincial health policy has developed into a third stage. It may be called the community health centres stage because these centres are the pivotal institutions in the evolving health care delivery system.

Costs. Since the institution of the National Health Grants Programme in 1948, the provinces have been encouraged by Ottawa to expand their health care systems. The object was to provide more facilities to meet growing demands for health services. During the insurance phase the key policy word was access. The overriding goal was to make the health care system accessible by removing individual financial constraints. In seeking to solve the cost problem for the individual, the insurance phase produced a public cost problem. The provincial hospital and medical care insurance plans were set up to regulate but not to control. They merely paid the bills generated by the private health system.

Rising costs were of concern to both federal and provincial governments,[85] but in the context of the existing arrangements there was little the provinces could do. Much of the cost problem could be traced back to attributes of the Medicare and HIDS plans in which Ottawa had entered into an agreement to pay fifty percent of total health costs that were determined almost entirely by the provinces. The only federal input into the determination of these costs was to define what were eligible or shareable costs. Ottawa stipulated it would share only the costs of hospital and physician services. The impact of federal eligibility restrictions has been to channel provincial health care into these two most costly forms of curative medical treatment and away from less costly nonshared health services. The open-ended federal agreement to pay half the provinces' eligible health bills had another unforeseen consequence: it provided an incentive for provincial policy-makers to spend "fifty-cent dollars." Health expenditures matched by Ottawa were seen as relatively inexpensive ways of helping economic growth and generating electoral support.[86]

In 1975 Ottawa gave notice to the provinces of changes in its sharing of health costs. It announced a ceiling on the annual rise in costs that it would share, and the replacement of the open-ended medical services agreement with a per capita grant. The provinces reacted sharply. All the earlier accusations of Ottawa initiating expensive programmes and then leaving the provinces holding the financial bag had come true. The federal action fueled provincial demands for greater autonomy and more tax room rather than cost-sharing grants. However, the real problem for the provinces is not so much getting Ottawa to guarantee its share of the ever increasing costs but to control these costs through changes in the health system. The Ontario Economic Council pinpoints the flaw that cannot be ignored: "At present, consumers receive medical service at zero or negligible direct costs. At the same time most of the providers are paid on a fee for service basis . . . the current system is the one most devoid of incentives to induce efficiency in the production of health care services and to encourage economy in the consumption of those services."[87]

The 1977 Fiscal Arrangements and Established Programmes Financing Act has placed the initiative for health policy clearly back in the hands of the provinces. The federal contribution for health costs is no longer based on closely defined conditional shared-cost programmes. Now, instead of matching provincial spending, federal funding will take the form of tax abatements and cash payments. Obviously this type of federal transfer permits the provinces much more latitude in the determination of their health policies and leaves to them the difficult problem of cost control.

Structure. From the point of view of the individual, hospital and medical insurance have helped to alleviate one problem of health systems, that of the financing of health care costs. But they have not touched another kind of problem, the nature of the health delivery system. Numerous studies of provincial health systems point to the following common failings.[88]

    (a) unequal access for the poor and for those living in rural areas, due in part to maldistribution of medical resources

    (b) lack of community participation

    (c) inadequate attention to local needs

    (d) fragmented and discontinuous health care

Two related structural reforms, regionalization and community health centres (CHC), have been the main responses to these criticisms. While also providing cost cuts, both regional organization and the CHC are based in part on consumer participation and are therefore potentially responsive to local community needs. The main objective of regionalization is to assure an effective utilization of health resources. The coordination of institutional and ambulatory services on a regional basis has been a major component in the more comprehensive approach to health services because such organization avoids costly duplication in busy areas and guarantees services in more remote districts. Although governmental reports in Quebec, Ontario, Manitoba, Nova Scotia, and

British Columbia have explicitly endorsed regionalization, and in the other provinces there has been an acceptance of the concept, Quebec is the only province to have established regionalization. Other provinces such as Ontario and Manitoba have tried to utilize the regionalism within their existing statutory frameworks. Several factors have impeded its implementation. Provincial governments have been reluctant to delegate authority and financial control to regional councils. Medical professionals tend to identify with a particular hospital and/or locality rather than the region, and hospitals have tended to function autonomously rather than as part of a system.

The Community Health Centre is a second organizational reform that has arisen in response to the structural and financial problems within the health care system. These centres are designed to provide a more accessible entry point. Using teams of health professionals, CHCs facilitate continuous and readily available one-stop medical service. The care is coordinated and potentially more effective than the fragmented forms of health service that characterize the existing insurance system. In this broader health care context the emphasis is on preventive as well as curative medicine.

Tailored to community needs, CHCs permit the transfer of some health functions from physicians and hospitals to less expensive personnel and facilities. The emphasis on prevention should reduce the demand for more costly curative services. As in the case of regionalization, all provinces have endorsed Community Health Centres in principle,[89] but few have taken any steps to implement the concept. Quebec, Saskatchewan, and Manitoba are the only provinces to have made any systematic efforts to employ the CHC concept. Slow provincial response to the CHC is not surprising, for the institutionalization of it requires a radical overhaul of the health care delivery system. Provision must be made for collective responsibility among the members of the health team. A major stumbling block has been the method of financing, since the group-oriented and preventive approaches of the CHC make fee for service payments unsuitable. Finally, there is the problem of integrating management responsibilities between health professionals and the centres' governing boards. As a consequence of these factors, the CHCs may be viewed as a challenge to the autonomy and power of the medical profession over the allocation of health functions and therefore as a threat to its dominance which was so much a part of earlier stages.[90]

The 1977 modification in the method of federal financing of health from shared-cost grants to unconditional tax points and cash payments is another signal of the end of the insurance stage. Provincial policy-makers are now dealing with a new set of conditions. The public-private distinction obscured in the insurance stage is being further obstructed by efforts to combine individually oriented curative health services with societally oriented, preventive services. In this current phase of health policy, the most important level of government is the province, with potentially greater decentralization to health regions than existed in the insurance era. The initiative that resided with the federal government has been returned to the provinces and most likely will eventually rest with the health regions and local centres. Finally, as we have seen, there are a number of reasons for assuming an increasing degree of regulation of the medical profession.

The current stage in the development of health policy promises to be a difficult and critical time for provincial decision-makers, for they have the primary functional responsibility for health services as well as the opportunity for initiative and creativity. Today the public agenda in each province reflects the search for solutions to the problems of cost and responsive delivery. Unfortunately, in some provinces the overriding importance of cost control and an unwillingness to do battle with the medical profession may result in cost-cutting being their only long-term policy with little regard for its effects on health care delivery.[91]

It is important to keep in mind that in the past the very policies that were the solutions to health care problems gave rise to a new set of difficulties. Even if the provinces do respond to the structural problems of the insurance phase there is no reason to doubt that regionalization and the CHC will likewise give rise to a new set of problems that will be the seeds of yet another phase of health policy.

EDUCATION

From about 1950 through 1972 Canada experienced an education explosion. The most dramatic policy changes occurred after 1960, but the factors creating the need for these reforms were taking shape in the previous decade. The post-war baby boom combined with large-scale immigration to create an irrepressible demand for more schools. Reinforcing such pressures for expansion were, of course, the continuing effects of industrialization and urbanization, which created needs for technical knowledge, expert training and, in general, a highly differentiated labour force and occupational structure. These social and economic transformations inevitably generated demands not only for more education, but for improved quality of educational services.

The growth of the educational sector broadly parallels the development of other social services and the rise of the welfare state. Just as the creation of minimum standards of health and welfare services is, in part, an effort to reduce the differences between rich and poor, the expansion of education is also an attempt to bring about greater equality. However, many of the demands for more and better education are related to the ideal of equal opportunity rather than to absolute equality.

Although there are many ways of describing how Canadian education developed in these years, figures on enrolment trends and public spending provide us with some concise measures indicative of the growth in this policy area. Tables 6.6 and 6.7 present an overview of educational trends from the perspective of enrolments. From the first of these, it is clear that the most extraordinary increases occurred in higher education. But even the elementary-secondary enrolment increases, which had started earlier, far outstripped simple increases in population.

Table 6.7 looks at a different aspect of enrolments. All provinces have compulsory education through age fifteen or sixteen. The percentage of seventeen-year-olds remaining in school provides the first test of the social permeation of the educational process. Retention rates highlight a second aspect of the same phenomenon. All provinces increased the scope of education from 1960 through 1970, but some clearly were starting from a more undeveloped stage than others. The early seventies represent a high-water mark in enrolments, since by 1974-1975 fewer seventeen-year-olds were remaining in school in all provinces except Quebec.

The costs of education provide a second very useful way of summarizing the broad development of education. Expenditures in education increased even faster than did enrolments because growth was not just in terms of quantity, but in the creation of more sophisticated and diversified training, better qualified teachers and more elaborate equipment. Tables 6.8 and 6.9 provide some figures indicating how spending on education has developed. From the mid-1950s into the early 1970s education in Canada as a share of gross national product has increased from less than 3 percent to almost 9 percent[92] (receding slightly after that). Correspondingly, an individual by 1970 could expect to put more than 10 percent of his earnings into schooling through taxes, whereas a decade earlier education might have cost 5 to 6 percent of personal income.

Because of these developments, education as public policy took on a new urgency for all levels of government, but most particularly for the provinces, where the largest share of constitutional authority is found. Education is also the area in which provinces have maintained their greatest autonomy vis-à-vis the federal government.* Increasing costs coupled with the direct involvement of millions of people in the education process forced provincial policy-makers and educational experts to

*This is less so for post-secondary and vocational education where federal funds have played a key role through federal aid to universities (1951) and TVTA (1960).

Table 6.6: A Decade of Expansion In Education, 1961-1971

PROVINCE	PERCENT INCREASE IN POPULATION	PERCENT INCREASE IN ELEMENTARY-SECONDARY ENROLMENT	PERCENT INCREASE IN POST-SECONDARY ENROLMENT
B.C.	34.1	64.0	196.6
ALTA.	22.2	44.2	318.3
SASK.	00.1	18.5	107.3
MAN.	7.3	30.2	153.8
ONT.	23.5	45.6	258.6
QUE.	14.6	44.5	134.5
N.B.	6.2	15.5	146.3
N.S.	7.1	19.8	146.7
P.E.I.	6.6	24.9	162.5
NFLD.	14.0	24.8	358.8

Source: Adapted from David Monroe, *The Organization and Administration of Education in Canada* (Ottawa: Secretary of State, Education Support Branch, 1974).

Table 6.7: Enrolment Trends

PROVINCE	RATIO OF ENROLMENT IN GRADES 9-12 TO THE 14-17 AGE GROUP*			RETENTION RATES: PERCENT OF GRADE II ENROLLED IN GRADE XI (9 YEARS LATER)**	
	1951-52	1967-68	1980-81	1960-61	1970-71
B.C.	71	94	99	71	84
ALTA.	60	94	100	67	84
SASK.	56	89	97	56	79
MAN.	50	86	96	61	81
ONT.	62	101	101	57	82
QUE.	38	96	103	34	81
N.B.	44	75	97	44	68
N.S.	45	74	96	47	70
P.E.I.	44	79	98	34	64
NFLD.	51	75	97	38	66

*Relevant age groups and school grades vary slightly for Newfoundland, Quebec, Ontario and British Columbia. Enrolment ratios may exceed 100 percent because grades may include students outside the age group.
Source: Adapted from Z. E. Zsigmond and C. J. Wenaas, *Enrolment in Educational Institutions by Province 1951-52 to 1980-81* (Ottawa: Queen's Printer, 1970), Staff Study No. 25, Economic Council of Canada, p. 45.
**Source: Statistics Canada, *Education in Canada* (1973), Table 41, p. 358. Reprinted by permission of the Minister of Supply and Services Canada.

Table 6.8: Expenditures on Education, 1956-73

YEAR	AS PERCENTAGE OF GNP	AS PERCENTAGE OF PERSONAL INCOME
1956	2.9	4.0
1960	4.4	5.8
1970	8.8	11.4
1973	8.1	10.2

Source: *Review of Educational Policies in Canada: Foreword and Introduction* (Toronto: CMEC, 1975), p. 24.

comprehensively re-examine this policy area. The common objectives underlying these provincial policy concerns included equality of opportunity and the efficiency and efficacy of the educational process in producing the quality and levels of learning to meet the needs of an increasingly urban, industrialized, and complex society. Policy-makers began to raise questions about the adequacy of the educational process, ranging from the basic structures, especially of secondary and post-secondary education, to matters of curriculum reform and teacher qualifications. The very broad and sweeping concerns of the various Royal Commissions on education since 1960 attest to the fundamental nature of this policy review.

The discussion which follows sketches out the most important policy issues and concerns which have occupied provincial policy-makers. Although it refers to several historical circumstances which have critically shaped the politics of education in Canada, the intent is not so much to provide a history of public education as it is to delineate generally the dominant patterns of provincial education policy and the most fundamental points of policy change and development in recent times.

Despite the relative size of education as a policy area, and its recognized significance in social and economic impact, it has only intermittently been in the forefront of political controversy.[93] This is not to say that there have been no conflicts over education policy. Two social cleavages—religion and language—have often made education a politically sensitive matter. These divisions vary in importance and intensity from one province to another. But, from the 1890 Manitoba School Question to the recent Quebec language bills 22 (1974) and 101 (1977), these cleavages have been at the core of some of the most divisive and intensely felt issues in Canadian history. In contrast, when and where there are few expressed grievances along religious or ethnic lines, policy priorities in the field of education are likely to be handled through

Table 6.9a: Indicators of Educational Finance: Expenditures on Elementary-Secondary Education (all schools) in thousands of dollars

PROVINCE	TOTAL EXPENDITURES		PERCENTAGE INCREASE,
	1960	1970	1960-1970
BRITISH COLUMBIA	134,765	415,300	208%
ALBERTA	122,830	381,436	211
SASKATCHEWAN	79,670	193,832	143
MANITOBA	63,869	194,706	205
ONTARIO	481,844	1,901,254	295
QUEBEC	329,438	1,349,615	310
NEW BRUNSWICK	31,894	108,834	241
NOVA SCOTIA	44,048	136,892	211
PRINCE EDWARD ISLAND	4,214	16,428	290
NEWFOUNDLAND	19,881	66,584	235

Source: *Education in Canada* (1973), pp. 364-366. Reprinted by permission of the Minister of Supply and Services Canada.

Table 6.9b: Indicators of Educational Finance: Provincial Comparisons

	PER PUPIL COST*	
PROVINCE	1960-61	1969-70
BRITISH COLUMBIA	$384	$670
ALBERTA	391	779
SASKATCHEWAN	349	672
MANITOBA	302	645
ONTARIO	331	803
QUEBEC	264	701
NEW BRUNSWICK	194	542
NOVA SCOTIA	226	525
PRINCE EDWARD ISLAND	162	455
NEWFOUNDLAND	150	376
CANADA	305	797

*Source: *Education in Canada* (1973), pp. 375-376. Reprinted by permission of the Minister of Supply and Services Canada.

administrative expertise and the advice of professional educators. Where this is the case, policy-making will show few outward signs of controversy. Public and partisan involvement will be minimal, and the policy arena will be well defined and self-contained.

Patterns of Structural Development

It is not possible to fix precise dates to each major educational development in each province. One can, however, broadly outline the emergence of certain general objectives of education, most of which became reality during the nineteenth or early twentieth centuries. These include free public education, compulsory schooling to some minimum age, and the establishment of provincial departments or ministries of education. If we take the educational system of Ontario as an example, we can observe the gradual emergence of these principles starting with the early initiatives in Upper Canada through the efforts of Egerton Ryerson. The Schools Acts of 1850 and 1871, which realized the objective of free and compulsory education, can be seen as cornerstones of the modern provincial education system.[94] Although the timing and structural characteristics vary from province to province, with a few exceptions to be noted, all provinces gradually adopted these basic tenets of education.[95]

Ontario had established a Minister of Education by 1876. Over time the authority of the Minister was expanded by various pieces of legislation (*e.g.*, the Public Schools Act, the Schools Administration Act, the Separate Schools Act, and others). All Ministries of Education are

Table 6.9c: Indicators of Educational Finance: Expenditure on Post-Secondary Education

PROVINCE	TOTAL EXPENDITURE ($ 000)		PERCENT INCREASE	COST PER FULL-TIME STUDENT	
	1960	1970		1960-61	1970-71
BRITISH COLUMBIA	28,085	173,933	519	$1,412	$3,350
ALBERTA	29,388	205,090	586	1,508	3,359
SASKATCHEWAN	12,638	71,765	468	1,227	3,295
MANITOBA	15,206	85,040	459	1,512	3,289
ONTARIO	117,759	928,384	688	1,616	3,728
QUEBEC	99,691	468,384	370	1,270	2,671
NEW BRUNSWICK	7,922	45,684	476	1,044	2,590
NOVA SCOTIA	11,888	96,110	708	1,101	3,151
PRINCE EDWARD ISLAND	1,308	6,001	359	894	2,513
NEWFOUNDLAND	2,623	25,861	886	1,014	2,758
CANADA	272,940	1,767,301	548	1,389	3,226

Source: *Education in Canada* (1973), pp. 462-463, 468, 469. Reprinted by permission of the Minister of Supply and Services Canada.

primarily concerned with the enforcement and administration of such acts. This means that they are typically empowered to establish, organize, and regulate all schools and other educational institutions, to monitor and define guidelines for courses of study, to distribute provincial grants, to regulate and certify the status of teachers, to establish special education projects (for example, schools for the physically handicapped), and to regulate a wide variety of miscellaneous programmes related to educational objectives.

The development of centralized provincial control over education has not proceeded in the same way in all provinces. Quebec illustrates a pattern of development at great variance with that seen in Ontario. From 1875 until 1964 there existed no Minister of Education in Quebec. Policy-making authority was exercised by one Catholic and one Protestant permanent committee. The restricted nature of educational opportunity, primarily within the Catholic sector, is reflected in the fact that in 1950-51 only 16.5 percent of sixteen-year-olds were still attending school in Quebec. Secondary education remained an undeveloped public service. The *collèges classiques,* for the most part run by the Church, were the primary route to further education. Non-*collège* graduates were only eligible to enter science faculties and to a limited extent the commerce faculties. All others required the *baccalauréat ès arts* granted by the *collèges.*[96]

The 1960s witnessed a far-reaching transformation of public education in Quebec, although much of the dynamics of this change predates the Quiet Revolution. The report of the Tremblay Commission in 1956 provided an important stimulus for reform which gained momentum by the end of the Duplessis era. In response to such demands, as well as the recommendations of the Parent Commission, whose task it was to re-evaluate comprehensively the educational needs of a modernizing province, a series of major policy changes in the structure of education were implemented by the Lesage Liberal government.[97] The first and perhaps the most basic of these was the re-establishment of a Minister of Education. This made possible governmental control over planning and policy-making. Over the next few years there followed the organization of a comprehensive system of secondary education, including regional educational facilities, the consolidation of a multitude of small school districts into many fewer large ones, the establishment of a kindergarten system, the organization of a regional college system (CEGEPs) and the organization of a University of Quebec.[98]

The changes which took place in Quebec within a very short time contrast with the relatively incremental developments in Ontario and other provinces. We sometimes think of Quebec in the 1960s as the primary example of transformation in educational policy and structure. It is true that the Quiet Revolution and the Parent Commission were responsible for some very far-reaching, profound innovations. But at the same time it is inaccurate to think of other provinces as maintaining the status quo with respect to education policy in this period. Ontario, for example, while not repudiating many fundamental principles, developed through more than a century of public education, did institute very basic changes in the organization and policy directions of provincial education.[99]

Formal education originated as a concern of local communities and very often of sectarian groups. Neither organizational base was well adapted to satisfy the educational needs of an increasingly non-rural and secular society. It is hardly surprising to find, then, that along with the rapid expansion in enrolments, basic organizational reforms have also been necessary. One of the most fundamental of these has been the rationalization of local authority through a process of consolidation of many small districts into much larger ones.

In some cases, as in Quebec and Newfoundland, the decisions in favour of greater efficiency through consolidation have had potential for political controversy because they have threatened the traditional authority of denominational systems. In other provinces consolidation reforms were often seen as threats to de facto minority language rights. In areas like eastern and northern Ontario and northern New Brunswick, Francophones have often constituted a local majority where French has become the language of instruction in community schools. Consolidation meant that many of these smaller schools would be closed and that Francophone pupils would become a minority submerged within much larger English-speaking majority districts. In other cases, most particularly the three westernmost provinces, such policy change has come about with relative ease by regrouping of school districts. For example, by 1972 British Columbia had transformed six hundred and fifty school districts into seventy-four larger ones.[100] Ontario from 1960 to 1974 had gone from over 3600 to 200. Catholic school boards in Quebec declined from 1300 to about 180 between 1967 and 1972.[101] All other provinces had by this time achieved similar reorganization or had before them recommendations of royal commissions dealing with these questions.

A second very basic area of reform, of concern to all provinces, has been educational finance. There have traditionally been three sources: fees, local taxes, and grants from some higher level(s) of government. Fees assessed to individual students (or their families) were once widespread. But as education moved from a private to a public service most such fees were discarded. Only in Newfoundland were school fees paid until recently for basic education.[102] (Some financing through student tuition fees is, of course, still common for university education.)

But in Canada today almost all public and secondary education is supported by a combination of the latter two sources.[103]

As the scope and functions of the educational sector expanded in importance, its relative share of provincial budgets increased. Local school districts, as the traditional organizational units of a limited education system, were complemented by a pattern of local property taxes and sometimes school fees as the only means of financial support. This system had two serious weaknesses. First, local resources in many small communities were limited. While they might have been sufficient for supporting an old-fashioned one-room school house and the salaries of one or two teachers (typically with little training), they could never hope to pay for large schools including more expensive secondary facilities which depend on more and better qualified staff and equipment. The second weakness involves the unequal distribution of educational finances which inevitably was detrimental to the goal of equality of educational opportunity. Some communities have far more resources to tax than do others and, therefore, can provide better facilities and a higher quality of education.* Thus, all provinces sooner or later have had to face the difficult question of financing, which has become particularly acute with the rapid expansion of costly secondary education. Most provinces have relied heavily on both local and provincial sources. Where local property taxes have continued to provide an important share of the costs of education, problems of equity across school districts have become acute.[104]

Table 6.10 provides a comparison of the source of education funding. It is clear that all provinces except British Columbia have since 1960 moved towards greater reliance on provincial revenues as a means of compensating for the disparities among school districts. Most provinces have established foundation programmes having the common objective of guaranteeing minimum educational services through the equalization of school revenues across all districts.[105] Three of the Atlantic provinces (New Brunswick, Prince Edward Island, and Newfoundland) have dealt with this problem through centralization of school financing.[106]

Post-secondary Education and Public Policy

Many of the same forces responsible for the extraordinary growth of secondary education produced a correspondingly significant expansion in

*Recognition of comparable disparities on a provincial and regional level encouraged federal initiatives, especially in post-secondary and vocational education.

Table 6.10 Financing of Elementary and Secondary Education by Source of Funds

	FEDERAL	PROVINCIAL	MUNICIPAL	FEES	OTHER
B.C.					
1960	4.9%	45.6%	44.1%	2.3%	3.1%
1970	2.9	44.3	47.5	2.1	3.2
ALTA.					
1960	4.1	48.5	44.3	1.5	1.6
1970	3.4	58.1	35.3	2.0	1.2
SASK.					
1960	5.6	40.5	48.7	2.2	3.0
1970	7.4	47.4	43.6	1.1	0.5
MAN.					
1960	7.8	42.0	48.4	1.8	—
1970	6.1	49.3	39.0	2.2	3.4
ONT.					
1960	1.9	38.6	55.4	2.6	1.5
1970	1.5	53.4	41.4	1.7	2.0
QUE.					
1960	1.4	36.9	49.6	7.9	4.2
1970	4.8	59.1	31.5	2.2	2.4
N.B.					
1960	2.3	34.3	56.1	3.0	4.3
1970	8.8	89.4	—	0.6	1.2
N.S.					
1960	3.8	49.1	43.8	1.6	1.7
1970	5.5	56.2	35.0	1.2	2.1
P.E.I.					
1960	4.5	60.7	31.6	3.1	0.1
1970	3.2	71.9	23.4	0.6	0.9
NFLD.					
1960	1.7	85.9	1.1	3.9	7.4
1970	0.3	89.3	1.1	1.7	7.6

Source: *Education in Canada* (1973), pp. 368-369. Reprinted by permission of the Minister of Supply and Services Canada.

higher education. Until World War II, university education in Canada remained quite limited and had shown no signs of dramatic change. The return to Canada of large numbers of veterans brought a revitalizing jolt to these institutions. Between 1945 and 1946 enrolments jumped by fifty percent. In the 1950s rapid population growth (through a high birth rate plus increased immigration), coupled with new manpower needs for highly specialized and highly educated personnel, combined to provide a solid foundation for the development of higher education.[107]

Table 6.11: Provincial Education Policy: Higher Education

PROVINCE	FULL-TIME POST-SECONDARY ENROLMENT AS PERCENTAGE OF 18-24 AGE GROUP		POST-SECONDARY COST PER FULL-TIME STUDENT	
	1960-61	1974-75	1960-61	1970-71
BRITISH COLUMBIA	10.8	15.1	$1,412	3,350
ALBERTA	7.9	19.9	1,508	3,359
SASKATCHEWAN	9.8	13.4	1,227	3,295
MANITOBA	9.5	15.6	1,512	3,289
ONTARIO	9.0	20.5	1,616	3,728
QUEBEC	11.0	22.1	1,270	2,671
NEW BRUNSWICK	9.7	12.4	1,044	2,590
NOVA SCOTIA	10.3	18.2	1,101	3,151
PRINCE EDWARD ISLAND	8.5	14.5	884	2,513
NEWFOUNDLAND	3.9	10.1	1,014	2,758
CANADA	9.7	18.4	1,389	3,246

Source: *Education in Canada* (1973), pp. 400-404, 468-470; (1975) p. 154. Reprinted by permission of the Minister of Supply and Services Canada.

Table 6.11, using enrolment figures and costs per student, gives an idea of how higher education grew in each province after 1960, the period of greatest development. This expansion is in a reality a combination of policy developments. Already existing universities, most of which originated as privately controlled denominational institutions, gradually passed from church to state control as a result of the exigencies of financial support. Existing institutions grew in size at the same time that new ones were being founded. A total of twenty-eight universities in 1945 grew into forty-seven by 1969. Total university enrolments went from less than 115,000 in 1960 to 355,000 in 1970.[107]

One of the most significant policy changes in post-secondary education in the 1960s was the establishment and growth of community colleges. Between 1964 and 1968, Ontario established a network of twenty Colleges of Applied Arts and Technology.[109] Quebec, following the recommendations of the Parent Commission, set up its CEGEPs (Collèges d'enseignement général et professionel), which numbered 37 by 1974. The Ontario system was originally designed as a terminal programme in vocational and technical training. The Quebec system, in contrast, became a new intermediate tier in the educational structure, offering both a terminal vocational programme and a pre-university programme.[110]

Institutions with functions similar to those of the Ontario system have been established in other provinces. British Columbia, for example, by 1972 had ten such vocational schools. Of the western provinces, British Columbia and Alberta have proceeded furthest with non-university post-secondary education.[111] Since 1964 several new technical colleges have been founded in the Atlantic provinces.[112]

Policy change in higher education cannot be seen as a purely provincial phenomenon. Much of the impetus for change came from Ottawa. In 1951-52 the Federal Government initiated a system of grants on a per capita basis to aid in the financing of university education. Over the years the formula used for calculating increased the federal contributions. Through the 1967 Federal Provincial Fiscal Arrangements Act, the Federal Government granted tax points to the provinces to cover fifty percent of the cost of higher education. This arrangement was renegotiated in 1977.[113]

A second federal decision of immense importance to the development of higher education in the provinces was the 1960 Technical and Vocational Training Assistance Act, according to which the federal government would finance seventy-five percent of capital and fifty percent of operating costs of technical and vocational training facilities. This made possible the creation of the complex array of community and technical colleges noted above.[114]

Religion and Education Policy

Education policy often goes unnoticed by the public because it is thought to involve professional matters, such as the optimal content, process, or structure which will assure given levels of knowledge and understanding in students. To the extent that these are technical matters, they are perhaps most appropriately handled by educational specialists. The latter typically include school boards, teachers, officials from the Ministry of Education, and pedagogic experts. At other times, however, interested publics become very sensitive to, even aroused by, issues of education policy,[115] because there is felt to be much more at stake than simply the relative excellence of the educational system. This is due to the fact that education policy has value implications for the larger society. Thus social groups may see in the struggle over education both material and emotive issues which impinge upon the future status of the group itself.

In the Canadian experience, education policy has tended to become the base for very intense controversy and conflict where it has been associated with religious and linguistic differences. The linkage between religion and education is recognized in the BNA Act (Section 93). The institutional variation in religious or sectarian involvement in Canadian schools can be summarized by a three-fold distinction in type of school system—denominational, separate, and non-sectarian.

In its simplest form, a denominational system is one in which the entire education process is organized and administered by a church or churches. Such systems are at the origin of many present-day educational structures and were common to most provinces when schools were first established in the nineteenth century. They have survived into the modern era in only two provinces, Quebec and Newfoundland, but in both of these cases, important policy innovations of the 1960s brought about substantial modifications which had the effect of lessening denominational control. Denominational control has never meant the total absence of state involvement, for in both provinces there has been a long-standing pattern of provincial financial support. In addition, not all facets of the educational system have been denominational. In Quebec, for example, a state-controlled sector including vocational schools, technical schools, and craft schools, can be dated from the turn of the century. Some post-elementary and secondary facilities were added later.

Despite such hybrid features, the denominational model does imply little or no governmental policy control over the education process. This represents a fundamental difference from a separate school system. The latter type also allows for the participation of religious organizations in schooling but within the principle of public accountability and public authority over the entire educational process. Typically in this situation governments through their Ministers of Education set general guidelines and supervise the conduct of all schools. Within these constraints, religious groups may establish and run their own separate schools with public financing. In simple terms the separate school system, in contrast to the denominational, assures public control but sectarian adminis-tration of parts of the education system.

Ontario, Saskatchewan, and Alberta all maintain this type of system, but separate schools are far more important in Ontario than in the other two.[116] Both separate and denominational school systems, where they exist, are recognized constitutionally either in the BNA Act (for the four original provinces) or in the various Acts conferring provincial status on former territories.[117]

The third type of system, which we have called non-sectarian, does not sanction any religious participation in the administration, teaching, or other school functions. Public education means secular control of education in all essential respects. Sectarian or church schools do exist in provinces having this system—but they do so as private schools without public financial support.* British Columbia, Manitoba, New Brunswick, Nova Scotia, and Prince Edward Island all maintain such systems.

The nature of religious involvement is a good deal more complex and varied than this broad distinction among three types of systems would suggest. Religious conflicts have produced some of the most contentious issues at the centre of education policy. Religious heterogeneity is in itself a poor predictor of sectarian-based conflicts over education policy. Some provinces with substantial religious minorities have developed a pattern of education policy which is virtually free of such divisions. This is the case for British Columbia, which established non-sectarian public schools early, a decision which has never been seriously questioned.[118] Similarly, none of the Maritime provinces had established a system of separate or denominational schools at the time of joining Confederation and, therefore, institutionalized the principle of non-sectarianism in their school systems.

In Nova Scotia, there also developed a tradition on the part of provincial governments of avoiding decisions with connotations of advantage or disadvantage to religious interests. Such matters have typically been left to local authorities.[119] One result of this pattern of decentralization of responsibility is that locally based accommodations have been common. Thus, Catholic minorities (which in some communities are local majorities) have been able to obtain Catholic teachers and even provide religious instruction after hours without having to struggle for the right to do so province-wide. Similar circumstances characterize Prince Edward Island, where the accepted practice of accommodating religious minority interests has often been at variance with the legal basis of non-sectarian education.[120]

In contrast to these four provinces, the pre-confederation origins of education in Saskatchewan and Alberta were denominational, following the Quebec model. However, various ordinances for the North West Territories between 1886 and 1901 succeeded in establishing the basis for a separate school system along the lines of Ontario's. This was confirmed in 1905 in the Acts granting provincial status to both.[121] Religion and education in these provinces have, from time to time, combined to produce political disagreements. For example, the status of separate schools was a matter of direct political concern in the pre-First World War years and again in the late 1920s in Saskatchewan,[122] although the separate school system never became as important a source of controversy as in Ontario.[123] In both Alberta and Saskatchewan

*This type of system is broadly similar to the dominant pattern in the United States, based on the principle of separation of church and state.

separate schools remained relatively few in number. One reason for this in the latter case was the development of Catholic participation within public schools much along the accommodative lines already noted in Nova Scotia and New Brunswick.[124]

The origins of education in Manitoba were, like those of its prairie neighbours, denominational. But as a result of the political struggles of the late nineteenth and early twentieth centuries, this province has today a non-sectarian school system. The Manitoba School Question stands as the most dramatic historical episode of this sort precisely because it incorporated in a highly polarized and intense way the division between Catholic-French and Protestant-English. It crystallized more acutely than any other issue the basic division in Canadian society, and it set a pattern of division to be repeated later and in much of the rest of Canada.[125] Some of the same kinds of conflict over education occurred around the same time in Ontario and in other provinces, and were to have profound influence on later developments.

Nowhere is the link between religion and politics more enduring than in Ontario.[126] The status of separate schools has provided the main policy arena for controversy, conflict and influence on the part of religious interests.[127] The Separate Schools Act of 1863 is part of the heritage from the formative pre-Confederation, Ryerson era in Ontario education. The status of separate schools was made permanent by the British North America Act, Section 93(1). Several problems were unforeseen by this early legislation and were to form the substance of later disagreement. Under the Ontario system parents may send their children to separate schools, pay school taxes to the local separate school board and remain exempt from what would otherwise amount to a double taxation to the public school system. Despite this assured source of revenue, the nature of school financing has remained the most fundamental difficulty and source of disagreement over the separate school system.[128]

In Ontario as elsewhere, school costs have traditionally been covered by a combination of local property taxes and provincial grants. (For a provincial comparison of the provincial-local shares see Table 6.10.) Local property taxes vary from community to community because of differences in assessed property values—which reflect differences in real wealth. Local Separate School revenues are based on the assessed values of separate school supporters. Property values (and, therefore, tax capacity) for these supporters have always been lower than for public school supporters.[129] This limited tax base has often been reduced even further by some Roman Catholic families opting for the public schools. The sharp post-war increases in school enrolment were especially great for Roman Catholic separate schools, which had 20 percent of all elementary pupils in 1953, 26.9 percent in 1963, and 30.4

percent in 1974. These increases magnified both the financial pressures and the perception of material disadvantage facing these schools.[130]

An additional source of difficulty has been legal constraints on school redistricting for separate schools. The original legislation had provided that separate school districts be defined by a three-mile radius around the school. This meant that potential separate school supporters beyond this circle were excluded. It also provided a constitutional impediment (or was so interpreted) against provincial efforts at consolidation of districts.[131]

The second major source of grievance, closely related to the problem of financial support, concerns the place of separate schools in secondary education. In the nineteenth century, public education most commonly meant elementary education. Secondary education existed for only a small, propertied segment of the population. But as high schools developed into institutions of mass education supported by public resources, the exclusion of the separate school system from a share in this financial support accentuated the discrepancy between the separate and common school systems. The 1871 High School Act made no provision for separate secondary education. Even into the present, all provincial grants for separate schools are set at the elementary per pupil rate and provide support for separate school pupils only through the tenth grade. Separate school supporters must pay a share of their taxes to the public secondary system for grades eleven through thirteen.[132]

During the 1960s the inequality of support for separate schooling at this level gave rise to organized pressure by separate school supporters for a basic change in policy by the Ontario government. In 1971, after considerable delay and reflection, Premier Davis decided against any extension of support.[133] The issue had become a clearly partisan one in which the Tories opted to oppose any extension in provincial support for separate schools while Liberals and New Democrats alike supported such a policy change.

In Quebec it is only in recent times that education policy, and especially the role of denominational interests in the school system, has become a focal point for controversy. Until the Quiet Revolution of the 1960s, conflict over the rights of religious and linguistic groups was kept out of the provincial policy arena by a combination of denominational control, which meant little state involvement in educational planning and policy, and an effectively decentralized division between French Catholics and English non-Catholics.[134] This division assured the minority group autonomy over its own schools.[135] The emphasis on local property taxes as the primary revenue source for education proved to be advantageous to the Protestant school system and is undoubtedly an important explanation for the lack of minority group grievance which has been so common within the Ontario separate school system.[136]

Between 1875 and 1964 there existed no Ministry of Education in Quebec. This absence reflected a situation in which the provincial government effectively gave up direct control over educational policy-making and delegated such authority to two permanent committees of the Public Education Council,[137] one Catholic and one Protestant. Much of secondary and higher education remained in private hands. Of the many innovations which characterized the 1960s in Quebec, one had particular significance for the place of the Church in the field of education, namely, the re-establishment of a Ministry of Education, because it provided a means for province-wide control, planning, and *public* policy-making.[138] Some of the structures of the old denominational system were left intact. But this change had the effect of secularizing policy-making in the field of education. It was followed by a number of major policy innovations, for example, the establishment of post-secondary CEGEPs and, by 1970, a provincial university system which transferred all of higher education from private to public hands.[139]

Newfoundland, like Quebec, entered the 1960s with a denominational system of education dating from the nineteenth century, which had gained constitutional legitimacy through the Terms of Union making Newfoundland a province. The traditional system was in fact a mix of church and state power for "while the schools were church-owned and operated, the Government held the power of the purse and, in fact, through the Minister, possessed a great deal of veto power."[140]

In contrast to Quebec, the denominational system in Newfoundland had evolved into a very fragmented arrangement in which the various denominations ran their own schools.[141] This produced an inefficient overabundance of small, often one- or two-room schools, located in outports that could ill-afford them.[142] As in Quebec, fundamental policy innovations in these years had dramatic implications for the policy-making authority of the denominations.[143]

The two most important changes in education in Newfoundland were consolidation and governmental reorganization. Consolidation meant reduction in both the number of districts and the number of schools. But, given the multiplicity of church schools in the province, effective consolidation required denominational compromise, that is, the merging together of small schools. The 1969 decision of the three largest Protestant churches to consolidate all educational facilities was a monumental step in the modernization of Newfoundland's schools.[144]

One of the most important recommendations of the Royal Commission on Education and Youth was for a reorganization along functional lines of the Department of Education. The Department had been organized along denominational groupings, but in 1968 the four largest denominations agreed to the recommended functional re-organization.[145] The effect of this was to shift denominational authorities out of a direct policy-making role and into an advisory one. Thus, both consolidation and structural reorganization have had a secularizing effect on the pattern of education policy in Newfoundland.

From a comparative provincial perspective, religion has influenced numerous issues in education policy-making. These issues include the right of church-run schools to exist; basic structural questions, such as consolidation, administrative reorganization, and the development of secondary education; questions of teacher certification and qualifications; and the basis and extent of public financing. For some provinces, like British Columbia, such matters have had few religious connotations for the broad pattern of provincial policy-making. In others, like Ontario, they have been of high sectarian salience and have helped shape the style and context of provincial politics.

Language and Education Policy

Religion and language have frequently been closely linked in political conflicts over educational and cultural policy. But it is useful to keep in mind that religious and linguistic interests are far from identical, and some policy problems, for example, the fight over separate schools, may involve both while others, such as the use of French as a second language of instruction, may involve primarily one.

An additional obstacle in analysing the role of language in the field of education is that the politics of language is much broader than this policy area. Linguistic-ethnic interests cross-cut several policy areas and levels of government. To the extent that the politics of language have impinged on educational policy, language issues have at certain epochs been a prime concern of provincial governments.[146] In several provinces—New Brunswick, Manitoba, Ontario, and Quebec—language has been a source of historic and deeply-felt divisions. Language has, of course, also been a concern of federal politics and language rights and bilingual/bicultural objectives have been grounds for some federal involvement in education—at times creating federal-provincial tensions. But at the federal level, much more than at the provincial, the language question has also involved issues of communication policy, bilingualism in the public service, cultural policy, and native peoples.[147]

Since our concern is primarily with provincial public policy, our consideration of the politics of language emphasizes those issues which have been and still are of major concern to provincial governments. This naturally means that some aspects of linguistic politics—those in which the federal government has been the main policy arena—will receive less attention.

In Ontario, the existing French-language schools were not the subject of dispute at the time of Confederation. They were, however, to become controversial by the end of the nineteenth century.[148] Controversy eventually led to Regulation 17 in 1912, which effectively abolished French as a language of instruction in Ontario schools and prompted an extended period of litigation and controversy.[149] An accommodation on French-language rights was reached in 1927, but the effect of conflict over this issue "resulted in what might be called a 'non-system' of education for Franco-Ontarians. These schools operated in isolation; they were not part of the English-language system of education in the province, and they lacked the planning, the guidance, and the co-ordination essential to an adequate educational regime."[150]

In recent years the Government of Ontario has taken several policy initiatives of considerable significance for minority language rights in education. Present legislation requires school boards to provide French language instruction where a minimum of twenty-five elementary pupils or twenty secondary students request it.[151] In 1975 French language enrolments represented 5.5 percent of total (combined elementary and secondary) enrolments in the province.[152] There has also been a greater effort to increase bilingual facility among anglophone students, and French is now an optional subject in all elementary and secondary schools. Selected schools offer French immersion programmes.[153]

In Manitoba the language issue has, as already noted, historically been tied to religious conflicts in education. The Laurier-Greenway compromise of 1897 allowed only token relief for French Catholic grievances. In 1916 all French-language instruction was banned. This situation was not altered until 1967 when the Roblin Government re-introduced French as a language of instruction. By 1970 Manitoba had extended minority language rights along the same lines as Ontario.[154]

The New Brunswick Common School Act of 1871 denied legal status to separate schools and precipitated a conflict based on the same religious-ethnic divisions which were to define a long-term crisis in Canadian education.[155] In its origins religion formed the primary cleavage in the politics of education. But the pattern of educational policy which emerged in New Brunswick had, at the very least, the effect of consistently neglecting the needs of the Acadian minority. Because Francophones represent more than a third of the province's population, it is hardly surprising that much of the demand for change would eventually reflect this fact. The 1960s witnessed fundamental changes in New Brunswick education. Today most Francophone children are taught in French-language elementary schools.[156] Until the last ten years the opportunity for secondary and higher education remained extremely limited for Acadians. Important changes, including the establishment of a French university in Moncton, have ameliorated this condition.[157]

In the other six predominantly anglophone provinces the French-speaking communities remain very small. French language is available in some localities but is not guaranteed legally.' In several of these provinces controversies over language have been of considerable historic importance, but now are no longer major issues on the provincial agenda.[158]

The development of bilingualism in the schools has been a policy change of profound importance in several provinces. But the focal point in recent years for the politics of language and education has undoubtedly become the province of Quebec. The status of both religious and linguistic minorities has traditionally not been a source of controversy because minority interests have been well guarded legally and in practice. The stimulus for the current policy conflict in Quebec derives from the perception of threat to the status of Québécois culture and to the future of the French language. The declining proportion of Francophones in Canada because of an extraordinary decline in the birth rate in Quebec from 1958 to 1970, along with a pronounced tendency for immigrants to adopt English as a second language and to enrol their children in English schools, precipitated an educational crisis. To some extent, the rise of separatist sentiment which brought the PQ to power in 1976 can be seen as a political effect of this issue. In direct response to these developments several governments from the late 1960s on have initiated a series of language policies. The first of these, Bill 63, which was introduced in 1969 by a fading Union Nationale government, confirmed the right of parents to choose the language of instruction for their children. It had the effect of intensifying Francophone feeling on the language question and in mobilizing opposition to the Bertrand government prior to the 1970 provincial election. Bill 22, passed by the Bourassa government in 1974, moved Quebec away from the principle of bilingualism by making French the sole official language. Some competence in the language was also set as a condition of entry into English-language schools. In addition, ministerial approval was required for any change in the size of English-language facilities.[159] These turned out to be half-way measures which left Francophone nationalists dissatisfied and Anglophones, as well as various immigrant groups, visibly angered.

The Parti Québécois election victory in November, 1976 escalated Quebec's internal divisions over language policy and expanded the policy arena to include the federal government and the other provinces. Bill 1 (later Bill 101), introduced in early 1977, represents a continuation of the initiatives of Bill 22 in further restricting the opportunity for education in English by denial of the right of parents to choose which language school their children would attend. Henceforth, all immigrants would be chanelled into the French school system. English language schools are to remain available only for pupils with at least one parent who received an English education in Quebec. Thus the school policy of the Parti Québécois rejects the principle of bilingualism. Minority language rights will not apply to new non-francophone immigrants. The long-term effect of this policy is clearly to bring about the gradual shrinking of anglophone education through a generational erosion and to assure that French would remain as the dominant language of everyday use.

CONCLUSIONS

Although differing in their patterns of development, welfare, health, and education policies have all had similar effects on two broad areas of Canadian politics and society. The first is their impact on the role and importance of the provinces as policy-making institutions. The second concerns the extent to which the social goals of security and equality have been achieved.

The advance of the welfare state is not unique to Canada. Indeed, in comparison with similar innovations in many European states, Canadian policy-makers have been laggard in the provision of social security. What may be unique in the Canadian case is the importance of the provinces in this process. In most nations increased centralization has been a concomitant of the emergence of the welfare state, the new or increased responsibilities being generally taken up by national governments. In Canada, in contrast, social policy development has led to the strengthening of the provinces. In the 1940s and 1950s it was often argued that the federal government had to assume responsibility for the social needs of Canadians. Despite this pressure for centralization and federal incursions through a universal family allowance programme and constitutional amendments giving Ottawa authority for unemployment insurance and old-age benefits, the provinces were able to retain the core of their jurisdictional authority over social policy. The problem of insufficient provincial revenues has been dealt with by increased federal transfers rather than by increased federal functions. The present arrangements for tax abatements and cash payments as the federal contributions to welfare, health, and post-secondary education recognize the primary policy role of the provinces. In sum, one impact of the social policies of the welfare state has been to augment the position of provincial governments by increasing the scope of provincial policy-making, and the development of these new services has helped to create provincial bureaucracies that can compete with experts in Ottawa.

The meaning of the welfare state has been defined in two alternative ways. For some, the welfare state is limited to the creation of a safety net for all members of society in which the state guarantees a minimum standard below which no individual should fall. For others the concept of the welfare state is broader and connotes policies directed toward a more equitable distribution of income in the society. Canadian decision-makers have, at some times, endorsed a minimum standard and at others, an equitable income distribution as policy goals. The question is the extent to which developments in welfare, health, and education have brought about the achievement of either goal. Several studies of policy and income distribution provide a basis for judgment. Analyses that compare the pre-tax, pre-transfer distribution of income with income distribution levels after taxes, and transfers, conclude that the net effect of governmental activities is a very modest redistribution of income toward the poor.[160] Much of the progressive effect (that is, from the well-off to the poor) of income-maintenance transfer programmes such as old-age pensions and unemployment insurance, is mitigated by the regressive impact of the tax system.

If we can conclude from these studies that there has been no major shift in income from the well-off to the poor, there remains the question of whether a minimum floor has been created. Certainly poverty still exists in Canada; even in the richest provinces, at least ten percent of the families live below the poverty line defined by Statistics Canada. Nonetheless, there is also evidence that since World War II there has been a significant decline in the extent of poverty, since today a lower percentage of family income fall below currently defined poverty lines than in earlier years.[161]

Studies of the health care system point in the same direction as welfare analyses.[162] There can be no doubt that public health insurance has raised the level of health care services for all income groups. However, the bias in health care utilization patterns has persisted. Upper and middle income Canadians continue to make more consistent use of health services than do lower income groups. As with welfare, it appears that, although there are important limitations stemming from both non-financial barriers to access and the maldistribution of medical resources, a minimum level of health care has been achieved.

The situation with regard to education is more complex. First, in the case of elementary and secondary schools the pattern of financing (municipal taxes and/or provincial revenues) is not progressive. Yet schools are available to all classes, and, therefore, the benefits are progressive. At the post-secondary level there is an overall regressive impact. Not only is the financing side (provincial and federal revenues) regressive, but the benefits are too. One observer of post-secondary systems has concluded, "The existing pattern of university education in Ontario strongly favours the rich and subsidizes the middle and high-income groups at the expense of the lower income groups."[163]

It is worth noting that the regressive impact of the post-secondary system is heightened when we move beyond a simple comparison of the costs and immediate benefits of education and consider long-term benefits. University education is related to later earnings, therefore, the present system provides the well-off with the skills to maintain their position in the future at the expense of the poor.

On the question as to what extent the goals of the welfare state have been achieved, it may be concluded that despite a large public sector and a significant government regulatory role, there has been only the most limited movement toward a redistribution of income. However, taken together these social policies do constitute a safety net which protects the public from certain universal risks.

NOTES

1. For general discussions of the rise of the welfare state, see Harold Wilensky, *The Welfare State and Equality*, University of California, Berkeley, 1975; Richard Titmuss, *Commitment to Welfare*, Allen and Unwin, London, 1968; Gaston Rimlinger, *Welfare Policy and Industrialization in Europe, America and Russia*, John Wiley, New York, 1971; Hugh Heclo, *Modern Social Politics in Britain and Sweden*, Yale University Press, New Haven, 1974; William Robson, *Welfare State and Welfare Society*, Allen and Unwin, London, 1976; and Maurice Bruce (ed.), *The Rise of the Welfare State*, Weidenfeld and Nicolson, London, 1973.

2. This conception of the role of the state is found in the two reports that formed much of the basis of the welfare state in Britain and Canada. See Sir Wm. Beveridge, *Social Insurance and Allied Services*, King's Printer, London, 1942; and Leonard Marsh, *Social Security for Canada*, King's Printer, Ottawa, 1943.

3. For example, see Arnold Heidenheimer, "The Politics of Public Education, Health and Welfare in the U.S.A. and Western Europe: How Growth and Reform Potentials have Differed," *British Journal of Political Science*, 3 July, 1973.

4. For a discussion of these and other politically significant needs see Ronald Manzer, *Canada: A Socio-Political Report*, McGraw-Hill Ryerson, Toronto, 1974.

5. Heclo, *op. cit.*, p. 13.

6. For a discussion of the early role of the municipalities and voluntary organizations in a province where they were especially important, see Richard Splane, *Social Welfare in Ontario, 1791-1893*, University of Toronto Press, Toronto, 1965, Chapter 3.

7. Henry Cassidy, *Public Health and Welfare Reorganization*, Ryerson, Toronto, 1945, p. 62.

8. These were put forward in the "Green Book" proposals at the Dominion-Provincial Conference on Reconstruction (1945).

9. See Piet Thoenes, *The Elite in the Welfare State,* Free Press, New York, 1966. Many political economists have also argued that welfare policies have both a legitimating and accumulating function. See, for example, James O'Connor, *The Fiscal Crisis of the State,* St. Martin's, New York, 1973; and essays by Panitch, Swartz, Finkel, and Schecter in Leo Panitch, (ed.), *The Canadian State: Political Economy and Political Power,* University of Toronto Press, Toronto, 1976.

10. Quoted in Splane, *op. cit.,* p. 16.

11. Richard Titmuss, *Social Policy,* Allen and Unwin, London, 1974, p. 74. The same belief was expressed in Canada when the Special Senate Committee on Poverty asserted the poor are "casualties of the way we manage our economy and society." *Poverty in Canada,* Information Canada, Ottawa, 1971, p. xxviii.

12. See Pierre Fournier, *The Quebec Establishment,* Black Rose Books, Montreal, 1976, p. 144.

13. See Richard Simeon, *Federal-Provincial Diplomacy: The Making of Recent Policy in Canada,* McGill-Queen's, Montreal, 1972, Chapter 3; and Kenneth Bryden, *Old Age Pensions and Policy-Making in Canada,* McGill-Queens, Montreal, 1972, Chapter 8.

14. These three policy principles are used to describe the development of Canadian social welfare policy by Ronald Manzer, "Public Policies in Canada: A Developmental Perspective," paper presented to CPSA, Edmonton, 1975.

15. Richard Bird, *Charging for Public Services: A New Look at an Old Idea,* Canadian Tax Foundation, Toronto, 1976, discusses this with regard to Canada's welfare insurance plans, pp. 174-185. See also A. Heidenheimer, *et al., Comparing Public Policy,* St. Martins, New York, 1975, Chapter 7 for a similar discussion with regard to Western Europe and the United States.

16. Andrew Armitage, *Social Welfare in Canada,* McClelland and Stewart, Toronto, 1976, p. 24.

17. Ontario's legislation was the first programme which made the insurance compulsory and administered by an independent board. Quebec had an earlier programme of workmen's compensation (1909), but it did not contain these two crucial elements.

18. Manzer, *op. cit.,* p. 23.

19. The other instances of universal provincial programmes are supplementary family allowance in Newfoundland, Prince Edward Island, and Quebec.

20. See David Kwavnick (ed.), *The Tremblay Report,* McClelland and Stewart, Toronto, 1973, pp. 63-78.

21. Special Senate Committee on Poverty, *Poverty in Canada,* Information Canada, Ottawa, 1971, p. 67.

22. However, within a province there may be municipal residence requirements for municipal assistance.

23. D.V. Smiley, *Canada in Question: Federalism in the Seventies*, Second Edition, McGraw-Hill Ryerson, Toronto, 1976, pp. 44-50.

24. Federal-Provincial Working Party on Income Maintenance, *Background Paper on Income Support and Supplementation*, Ottawa, 1975, p. 3.

25. "Groups working for handicapped will fight Ottawa's New Plan," in *Toronto Globe and Mail*, October 3, 1977, and "Keep funds control, social agencies tell Ottawa," in *Toronto Globe and Mail*, October 28, 1977. Bloc financing has also been criticized because it will contribute to greater inequality in the provincial provision of social services. That is, poorer provinces, requiring more federal assistance, would fall even further behind in the provision of social services. See "Lalonde's legacy: step to inequality," in *Toronto Globe and Mail*, November 10, 1977.

26. Cassidy, *op. cit.*, p. 142.

27. Statistics Canada, *Income Distribution by Size in Canada*, 1974, p. 136. This publication also provides the provincial distribution of low income families.

28. There is no agreed-upon single poverty standard in Canada. For a comparison of the various poverty lines that have been put forward see David Ross, *Canadian Fact Book on Poverty*, Canadian Council on Social Development, Ottawa, 1975.

29. The Canadian Council on Social Development proposes defining poverty as a family income that is fifty percent or less than the average Canadian income. See *Social Security for Canada 1973*, Ottawa, 1973, p. 147. Statistics Canada originally based its low income (poverty line) standard on the proportion of family income to be spent on food and shelter. Any family that must spend seventy percent or more of its income on food and shelter is considered low income. Although the actual determination of low income has been revised and updated the essential determination is still based on the proportion of income spent on food and shelter. See *Income Distribution by Size in Canada*, 1973, p. 17 for an explanation of current low income cut-offs.

30. Cassidy, *op. cit.*, p. 46.

31. For a discussion of the policy impact of socialist parties in Canada see W.M. Chandler, "Canadian Socialism and Policy Impact: Contagion from the Left?" in *Canadian Journal of Political Science* 10, December, 1977, pp. 755-780.

32. Bryden, *op. cit.*, p. 15.

33. For a discussion of early efforts in children's welfare see Splane, *op. cit.*, and M.K. Strong, *Public Welfare Administration in Canada*, University of Chicago, Chicago, 1930, Chapter 13.

34. For an excellent analysis of Ontario's profitable response to a shared-cost programme see Stefan Dupré *et al.*, *Federalism and Policy*

    Development: The Case of Adult Occupational Training in Ontario,
    University of Toronto, Toronto, 1973.
35. See Terry Copp, *Anatomy of Poverty,* McClelland and Stewart,
    Toronto, 1974, and Dale Posgate and Ken McRoberts, *Quebec: Social
    Change and Political Crisis,* McClelland and Stewart, Toronto, 1976,
    pp. 43-64.
36. Ramsay Cook, *Maple Leaf Forever,* Macmillan, Toronto, 1971, p. 86.
37. Armitage, *op. cit.,* pp. 167-169.
38. Cassidy, *op. cit.,* pp. 392-440.
39. For a discussion of the party systems in each of the Atlantic
    Provinces see: P.J. Fitzpatrick, "The Policies of Pragmatism," Susan
    McCorquodale, "The Only Father's Living Realm," J.M. Beck, "The
    Party System in Nova Scotia: Tradition and Conservatism," and
    Frank MacKinnon, "Big Engine Little Body," all in Martin Robin
    (ed.), *Canadian Provincial Politics,* Prentice-Hall, Toronto, 1972.
40. This description is drawn from Ontario Welfare Council, *The
    Province of Ontario: Its Social Services,* Toronto, 1974.
41. For discussions of the variations in Ontario and across Canada
    see Ontario Economic Council, *Issues and Alternatives 1976: Social
    Security,* Toronto, 1976, p. 16, and Marc Lalonde, *Working Paper on
    Social Security,* Queen's Printer, Ottawa, 1973, p. 13.
42. Bird, *op. cit.,* p. 162. See also Simon McInnes, "Canadian Social
    Policy Studies: A Classificatory Exercise," paper presented to
    C.P.S.A., Fredericton, 1977.
43. As has been pointed out in many criticisms of the social security
    system, full time employment for one person at the minimum wage
    guarantees an income above the poverty line only in the case of an
    unattached individual. Furthermore, minimum wage earnings are
    not related to family size, but social assistance does vary with
    family size.
48. *Income Support and Supplementation,* Ottawa, 1975. For contrasting
    assessments of the Social Security Review see Johnson, *op. cit.,;*
    A.M. Moore, "Income Security and Federal Finance," pp. 473-479;
    and R.C. Baetz and K. Collins, "Equity Aspects of Income Security
    Programs," pp. 487-497, *Canadian Public Policy,* I:4 Autumn, 1975.
49. *Poverty in Canada,* p. 169.
50. For descriptions of the beginnings of public health services see
    J. Hastings and W. Mosley, *Organized Community Health Services,* a
    study prepared for the Royal Commission on Health Services (Hall
    Commission), Queen's Printer, Ottawa, 1964; R. Defries (ed.), *The
    Federal and Provincial Health Services in Canada,* Canadian Public
    Health Association, Toronto, 1962; and Canadian Public Health
    Association, *The Development of Public Health in Canada,* Toronto, 1940.

51. *Emerging Patterns of Health Care*, a study prepared for the Hall Commission, Queen's Printer, Ottawa, 1964, p. 38.
52. *Canada Yearbook, 1975*, Information Canada, 1976, p. 200. See also *Review of Health Services in Canada*, an annual publication of the Department of National Health and Welfare.
53. Canadian Tax Foundation, *Provincial and Municipal Finances, 1977*, Toronto, 1977.
54. The broad objectives of the federal government, to be pursued in cooperation with the provinces, are described in Marc Lalonde, *A New Perspective on the Health of Canadians*, Department of National Health and Welfare, 1974.
55. *Canada Yearbook 1975, op. cit.*, p. 214.
56. Changing policies toward the medical profession are discussed at length in a provocative article by G.R. Weller, "From Pressure Group Politics' to 'Medical Industrial Complex': The Development of Approaches to the Politics of Health," *Journal of Health Politics, Policy and Law 1*, Winter, 1977, pp. 444-470. Weller distinguishes three stages, which are benign neglect, insurance, and holistic. The central characteristic of each stage is the "extent of politicization of health care". We have broken this concept down into two parts—the extent of public vs. private health services and the relationship between the medical profession and the state.
57. See Richard Splane, *Social Welfare in Ontario 1791-1893*, University of Toronto Press, Toronto, 1965, for a discussion of the early period of self-regulation. See Carolyn Tuohy, "Pluralism and Corporatism in Ontario Medical Politics" in K. Rea and J.T. McLeod (eds.), *Business and Government in Canada*, Methuen, Toronto, 1976, pp. 395-413, for an analysis of the evolution of the medical profession's self-regulatory activities.
58. Weller, *op. cit.*, p. 445.
59. H. Cassidy, *Public Health and Welfare Organization in Canada*, Ryerson, Toronto, 1945, p. 154.
60. *Report of Hall Commission*, p. 384.
61. *Ibid.*, p. 385.
62. Alberta 1919, Saskatchewan and Ontario 1923, Manitoba 1928, PEI 1931, Newfoundland 1934, Quebec 1936, Nova Scotia 1943, B.C. 1946.
63. These are drawn from descriptions of each province's system contained in Cassidy, *op. cit.*
64. In 1926 Quebec established a system of county health units which operated through the province. These county units were considered a major organizational indication in the field of public health.

65. See T. Copp, *Anatomy of Poverty*, McClelland and Stewart, Toronto, 1975.

66. Cassidy, *op. cit.*, p. 349.

67. Prior to provincial legislation public medical services to the indigent were left to the discretion and resources of the municipalities or the poor districts.

68. For a description of the medical market model see R. Klein, "*The Political Economy of National Health*," *The Public Interest*, Winter, 1972, pp. 112-125.

69. Weller, *op. cit.*, p. 446.

70. *Report of the Hall Commission*, p. 411.

71. For a discussion of B.C.'s early entry into the field see D. Swartz, "The Politics of Reform: Conflict and Accommodation in Canadian Health Policy" in L. Panitch (ed.), *The Canadian State: Political Power and Political Economy*, University of Toronto Press, Toronto, 1976, pp. 311-343. The conflicts surrounding the plan are described in Martin Robin, *Pillars of Profit*, McClelland and Stewart, Toronto, 1973, pp. 20-30.

72. J. McLeod "Health, Wealth and Politics," L. LaPierre (ed.), *Essays on the Left*, McClelland and Stewart, Toronto, 1971, pp. 81-99.

73. See Charles Berry, *Voluntary Medical Insurance and Prepayment*, a study prepared for the Hall Commission, 1965. Berry notes that by 1961 53% of the population had some form of voluntary medical insurance, p. 22.

74. This discussion of the National Health Grants Programme comes from M. LeClair, "The Canadian Health Care System," in S. Andreopoulos (ed.), *National Health Insurance: Can We Learn from Canada?*, John Wiley and Sons, New York, 1975, pp. 11-92.

75. *Canada Yearbook, 1972*, Information Canada, Ottawa, 1973.

76. Caroline Tuohy, "Medical Politics After Medicare", *Canadian Public Policy 2*, Spring 1976.

77. See R.F. Bagley and S. Wolfe, *Doctor's Strike: Medical Care and Conflict in Saskatchewan*, Macmillan, Toronto, 1967, and E.A. Tollefson, *Bitter Medicine*, Modern Press, Saskatoon, 1963, and E.A. Tollefson "The Medicare Dispute" in Norman Ward and Duff Spafford, *Politics in Saskatchewan*, Longman, Toronto, 1968, pp. 238-279.

78. *Report of the Hall Commission*, Vol. 1, recommendations, pp. 18-96.

79. Le Clair, *op. cit.*, p. 48.

80. For a useful discussion of Ontario response to federal initiatives, see G.R. Weller, "Health Care and Medicare Policy in Ontario" in G.B. Doern and S.V. Wilson (eds.), *Issues in Canadian Public Policy*, Macmillan, Toronto, 1974, pp. 85-114. On Quebec see Malcolm Taylor, "Quebec Medicare: Policy Formulations in Conflict and Crisis," *Canadian Public Administration* xv, Summer 1972, pp. 211-250.

The general argument is presented in Claude Morin, *Quebec vs. Ottawa, the Struggle for Self-Government 1960-72*, University of Toronto Press, Toronto, 1976.

81. The negotiating agents for the profession differ from province to province. The Federation of General Practitioners and the Federation of Medical Specialists are professional unions chartered by the Province of Quebec to represent physicians. In B.C., the British Columbia Medical Association handles fee negotiations. In Ontario the negotiations are carried out by the Joint Committee on Physicians' Compensation committee made up of representatives of the government and the O.M.A.).

82. See P. Manga, *The Income Distribution Effect of Medical Insurance in Ontario*, Ontario Economic Council, Toronto, 1978, and R.G. Beck, "Economic Class and Access to Physicians' Services and Public Medical Care Insurance," *International Journal of Health Services* 3, 1973, pp. 341-355.

83. Swartz, *op. cit.*, and Tuohy, "Medical Policies After Medicare", *op. cit.*

84. On the problems of access see Government of Manitoba, *White Paper on Health Policy*, Winnipeg 1972; Government of Ontario, Health Planning, Task Force *Report* (Mustard Report), Toronto, 1974; Claude Castonguay, "The Quebec Experience" in Andrepoulos, *op. cit.*, pp. 97-121; and Government of British Columbia, *Health Security for British Columbians*, (Foulkes Report), Victoria, 1973. Responsiveness was a concern that figured prominently in the Manitoba *White Paper on Health Policy*, Quebec Commission of Enquiry on Health and Social Welfare *Report of the Commission of Inquiry on Health and Social Welfare*, (Castonguay-Nepveu Report), Quebec City, 1970, and E. Pickering, *Special Study Regarding the Medical Profession in Ontario*, Ontario Medical Association, Toronto, 1973.

85. See for example Task Force Reports on the cost of Health Services in Canada, *Delivery of Medical Care, Price of Medical Care and Public Health*, Information Canada, 1970. Economic Council of Canada, *Patterns of Growth*, 7th Annual Report, Information Canada, 1970. See also *Manitoba White Paper on Health Policy*, and Ontario Economic Council, *Issues and Alternatives in 1976: Health*, Toronto, 1976.

86. Weller, "Health Care in Ontario," p. 98.

87. Ontario Economic Council, *op. cit.*, p. 17.

88. *Ibid.*, *Manitoba White Paper on Health Policy, op. cit.*, *Foukes Report, op. cit.*, and R.G. Evans, "Health Services in Nova Scotia," *Canadian Public Policy* 1, Summer, 1975.

89. *Report of the Community Health Centre Project*, Information Canada, Ottawa, 1972 (Hastings Report).

90. "Medical Politics After Medicare: The Case of Ontario" *op. cit.*
91. P. Manga and G. Weller, "The Failure of the Equity Objective in Health: A Comparative Analysis". Paper presented at the American Political Science Association meetings, 1978, pp. 38-56.
92. See also *Canada Year Book, 1975*, p. 262.
93. From a comparative perspective, education in many political systems, for example, France and Germany, has been an arena for intensely felt ideological divisions and has been a traditional source of political conflict. Although in Canada there have been some roughly similar instances like the Manitoba School Question and perhaps today language and education in Quebec, the overall pattern of policy-making cannot be described as heavily ideological. For a comparative example, see Arnold J. Heidenheimer, Hugh Heclo and Carolyn T. Adams, *Comparative Public Policy, the Politics of Social Choice in Europe and America*, St. Martin's Press, New York, 1975, chapters 2 and 5.
94. Statistics Canada, *The Organization and Administration of Public Schools in Canada*, 1966, 81-535 provides a historical sketch of basic educational structures; David Munroe, *The Organization and Administration of Education*, Information Canada, Ottawa, 1974 is the most recent update of this review.
95. On the history of educational development in Canada see J. Donald Wilson, Robert M. Stamp and Louis-Phillipe Audet (eds.), *Canadian Education: A History*, Prentice-Hall, Scarborough, 1970. For a useful analysis of policy developments see also Ronald Manzer, "Public School Policies in Canada: A Comparative, Developmental Perspective," paper presented at the International Studies Association Convention, Toronto, February, 1976.
96. Quebec, Ministry of Education, Planning Branch, *Review of Educational Policies in Canada: Quebec*, Council of Ministers of Education, Toronto, mimeographed, 1975, pp. 4-5.
97. *Ibid.*, Chapter IV on the impact of the Parent Commission.
98. *Ibid.*, pp. 67-70.
99. David M. Cameron, *Schools for Ontario*, University of Toronto Press, Toronto, 1974, analyses the major patterns of policy change in Ontario in the 1960s.
100. Monroe, *op. cit.*, pp. 103, 108. On consolidation in Alberta, see John W. Chalmers, *Schools for the Foothills Province*, University of Toronto Press, Toronto, 1967, pp. 283-303.
101. Ontario, Minister of Education and the Minister of Colleges and Universities, *Review of Educational Policies in Canada: Ontario*, Council of Ministers of Education, Toronto, 1975, p. 26; Quebec, Minister of Education, *op. cit.*, p. 69.

102. On Newfoundland see F.W. Rowe, *Education and Culture in New-foundland*, McGraw-Hill Ryerson, Toronto, 1976, pp. 74-77. For a general overview of educational finance, see Monroe, *op. cit.*, passim; *Provincial and Municipal Finances 1975*, Canadian Tax Foundation, Toronto, 1975, pp. 172-188.

103. In Quebec in the 1970s the percentage of secondary and CEGEP level students enrolled in privately-run Church-controlled institutions has represented up to fifteen percent of total enrolments. These students tend to be overwhelmingly drawn from the upper classes and are concentrated in the general (university) stream. These private institutions receive almost full financial support from the provincial government.

104. Cameron, *op. cit.*, chapters 3, 6, 7 analyses the extent of the disparities created by a reliance on local taxation.

105. Canadian Tax Foundation, *Provincial and Municipal Finances 1977*, Toronto, 1977, chapter 9. W.B.W. Martin and A.J. Macdonnell, *Canadian Education*, Prentice-Hall, Toronto, 1978, pp. 119-122.

106. Newfoundland has never developed a strong local base for the financing of education. See Rowe, *op. cit.*, chapter 5; Ministers of Education for the provinces of New Brunswick, Newfoundland, Nova Scotia, and Prince Edward Island, *Review of Educational Policies in Canada: Atlantic Region*, Council of Ministers of Education, Toronto, 1975, pp. 70-77.

107. E.F. Sheffield, "The Post-War Surge in Post-Secondary Education: 1945-1969," in Wilson et al., *op. cit.*, pp. 416-443 provides a useful overview of these changes. See also Economic Council of Canada, *Seventh Annual Report*, Queen's Printer, Ottawa, 1970, chapter 5.

108. Sheffield, *Ibid.*, p. 422; Economic Council, *op. cit.*, p. 60.

109. Glenda M. Patrick, "The Politics of Higher Education in Ontario: an Analysis of Public Policy in the Post-War Period 1945-1964," mimeo., Annual Meeting of the Canadian Political Science Association, Fredericton, New Brunswick, June 1977, examines in detail the background conditions and organized group inputs which led to the developments of the CAATS.

110. For a description of CEGEPs see Quebec Minister of Education, *Review of Educational Policies, op. cit.*, pp. 97-103.

111. Munroe, *op. cit.*, p. 113; on the development of community colleges in the western provinces see Ministers of Education for British Columbia, Alberta, Saskatchewan, and Manitoba, *Review of Educational Policies, op. cit.*, pp. 53-60.

112. Ministers of Education for the provinces of New Brunswick, Newfoundland, Nova Scotia, and Prince Edward Island, *Review of Educational Policies, op. cit.*, p. 38.

113. Ontario Economic Council, *Issues and Alternatives 1976: Education*, p. 17; George E. Carter, "Financing Post Secondary Education Under the Federal-Provincial Fiscal Arrangements Act: An Appraisal," *Canadian Tax Journal* 24, 1976, pp. 505-522.

114. Patrick, *op. cit.*, pp. 29-30; Cameron, *op. cit.*, pp. 163-178. J.S. Dupré, *Federalism and Policy Development: the Case of Adult Occupational Training in Ontario*, University of Toronto Press, Toronto, 1973.

115. Lawrence W. Downey, "Politics and Expertise in Educational Policy-Making," in J.H.A. Wallin, ed., *The Politics of Canadian Education* Canadian Society for the Study of Education, Edmonton, 1977, pp. 138-140, distinguishes between political and rational modes of policy-making in education. For an analysis of the role of experts in education policy formation, see David M. Cameron, *Schools for Ontario, Policy-making, Administration and Finance in the 1960s* University of Toronto Press, Toronto, 1972.

116. On the Ontario origins of separate schools see C.B. Sissons, *Church and State in Canadian Education*, Ryerson, Toronto, 1959, chapter 1.

117. British North America Act, Section 93 (1); Manitoba Act, Section 22; Alberta Act, Section 17; Saskatchewan Act, Section 17; Term 17 of the Terms of Union of Newfoundland with Canada. These provisions represent the constitutional status of the various sectarian school systems and were the source of some of the most controversial decisions in Canadian constitutional history.

118. Sissons, *op. cit.*, p. 371. See also Statistics Canada, *A Century of Education in British Columbia, 1871-1971*, Information Canada, Ottawa, 1971.

119. Beck, p. 205-207; Sissons op. cit., pp. 303-304; D.A. Schmeiser, *Civil Liberties in Canada*, Oxford University Press, Oxford, 1964, pp. 157-158.

120. Sissons, *op. cit.*, pp. 357, 364.

121. *Ibid.*, p. 256; Schmeiser, *op. cit.*, pp. 169-182.

122. Sissons, *op. cit.*, pp. 276-277, 293.

123. 1974 figures for Ontario indicate that 30.4 percent of pupils (junior kindergarten through grade ten) were enrolled in separate schools and 69.6 percent in public schools. Ontario, Minister of Education, *Roman Catholic School Enrolment* (76-0235) and *Public School Enrolment* (76-0236).

124. Sissons, p. 277.

125. Lovell Clark, "Introduction," *The Manitoba School Question: Majority Rule or Minority Rights?*, Copp Clark, Toronto, 1968, pp. 1-9; Skelton, p. 19.

126. Evidence presented in Chapter Three demonstrates the persistence of the religious basis of party politics in several provinces including Ontario. Other studies have shown the religious factor to exist in federal politics. See John Meisel, *Working Papers on Canadian Politics*,

McGill-Queen's, Montreal, 1975, Second Edition, Chapter Six; William P. Irvine, "Explaining the Religious Basis of the Canadian Partisan Identity: Success on the Third Try," VII *Canadian Journal of Political Science*, September, 1974, pp. 560-563.

127. The late nineteenth century represents an era in which religious feelings ran high in much of Canada. Some of this sentiment was polarized into partisanship, as in the Ontario "no popery" elections of 1886 through 1894. Mowat's Liberal government, by amending the Separate School Act to ameliorate the financial situation of separate schools, incurred considerable Catholic sympathy and some Protestant hostility. Religious divisions were further aroused and polarized by the Conservative attempt to capitalize on anti-Catholic sentiment. This campaign earned the Conservatives some support from the Orange Order and the Protestant Protective Association but was insufficient to oust the dominant Liberals from office. For an account of this period see Franklin A. Walker, *Catholic Education and Politics in Ontario*, Thomas Nelson, Toronto, 1964, Chapters 5-7.

128. For a useful discussion of this problem see David M. Cameron, *Schools for Ontario, op. cit.*, pp. 57-66.

129. *Ibid.*, pp. 64-65.

130. *Ibid.*, pp. 69-72. Cameron reports the per-pupil expenditure disparity for selected years as follows: 1945 Public: $84.78, Separate: $53.21. 1963 Public: $315.08; Separate $232.52, p. 80.

131. *Ibid.*, pp. 28-31, discusses the constitutional-political problems of consolidation of separate school districts.

132. Minister of Education and Minister of Colleges and Universities, Ontario, *Review of Educational Policies in Canada: Ontario*, Council of Ministers of Education, Toronto, mimeo, 1975, pp. 24-25.

133. Some observers read Davis' decision as an attempt to mobilize latent anti-Catholic sentiment prior to the 1971 provincial election. It is doubtful that this was the case. Certainly, there is little to indicate that the separate school issue ignited any widespread feelings that were translated into votes. Public opinion findings suggest instead that the issue was of comparatively low popular interest. Jonathan Manthorpe, *The Power and the Tories*, Macmillan, Toronto, 1974, pp. 155-159; Walter Pitman, "The Limits of Diversity: the Separate School Issue in the Politics of Ontario," in Donald C. MacDonald, ed., *Government and Politics of Ontario*, Macmillan, Toronto, 1975, pp. 17-32.

134. Ministry of Education, Planning Branch, Government of Quebec, *Review of Educational Policies in Canada: Quebec*, Council of the Ministers of Education, Toronto, mimeo, 1975, pp. 5-7. Sissons, *op. cit.*, pp. 129-160; Schmeiser, *op. cit.*, pp. 148-155.

135. Montreal and Quebec City, both with anglophone minorities,

established Catholic and Protestant school boards each with authority over its own taxes, curriculum, and other policy matters. Outside of these cities, minority group schools were established on a voluntary basis. Sissons, *op. cit.*, p. 135. English Catholic schools developed under the administration of the Catholic committee of the Council of Education. Such schools, mainly in Montreal, were permitted their own autonomy and evolved programs similar to those of the Protestant schools. Schmeiser, *op. cit.*, p. 151.

136. *Ibid.*, p. 150; Cameron, *op. cit.*, p. 57-66 describes contrasting circumstances in Ontario.

137. Quebec Ministry of Education, *op. cit.*, p. 5.

138. *Ibid.*, pp. 67-68; Dale Posgate and Kenneth McRoberts, *Quebec, Social Change and Political Crisis,* McClelland and Stewart, Toronto, 1976, p. 111.

139. Quebec Ministry of Education, *op. cit.*, pp. 97-106.

140. Frederick Rowe, *Education and Culture in Newfoundland,* op. cit. p. 160.

141. The most important churches and their approximate share of the population were the Roman Catholic (36%), the Anglican (30%), the United Church (20%), the Salvation Army and Pentacostal (10% together). *Ibid.*, pp. 154-155.

142. "The strongest objection that critics of the system brought against it was that in hundreds of villages and hamlets, two, three or even four one- or two-room schools were being operated under impossible conditions. Untrained teachers tried to cope with a range of grades sometimes extending from kindergarten to X or XI; there was a waste of effort and an unnecessary duplication of services; often a school's enrolment was so small that the school operated only for half a year; it was difficult to find even untrained teachers to work under so many adversities, so that not infrequently the small schools were closed for part or the whole of the year, leaving the children out in the cold, literally and figuratively." *Ibid.*, p. 155.

143. Rowe refers to the "Revolution of the 1960's" to encapsulate the scope of these policy cleavages. *Ibid.*, Chapter 9.

144. *Ibid.*, pp. 153-159.

145. The secularization of the Department of Education through reorganization had the support of the three largest Protestant churches but was strongly opposed by the Roman Catholic and Pentacostal churches, *ibid.*, pp. 159-164.

146. On the implications of demographic developments and educational reforms on language rights see Richard J. Joy, *Languages in Conflict,* McClelland and Stewart, Toronto, 1972, pp. 37-44.

147. On federal language policy see V. Seymour Wilson, "Language

Policy," in G. Bruce Doern and V. Seymour Wilson, eds., *Issues in Canadian Public Policy*, Macmillan, Toronto, 1974, pp. 253-285.

148. Wilson et. al., *op. cit.*, p. 353.

149. Schmeiser, *op. cit.*, p. 143; *Report of the Royal Commission on Bilingualism and Biculturalism*, Vol. II, p. 47-53.

150. *Ibid.*, p. 51.

151. *Report of the Minister of Education*, 1976-1977, p. 9.

152. Ministry of Education, *Education Statistics, Ontario 1975*, p. 41.

153. As of 1975 there were over 650,000 elementary pupils and 195,000 secondary students enrolled in French classes, *ibid.*, p. 60. Federal financing assists French language training across Canada.

154. Wilson et al., *op. cit.*, p. 355; Vincent Price, "Manitoba Celebrates Its Centenary by Doing Justice to French Schools," in Hugh A. Stevenson, Robert M. Stamp and I. Donald Wilson, eds., *The Best of Times the Worst of Times: Contemporary Issues in Canadian Education*, Holt, Rinehart and Winston, Toronto, 1972, pp. 158-160 (reprinted from *Le Devoir*, July 4, 1970).

155. For an overview of these early developments see M.R. Lupul, "Educational Crisis in the New Dominion to 1917," in Wilson et al., *op. cit.*, chapter 13.

156. On recent changes in language policy see *Report of the Royal Commission on Bilingualism and Biculturalism*, pp. 98-108.

157. *Ibid.*, pp. 104-108. The 1963 Royal Commission on Finance and Municipal Taxation (Bryne) was instrumental in bringing into the policy arena the need to respond to existing disparities in educational services. The Deutsch Commission on Higher Education (1962) recommended the establishment of a Francophone University.

158. The history of the language issue in Saskatchewan is analyzed in Keith A. McLeod, "Politics, Schools and the French Language, 1881-1931" in Norman Ward and Duff Spafford, eds., *Politics in Saskatchewan*, University of Toronto Press, Toronto, 1968 pp. 124-150; and David E. Smith, *Prairie Liberalism, The Liberal Party in Saskatchewan 1905-1971*, University of Toronto Press, Toronto, 1975, pp. 109-124.

159. Posgate and McRoberts, *op. cit.*, pp. 172, 184-185.

160. See W.I. Gillespie, "On the Redistribution of Income in Canada," XCIII *Canadian Tax Journal* 93, July/August 1976, pp. 419-450; Alan Maslove, *The Pattern of Taxation in Canada*, Economic Council of Canada, Ottawa, 1972; Grant Reuber, "The Impact of Government Policies on the Distribution of Income in Canada: A Review," mimeo, 1977. For these and other indicators of policy impact see R. Manzer, *Canada: A Socio-Political Report*, McGraw-Hill Ryerson, Toronto, 1974, pp. 25-67.

161. Statistics Canada, *Family Incomes*, DBS 13-538, 13-208.
162. Beck, *op. cit.* and Manzer, *op. cit.*. For a good summary of the other studies see Manga and Weller, *op. cit.*
163. O. Mehmet, *Who Benefits from the Ontario University System?*, Ontario Economic Council, Toronto, 1978, p. 38.

Chapter 7

Resource Development Policies

The growth of provincial governments is most commonly associated with the post World War II expansion of the social policies of health, welfare, and education. It is important, however, to realize that provincial governments have had a long tradition of public involvement in the mobilization of physical resources.[1] By the beginning of the twentieth century, long before the welfare state had appeared, the provinces were already concerned with the development of their economies. They sought to facilitate this development through encouraging the exploitation of natural resources, the promotion of agriculture and industry, and the creation of a transportation infrastructure.

The contrast between the social policies and the mobilization of physical resources goes beyond the temporal question of which came first. The evolutionary pattern of each broad policy area also differs. In the case of social policy, the dominant trend for all government has been in the direction of maximizing the number of people who benefit by expanding the kind of coverage available and in ensuring national minimum standards. Thus, the pattern of political demands and policy responses has had a broad continuity and similarity for all governments. In the area of resource development this is much less true. The distinctive resource bases of the provinces (and the resulting differentials in potential for resource exploitation) have made the policy pattern from province to province non-uniform. In other words, the pressures which have stimulated the state into an increasingly active policy role have not necessarily been framed within common issues or common responses because their starting points are fundamentally divergent.

Provincial intervention to promote economic development through resource mobilization has not necessarily meant effective public control (that is, the substitution of public for private authority); nor has it meant that all segments of the population have benefitted equally. The role of the state has been to facilitate economic development primarily through the private sector.[2]

THE POLITICS OF NATURAL RESOURCES AND ENERGY

Resource exploitation and the export of resource staples have been keystones of Canadian economic growth and have been long-standing matters of public concern. Resource policy quickly became a field of active interest group involvement—often resulting in close clientele relationships between business and government. Where the objectives of resource exploitation impinged on the interests of other groups, for example, farmers, conservationists, native peoples or the general public, they created the potential for political conflict. The need to resolve or contain such conflicts has meant that provincial governments have had to maintain a more or less permanent interest in the conditions and rate of resource exploitation. Thus Nelles, in his monumental history of the politics of forests, mines, and hydro-electric power in Ontario, is able to document a strong tradition of direct state intervention and extensive patterns of cooperation and conflict between government and resource-based industries.[3]

Governments have been more than simple mediators of conflicting group interests. In this field as in others, provinces have had their own sets of objectives and have acted at times as independent participants both in conflict and in cooperation with private economic interests in the evolution of policies. As such, resource policy has constituted an area in which governments have had to define the "public interest," the meaning of which has varied greatly over time and place. In some cases it has been synonymous with job creation; in other cases it has been expressed in terms of conservation, environmental standards, pollution control, and the assurance of the renewability of certain resources. In still other circumstances, it has been seen as the problem of foreign ownership or the guarantee of public return on use and depletion of public resources. Perhaps the most direct reason for the early active interest of provincial governments in this policy area is that natural resources have always represented an attractive, and in many instances a substantial, source of public revenue. It has been estimated that in 1913 natural resources accounted for an average of over 20% of provincial revenues. By 1970 this figure had declined to about 6%—although as a result of price increases it had risen to 8.1% by 1975.[4]

Reinforcing the relative decline in importance of this policy area was a popular complacency which minimized the significance of natural resource issues. In Canada, the world's second highest per capita consumer of energy, the belief was widespread that vast resource holdings, both discovered and potential, would insulate the nation against any imaginable world shortages. This downward trend in the saliency of natural resource issues may be at an end. The energy crisis of the early 1970s provoked at all levels of government a new awareness of the immediacy and seriousness of energy- and resource-related issues.

Although the public sector has traditionally played a reactive and facilitative role for resource development and exploitation, the implications of the energy crisis demonstrated that, in the future, governments would require the ability to define policy options and avoid policy-making by crisis management. The oil embargo by the OPEC nations in 1973-1974 may not have been the fundamental cause of the energy crisis, but, it undoubtedly served as a stimulus for a serious reassessment of existing patterns of resource depletion, high and wasteful patterns of energy consumption, and the need for governments to develop a planning capacity.

The problem of ultimate scarcity of non-renewable natural resources is, of course, not new. But policy-makers and to a large extent interested publics have a strong tendency to view issues in the short-term. This has meant that the benefits of resource development and economic growth have traditionally overshadowed the danger of exhausting these resources. What is new is the increasing recognition that there are very real costs to a policy of maximum exploitation and that the public interest may be better served by policies of conservation than by unrestrained consumption.[5]

In exploring the character of provincial resource politics, an essential starting point is, therefore, the extent and quality of natural resource endowments. It should be clear, for example, that forestry, mining, or energy issues will arise primarily in those provinces having a substantial base in those resources (although the *lack* of a crucial resource like petroleum may generate its own policy issues.) A second major point in understanding resource politics involves the fact of federal-provincial relations. Provinces are not fully independent in determining resource policy directions. Thus, the jurisdictional question constitutes another basic condition for analysing resource policy and politics. And thirdly, especially in recent times, the energy sector has taken on such an overriding urgency and importance within the broader area of resource policy that it deserves some special comment.

Natural Resource Endowments

Many of the basic policy differences among the provinces in the fields of natural resources and energy stem in large part from the simple fact that the provinces differ sharply in the quantity, variety, and exploitive value of the resources which they possess. Their resource bases are the origin both of economic growth and prosperity and of distinct political interests. Thus, it is not surprising that energy-rich Alberta may, at times, be in conflict with energy-dependent Ontario, or more generally

Table 7.1: The Provincial Distribution of Mineral Resources: Production Shares as Percent of Total Canadian Value (1975)

	FUELS			METALLICS				NON-METALLICS		TOTAL VALUE OF MINERAL PRODUCTS ($ 000)
	PETROLEUM	NATURAL GAS	COAL	NICKEL	COPPER	ZINC	IRON ORE	ASBESTOS	POTASH	
NFLD.	—	—	—	—	1.0	2.3	52.7	6.8	—	$ 568,212
P.E.I.	—	—	—	—	—	—	—	—	—	1,540
N.S.	—	—	8.2	—	—	—	—	—	—	96,688
N.B.	—	—	1.2	—	1.6	17.0	—	—	—	251,393
QUE.	—	—	—	—	16.3	11.0	22.5	66.2	—	1,142,457
ONT.	0.1	0.4	—	73.6	36.6	31.1	23.2	0.5	—	2,339,449
MAN.	0.8	—	—	26.4	8.9	6.1	—	—	—	533,189
SASK.	10.3	0.5	1.5	—	1.1	0.4	—	—	100	826,536
ALTA.	86.1	94.8	32.1	—	—	—	—	—	—	6,000,849
B.C.	2.5	4.1	56.8	—	33.3	9.2	1.6	14.5	—	1,223,915
YUKON	—	—	—	—	1.1	10.6	—	12.0	—	228,898
N.W.T.	0.1	0.2	—	—	—	12.3	—	—	—	189,477
CANADA	3,781,067	1,729,631	575,800	1,109,203	1,016,819	895,357	923,184	266,943	346,806	13,402,603
% OF TOTAL VALUE	28.2	12.9	4.3	8.3	7.6	6.7	6.9	2.0	2.6	

Source: *Canada Year Book, 1976-77*, pp. 618-628. Reprinted by permission of the Minister of Supply and Services Canada.

that resource-producing provinces may be at odds with the federal government and indirectly with the resource-consuming areas of the country.

The significance of resource development for provincial and national wealth means that resource policy will be inextricably tied to questions of equalization and regional development. And as the threat of resource scarcity is felt to be increasingly pressing, resource policy issues will also become more redistributive in their implications. It is, therefore, crucial to understand the nature of the differences which exist between resource-rich provinces and the resource poor.

Table 7.1 provides an overview of the major economically exploitable, non-renewable mineral resources in each province. These are by no means the only resources available for exploitation, but the comparison does provide an approximation of provincial differences. The data reflect the very uneven distribution of resource wealth. Provinces can be roughly divided into several categories—those with little or no significant mineral production (Prince Edward Island, Nova Scotia, and New Brunswick), those with significant production from one or two key resources (Newfoundland and Saskatchewan), those with a wider variety of productive resources (Ontario, Quebec, Manitoba, and British Columbia), and one (Alberta) with an extraordinary natural inheritance of energy resources.

Table 7.2 is designed to provide some additional perspectives to these figures. The first two columns indicate the change in the relative standing of provinces with respect to resource wealth. The rapid excalation in energy prices between 1973 and 1975 had the effect of accentuating Alberta's already dominant resource position. By 1975 it accounted for about 45% of Canada's total mineral production value. The relative position of the three next most important producing provinces (Ontario, British Columbia, and Quebec) had slipped correspondingly. Another way of looking at provincial non-renewable resources is on a per capita basis (as in column 3 of Table 7.2). These figures indicate the importance of resources for two provinces, Newfoundland and Saskatchewan, which tend to be underestimated by total production figures. The last column links resource value to politics by estimating the degree to which provinces rely on this base as a source of public revenues. Not accounted for in these comparisons are the renewable natural resources. In this category the most economically significant sectors are forestry, fisheries, hydro power, and agriculture (Table 7.3).

What do these differences in natural resource and energy characteristics mean for provincial politics? Broadly speaking, such resource wealth is the basis for economic growth and prosperity, and in this sense it has diffuse effects for governments. More specifically, natural resources represent a significant non-tax revenue. The ability of

Table 7.2: Provincial Comparisons of Resource Value

	% OF TOTAL CANADIAN MINERAL VALUE (1975)	(1973)	TOTAL MINERAL VALUE PER CAPITA (1975)	NATURAL RESOURCE REVENUE AS % OF GROSS PROVINCIAL REVENUE (1976-77)*
NFLD.	4.2	4.5	$1,019.	1.3
P.E.I.	—	—	13.	.1
N.S.	0.7	0.7	117.	.5
N.B.	1.9	1.9	371.	1.5
QUE.	8.5	11.1	183.	1.0
ONT.	17.5	22.2	283.	1.4
MAN.	4.0	5.0	522.	2.1
SASK.	6.2	6.1	897.	21.6
ALTA.	44.8	33.0	3,265.	50.8
B.C.	9.1	11.7	496.	5.3
ALL PROVINCES			588+	8.1

Source: *Canada Year Book, 1975, 1976-77.* Reprinted by permission of the Minister of Supply and Services Canada.
*Provincial and Municipal Finances, 1977, p. 33.
+Canadian per capita value.

Table 7.3: Provincial Shares of Major Renewable Resources as Percent of National Totals

	FORESTRY*	FISHERIES†	HYDRO POWER (GENERATING CAPACITY IN MEGAWATTS)	AGRICULTURE**
NFLD.	0.1	16.7	16.7	—
P.E.I.	—	3.0	—	0.4
N.S.	1.1	26.8	0.4	0.5
N.B.	2.7	14.7	1.8	0.4
QUE.	15.3	4.4	37.3	10.4
ONT.	7.7	2.8	18.9	21.3
MAN.	0.4 ⎫		6.7	9.7
SASK.	1.0 ⎬	2.8	1.5	35.1
ALTA.	3.6 ⎭		1.9	18.8
B.C.	67.9	32.2	14.4	3.4
CANADA ($ 000)	$2,558,545	$685,416	37090mw***	$4,327,875

Source: *Canada Year Book, 1976-77.* Reprinted by permission of the Minister of Supply and Services Canada.
*based on $ values for 1973 and 1974, p. 494.
**based on net income 1975, p. 546.
***total generating capacity 1975, p. 690.
†based on $ value of fishery products, 1974, p. 500.
N.B. Percentage totals may not equal 100% due to rounding.

governments to tap this source frees other funds for the financing of otherwise unviable programs and allows governments greater freedom in tax policy and industrial incentives. Alberta has benefitted most from resource revenues, which by 1976-77 represented just over 50% of gross general revenues. This income source has allowed Alberta to eliminate retail sales taxes and to maintain the lowest rate of personal income taxes (38.5% of federal tax in 1977).

Alberta has also been able to devote much of this resource revenue to encouraging industrial diversification and development of the provincial economy, and has re-invested in new resource development, such as the Syncrude project.[6] A second political consequence may, therefore, be that resource production serves to expand the policy options open to a government.

Thirdly, and of considerable importance to the provincial political process, is the fact that variations in natural resource wealth will inevitably produce very different sets of influences on provincial governments in the form of organized interest groups with a vital stake in policy priorities.[7] Saskatchewan shares with Alberta petroleum resources, and has, on a much more limited scale, been able to rely on resource revenues (over 20% in 1976-77). In addition to oil, the development of potash and uranium resources have opened to Saskatchewan the possibility of becoming a "have" province.

Several provinces, although lacking in energy resources, are nevertheless resource rich. British Columbia has a limited petroleum production and is rich in coal deposits, but its most significant resource sectors have been timber and minerals. Forest resources (along with the associated industries of lumber and pulp and paper) have been more central to the economic growth of British Columbia than to any other province. It is, therefore, not suprising that the relationship between this economic sector and government has been a matter of recurrent public concern. Because the province has retained Crown ownership of most of the commercially valuable forest lands, a government-private industry partnership has built up. Several commissions and task forces have from time to time examined and proposed revision in the resource rents, taxes, subsidies, and licensing practices which make up this partnership.[8] The policy principle which has characterized the post-war era has been described as sustained yield through which the government, via leasing and regulation, ensures the ultimate renewability of timber reserves.[9]

The past three decades have witnessed a rapid expansion of both the timber and mining industries and their resource-based manufacturing sectors.[10] Provincial politics during most of this era was dominated by Premier W.A.C. Bennett, who articulated a policy credo of prosperity founded on rapid growth and development.[11] In this climate, provincial policy sought to maximize private resource development though favourable government financial incentives and the provision of supporting public works—highways, bridges, and schools. The thrust of government initiative into the 1970s was, therefore, a continuation of the traditional pattern of resource exploitation, often based on extensive foreign investment, for immediate economic rewards. It is in part this tradition which led one observer to label British Columbia as an example of "the politics of exploitation."[12]

Ontario and Quebec, like British Columbia, can be described as resource rich. Both have varied sources of natural wealth. With the exception of large sources of hydro-electric power, they are highly dependent on external energy resources. Along with the development of hydro power, timber resources, the pulp and paper industry, and mining have all been vital to economic growth.[13] In all three provinces natural resource wealth has resulted in a complex set of issues which have shaped the character of resource policy. One of the most general of these has been the question of the appropriate role of government. Should it play an essentially passive-permissive role in which interest groups (that is, the extractive industries) dictate effective policy? Or should government assume a controlling and planning role in which the "public interest" is expressed by an activist state and in which pressure groups are, therefore, constrained in their political influence? Linked with this pervasive issue are two more specific sub-issues. What is the desired role of foreign investment and ownership in the resource industries? To what extent should profits and immediate economic benefits determine the inflow of foreign capital? Conversely, to what extent should environmental costs, resource depletion, and social costs (for example the impact on native peoples) be taken into account in the formulation of provincial resource policies?

None of these issues has been definitively settled and only rarely have they been systematically considered within the provincial policy process. Nevertheless, in Ontario, for example, there is a tendency towards a more coordinated and long-term policy orientation.

In the three Maritime provinces there is a scarcity of economically exploitable natural resources.[14] Those that do exist, such as coal in Nova Scotia, are of comparatively low value. This is less true in Newfoundland (and particularly in Labrador) where important iron ore deposits and hydro power have provided greater potential for natural resource development. Indeed, the post-Confederation Smallwood era in Newfoundland politics was in many ways dominated by various plans for economic growth through the exploitation of iron ore, and the building of the massive Churchill Falls hydro project.[15] Despite the success of some of these efforts, it cannot be said that the basic economic difficulties of Newfoundland or the other three eastern provinces have been resolved. One consequence of this persisting issue (and certainly a factor in accentuating its severity) has been the gradual decline of these provinces as population and economic centres within Canada.

The combination of a lack of exploitable resources and chronic unemployment helps to explain why the Maritimes in particular have become directly and indirectly involved in a wide range of economic enterprises with the intent of stimulating secondary manufacturing.[16] Among the best known of these efforts are Nova Scotia's Industrial Estates Limited (IEL), a policy innovation of the Stanfield government in 1957, and New Brunswick's abortive involvement in the Bricklin sportscar.[17]

Renewable resources, particularly fisheries and forests, have traditionally played an important role in the political economy of Atlantic Canada. Although fishery policy falls constitutionally within federal jurisdiction, in practice the provinces have played an active role in both administration and policy formulation.

The seas surrounding the four eastern provinces are rich in fish resources. These continue to form a vital sector of economic activity in these provinces. However, fisheries have been beset by a serious problem of overfishing and gradual resource depletion. The 1977 establishment of a 200-mile zone restricting foreign access to fishing rights promises to remove one of the most serious causes of depletion. Another major problem, that of too many fishermen receiving very low income, remains to be resolved. Open access to the seas coupled with endemic high unemployment and widespread but relatively inefficient inshore fishing have made any solution to this problem difficult.

The problem of high unemployment represents a major policy constraint on effective fishery resource management. But the 200-mile limit means that eastern Canada, and especially Newfoundland and Nova Scotia, will be able to reap direct economic benefits which have previously eluded them. This may provide an opportunity for rationalization of the industry and effective resource management, which have often seemed in the past to be unobtainable.[18]

The Problem of Jurisdiction

The question of who has legitimate authority to allocate and make laws concerning natural resources has been a source of recurrent dispute between federal and provincial governments. In recent years this issue has been the focus of renewed controversy in the wake of a heightened sense of resource scarcity and the rapid rise in energy prices, both of which have sharpened the implications for public revenues at both levels of government.

A brief review of the constitutionally prescribed divisions of authority is the most direct route to understanding the significance of the jurisdictional issue.[19] Provincial authority derives from several sections of the B.N.A. Act of 1867, but perhaps most centrally from section 109, which granted to the four original provinces control over "all Lands, Mines, Minerals, and Royalties belonging" to them. British Columbia, Prince Edward Island, and Newfoundland were granted similar powers upon joining Confederation. The prairie provinces were not, however, granted equivalent rights until the B.N.A. Act of 1930.[20] The effect of section 109 and these later extensions of the same principle was to accord to the provinces proprietary status over the bulk of public lands and resources within their boundaries, with the same rights that a private owner would have.[21] In addition to this proprietary power, Section 92 provides the provinces with legislative and executive authority over "the Management and Sale of Public Lands belonging to the Province," "Property and Civil Rights," and "All Matters of a merely local and private Nature in the Province."

Federal power also derives in part from the public ownership of property and in part from provisions of legislative and executive authority. Numerous provisions of section 91 have clear relevance to natural resource policy. By these provisions the federal government retains policy competence over the regulation of trade and commerce, militia, military and naval service, and defence, navigation and shipping, sea coast and inland fisheries, Indians and lands reserved and matters beyond those enumerated to the provinces. Less direct but perhaps more pervasive in their implications for shaping natural resource policy are the federal government's powers over spending, taxation, and lending, and the broad umbrella clauses, "peace, order and good government" and works "declared by the Parliament of Canada to be for the general advantage of Canada. . . ."

Thus, although it would appear that the provinces have adequate constitutional grounds to decide how, when, and under what conditions natural resources will be developed, there are also ample grounds to justify federal involvement in these policies. The effect is one of considerable jurisdictional overlap which carries with it the potential for federal-provincial conflict.[22]

An important recent example of this sort of conflict involved Alberta and Ottawa in disagreements over oil pricing and export policies. Alberta, as the major oil-producing province, has a natural interest in high prices and large markets through export. Much of the rest of Canada, as for example an energy-dependent but heavily industrialized province like Ontario, favours prices below world prices and, therefore, a two-price system.[23]

The federal government, while recognizing the eventual need to raise Canadian oil to something close to world price levels, sought in the short term to assure a two-price system. Alberta and Saskatchewan naturally saw this as their loss and as a subsidy to the central and eastern provinces.[24] National Energy Board restrictions on oil and gas exports have also, of course, constrained potential sales. The issue of the distribution of resource revenues has been at the core of federal-provincial differences in this policy area. Increasing world prices for various minerals and energy products during the early 1970s stimulated governmental interest in capturing a larger public share of windfall profits. By 1974 all of the major resource-producing provinces had either increased their taxation or were in the process of doing so.[25] The federal-provincial struggle in this regard became apparent in May of 1974 when Finance Minister John Turner announced a number of revisions in federal taxation of resource income.[26]

Federal concern involved most importantly the implications for the system of equalization payments. Given the method of calculation in use prior to 1973-74, a rapid increase in resource revenue within the producing provinces would automatically boost federal payments to the energy-poor provinces. Without a federal mechanism for tapping this new resource wealth, the situation created a heavy burden on federal finances. During 1974-75 several federal initiatives were taken to alleviate this condition. The two-price system for oil limited provincial revenues. The export tax on oil set exports at world prices and also provided funds to subsidize the eastern provinces dependent on foreign oil. As well, the federal government amended the equalization formula so that only one third of new royalties would be used to calculate equalization rates.[27] But the most controversial reform proposal was that provincial royalties would no longer be deductible in the calculation of corporate taxable income.[28] This federal initiative represented a response to various provincial attempts to gain a larger share of resource-based income and was an attempt at a national redistribution of the benefits of resource industries. The resource-rich provinces, on the other hand, saw this action as a challenge to their legitimate control over natural resources.

The Federal-Provincial Fiscal Arrangements and Established Program Financing Act, 1977 brought about a major redefinition of financial arrangements. According to Thomas J. Courchene, one of the difficulties with the old scheme was that "Ottawa had undertaken to equalize some categories of revenues that are entirely out of its control. Energy is the obvious example, but it applies more generally to all natural resource revenues."[29]

The new arrangements expand the number of revenue sources from 22 to 29. But most crucial from the perspective of natural resource policy is the provision that one half of provincial revenues from all non-renewable resources will be included in the equalization calculations. This will reduce the disincentives on the part of the energy-poor provinces to engage in resource development.[30]

A second major jurisdictional dispute arose out of Saskatchewan's mineral tax and royalty policies. In 1974, following price increases coupled with federal initiatives to claim a larger share of resource revenues, the Blakeney government passed the Oil and Gas Conservation, Stabilization and Development Act, which included a mineral income tax and coincident royalty surcharge. The effect of this law was to tax the large windfall profits resulting from post-1973 price increases at a 100% rate.[31] This generated a conflict between the oil industry on one side and the provincial government on the other. As the issue became a constitutional one of jurisdictional authority, the federal government joined with the producers in litigation while several other provinces, Quebec, Manitoba, and Alberta, joined in defence of Saskatchewan's right to manage natural resources. In 1977 the Supreme Court of Canada, in a 7 to 2 decision, ruled the Saskatchewan royalty surcharge on oil to be an indirect tax and an infringement on federal authority over the regulation of interprovincial and international trade and, therefore, unconstitutional.

During roughly the same period of time, the initiatives of the Saskatchewan government to establish a prorationing scheme for setting production quotas and a reserve tax were also challenged by the privately owned potash industry.[32] Although the basic constitutional question regarding the extent of provincial authority was the same as in the oil super royalty issue, the response of the Saskatchewan government was quite different. The Blakeney government had made resource policy a central issue in the 1975 provincial election. Following the NDP victory, the government moved to nationalize part of the potash industry. A public Potash Corporation of Saskatchewan was created in 1976, and the government bought out one mine, and had plans of purchasing at least two more.

The Energy Crisis

Although in its broadest form the energy crisis of the 1970s is of course a set of complex world-wide economic and political problems, it has very different meaning and urgency for different parts of the world. This is no less true within Canada, for the energy crisis has raised distinctive concerns for those provinces which are energy-rich as well as for those which are energy-poor. Our task is, therefore, twofold: first to describe the nature of the crisis generally and second to observe its particular significance for provincial decision-making.

Evaluations of how critical the energy problem is depend fundamentally on estimates of future abundance or scarcity of resources. These conditions are in turn a function of the availability of existing reserves, the discovery of new ones, present and future patterns of consumption, and costs. Thus, the energy crisis may be thought of as two sub-crises: of supply and demand.[33] It is the latter which represents the biggest question mark; for international oil prices, beyond the control of Canadian policy-makers, will largely condition both supply and demand.

In the 1970s about two-thirds of Canada's energy consumption was from oil and gas. Another quarter was based on hydro electricity with the remainder based on coal and nuclear sources. During the decade preceding the OPEC-induced crisis, total Canadian consumption had been increasing at the rate of about 5.5% a year. Domestic consumption of oil jumped from about one million (1963) to about 1.7 million barrels per day in 1973. Estimates of future energy demands are problematic because they depend on unknown price trends and on levels of economic growth. Nevertheless, it is clear that energy consumption will continue to increase although at a slightly slower rate than in the past. It is estimated, for example, that in 1990 oil will be consumed at the rate of between 2.6 and 3.0 million barrels per day.[34]

Statements of future available resources are necessarily problematic since they depend on discoveries not yet made and on technologies not yet developed. Even where there is a high degree of certainty about the physical volume of existing reserves, only a portion of this may be economically recoverable given prevailing prices. Moreover, the oil companies retain control over information on supply. This leaves provincial and federal governments alike in a dependent position. It also leaves open the possibility of crisis either orchestrated or intensified by companies seeking increased profits.

Several facts about oil supply are clear, however. By 1975 Canada had become a net importer of oil with the prospects of a rapid increase in import dependency into the 1980s. There is no doubt that reserves of conventional crude oil in the three western provinces are being rapidly depleted. The 1975 production of 1.7 million barrels per day is expected to dwindle to less than one third that level by 1990.[35]

These supplies will have to be supplemented by new discoveries in frontier regions (that is, the Mackenzie Delta, Beaufort Sea, Arctic islands, and the east coast) and by the development of nonconventional synthetic crude oil. Both of these options involve very high costs and considerable uncertainty. The problem of escalating development costs became clear in the Syncrude case. Cost estimates for this project, basic to the future exploitation of the Athabasca tar sands, jumped from a 1973 figure of about $500 million to $2.3 billion in October of 1974.[36]

Industry estimates of oil sands producibility vary greatly. The success of Syncrude, the development policy of the Alberta government and, of course, economic factors will shape these prospects. The National Energy Board has since 1975 become more cautious in its forecast of synthetic crude production, estimating under 400 thousand barrels per day by 1990.[37] The prospects for frontier reserves are even more problematic with very limited discoveries to date.

The situation with respect to other forms of energy is not as acute. Natural gas accounts for about one-fifth of total energy use. Known reserves, although limited, are more extensive in comparison with conventional crude oil.[38] Moreover, frontier exploration has already shown extensive new reserves.

Oil and gas reserves will, over time, be depleted. This inevitably will lead to increased dependence on other energy forms—most notably coal, hydro, nuclear, and possibly solar and wind sources.* Coal supplies are abundant and substantially unexploited. Almost all of Canada's coal reserves are located in the three westernmost provinces. These provincial governments have pursued a policy of restraint partly because of increasing prices, but also because the coal industry carries with it

*There is, of course, a limit to the substitutability of energy sources. Transportation, for example, is almost 100% dependent on petroleum, for which there is as yet no satisfactory alternative.

direct implications for land use and environmental policy concerns.

Hydro-electric power represents about 23% of Canadian energy supplies and is the only major indigenous energy resource found in the two most industrialized and populous provinces. This fact helps to explain the prominent policy role of Ontario Hydro and Hydro Quebec.

Trends in Natural Resource Policy

There exists no systematic provincial comparison which would permit us to conclude how far each province has moved toward controlling its own natural resource future. There is no doubt that all provinces today have abandoned the nineteenth century belief in private interest as public policy for greater regulation and more conscious assessment of the social and environmental costs of resource exploitation. But the politics of scarcity have not yet brought provincial resource policy to the stage where it can be described as comprehensive, rational planning.

It would be simplistic to view provincial policy-makers as autonomous in the field of natural resources. They cannot consistently control all the factors shaping resource issues and policy and, therefore, cannot be said to be totally in control of their own decisional process. There are at least three very basic independent elements, any one of which might be sufficient to vitiate the will of a provincial government:

The rate and extent of development in resource industries are subject to short-term fluctuations in international resource markets. Recent changes in the supply and demand for such key export staples as potash, copper, or nickel have had rather direct consequences in terms of job lay-offs and capital investments for the economies of the producing provinces. Second, private resource industries and financial institutions have by and large retained complete authority over long-range investment decisions. These may be influenced by provincial incentives to attract industry, but basic development policy choices remain in multi-national corporate hands. And thirdly, as has been noted in the discussions of jurisdictional issues, provincial resource policy must take account of and often respond to the constraints imposed by federal policy.

But even allowing for these crucial limitations on the autonomy of provincial action in the natural resource sector, one can observe at least one broad trend in the evolution of policy-making. The traditional style of pork-barrel, distributive policy-making in which tight, stable government-industry clientele relationships determined policy outcomes in a closed, secret, and largely *ad hoc* manner seems to be on the wane. One can certainly find important remnants of it today, and it is no doubt true that this patronage-based style of distributive politics has been more effectively eroded in some provinces than in others. Nevertheless, there clearly is a trend toward a more open, more public, and sometimes more partisan quality to natural resource policy-making. Public opinion is today increasingly aware of the need for conservation and the environmental and social dangers of resource exploitation. One can think, for example, of the controversy over James Bay, over the development of nuclear energy projects in several provinces, or over the Reed paper controversy in Ontario. Some of the political sensitivity of these issues may be related to the insecurity of minority governments or the appearance of widespread corruption, but in general such cases indicate that conflicting interests and opinions are now articulated in the policy process. When this happens, policy is no longer resolved in the arena of closed, clientistic agreements. Rather, general rules and guidelines become more common. And as political participants perceive the costs to them (and to their constituents), the redistributive nature of the issues forces policy into the wider, more politicized arenas of party politics and cabinet decision-making.

AGRICULTURE

Agriculture comprises a distinct sector within resource mobilization policies because of its constitutional status and economic and social context. Section 95 of the British North America Act places agriculture and immigration under the shared jurisdiction of both federal and provincial governments, with federal legislation taking precedence. For many years the two levels pursued separate agriculture policies. Ottawa was primarily concerned with agriculture as an instrument of nation-building. (The constitutional link to immigration is significant.)

> The federal government's interest in agriculture was essentially an interest in agricultural commerce and finance, in opportunities for the profitable servicing of a rapidly expanding agricultural frontier. . . . To a very considerable extent [it] was but an amplification of the clause which gave the Dominion government exclusive jurisdiction over trade and commerce.[39]

The provinces focussed on the productive aspects of agriculture. Their policies provided assistance through agricultural extension and education. Early provincial activities were directed toward the encouragement of agricultural societies and exhibitions. Today, the problems of agriculture are such that both levels have expanded their interests and the distinctions between provincial and federal activities have been eroded.

What are the problems facing Canadian agriculture? To some extent the answer depends on one's perspective. Farmers, agribusiness, consumers and politicians have tended to conceive agricultural problems rather differently. There are, however, some points of agreement including "low farm income, rigidities inhibiting resource transfer, over-production, unstable and uncertain prices, the existence and prevalence of small, non-viable farms, increasing regional disparities, the cost-price squeeze, slow market growth, declining farm share of the national income, and the ineffectiveness of government policies and programs."[40]

In the prairie provinces, agriculture has been more than just another set of problems for decision-makers. By 1900 wheat had been established as a staple, and since that time agriculture has continued to be a central source of policy issues, such as the problems posed by grain handling, which are as salient today as they were fifty years ago.[41] In addition, agriculture has also affected other policy areas. For example, the early introduction of public health care was a response to the special needs of scattered agricultural populations. Similarly, demands concerning transportation rates and services are directly linked to the needs of farming. In general, the agricultural sector has had a profound effect on all aspects of prairie politics including the character of party competition and provincial relations with Ottawa.[42]

State involvement in agriculture stems from two factors: the traditional structure of agriculture and the popular salience of food prices. A large number of small farms, variable demands and prices, and changing technology have made agriculture very dependent on state protection.[43] Policy responses to producer problems have been tempered by public concern with rising food costs.[44] Faced with what at times appear to be conflicting demands for higher farm incomes and stable food prices, federal and provincial governments have responded with three broad types of activities.[45] The first type consists of programmes for research extension and education. Although there is some federal involvement, provincial agricultural departments are the main communicators of technological advances. They provide advice and assistance to interested members of farm communities.[46]

The second type involves direct assistance for farm income maintenance and has tended to come from Ottawa rather than from provincial governments. Federal price supports for agricultural products were introduced in 1944. In 1958, under the Agricultural Stabilization Act, Ottawa began a programme to guarantee a minimum price to farmers regardless of the market price of the particular product. In 1977 the Stabilization Board paid farmers 262 million dollars. Provincial activities for income assistance have centred on crop insurance and farm credit. Since the Crop Insurance Act in 1959 Ottawa and the provinces have shared the cost of provincial crop insurance schemes. Early provincial involvement in farm credit ended during the Depression (except in Quebec). However, in the 1950s the provinces once again took up farm credit and today most provinces have direct loan programmes for farmers.

It is the third type of activity, production and marketing assistance, where the greatest change has taken place in the policy role of the provinces. Production assistance, mainly through resource development, has been tied to federal-provincial joint programmes. Although Ottawa provided some earlier assistance with the Prairie Farm Rehabilitation Act (1935) and the Maritime Marshland Rehabilitation Act (1948), the provinces did not become directly involved until the 1961 Agricultural and Rural Development Act. Under ARDA, federally approved provincial projects are implemented by the provinces with Ottawa and the province sharing the cost.

Initial provincial action in marketing assistance consisted of statutes authorizing cooperation. Manitoba was the first province to incorporate cooperatives in 1887, followed by Quebec in 1906. Because they were not compulsory, cooperatives could not effectively facilitate commodity marketing. To alleviate this problem, provinces attempted to bring all producers of a commodity under a single marketing board. Producer-controlled marketing boards are established by statute and are empowered to control the production and sale of an agricultural product. Boards often advertise and promote the product, improve marketing facilities, establish supply quotas, set prices, and collectively bargain with processors.[47]

British Columbia established the first provincial marketing board in 1927. The enabling legislation was, however, declared *ultra vires* in 1931 because it interfered with interprovincial trade. A narrower Natural Products Marketing Act Amendment Act was passed in British Columbia in 1936. This Act served as a model for other provinces for the establishment of intra-provincial marketing schemes. In 1949 the federal Agricultural Products Marketing Act expanded the intra-provincial power of provincial boards by allowing them authority over inter-provincial and export trade of their commodities. In 1974 over half of farm cash income came from sales under provincial marketing boards. In that year there were 108 provincial marketing boards. Every province has at least one board, Quebec has twenty-six, and Ontario twenty-two. Seventy-nine of these provincial boards have been delegated federal authority over interprovincial and export trade.[48]

In summary, it should be noted that public spending in this area has never been a significant budgetary component; nor is it a useful indicator of agricultural policy patterns. The more significant side of provincial agriculture policy is found in its regulatory elements. Marketing boards are the most important aspect of provincial agricultural regulation, although land use policies to preserve agricultural land are becoming an issue of increased conflict and concern.[49] It can also be observed that because provincial agriculture has been oriented towards small-scale extension, research and educational projects much of the policy arena has been highly distributive in character. By focusing on benefits and services to producers, agricultural policy in the provinces has sometimes appeared to be non-conflictual. Indeed, some of the most bitter issues involving farm financing and product marketing have normally been federal areas of concern. Disagreements and conflicts over farm policy have, therefore, often been expressed through federal-provincial relations. Although historically farmer protests have been the source of major upheavals in provincial politics, recent farmer discontent with political leadership has often been directed primarily at federal parties and governments.

TRANSPORTATION

The staple character of the Canadian economy has meant that economic viability has always depended on the efficient transport of goods across vast distances for eventual export (originally to Britain and later to the United States). Thus, economic necessity has made transportation loom large as a critical issue area in the context of Canadian development. Not only is a viable transport system a prerequisite for economic well-being, it also provides services that bear on the goals of regional equity and national unity.

Governmental activities in transportation have been directed toward two kinds of objectives, those related to the efficient allocation of resources *within* the transport system (which may be called endogenous) and those related to larger purposes, *e.g.*, regional development, outside of the transport system (which may be called exogenous).[50] With regard to the former, government intervention seeks to compensate for the ways in which transport does *not* conform to a perfectly competitive market situation which would efficiently allocate resources.

Monopoly, destructive competition, and externalities are the three economic grounds for transport regulation.[51] The absence of alternative modes of transport gave rise to the monopoly basis for railroad regulation. The main concern is to regulate prices and discriminatory rates. In the case of destructive competition, easy entry permits firms to come in and skim off low-cost business. This, it is alleged, leads to unstable services and prices which are too low for an industry's long term survival. Externalities constitute the third basis for state action. In this case the market price does not include the costs or benefits to those who are not the direct consumers of the product. In other words, social costs or benefits are not included in the price. Regulation and subsidization can be used to build in the consideration of such costs and benefits. For example, compliance with pollution standards results in higher prices for a firm's products, whereas previously unidentified costs were simple passed on to society in the form of pollution.

Generally, policies geared toward improving allocative efficiency (endogenous objectives) are corrections aimed at attaining a purely competitive market economy. Promotional policies, on the other hand, aim to change the pattern of economic development. A distortion is introduced into the market in order to use transportation for external or exogenous purposes.

Much of the importance of transportation policy is due to its perceived impact on external objectives. Transportation has been used as an instrument for the preservation of national unity and for achieving macro-policy goals. Included in the latter are promotion of economic development and other socio-economic objectives, for example, income redistribution, mobility of disadvantaged groups, and reduction in regional disparities.[52]

Historically, transportation has been viewed by federal and provincial decision-makers as a crucial element in the economic development of the nation and its particular regions.[53] The promise of a railway system to connect the region to central markets was part of the lure of Confederation for Nova Scotia and New Brunswick. Similarly, upon its entering Confederation, British Columbia was promised a railway linkage with the rest of Canada. The transcontinental railroad was a cornerstone of Macdonald's National Policy of linking resource-rich hinterlands to the manufacturing economies of central Canada. A transcontinental railway was to bring people west and raw materials east. Compensatory rail freight rates for regions disadvantaged by both their distance from the centre and the absence of transport competition were provided for in the Crow's Nest Pass Agreement (1897) and the Maritime Freight Rates Act (1927). The subsidized rates for moving the raw materials of the Prairies to the east and the products of the Maritimes west have been characterized as symbols of Ottawa's recognition of special regional economic needs. These subsidies have continued and remain a source of controversy. They are defended by some as necessary for the economic well-being of both regions, but are criticized by others as distorting the development of regional economies.

The structural setting of transportation policy differs from that of social policy areas in two fundamental respects: One is the jurisdictional division, and the other is the public-private sector mix. Although transportation has typically been a primary concern for provincial governments, it is essentially a federal power. Unlike social welfare, health, and education, in which the provinces constitutionally predominate and in which Ottawa plays an ancillary role, in the transportation sphere Ottawa is the primary authority and the provinces have had to play a more peripheral role. However, in each of these policy spheres, inferior constitutional status does not prevent the "secondary" level from arguing that it has legitimate concerns and therefore requires input into the actions of the dominant level of government. Just as Ottawa has maintained that health and social welfare are national concerns and has emphasized the need for national minimum standards, the provinces have contended that transportation is an important element in provincial development, and therefore provincial needs must be incorporated into national transportation policies.[54]

Transportation also differs from social development policies in the extent to which it is a mixed system of elements from the public and private sectors. Health, welfare, and education have come to be more squarely in the public sector with the state as the main provider of services. In contrast, significant aspects of transportation services remain in private hands, and public ownership often exists alongside private. Both are subject to varying degrees of regulation.[55] Thus in transportation, public involvement ranges from minimal regulation of private firms to public ownership and provision of transport services. Unlike social policies in which level of expenditure is a good synoptic indicator of public concern, in the field of transportation, the nature and extent of public activity is best reflected by the regulatory side of policy-making.

Jurisdictional Questions

There is no doubt that transportation is, in the main, a power of the federal government. Its jurisdiction extends over air, rail, water, road, and pipeline transportation. Intraprovincial transportation, unless otherwise specified, is left to the provinces. Although constitutionally interprovincial road transportation is a federal concern, control over interprovincial motor transport has been retained by the provinces. In 1938, the Transport Act provided for the federal regulation of railway, ship, and aircraft traffic. Trucking was omitted from the legislation and the scope of the newly created Board of Transport Commissioners. Any doubts concerning the right of Ottawa to regulate trucking, however, were removed by the ruling in the Winner case (1951). Not only did the decision provide for federal regulation of interprovincial trucking, it also ruled that Ottawa's power extended to the intraprovincial activities of the regulated firms.[56]

The federal government at that time felt unable to take on the burdensome task of trucking regulation and delegated its power to provincial regulatory boards. In 1954, the Motor Vehicle Transport Act permitted each province to establish its own trucking regulations. This resulted in a lack of uniformity which, according to the Canadian Trucking Association, placed truckers at a competitive disadvantage vis-à-vis the railways.[57]

Throughout the fifties and sixties transportation policy was based on a jurisdictional division in which the provinces were responsible for road transport while other modes of transportation (air, water, rail, pipelines) were Ottawa's domain. This arrangement became less satisfactory as Canadian transportation patterns changed. In 1960, rail accounted for fifty-one percent of freight revenues and highways for thirty-two percent; by 1974 the rails' share was down to thirty-five percent and the truckers' portion had risen to forty-six percent.[58] The increase in competition and interdependence among all modes of transport created a need for more integrated policy. The proposals of the MacPherson Royal Commission on Transportation (1961) reflected an understanding of the changing transportation scene: the Commission recommended that, whenever possible, increased competition rather than regulation should allocate resources, and where regulation was necessary it should be based on a recognition of the interdependence and possible substitutability of various means of transportation.[59] Thus the regulations affecting any one mode of transportation must be seen as having a likely impact on other modes.

The 1967 National Transportation Act was directed toward the establishment of an economic, efficient, and adequate transportation system. The regulation of that system was to be the function of a single federal agency, the Canadian Transport Commission. Wherever possible, competition rather than government fiat was to determine rates and services. The new emphasis on interdependence and competition as opposed to regulation had one very direct consequence for the provinces. Part III of the NTA provided that the regulation of extra-provincial trucking be returned to federal jurisdiction. Trucking had become too important to be left outside of a general transportation scheme. Although Ottawa went to a great deal of trouble to persuade the provinces and trucking pressure groups to accept federal regulation of trucking, Part III of the NTA was proclaimed but never implemented. Angered by Ottawa's slowness in proposing uniform trucking regulations, the Canadian Trucking Association withdrew its support for Ottawa's new role and made it virtually impossible for the federal government to proceed as the regulator of the trucking industry.[60] Today road transportation remains in the provincial sphere.

Given the predominance of the federal government in transportation, it becomes important to consider how provincial interests are represented in the federal decision-making arena. Unfortunately there are very few mechanisms for effective provincial input into federal transportation policy. Although the special rates from the Crow's Nest Pass Agreement and the Maritime Freight Rates Act have been effectively defended by the provinces, the provinces seek a more general impact on national transportation policies. If nothing else there is a growing recognition that federal policies that change the usage of rail, air, and water facilities also affect the utilization of the roads and therefore have a direct effect on provincial budgets. Beyond those members of the CTC who are seen as regional representatives, the only formal roles for the provinces in federal transportation are as recipients of shared-cost grants for commuter services, road construction, and railway crossings and as intervenors in cases before the CTC.[61]

It was not until the late fifties and sixties that any intergovernmental consultations on transportation took place. The interactions between Ottawa and the Atlantic Provinces Economic Council represented an important beginning in making Ottawa formally aware of regional transportation interests. At the Western Economic Opportunities Conference in 1973, transportation was one of the major policy areas that the Prairie Provinces discussed with Ottawa. In their position paper these provinces put together four demands for amendments to the National Transportation Act, which provided some insight into provincial desire for access to federal decision-making: (i) establishment of regional economic development as one goal of national transportation policy, (ii) full disclosure of costs incurred by the railways, (iii) examination of legislative provisions setting criteria for establishment of rates, (iv) creation of a permanent federal-provincial transportation committee.[62]

Impetus for change in federal-provincial relations in transportation comes from three sources. First, stronger, more competent provincial governments have gone beyond the traditional emphasis on road building. In provincial bureaucracies resides much of the expertise for dealing with modern transport problems. Thus the provinces now have not only a greater awareness of their unique interests, they are more able to act on these interests. One of the enduring sources of tension within Canadian confederation has been the perceived disadvantage of the peripheral regions against the dominant central provinces. This centrifugal tendency is nowhere more apparent than in transportation policy where the non-central provinces allege that federal agencies tend to reflect the views of central Canada because there is no effective mechanism for the articulation of regional interests. A third source of dissatisfaction and pressure for change involves the lack of accountability of the CTC. Because this agency has a quasi-autonomous status as an independent regulatory body, it is not directly responsible to any political authority.[63]

Criticism of the federal policy patterns and the lack of access by the provinces have generated a number of proposals for reform. Some pose relatively minor changes like allowing the provinces access to cost data in order to improve their briefs to the CTC or the creation of an advisory National Transportation Council comparable to the Economic

Council of Canada. A more fundamental suggestion has been to replace the CTC with a joint federal-provincial regulatory board.[64] The proposals for reform have sought both to establish a forum for the accommodation of federal-provincial interests and to improve the likelihood of reasonable regulatory decisions. These goals can best be achieved through some institutional arrangement based on what Richard Schultz calls "regulatory sharing"—involvement of both levels of government in regulatory programmes created after a process of joint consultations.[65]

The Public/Private Mix

In many sections of the Canadian economy public ownership and involvement exist alongside private enterprise. The field of transportation is a good example of this coexistence. There are several reasons for public involvement in the transportation sector: (1) transportation is social overhead (i.e. it is necessary for economic and social development), (2) transportation has direct and indirect effects on the regional distribution of wealth, (3) massive capital investment is often required, and (4) the large scale often means the usual competitive forces may not reliably control behaviour, creating a need to regulate.[66]

Although Ottawa has been the main agent in the creation of the transportation public sector, the provinces have in their own right been active participants. Each province has a Department of Transportation. For many years, transportation and communication was the single largest expenditure category in provincial budgets. From the 1940s through the 1960s the provinces spent on an average over 20% of their budget on transportation. Prior to the full development of the welfare state most government services were directed toward building a suitable infrastructure for economic development. Moreover, road building has always been an important source of patronage for the provinces. The fifty-cent dollars available from Ottawa under the TransCanada Highway Programme (1950) were an additional incentive for provincial decision-makers to channel their resources into transportation. During the 1950s this policy area increased to almost 1/3 (28.8%) of annual provincial expenditures. By the 1970s, however, transportation had been dwarfed by health and education spending. From 1970 to 1974 the provinces spent on average 11.7% of the budget on transportation and communication. New Brunswick spent the most, (15.9 percent) and Manitoba the least (8.6 percent).[67] In terms of provincial employment, in 1957 transportation accounted for 12% of all provincial employees; in 1967 15% and in 1976 8.5%.[68]

From what has already been said about the federal constitutional predominance in the field of transportation, it may seem odd to discover that the provinces actually spend about 75% of the total dollars allocated to transportation for all levels of government. The reason for this is simply that the most expensive budgetary items happen to include construction and maintenance of highways and roads. But these dollars do not reflect a corresponding importance in decision-making. In fact, some of the most controversial and important transport policy decisions are primarily regulatory in nature and therefore are not manifested in budgetary terms. The most important instruments of provincial transportation policies are regulation, provision of facilities, and public ownership.

Regulation

Surface transport is the sole mode of transportation regulated by the provinces. The trucking industry is the main industry to come under these regulations. There are several dimensions in trucking regulations, including: control of entry to the industry, price determination, quality of service, safety, finance and acquisitions, and operating rights.[69] Control of the entry of firms into the industry and control of rates are fundamental to effective public regulation. Provincial comparisons have shown that although all provinces but Newfoundland have entry control, only three — Manitoba, B.C., and Saskatchewan — can effectively be considered "regulatory" provinces because they are the only ones that also control rates.[70] The lack of uniformity across provincial jurisdiction has been a source of discontent for firms engaged in interprovincial traffic. As we have noted, the Canadian Trucking Association's support for the federal takeover of trucking regulation was based in part on a desire to impose some order and uniformity on the chaotic provincial situation.

Trucking regulation, similar to most other instances of federal or provincial regulation, has developed outside the regular departmental structure. All the provinces except Nova Scotia, P.E.I., and Newfoundland have created separate regulatory commissions or boards to deal with transportation. In Quebec and New Brunswick, for example, there is a single umbrella agency that deals with all aspects of provincial transport regulation, whereas in Ontario, Alberta, Saskatchewan, British Columbia, and Manitoba there are several agencies. British Columbia and Manitoba each have four boards that handle separate aspects of transportation which include ferries, harbour, taxis, and highway transportation.[71]

Public Provision of Facilities

Sometimes state involvement has meant that the provinces finance the capital facility but private firms continue to compete. According to Paul Phillips, "in the development of transportation and communication, provincial and federal governments have been the major domestic financial intermediary for most large scale capital intensive development."[72] One of the early instances of provincial action in this regard was the building in the 1890s of a railway by Manitoba. As a result of the discontent with the CPR monopoly in the West, the Liberal government of Manitoba started in 1888 to build a railway to compete with CPR. An American company, the Northern Pacific Railroad, was given the running rights.[73]

Roads are the main transportation facility provided by the provinces. Generally the provinces are responsible for all roads outside of town limits and they also assist the municipalities for roads within city limits. Compared to the other modes of transportation, the users of roads come closest to bearing the full cost of travel. Roads have the lowest proportion of indirect costs (which are the costs of facilities not covered by users and therefore borne by the taxpayer). In 1965 it was estimated only 6 percent of the cost of roads are passed on to the public purse whereas air travellers pass on 26%; for the rails, the cost to the taxpayer is 18%. Of course the six percent road figure is somewhat misleading because private car users bear a disproportionate share of road costs as compared to commercial truck users. Based on costs per ton mile, truckers' pay, depending on the province, anywhere from 31¢ to 44¢ whereas the lowest rate for cars is 53¢ and the highest is 87¢.[74] Therefore it is the "driving public" as opposed to the general public that subsidizes trucking.

The provinces are very wary of federal actions that may divert rail, air, and water users to the roads. The announced federal policy to have users pay more of the costs will mean higher prices for modes of transportation under federal jurisdiction and a likely turning to the roads as an alternative.[75] Similarly plans for railway line abandonment generally mean increased road use and therefore greater costs to the provinces.[76] Transportation is very much a federal-provincial issue area; decisions by either level affecting the use and/or costs of any mode of transport have ramifications for the other governments' responsibilities.

Public Ownership

The third instrument of provincial involvement in transportation is public ownership. Here government itself directly provides the transportation services. In the other two instances, regulation and provision of facilities, the state works within the context of the private sector. In the case of public ownership, the state takes the place of the private firm. (A state-owned service may exist either in competition with other, private firms or as a monopoly.) Public ownership at the provincial level is not very widespread and most provinces do not provide or own any transportation service. The British Columbia Railway, Ontario Northland Railway, Ontario GO Transit, Alberta Western Airlines Ltd., and

Northern Alberta Railway are some of the relatively few examples of provincial ownership.

The most common form of public ownership occurs in municipal transit systems. Most municipal transit systems began as privately owned street railways. Today, virtually all are publicly owned.[77] Since the fifties most Canadian urban centres have initiated studies of their transportation needs, but so far only Montreal, Toronto, and Edmonton have developed electric mass transit systems. The car thus remains the major mode of transportation in urban centres, and the major government investment is in roads. This policy direction appears to be slowly shifting as energy and environmental concerns are making mass transit more attractive. The low profitability of mass transit has made it unappealing to the private sector, so there can be no public transit unless provided by the government.

The provinces have become involved in municipal transit mainly through cost-sharing. Alberta, B.C., N.S., Manitoba, and Ontario provide subsidies to the municipalities to cover capital costs and in some cases operating deficits. The Ontario Transportation Development Corporation was established in 1975 to stimulate research and development in this area. British Columbia is the only province to have a central planning agency (located in the Ministry of Municipal Affairs and Housing) for transit in all municipalities.

Ottawa has also become involved in assisting the municipalities with their transportation needs. In the tri-level consultations of 1972 and 1973 one of the major topics was transportation. The National Urban Transportation Development Corporation was created to promote innovation in urban transit. The federal government under the 1974 Railway Relocation and Crossing Act makes funds available to municipalities to assist in some phases of urban transport development.

Transportation Issues

Beyond those immediate and highly visible conflicts that arise over the termination of local bus services or the location of a new highway, two issues — representation of the public interest and the impact of regulations — have proven especially contentious for provincial decision-makers. These issues are of special interest because they pose questions that are also raised in other areas under provincial regulation.

Regulatory boards generally have a statutory responsibility to serve the public interest. The effectiveness with which this principle has been implemented is open to serious question.[78] The regulatory process has tended to operate in a rather one-sided fashion, weighted in favour of the interests being regulated. The membership of the boards tends to be drawn from those likely to be sympathetic to the regulated industry. The staff of the agency is also likely to be drawn from industry sources, and in its own self-interest it is unlikely to pursue consumer interests. There is rarely any representation of the consumer on the boards, nor is there much provision for effective participation at hearings. In recent years, however, there have been notable efforts by some provinces to include the public. Ontario in 1972 established channels for the formal inclusion of consumer representation. In Saskatchewan the Advisory Council to the Government for Transportation Policy has been holding open meetings in order to tap public opinion on transport issues.

As is the case in regulation of other sectors, large unorganized groups tend to remain ineffective because the benefits of participation are not sufficient to induce an individual to pay the costs of consumer participation. In transportation as in other areas, an institutionalized consumer advocate is needed.[79]

As we have seen, government involvement in transportation has been directed toward two purposes: to make the allocation of resources more efficient and to use transportation as a means toward a number of external goals, namely regional development and equity. The impact of transportation policies must be considered in the light of these two sets of objectives. Much of the evidence obtained from economic and political analysis points on balance to a negative assessment. Unlike the case of railroads, where the main objective of regulation was to protect the public from monopoly power, in the case of trucking, "economic theory does not suggest that regulation is required or desirable."[80] For the railways high capital costs prohibit entry, but for trucking firms entry is relatively easy, and thus competition among firms is virtually assured. The impact of regulation has tended to protect existing firms *from* competition. For the consumer the impact is not very favourable. Comparisons of those provinces in which there is little direct regulation of trucking and those in which there is a great deal draw similar conclusions: rates are higher in the regulating provinces.[81] Moreover, in his work in Northern Ontario, Bonsor found that "entry restrictions and rate regulation in the highway trucking industry are thus seen as causes for both high trucking and rail rates . . . Deregulation would, therefore, yield two important benefits: lower truck rates and lower rail rates."[82]

What about the external objectives? Have transportation policies facilitated regional development and helped to compensate for distance from central markets? There are varying assessments. In a study of Prairie development for the Royal Commission on Consumer Prices and Inflation, Wilson and Darby conclude that transportation is not a very important factor in stimulating economic growth and that in order to bring about further development other inducements are required.[83] Alternatively, there are those who maintain subsidies and regulation badly distort the allocation of resources and prevent regional economic development and diversity. They argue that transportation factors do have an important effect on development and that, unfortunately, the effect has been negative. The present structure of rates in the West and Northern Ontario has been criticized as a barrier to regional economic diversity and as an arrangement that leads to suboptimal location of industries.[84] Analysis of the Atlantic provinces points to equally negative conclusions.[85] The present structure does not benefit industry. It is argued that, although the Atlantic provinces need help, such assistance would be more effective if it were in the form of a direct subsidy to producers.

Although each new technology may generate its own particular transportation problems there have been certain long-standing factors of provincial transportation policy. Transportation has always been viewed by provincial decision-makers as a crucial element in regional economic development. As is the case in most areas of economic policy Ottawa is the dominant government and its decisions weigh heavily on the well-being of all the provinces. In the past, subsidies for those services believed to be necessary to a region were a major part of federal transportation policy. Today, Ottawa is leading the push to slash subsidies and to have users pay the full cost of transportation services. Thus, more conflict has emerged in the federal-provincial transportation arena. Today, more than ever before, strengthened provincial governments are demanding to play a significant role in the determination of national transportation policy.

CONCLUSIONS

Provincial involvement in the mobilization of physical resources has created a service state which, for the most part, has facilitated rather than supplanted the private sector. The appropriation of land and other resources and the promotion of capital accumulation were the earliest forms of state support designed to stimulate private economic development.[86] This has meant that the provinces have in general pursued resource mobilization indirectly.

In order to encourage sufficient private capital investment in natural resource development, the provinces have sought to provide the private sector with economic incentives and a transportation infrastructure. Similarly, the provinces have encouraged the agricultural sector through research development and marketing boards. However, with the heightened awareness of the social consequences of resource exploitation and of the inevitable depletion of reserves, there is increasing pressure to impose restraints on resource exploitation. This new concern for conservation has increased the extent of public involvement and the level of conflict in resource policy-making because it has generated divergent views of the public interests.

NOTES

1. On the general notion of resource mobilization as an area of policy, see Richard Rose, "On the Priorities of Government: A Developmental Analysis of Public Policies," *European Journal of Political Research,* 4 1976, pp. 247-289. For analyses in the Canadian setting see H. Aitken, "Defensive Expansion: The State and Economic Growth in Canada" in W. Easterbrook and M.H. Watkins (eds.), *Approaches to Canadian Economic History,* McClelland and Stewart, Toronto, 1967, pp. 183-221; Glenn Porter and Robert Cuff (eds.), *Enterprise and National Development,* Hakkert, Toronto, 1973, and Ronald Manzer. "Public Policies in Canada: A Developmental Perspective," paper presented at the Canadian Political Science Association meetings, 1975.

2. See Pierre Fournier, *The Quebec Establishment,* Black Rose Books, Montreal, 1976, p. 164.

3. H.V. Nelles, *The Politics of Development: Forests, Mines and Hydro-Electric Power in Ontario, 1849-1941,* Macmillan, Toronto, 1974.

4. Anthony Scott, "Who Should Get Natural Resource Revenues?" in Scott (ed.), *Natural Resource Revenues, A Test of Federalism,* University of British Columbia Press, Vancouver, 1976, p. 19. This trend does not apply to the energy-rich provinces which have gradually drawn more heavily on natural resource revenues.

5. Thomas L. Burton, *Natural Resource Policy in Canada, Issues and Perspectives,* McClelland and Stewart, Toronto, 1972, provides a historical summary of the evolving balance between exploitation and conservation, chapter 1. See also Energy, Mines and Resources Canada, *Minerals and the Environment: Current Problems and Policies,* Mineral Policy Series, MR 163, Ottawa, 1976.

6. Judith Maxwell, *Policy Review and Outlook, 1976, Challenges to Complacency,* C.D. Howe Institute, Montreal, 1976, pp. 130-161; John Helliwell and Gerry May, "Taxes, Royalties, and Equity Participation as Alternative Methods of Dividing Resource Revenues: The Syncrude Example," in Scott (ed.), *op. cit.,* pp. 153-180; and Larry Pratt, *The Tar Sands: Syncrude and the Politics of Oil,* Hurtig, Edmonton, 1976.

7. There exists no systematic assessment of the role of resource industries across all provinces. Case studies do, however, confirm the importance of this role in the policy process. See, for example, M.W. Bucovetsky, "The Mining Industry and the Great Tax Reform Debate," pp. 87-114, and A. Paul Pross, "Input versus Withinput: Pressure Group Demands and Administrative Survival," pp. 148-171 in A. Paul Pross (ed.), *Pressure Group Behaviour in Canadian Politics,* McGraw-Hill Ryerson, Toronto, 1975; Larry Pratt, "The State and

Province Building: Alberta's Development Strategy," in Leo Panitch (ed.), *The Canadian State: Political Economy and Political Power*, University of Toronto Press, Toronto, 1977, pp. 133-162.

8. The most recent task force on forest policy was established by the NDP government in 1974 and chaired by P.H. Pearse. See British Columbia Royal Commission on Forest Resource, *Timber Rights and Forest Policy in British Columbia*, Queen's Printer, Victoria, 1976. See also William McKillop and Walter J. Mead, *Timber Policy Issues in British Columbia*, University of British Columbia Press, Vancouver, 1974.

9. G.W. Taylor, *Timber: History of the Forest Industry in B.C.*, Douglas, Vancouver, 1975, p. 184.

10. General descriptions of these sectors and their growth are found in Mary L. Barker, *Natural Resources of British Columbia and the Yukon*, Douglas, David and Charles, Vancouver, 1977, and Taylor, *ibid*. For studies which systematically examine policy issues of natural resources, see M. Crommelin and A. Thompson (eds.), *Mineral Leasing Policy as an Instrument of Public Policy*, University of British Columbia Press, Vancouver, 1977.

11. Martin Robin, *Pillars of Profit*, McClelland and Stewart, Toronto, 1973, pp. 172-175.

12. E.R Black, "British Columbia, The Politics of Exploitation," in W.E. Mann (ed.), *Social and Cultural Change in Canada, I*, Copp Clark, Toronto, 1970, pp. 112-119.

13. A brief account of the evolution of natural resource policy in Ontario is in W.R. Smithies, *The Protection and Use of Natural Resources in Ontario*, Ontario Economic Council, Toronto, 1974. Nelles, *op. cit.*, offers detailed historical evidence on government-industry interrelationships.

14. Atlantic Canada must also be described as energy dependent. These provinces do, however, have the possibility of some future energy developments in offshore oil and in the harnessing of tidal power. See Atlantic Provinces Economic Council, *Energy: Its Sources, Production, Distribution and Financing in Atlantic Canada*, Halifax, 1976. See also W.A. Black and J.W. Maxwell, "Resource Utilization: Change and Adaptation," in Alan Macpherson (ed.), *The Atlantic Provinces*, University of Toronto Press, Toronto, 1972, pp. 73-136.

15. Peter Neary (ed.), *The Political Economy of Newfoundland, 1929-1972*, Copp Clark, Toronto, 1973, pp. 174-221; Philip Smith, *Brinco, the Story of Churchill Falls*, McClelland and Stewart, Toronto, 1975.

16. It has been argued that the problem of economic lag in the Maritimes stems not only from a lack of resources and from geographic isolation, but also from the centralist bias of national economic policies.

17. Examples of such public sector participation in several provinces are

found in Philip Mathias, *Forced Growth*, McClelland and Stewart, Toronto, 1975. Chapter Two above also considers the extent of government economic involvement. See also Roy George, *The Life and Times of Industrial Estates Limited*, Institute of Public Affairs, Dalhousie, Halifax, 1974; and H.A. Fredericks with Allen Chambers, *Bricklin*, Brunswick Press, Fredericton, 1977.

18. Parzival Copes, "Canada's Atlantic Coast Fisheries: Policy Developments and the Impact of Extended Jurisdiction," *Canadian Public Policy* 4, Spring, 1978, pp. 155-171; and C.L. Mitchell, "The 200-mile Limit: New Issues, Old Problems for Canada's East Coast Fisheries," *Canadian Public Policy* 4, Spring, 1978, pp. 172-183.

19. Analyses of jurisdictional questions are found in W.R. Lederman, "The Constitution: A Basis for Bargaining," pp. 52-60; Donald V. Smiley, "The Political Context of Resource Development in Canada," pp. 61-72 in Scott (ed.), *op. cit.*, and A.R. Thompson and H.R. Eddy, "Jurisdictional Problems in Natural Resource Management in Canada," in W.D. Bennett *et al.*, *Essays on Aspects of Resource Policy*, Science Council of Canada, Ottawa, 1973, pp. 67-96.

20. For an explanation of the differential treatment of provincial property rights prior to 1930 in the prairie provinces and, to a limited extent, in British Columbia, see Gerard V. La Forest, *Natural Resources and Public Property under the Canadian Constitution*, University of Toronto Press, Toronto, 1969, pp. 27-45, 182-189.

21. An important exception is uranium, which is predominantly under federal control. See G.B. Doern, "Science and Technology in the Nuclear Regulatory Process: the Case of Canadian Uranium Miners," *Canadian Public Administration*, 21, Spring, 1978, pp. 51-82.

22. For contrasting governmental positions see J. Peter Meekison (ed.), *Canadian Federalism: Myth or Reality*, Third edition, Methuen, Toronto, 1977, pp. 397-416.

23. On the significance of the two-price system see L. Waverman, "The Two Price System in Energy: Subsidies Forgotten," *Canadian Public Policy* 1, Winter, 1975, pp. 76-96.

24. Allan Blakeney, "Resources, the Constitution and Canadian Federalism," in Meekison, *op. cit.*, pp. 179-188.

25. In April 1974 Alberta raised its royalty rate to 65% on the price over $3.80 per barrel. Later adjustments reduced the average royalty to 38.9% of wellhead price. Saskatchewan at first set the royalty on price increments at 100%, but later reduced the rate to 66 2/3%. These policy initiatives are discussed in R.W. Cochrane, "Provincial Tax and Royalty Developments, Oil and Gas Resource Operations," Canadian Tax Foundation, *Conference Report, 1975*, pp. 137-156.

26. An account of these developments is found in R.D. Brown, "The Fight Over Resource Profits," *Canadian Tax Journal* 22, July-August,

1974, pp. 315-337. The Federal Government's position is expressed by T.S. Tuschak, "A Federal Perspective on the Tax Treatment of the Petroleum Industry," Canadian Tax Foundation, *Conference Report,* *1975,* pp. 157-173.

27. An excellent discussion of this linkage is Thomas J. Courchene, "Equalization Payments and Energy Royalties" in Scott (ed.), *op. cit.,* pp. 73-107. See also Thomas J. Courchene, "The New Fiscal Arrangement and the Economics of Federalism," paper presented at the Conference on the Future of the Canadian Federation, Toronto, October 1977, p. 15.

28. The Government was defeated on the proposed budget two days later. The budget of November 1974 modified the effects of these proposals by reducing the federal tax rate. The June 1975 budget again revised these arrangements. For a review of these developments, see Sydney E. Ewans et al., "Tax and Royalty Treatment of the Petroleum Industry 1974-75" in Canadian Tax Foundation, *1975 Conference Report,* pp. 122-187.

29. Courchene (1977), *op. cit.,* pp. 13-14.

30. *Ibid.,* p. 16. For an overview of the 1977 Act see David B. Perry, "The Federal-Provincial Fiscal Arrangements Introduced in 1977," *Canadian Tax Journal* 25, July-August, 1977, pp. 429-440.

31. Canadian Tax Foundation, *Provincial and Municipal Finance, 1975,* pp. 117-118.

32. Prorationing was introduced in 1969 and the reserve tax in 1974. George R. Fraser, "Recent Developments and Royalty Measures in the Mining Industry," Canadian Tax Foundation, *Conference Report* *1975,* pp. 423-427. See also Richard Schaffner, *New Risks in Resource Development: the Potash Case,* C.D. Howe Research Institute, Montreal, 1976; John Richards, "Potash, Populists and Fabians," *Canadian Forum,* November, 1977, pp. 14-21.

33. Energy, Mines and Resources, *An Energy Strategy for Canada, Policies for Self-Reliance,* Ottawa, 1976, p. 3. Other general sources on Canada's energy position include: Science Council of Canada, *Canada's Energy Opportunities,* Information Canada, Ottawa, 1975; National Energy Board, *Canadian Oil, Supply and Requirements,* Ottawa, 1977.

34. Energy, Mines and Resources, *ibid.* provides two alternative scenarios of energy demands to 1990 and suggests a total rate of annual growth between 3.7 and 4.8%, pp. 48-60.

35. National Energy Board (1977), pp. 9-13, 25.

36. Maxwell, *op. cit.,* p. 133.

37. National Energy Board, *op. cit.* (1977), pp. 20-23.

38. Excluding frontier reserves, about 53 Tcf with a 1975 annual production of 2.5 Tcf NEB *ibid.,* p. 67; Science Council of Canada, *op. cit.,* p. 19.

39. V.C. Fowke, *Canadian Agricultural Policy: The Historical Pattern*, University of Toronto Press, Toronto, 1946, p. 156. See also David MacFarlane and J.D. Black, *The Development of Canadian Agriculture to 1970*, Macdonald College-McGill University, Montreal, 1958.

40. W. Craddock and E.T. Lewis, "Agriculture in the Canadian Economy" in L. Officer and L. Smith (eds.), *Issues in Canadian Economics* McGraw-Hill Ryerson, Toronto, 1974, p. 163.

41. See for example, Royal Commission on Grain Handling and Transportation, *Grain and Rail in Western Canada*, vol. 1, Ottawa, 1977, pp. 19-24.

42. See for example, David Smith, *Prairie Liberalism*, University of Toronto Press, Toronto, 1975; Norman Ward and Duff Spafford, *Politics in Saskatchewan*, Longman, Toronto, 1968, and Denis Smith, "Prairie Revolt, Federalism and the Party System" in H. Thorburn (ed.), *Party Politics in Canada*, Third Edition, Prentice-Hall, Scarborough, 1972, pp. 204-215; S.M. Lipset, *Agrarian Socialism*, University of California Press, Berkeley, 1950; C.B. Macpherson, *Democracy in Alberta: Social Credit and the Party System*, University of Toronto Press, Toronto, 1962; Wm. Irvine, *The Farmers in Politics*, McClelland and Stewart, Toronto, 1976; and Martin Westmacott, "The National Transportation Act and Western Canada: A Case-study in Co-operative Federalism," *CPA*, Fall, 1973, pp. 447-467.

43. S.W. Garland and S.C. Hudson, *Government Involvement in Agriculture*, A Study for the Federal Task Force on Agriculture, Queen's Printer, Ottawa, 1968, p. 315.

44. Don Mitchell, *The Politics of Food*, Lorimer, Toronto, 1975. See also Grace Skogstad, "The Farm Products Marketing Agencies Act and the Food Policy Debate: Case Studies of Agricultural Policy," paper presented at the Canadian Political Science Association Meetings, London, May 1978; and M Veeman and T. Veeman, "The Directions of Canadian Agricultural Policy," *Canadian Journal of Agricultural Economics*, July, 1976, pp. 78-90.

45. Federal Task Force on Agriculture, *Canadian Agriculture in the Seventies*, Queen's Printer, Ottawa, 1969, p. 276.

46. See W.E. Drummond, *et al.*, *A Review of Agricultural Policy in Canada*, The Agricultural Research Council of Canada, 1966; Hughes Morrissette, *Les Conditions du Développement Agricole au Quebec* Les Presses de L'Université Laval, Québec, 1972; and G. Elmore Reaman, *A History of Agriculture in Ontario*, Vol. II Saunders, Toronto, 1970.

47. On marketing boards see A.E. Safarian, "Agricultural Marketing Legislation: A Case Study," in P. Meekison (ed.), *Canadian Federalism: Myth or Reality*, Third Edition, Methuen, Toronto, 1977, pp. 430-439; Broadwith, Hughes and Associates, "The Ontario Milk Marketing Board: An Economic Analysis," in Ontario Economic Council, *Government Regulation*, Toronto, 1978, pp. 67-102.

48. *Canada Yearbook, 1976-77,* Statistics Canada, Ottawa, 1977, p. 549. There is some pressure for Ottawa not to delegate its authority to various provincial boards but rather to establish national marketing boards. The Canadian Wheat Board (1935) is the oldest national board. In 1972 the Farm Products Marketing Agencies Act provided for the establishment of national boards for poultry and poultry products.

49. For an introduction to the land use issue see Ralph Krueger, "The Preservation of Agricultural Land in Canada" and J.L. Nowland and J.A. McKeague, "Canada's Limited Agricultural Land Resource," both in R. Krueger and B. Mitchell (eds.), *Managing Canada's Renewable Resources,* Methuen, Toronto, 1977, pp. 109-131; and A.D. Crerar, "The Loss of Farmland in the Metropolitan Regions of Canada" in R. Krueger, *et al.* (eds.), *Regional and Resource Planning in Canada,* Revised Edition, Holt, Rinehart and Winston, Toronto, 1970, pp. 126-133.

50. See K. Studnicki-Gizbert, "Administration of Transport Policy: The Regulatory Problems" in K. Rea and J.T. McLeod, *Business and Government in Canada,* Second Edition, Methuen, Toronto, 1976, 259-268.

51. W.G. Waters II, "Public Policy and Transport Regulation: An Economic Perspective," in K. Ruppenthal and Wm. Stanbury (eds.), *Transportation Policy: Regulation, Competition and the Public Interest,* University of British Columbia Centre for Transportation Studies, Vancouver, 1976, pp. 11-14.

52. *Ibid.,* pp. 20-24.

53. See G.P. de T. Glazebrook, *A History of Transportation in Canada,* McClelland and Stewart, Toronto, 1938; A.W. Currie, *Canadian Transportation Economics,* University of Toronto Press, Toronto, 1967; David Bercuson (ed.), *Canada and the Burden of Unity* Macmillan, Toronto, 1977, Chapters 4 and 6. For a different view see Howard Darling, "What Belongs in Transportation Policy?" *Canadian Public Administration* 18, Winter, 1975, 659-668.

54. Westmacott, *op. cit.*

55. In a recent essay on the evolution of transportation policy, Baldwin contends that generally the degree of regulation is diminishing. See J. Baldwin, "The Evolution of Transportation Policy in Canada," *Canadian Public Administration* 20, Winter, 1977, 600-631.

56. Arthur Wright, "An Examination of the Role of the Board of Transport Commissions for Canada as a Regulatory Tribunal," *Canadian Public Administration,* December, 1963, 349-385 for a useful summary of Canadian transport regulation. See also John C. McManus, *Federal Regulation of Transport in Canada,* Canadian Consumer Council, Ottawa, 1972.

57. Richard Schultz, "Interest Groups and Intergovernmental Negotiations Caught in the Vise of Federalism" in P. Meekison (ed.), *Canadian Federalism: Myth or Reality?,* Third Edition, Methuen, Toronto, 1977.

58. Canadian Transport Commission, *Transport Review: Trends and Selected Issues*, Ottawa, 1977.

59. Royal Commission on Transportation, *Report*, Ottawa, 1961. See also K. Studnicki-Gizbert, "Transport Policy: Objectives and Policy Instruments" in K. Studnicki-Gizbert (ed.), *Issues in Canadian Transport Policy*, Macmillan, Toronto, 1974, 361-407; and H.L. Purdy, *Transport Competition and Public Policy in Canada*, University of British Columbia Press, Vancouver, 1972.

60. Schultz, *op. cit.*

61. See M.W. Westmacott, "The Canadian Transport Commission, Freight Rates and the Public Interest," p. 56; and J.W. Langford, "The National Transportation System: Restructuring for Effective Regulation," p. 102, in Ruppenthal and Stanbury, *op. cit.*

62. As quoted in Westmacott, "The Canadian Transport Commission, Freight Rates and the Public Interest," p. 82.

63. *Ibid.*; Ivan Feltham, "Transport-Regulation in Canada" in Studnicki-Gizbert (ed.), *op. cit.*, 309-343. See also John Langford, *Transport in Transition: The Reorganization of the Federal Transport Portfolio*, McGill-Queen's, Montreal, 1976.

64. See Karl Ruppenthal, "Transport in Canada: Needs, Trends and Problems" and J. Baldwin, "Transportation Policy and Jurisdictional Issues," *Canadian Public Administration* 18, Winter, 1975, 587-600 and 630-641; and Langford, *op. cit.*, 102.

65. R. Schultz, "Intergovernmental Cooperation, Regulatory Agencies and Transportation Regulation in Canada: The Case of Part III of the National Transportation Act," *Canadian Public Administration* 19, Summer, 1976, 183-207.

66. James Seldon, "Transportation in Canada," in F. Officer and L. Smith, *Issues in Canadian Economics*, McGraw-Hill Ryerson, Toronto, 1974.

67. Canadian Tax Foundation, *Provincial and Municipal Finances 1977*, Toronto, 1977.

68. See J. Hodgetts and O.P. Dwivedi, *Provincial Governments as Employers*, McGill—Queen's, Montreal, 1974, 12; and Canadian Tax Foundation, *National Finances 1976*, Toronto, 1977.

69. Gayton Germane, "The Rationale for Transport Regulation" in Ruppenthal and Stanbury, *op. cit.*, 39-48; and G.B. Reschenthaler, *The Performance of Selected Independent Regulatory Commissions in Alberta, Saskatchewan and Manitoba*, Canadian Consumer Council, Ottawa, 1972.

70. James Sloss, "Regulation of Motor Freight Transportation: A Further Analysis of Provincial Trucking Regulation," *Bell Journal of Economics and Management*, 1973, 655-664.

71. K. Rubin, *Report on Inventory of Regulatory Boards*, Canadian Consumer Council, Ottawa, 1971.

72. "National Policy, Continental Economics and National Disintegration" in D.J. Bercuson, *op. cit.*, 35.
73. T.D. Regehr, "Western Canada and the Burden of National Transportation Policies" in *ibid.*, 115-142.
74. Purdy, *op. cit.*, 140-152. There are many models for estimating user costs. Although there are differences in the amounts attributed to users, one consistent finding is that road users pay a significantly larger portion of costs than users of other modes of transportation. See Z. Haritos, "Transport Costs and Revenues in Canada," *Journal of Transport Economics and Policy*, January, 1975, 16-33.
75. Nancy Bryan, *More Taxes and More Traffic*, Canadian Tax Foundation, Toronto, 1972, 175.
76. The Hall Royal Commission on Grain Handling and Transportation recommended specific compensation for the provinces for decisions that result in increased road use. Hall Commission, *op. cit.*, Vol. 1, 534. See also *Globe and Mail*, 18 May 1977, B1.
77. See Donald Levy, "Innovation in Transit in Medium Size Canadian Cities," Research Report #31, University of Toronto, York Joint Programme in Transportation, June 1976; Roads and Transportation Association of Canada, *Nation on the Move 1975*, Ottawa, 1976; and D.J. Reynolds, *The Urban Transportation Problem 1970-2000* Ottawa, 1971.
78. See K. Studnicki-Gizbert, "Transport Policy", *op. cit.*, Stanbury, *op. cit.*, and J. Grafstein, "Some Issues in the Development of Regulatory Policies: Who is Regulating What?" in Studnicki-Gizbert, *op. cit.*, 340-356.
79. G. Reschenthaler, *op. cit.*; and Michael Trebilcock, "Winners and Losers in the Modern Regulatory State," in K. Rae and J.T. McLeod, *op. cit.*, pp. 362-378.
80. N.C. Bonsor, *Transportation Rates and Economic Development in Northern Ontario*, Ontario Economic Council, Toronto, 1976, 20.
81. Sloss, *op. cit.*, and John Palmer, *Empirically Testing the Effects of Provincial Trucking Regulation: A Further Analysis*, Canadian Consumer Council, Ottawa, 1975.
82. Bonsor, *op. cit.*, 65.
83. *Transportation in the Prairies*, Report prepared for the Prairies Royal Commission on Consumer Problems and Inflation, Edmonton, 1968, 14-15.
84. Bonsor, *op. cit.*, Regehr, *op. cit.*, and G. Weller, "Hinterland Politics of Northwestern Ontario," *Canadian Journal of Political Science* 10, December, 1977, 727-754.
85. Mohring Herbert, "Transport Subsidies and the Economic Development of the Atlantic Provinces," in Studnicki-Gizbert, *op. cit.*, 263-304 and Economist Intelligence Unit, *Atlantic Provinces Transportation*

Study, Ottawa, 1967, vol. V; see also Atlantic Provinces Economic Council, *Aspects of Transportation in Atlantic Canada,* Halifax, 1975; and Forbes, *op. cit.*

86. See Manzer, *op. cit.* for an analysis of the changing policy principles associated with economic development.

Chapter 8

Perspectives on Provincial Policy

Policy Development

In the evolution of the modern state the scope of public activity has expanded from a core of essential functions concerning defense and internal order through a secondary range of activity typified by resource development and exploitation to the provision of social benefits and services.[1] These three stages, each characterized by the primacy of certain issues, apply to the general expansion of the public sector. The major areas of provincial policy growth can be associated with these second and third stages. Provincial governments became deeply involved in resource development issues at a very early stage; social problems generally were politicized at a much later date. There is today a standing acceptance of the provincial service state as a facilitator of economic development and of the provincial welfare state as an instrument for individual and social betterment. Although together social and resource policy account for the bulk of the expansion of the provincial public sector, they have reflected distinct patterns of policy activity.

Decision-makers in these fields have tended to employ different policy means to achieve social and economic goals. In the case of social policies government action is designed to benefit individuals directly.[2] Since social policies entail income transfers and the provision of facilities and services, expenditures are the most important instruments of policy. Changing policy priorities can, therefore, be gauged through budgetary indicators.

The scope of provincial involvement in resource mobilization, on the other hand, has always been greater than expenditure analysis alone would indicate, and has tended to rely on indirect means to promote economic growth. Early public involvement in these areas often took the form of subsidies and other fiscal incentives for selected economic sectors. But over time there has been a gradual shift away from these distributive modes in favour of general guidelines and rules designed to control as well as to facilitate resource development. Many crucial provincial initiatives in natural resource exploitation, agriculture, and transportation have been regulatory in nature.

The comparison of social and resource development policies also indicates differing patterns of political conflict. Social policies, especially health and welfare, have typically been controversial because they are often seen in redistributive terms, with collective consequences beyond the benefits accruing to the individual. Education, too, has been an arena for conflict because of its significance for linguistic and religious communities.

In contrast, resource mobilization has often shown minimal levels of conflict. Traditionally, involvement in many of the policy developments in this area has been restricted to a narrow range of producer groups operating in close cooperation with government. However, as the social costs of resource policies have become apparent, many resources issues have gradually become matters of increased public concern and involvement. This has meant that arenas of policy-making have been expanded to include previously excluded interests with the result that political controversy over such issues has become more common.

Whether we compare social and resource development or even the specific policies within either one of these broad fields, we find there has been no single path of policy evolution and no common policy-making process. Just as there are multiple patterns of policy, there are multiple determinants of any policy. A number of factors have commonly been employed in the explanation of public policy.

Socio-economic conditions have been of fundamental significance for social and resource policy development. There is little doubt that industrialization and urbanization have served as basic stimuli for social policy development because they have generated a common set of needs (although differing in intensity) in all provinces and have, therefore, created the conditions for the emergence of the welfare state. Socio-economic factors have had a less uniform effect within the resource development fields. Because of dissimilar resource bases, there developed in each province a distinct set of issues and interests. In the case of resource policies, the link with social and economic change is especially difficult to decipher since policies of resource exploitation have themselves generated social and economic transformations. This means, in addition, that there has been an inevitable interdependence between social policy change and resource mobilization.

The second broad category of policy determinants is represented by political forces. As seen in Chapter 3, these include political ideas and values, pressure groups, and parties. The rise of the welfare state must be seen as in part a response to changing political ideas and values.[3] Prevailing views of appropriate forms of state activity and of the extent of public social responsibility help to define the direction and content of policy. The evidence of this impact is particularly clear in the emergence of systems of public health care and income maintenance, but it is also identifiable in the context of resource mobilization, where a growing awareness, on the part of both the general public and political elites, of the ultimate scarcity of resource wealth has led to emphasis on conservation as a policy goal.[4]

Organized pressure groups are a second category of political forces which are often thought to have a decisive impact on policy-making. Despite extensive speculation, surprisingly little is known about group influence because groups have rarely been the subject of systematic research. However, their active influence is documented in a limited number of case studies of specific policy decisions in such fields as health, natural resources, agriculture, and transportation. In many of these examples, interest group influence is not the product of the give-and-take of pluralist conflict; instead it is achieved through a corporatist sharing of power with government or a close clientele relationship between an agency and the sector it regulates.

There has been great controversy over the impact of political parties on public policy. On one side is the negative argument that parties have had little or no effect on shaping policy directions. The brokerage style and the absence of creative politics imply that there are no substantial policy differences between parties and that no identifiable policy change will result from a new party forming a government.[5] On the other side, in provincial politics there seems to be reason to argue that sometimes and under certain conditions parties may have a decisive and distinctive policy role. The impact of the Saskatchewan CCF after 1944 and of the Quebec Liberals after 1960 is beyond dispute. More recently the actions of the Blakeney government in resource policy and the Lyon government's cutbacks in the public sector imply considerable, albeit very different, policy shifts. Such examples notwithstanding, in general change in governing party does not necessarily portend policy change.

Finally, the structure of government itself must be viewed as a determinant of policy. Government institutions, which represent the standing mobilization of bias, and the established "rules of the game" place constraints on participants and affect their access and influence in the policy-making process. There is general agreement on the primacy of the cabinet and bureaucracy as decisional arenas. In health and welfare policy, for example, there is substantial evidence that policy-making is a corrective process of reform through "social-learning" that indicates the crucial role of bureaucratic expertise.[6] In addition, the developing structure of cabinet and administration has been the central instrument for province-building because it has permitted an increased decisional capacity for dealing with increasingly complex and large-scale policy problems.

In spite of some evidence on the determinants of policy, there remain serious limitations to explanations of policy development in the provincial context. One is that there is as yet an inadequate basis in existing research for understanding and establishing the impact of each apparent determinant. With regard to almost all of these (whether pressure groups, bureaucracy, public opinion, etc.), systematic evidence that would permit comparisons across provinces is to a large extent not yet available. There is, in short, an immediate need for more descriptive material on most aspects of provincial politics.

Even with more complete information about the components of provincial politics, there would remain a second problem for policy analysis, that the relative importance of each factor cannot be assessed, nor can the conditions under which the relative importance changes. This means that there is as yet no generally accepted model with which to fully analyse the question of policy determinants.

The various determinants of policy must, therefore, be viewed not as competing explanations but as a set of dynamics and constraints for decision-makers. Some are of a long-term and enduring nature which set broad limits on viable options and on the scope and content of the policy agenda. Others are much more immediate, visible, and short-term in character. It has often been observed that politicians tend to be preoccupied by these proximate factors with the result that policy change commonly appears to be a composite of limited and incremental modifications which reflect reactive responses to the most apparent and immediate concerns of policy-makers. There is little doubt that a great deal of government activity takes the form of crisis management. But even if policy-makers are rarely afforded the luxury of reflection and the opportunity to examine basic causes or to engage on a regular basis in long-range planning, it would be extremely short-sighted for observers to take the insiders' perspective at face value as a comprehensive and accurate assessment of the entire process. Long-term and distal factors clearly do set the broad directions and the standing priorities for what governments do. When a new government comes to power, it is never really free to start with a clean slate and to redefine its tasks. It inherits instead a policy legacy of existing programmes and committed expenditures, each of which may be the result of a long policy evolution.

The Changing Provincial State

Province-building, which denotes the coming of age of provincial governments, is both a product of policy development and an influence on future policies. The evolution of the provinces towards more capable and more complex organizations is the consequence of several factors. First, the increased responsibilities associated with the welfare state remain within provincial jurisdictions and have resulted in an expanded provincial public sector. Second, much of the wealth stemming from the exploitation of natural resources has strengthened provincial economies and increased their revenues. And third, many of the problems associated with urban life have created a need for greater initiative and planning on the part of provincial governments. Increases in the size and competence of provincial bureaucracy have accompanied expanded provincial activities. Several provinces now have civil services with skills and capabilities comparable to Ottawa's. These changes become all the more significant when they are coupled with a growing sense of public purpose and a cabinet orientation toward long-range planning.

As described in Chapter 4, the unaided politician in an unaided cabinet is becoming a vestige of the past. The evolution of policy machinery into comprehensive and sophisticated structures can be traced to the enlarged scope of provincial concerns. Within the confines of what are sometimes very limited resources, all the provinces are involved in the development of their central decisional apparatus. One effect of such institutional change may be to enhance the power of the already dominant executive.

Another change associated with province-building is a tendency towards policy homogenization. Socio-economic development, combined with important social policy initiatives by the federal government, has led to a common set of provincial policy obligations. The extent to which this means an eventual convergence of provincial policy patterns is, however, open to question. For as provincial structures have matured, they have also gradually maximized their capacity to set their own policy directions.

Because the provinces have been the primary channels for the articulation of regional interests, the increasing strength and effectiveness of these governments create centrifugal forces within Canadian federalism. These tendencies have been exacerbated because the federal government has neither effectively accommodated regional interests, nor provided consistent representation of non-territorially based interests.[7] The result has been that conflict resolution and many significant policy decisions take place in the federal-provincial arena.

The Future of the Provinces within the Federal System

In the context of social and resource mobilization policies, there have been differing patterns of federal-provincial relations. Health, welfare, and education have been crucial arenas for federal entry into provincial jurisdiction. Predominantly through the device of conditional grants, Ottawa has been a key initiator of social reform. The latest trend, however, has been away from direct federal involvement in social policy. The major shared-cost programmes of health and post-secondary education no longer exist and conditional grants for social welfare services are following a similar course. The message is clear: Ottawa will no longer use share-cost grants to force the provinces to provide certain social services. These decisions are now up to the provinces. With regard to resource development issues, Ottawa's role has been more direct. Agriculture is a concurrent power and transportation is predominantly federal. The powers to tax and to regulate trade and commerce are the constitutional basis for federal influence over resource development.

Although provincial initiatives may often compete with federal policy-making, this should not obscure the enduring changes that have occurred at the provincial level. The history of Canadian federalism has been characterized by pendular shifts between centralization and decentralization. The maturation of the provinces may mean an end to this cyclical quality in Canadian federalism, for it makes impossible any return to the centralism of the past. The provinces are no longer willing (nor do they need) to deal with Ottawa as junior members who carry out the lesser government functions. They demand to be consulted by Ottawa not only in those areas of shared jurisdiction and programmes but also in those normally within federal authority. In their efforts to provide inputs into national policies and to deal more systematically with their own jurisdictions, they have become more equal participants within the federal system. They perceive their own legitimate interests as essential ingredients to be considered in the formulation of national policies. Cairns has described this new relationship in the following way:

> Both levels of government are strong. Neither can dominate the other. Both pursue increasingly comprehensive and integrated goals with a consequent decline in their willingness to defer to the interests of external governments.[8]

Ottawa has at least partially recognized this emergent provincial role. In the words of the Minister of State for Federal-Provincial Relations,

> ... We are laying the groundwork for a new approach to the making of national economic policies for Canada.... A century ago, Sir John A. simply announced what his national policy was going to be: no discussions with provincial governments, no series of visits to provincial capitals and no federal-provincial conferences preceded his announcement and no one seems to have expected that they would. By contrast, any policies and processes we decide upon in this area today will emerge as a result of the process of federal and provincial consultation and as a result of a continuing process of consultation.[9]

Even a more positive federal attitude towards provincial consultation cannot resolve the basic conflicts resulting from substantial differences in regional interests. Given this dilemma a more productive approach may be a renewed effort towards what has been described as "project disentanglement,"[10] which involves a clarification of the division of power between Ottawa and the provinces. At Confederation, the division of powers was based on the notion of the provinces having jurisdiction over those matters separating the French and English communities and those areas of a predominantly local nature.[11] Although suitable then, such a division of authority has long since become outmoded. Today, as we have seen at several points in this book, virtually all aspects of provincial policy-making demonstrate the convoluted and confusing nature of federal and provincial jurisdiction.

Because of the intricate intertwining of federal and provincial authority, any disentanglement of jurisdictions must proceed step by step, handling one policy field at a time. This means that no single rule or formula is likely to provide a workable solution for each step. Policy disentanglement can have several benefits, including the reduction in conflict resulting from overlapping authorities, the rechanneling of government resources previously devoted to intergovernmental relations, and the provision of clearer lines of public responsibility.

Canadian federalism is in a period of uncertainty and transition. Demands for autonomy from Quebec alongside persisting disparities and dissatisfaction in other regions create a climate in which it is very unclear precisely how power relationships between federal and provincial governments will evolve. But whatever change occurs it is reasonable to expect the provinces to continue to occupy a key policy-making role. Some decentralizing trends are likely, and these will inevitably devolve greater authority to the provinces. On the other hand, as the provinces increase their effectiveness, they are likely also to maximize their participation and influence in national policy formation. Thus, a dialectic of decentralization through constitutional reform, reinforced by the political energy of the provinces, will stimulate stronger and more effective provincial representation in national policy. This could, in the long run, have the effect of strengthening the process of national conflict resolution and of revitalizing Canadian federalism.

NOTES

1. Richard Rose, "On the Priorities of Government: A Developmental Analysis of Public Policies," *European Journal of Political Research*, 4, 1976, pp. 247-289.
2. Richard Simeon, "Studying Public Policy," *Canadian Journal of Political Science* 9, December, 1976, pp. 561-562.
3. Ronald Manzer, "Public Policies in Canada: A Developmental Perspective," paper presented at the Annual Meetings of the Canadian Political Science Association, Edmonton, 1975; Kenneth Bryden, *Old Age Pensions and Policy-Making in Canada*, McGill-Queen's,

Montreal, 1974, pp. 15, 19-24; and Gaston Rimlinger, *Welfare Policy and Industrialization in Europe, America and Russia,* Wiley, New York, 1971.

4. Manzer, *ibid.*
5. J. Porter, *The Vertical Mosaic,* University of Toronto Press, Toronto, 1965, pp. 368-370.
6. H. Heclo, *Modern Social Politics in Britain and Sweden,* Yale University Press, New Haven, 1974, chapter 6.
7. D.V. Smiley, "Territorialism and Canadian Political Institutions," in *Canadian Public Policy* 3, Fall, 1977, pp. 449-457.
8. Alan Cairns, "Governments and Societies of Canadian Federalism," *Canadian Journal of Political Science* 10, December, 1977, p. 721.
9. Hon. Marc Lalonde, *Conference of First Ministers on theEconomy,* Ottawa, February 13-15, 1978. Reproduced by permission of the Minister of Supply and Services Canada.
10. Smiley, *op. cit.;* Richard Simeon, "The Federal-Provincial Decision-Making Process," *Issues and Alternatives 1977, Intergovernmental Relations,* Ontario Economic Council, Toronto, 1977, pp. 25-37.
11. D.V. Smiley, *Canada in Question: Federalism in the Seventies,* Second Edition, McGraw-Hill Ryerson, Toronto, 1976, p. 4.

Selected Bibliography

GENERAL REFERENCES ON PROVINCIAL POLITICS

Beck, J. Murray, *The Government of Nova Scotia*, University of Toronto Press, Toronto, 1957.

Bellamy, David, Jon Pammett and D. Rowat, Editors, *Comparative Provincial Political Systems*, Methuen, Toronto, 1976.

Bernard, André, *La Politique au Canada et au Québec*, Les Presses de l'Université du Québec, Montreal, 1977.

Bernard, André, *What Does Quebec Want?* Lorimer, Toronto, 1978.

Dion, Léon, *Quebec: The Unfinished Revolution*, McGill-Queen's University Press, Montreal, 1976.

Donnelly, M., *The Government of Manitoba*, University of Toronto Press, Toronto, 1963.

Fournier, Pierre, *The Quebec Establishment*, Black Rose Books, Montreal, 1976.

Gagan, D.P., Editor, *Prairie Perspectives*, Holt, Rinehart and Winston, Toronto, 1970.

Hockin, Thomas, *Government in Canada*, McGraw-Hill Ryerson, Toronto, 1976.

Kwavnick, David, Editor, *The Tremblay Report*, McClelland and Stewart, Toronto, 1973.

Lipset, S.M., *Agrarian Socialism*, Anchor Books, New York, 1968.

MacDonald, Donald, Editor, *Government and Politics of Ontario*, Macmillan of Canada, Toronto, 1974.

MacKinnon, Frank, *The Government of Prince Edward Island*, University of Toronto Press, Toronto, 1951.

Macpherson, Alan, *The Atlantic Provinces*, University of Toronto Press, Toronto, 1972.

Macpherson, C.B., *Democracy in Alberta*, University of Toronto Press, Toronto, 1962.

Milner, Henry, *Politics in the New Quebec*, McClelland and Stewart, Toronto, 1978.

Neary, Peter, Editor, *The Political Economy of Newfoundland 1929-1972*, Copp Clark, Toronto, 1973.

Noel, S.J.R., *Politics in Newfoundland*, University of Toronto Press, Toronto, 1971.

Posgate, Dale and Kenneth McRoberts, *Quebec: Social Change and Political Crisis*, McClelland and Stewart, Toronto, 1976.

Robin, Martin, *The Rush for Spoils*, McClelland and Stewart, Toronto, 1972.

Robin, Martin, *Pillars of Profit*, McClelland and Stewart, Toronto, 1973.

Robin, Martin, Editor, *Canadian Provincial Politics*, Second Edition, Prentice-Hall of Canada, Scarborough, 1978.

Rowat, Donald, Editor, *Provincial Government and Politics: Comparative Essays*, Department of Political Science, Carleton University, Ottawa, 1972.

Schindeler, Fred, *Responsible Government in Ontario*, University of Toronto Press, Toronto, 1969.

Thorburn, Hugh, *Politics in New Brunswick*, University of Toronto Press, Toronto, 1961.

Thomson, Dale, Editor, *Quebec Society and Politics: Views from the Inside*, McClelland and Stewart, Toronto, 1973.

Ward, Norman and D. Spafford, Editors, *Politics in Saskatchewan*, Longman Canada, Don Mills, 1968.

CHAPTER 1. THE ANALYSIS OF PROVINCIAL POLICY-MAKING.

Anderson, James, *Public Policy-Making*, Praeger, New York, 1975.

Ashford, Douglas, Editor, *Comparing Public Policies*, Sage, Beverley Hills, 1978.

Bauer, Raymond and K. Gergen, Editors, *The Study of Policy Formation*, The Free Press, New York, 1968.

Bird, Richard, *The Growth of Government Spending in Canada*, Canadian Tax Foundation, Toronto, 1970.

Braybrooke, David and Charles Lindblom, *A Strategy of Decision*, Free Press, New York, 1970.

Cairns, Alan, "Governments and Societies of Canadian Federalism," *Canadian Journal of Political Science* 10, December 1977, pp. 695-727.

Chandler, Marsha, William Chandler, and David Vogler, "Policy Analysis and the Search for Theory," *American Politics Quarterly* 2, January, 1974, pp. 107-118.

Doern, G.B. and S.V. Wilson, Editors, *Issues in Canadian Public Policy*, Macmillan of Canada, Toronto, 1974.

Godwin, R.K. and W. Bruce Shepard, "Political Process and Public Expenditure: A re-examination Based on Theories of Representative Government," *American Political Science Review* 64, December 1970.

Groth, Alex, *Comparative Politics: A Distributive Approach*, Macmillan, New York, 1971.

Heindenheimer, Arnold, Hugh Heclo, and Carolyn Adams, *Comparative Public Policy*, St. Martins, New York, 1975.

Hofferbert, R., *The Study of Public Policy*, Bobbs-Merrill, Indianapolis, 1975.

King, Anthony, "Ideas, Institutions and Policies of Governments: A Comparative Analysis," *British Journal of Political Science* 3, July, Oct. 1973, pp. 291-313, 409-423.

Lindberg, Leon, Editor, *Stress and Contradiction in Modern Capitalism*, Heath, Lexington, Massachusetts, 1975.

Lowi, Theodore, "American Business, Public Policy, Case Studies and Political Theory," *World Politics* 16, July 1964, pp. 677-715.

Lowi, Theodore, "Decision-Making vs. Policy-Making: An Antidote for Technocracy," *Public Administration Review* 30, May/June 1970, pp. 314-325.

Manzer, Ronald, "Public Policies in Canada: A Developmental Perspective," paper presented to Canadian Political Science Association, 1975.

Nettle, J.P. *Political Mobilization*, Basic Books, New York, 1967.

O'Connor, James, *The Fiscal Crisis of the State*, St. Martin's Press, New York, 1973.

Panitch, Leo, Editor, *The Canadian State: Political Economy and Political Power*, University of Toronto Press, Toronto, 1977.

Rae, Kenneth and J. McLeod, Editors, *Business and Government in Canada*, Second Edition, Methuen, Toronto, 1976.

Ranney, Austin, Editor, *Political Science and Public Policy*, Markham, Chicago, 1970.

Rose, Richard, "On the Priorities of Government: A Developmental Analysis of Public Policies," *European Journal of Political Research* 4, September 1976, pp. 247-289.

Rose, Richard, "Comparing Public Policy," *European Journal of Political Research* 1, April 1973, pp. 67-93.

Rose, Richard, Editor, *The Dynamics of Public Policy: A Comparative Analysis*, Sage, Beverly Hills, Ca., 1976.

Schattschneider, E.E., *The Semi-Sovereign People*, Holt, Rinehart and Winston, New York, 1960.

Simeon, Richard, "Studying Public Policy," *Canadian Journal of Political Science* 9, December, 1976, pp. 548-580.

Smith, T.A., *The Comparative Policy Process*, ABC Clio, Santa Barbara, Ca., 1975.

CHAPTER 2. THE SOCIAL AND ECONOMIC ENVIRONMENT OF PROVINCIAL PUBLIC POLICY.

Brewis, T.N., *Regional Economic Policies in Canada*, Macmillan of Canada, Toronto, 1969.

Canada, *Report of the Royal Commission on Bilingualism and Biculturalism,* Ottawa, 1968.

Clark, S.D., *The Developing Canadian Community,* Second Edition, University of Toronto, Toronto, 1962.

Dahrendorf, Ralf, *Class and Class Conflict in Industrial Society,* Stanford University Press, Palo Alto, 1959.

Deutsch, Karl, "Social Mobilization and Political Development," *American Political Science Review* 55, September 1961, pp. 193-514.

Durkheim, Emile, *Division of Labor in Society,* trans. by G. Simpson, Free Press, New York, 1964.

Dye, Thomas, *Politics, Economics and the Public: Policy Outcomes in the American States,* Rand McNally, Chicago, 1966.

Easterbrook, W.T. and Hugh Aitkin, *Canadian Economic History,* Macmillan, Toronto, 1956.

Easterbrook, W.T. and M.H. Watkins, Editors, *Approaches to Canadian Economic History,* McClelland and Stewart, Toronto, 1962.

Economic Council of Canada, *Living Together: A Study of Regional Disparities,* Supply and Services Canada, Ottawa, 1977.

Innis, H., *Essays in Canadian Economic History,* University of Toronto Press, Toronto, 1956.

Joy, Richard, *Languages in Conflict: The Canadian Experience,* McClelland and Stewart, Toronto, 1972.

Lieberson, Stanley, *Languages and Ethnic Relations in Canada,* Wiley, New York, 1970.

Lipset, S.M., *Political Man,* Doubleday, Garden City, 1960.

Mackintosh, W.A., *The Economic Background of Dominion-Provincial Relations,* McClelland and Stewart, Toronto, 1964.

Manzer, Ronald, *Canada: A Socio-Political Report,* McGraw-Hill Ryerson, Toronto, 1974.

Officer, L. and L. Smith, Editors, *Issues in Canadian Economics,* McGraw-Hill Ryerson, Toronto, 1974.

Peters, B. Guy, "Political and Economic Effects on the Development of Social Expenditures in France, Sweden and the U.K.," *Midwest Journal of Political Science* 16, May 1972, pp. 225-238.

Porter, John, *The Vertical Mosaic,* University of Toronto Press, Toronto, 1965.

Porter, John, *Canadian Social Structure: A Statistical Profile,* McClelland and Stewart, Toronto, 1969.

Rioux, M. and Yves Martin, Editors, *French Canadian Society, vol. 1,* McClelland and Stewart, Toronto, 1964.

Schwartz, Mildred, *Politics and Territory,* Macmillan of Canada, Toronto, 1969.

Stone, Leroy and C. Marceau, *Canadian Population Trends and Public Policy,* McGill-Queen's University Press, Montreal, 1977.

Wade, M., *Regionalism in the Canadian Community 1867-1967*, University of Toronto Press, Toronto, 1969.

Warkentin, John, Editor, *Canada: A Geographical Interpretation*, Methuen, Toronto, 1968.

CHAPTER 3. POLITICAL FORCES IN THE PROVINCES.

Avakumovic, Ivan, *Socialism in Canada, A Study of the CCF-NDP in Federal and Provincial Politics*, McClelland and Stewart, Toronto, 1978.

Cairns, Alan, "The Electoral System and the Party System in Canada, 1921-1965," *Canadian Journal of Political Science* 1, March 1968, pp. 55-80.

Caplan, Gerald, *The Dilemma of Canadian Socialism: the CCF in Ontario*, McClelland and Stewart, Toronto, 1973.

Chandler, W.M., "Canadian Socialism and Policy Impact: Contagion from the Left?," *Canadian Journal of Political Science* 10, December 1977, pp. 755-780.

Christian, W. and C. Campbell, *Political Parties and Ideologies in Canada: Liberals, Conservatives, Socialists, Nationalists*, McGraw-Hill Ryerson, Toronto, 1974.

Elkins, David, "The Perceived Structure of Canadian Party Systems," *Canadian Journal of Political Science* 7, September 1974, pp. 502-524.

Elkins, David, "Politics Makes Strange Bedfellows: the B.C. Party System in the 1952 and 1953 Provincial Elections," *B.C. Studies*, 30 Summer 1976, pp. 3-26.

Engelmann, Frederick and Mildred Schwartz, *Canadian Political Parties: Origin, Character, Impact*, Prentice-Hall, Scarborough, 1975.

Fox, Paul, Editor, *Politics: Canada*, Fourth Edition, McGraw-Hill Ryerson, Toronto, 1977.

Hamilton, Richard and Maurice Pinard, "The Bases of Parti Québecois Support in Recent Quebec Elections," *Canadian Journal of Political Science* 9, March 1976, pp. 3-26.

Irving, John, *The Social Credit Movement in Alberta*, University of Toronto Press, 1959.

Laponce, Jean, "Ethnicity, Religion and Politics in Canada: A Comparative Analysis of Survey and Census Data" in M. Dogan and S. Rokkan, Editors, *Social Ecology*, MIT Press, Boston, 1969, pp. 187-216.

Leduc, Lawrence, Jr. and Walter L. White, "The Role of Opposition in a One-Party Dominant System: the Case of Ontario," *Canadian Journal of Political Science* 7, March 1974, pp. 86-100.

Lemieux, Vincent, Marcel Gilbert and André Blais, *Une élection de réalignement*, Editions du Jour, Montréal, 1970.

Meisel, John, *Cleavages, Parties and Values in Canada*, Sage, London, 1974.

Meisel, John, *Working Papers on Canadian Politics*, Second Edition, McGill-Queen's University Press, Montreal, 1975.

McRae, Kenneth, Editor, *Consociational Democracy, Political Accommodation in Segmented Societies*, McClelland and Stewart, Toronto, 1974.

Morton, Desmond, *NDP, The Dream of Power*, A.M. Hakkert, Toronto, 1974.

Morton, W.L., *The Progressive Party in Canada*, University of Toronto Press, Toronto, 1950.

Pinard, Maurice, *The Rise of a Third Party, A Study in Crisis Politics*, Enlarged Edition, McGill-Queen's University Press, Montreal, 1975.

Presthus, Robert, *Elite Accommodation in Canadian Politics*, Macmillan of Canada, Toronto, 1973.

Pross, A. Paul, Editor, *Pressure Group Behaviour in Canadian Politics*, McGraw-Hill Ryerson, Toronto, 1975.

Quinn, Herbert, F., *The Union Nationale, A Study in Quebec Nationalism*, University of Toronto Press, Toronto, 1963.

Rose, Richard and Derek Urwin, "Social Cohesion, Political Parties and Strains in Regimes," *Comparative Political Studies* 2, April, 1969, pp. 7-67.

Schwartz, Mildred, *Public Opinion and Canadian Identity*, University of California, Berkeley, 1967.

Simeon, Richard and David Elkins, "Regional Political Culture in Canada," *Canadian Journal of Political Science* 7, September 1974, pp. 397-437.

Stein, Michael, *The Dynamics of Right-wing Protest: A Political Analysis of Social Credit in Quebec*, University of Toronto Press, 1973.

Rae, Douglas, *The Political Consequences of Electoral Laws*, Yale University Press, New Haven, 1967.

Thorburn, Hugh, Editor, *Party Politics in Canada*, Third Edition, Prentice-Hall, Scarborough, 1972.

Wilson, John, "The Canadian Political Cultures: Towards a Redefinition of the Nature of the Canadian Political System," *Canadian Journal of Political Science* 7, September, 1974, pp. 438-483.

Wilson, John and David Hoffman, "The Liberal Party in Contemporary Ontario Politics," *Canadian Journal of Political Science* 3, June 1970, pp. 177-204.

Winn, Conrad and John McMenemy, Editors, *Political Parties in Canada*, McGraw-Hill Ryerson, Toronto, 1976.

Young, Walter, *Democracy and Discontent: Progressivism, Socialism and Social Credit in the Canadian West*, Ryerson, Toronto, 1969.

CHAPTER 4. STRUCTURES OF POLICY-MAKING

Atkinson, Michael, "The Policy Interests of Provincial Backbenchers," *Legislative Studies Quarterly* 3, November, 1978, pp. 629-646.

Benjamin, Jacques, "La Rationalisation des Choix Budgetaires: Les Cas Québecois et Canadien," *Canadian Journal of Political Science* 5 September, 1972, pp. 348-364.

Bryden, Kenneth, "Executive and Legislature in Ontario: A Case Study in Governmental Reform," *Canadian Public Administration* 18, 1975, pp. 235-252.

Bryden, Kenneth, "Cabinets," in David Bellamy *et al.*, *Comparative Provincial Political Systems*, Methuen, Toronto, 1976, pp. 310-322.

Burns, R.M., "The Operation of Fiscal and Economic Policy", in G.B. Doern and S.V. Wilson, Editors, *Issues in Canadian Public Policy*, Macmillan of Canada, Toronto, 1974, pp. 286-309.

Burns, R.M., "Budgeting and Finance" in David Bellamy *et al.*, *Comparative Provincial Political Systems*, Methuen, Toronto, 1976, pp. 323-340.

Campbell, D.S., "Planning Programming and Budgeting — the Ontario Government," *Cost and Management* 49, July-August, 1975, pp. 6-13.

Conseil, du Trésor: *Le Système du Budget par programme et son application au Gouvernement du Québec*, Quebec City, 1972.

Doern, G. Bruce, Editor, *The Regulatory Process in Canada*, Macmillan of Canada, Toronto, 1978.

Doern, G.B. and Peter Aucoin, *The Structure of Policy-Making in Canada*, Macmillan of Canada, Toronto, 1971.

Falcone, D. and Wm. Mishler, "Legislative Determinants of Provincial Health Policy in Canada," *Journal of Politics* 39, August 1977, pp. 345-367.

Fleck, James, "Restructuring the Ontario Government," *Canadian Public Administration* 16, 1973, pp. 56-72.

Gow, D., *The Progress of Budgetary Reform in the Government of Canada*, Economic Council of Canada, Ottawa, 1973.

Hodgetts, J.E. and O.P. Dwivedi, *Provincial Governments as Employers*, McGill-Queen's University Press, Montreal, 1974.

Jackson, Robert and Michael Atkinson, *The Canadian Legislative System*, Macmillan of Canada, Toronto, 1974.

Kernaghan, Kenneth, Editor, *Public Administration in Canada: Selected Readings*, Third Edition, Methuen, Toronto, 1977.

Kornberg, Alan, David Falcone and William Mishler, *Legislatures and Societal Change: The Case of Canada*, Sage Publications, Beverley Hills, Ca., 1973.

Lapierre, Laurier, Editor, *Essays on the Left,* McClelland and Stewart, Toronto, 1971.

Leman, Christopher, "Patterns of Policy Development: Social Security in the United States and Canada," *Public Policy* 25, Spring, 1977, pp. 261-291.

McInnes, Simon, "Improving Legislative Surveillance of Provincial Public Expenditure: The Performance of the Public Accounts Committee and Auditors General," *Canadian Public Administration* 20, Spring 1977, pp. 36-86.

McLeod, Alex: "Reform of the Standing Committees of the Quebec National Assembly," *Canadian Journal of Political Science* 8, March 1975, pp. 22-39.

Ontario Committee on Government Productivity, *Reports,* Toronto, 1973.

Ontario Economic Council, *Issues and Alternatives 1978: Government Regulation,* Toronto, 1978.

Reschenthaler, B.G., *The Performance of Selected Independent Regulatory Commissions in Alberta, Saskatchewan and Manitoba,* Canadian Consumer Council, Ottawa, 1972.

Rubin, K., *Inventory of Provincial Regulatory Agencies,* Canadian Consumer Council, Ottawa, 1971.

Silcox, Peter, "The Proliferation of Boards and Commissions," in T. Lloyd and J. McLeod, Editors, *Agenda 1970: Proposals for a Creative Politics,* University of Toronto Press, Toronto, 1968.

Silcox, Peter, "The ABCs of Ontario: Provincial Agencies, Boards and Commissions," in Donald MacDonald, Editor, *Government and Politics of Ontario,* Macmillan of Canada, Toronto, 1975, pp. 135-152.

Simeon, Richard, "The Overload Thesis and Canadian Government," *Canadian Public Policy* 2, Fall 1976, pp. 541-552.

Szablowski, George, "Policy-Making and Cabinet," in Donald MacDonald, Editor, *Government and Politics in Ontario,* Macmillan of Canada, Toronto, 1975, pp. 114-134.

Tennant, Paul, "The NDP Government of British Columbia: Unaided Politicians in an Unaided Cabinet," *Canadian Public Policy* 3, Fall, 1977.

Wallace, D.M., "Budget Reform in Saskatchewan: A New Approach to Program Based Management," *Canadian Public Administration* 17, Winter 1974, pp. 586-599.

CHAPTER 5. THE FEDERAL SYSTEM.

Black, Edwin, *Divided Loyalties, Canadian Concepts of Federalism,* McGill-Queen's University Press, Montreal, 1975.

Black, Edwin and Alan Cairns, "A Different Perspective on Canadian

Federalism," *Canadian Public Administration* 9, March 1966.

Canadian Tax Foundation, *Provincial and Municipal Finances, 1977*, Toronto, 1977.

Careless, Anthony, *Initiative and Response: The Adaptation of Canadian Federalism to Regional Economic Development*, McGill-Queen's University Press, Montreal, 1977.

Carter, George, *Canadian Conditional Grants Since World War II*, Canadian Tax Foundation, Toronto, 1971.

Carter, George, "Financing Health and Post-Secondary Education: A New and Complex Fiscal Arrangement," *Canadian Tax Journal* September-October 1977, 25, pp. 534-550.

Courchene, T., "The New Fiscal Arrangements and the Economics of Federalism," paper presented at the Conference on the Future of the Canadian Federation, University of Toronto, 1977.

Dupré, Stefan, *et al.*, *Federalism and Policy Development: The Case of Adult Occupational Training in Ontario*, University of Toronto, 1973.

Elton, D.K., Editor, *One Prairie Province?*, Lethbridge Herald, Lethbridge, 1970.

Hodgetts, J.E., "Regional Interests in a Federal Structure," *Canadian Journal of Economics and Political Science* 32, February 1966, pp. 3-14.

Husband, D.D., "National versus regional growth: Some issues," *Canadian Public Administration* 15, Winter 1971, pp. 538-555.

Mallory, J.S., *Social Credit and the Federal Power in Canada*, University of Toronto, 1954.

Meekison, Peter, Editor, *Canadian Federalism: Myth or Reality?*, Third Edition, Methuen, Toronto, 1977.

Moore, A.M., J.H. Perry, and D. Beach, *The Financing of Canadian Federation: The First Hundred Years*, Canadian Tax Foundation, Toronto, 1966.

Morin, Claude, *Quebec vs. Ottawa: the Struggle for Self-government, 1960-1972*, University of Toronto, 1976.

Ontario Advisory Committee on Confederation, *The Confederation Challenge, Background Papers and Reports*, Volumes I and II, Toronto, 1967, 1970.

Ontario Economic Council, *Issues and Alternatives 1977: Intergovernmental Relations*, Toronto, 1977.

Perry, David, "The Federal-Provincial Fiscal Arrangements Introduced in 1977," *Canadian Tax Journal* 25, July-August 1977, pp. 429-440.

Schultz, Richard, "The Regulatory Process and Federal Provincial Relations," in G. Bruce Doern, Editor, *The Regulatory Process in Canada*, Macmillan of Canada, Toronto, 1978, pp. 128-146.

Simeon, Richard, *Federal-Provincial Diplomacy: The Making of Recent Policy in Canada*, University of Toronto Press, Toronto, 1972.

Simeon, Richard, "Regionalism and Canadian Political Institutions," *Queen's Quarterly* 82, Winter 1975, pp. 499-511.

Simeon, Richard, Editor, *Must Canada Fail?*, McGill-Queen's University Press, Montreal, 1978.

Smiley, Donald, *The Canadian Political Nationality*, Methuen, Toronto, 1967.

Smiley, Donald, *Canada in Question: Federalism in the Seventies*, Second Edition, McGraw-Hill Ryerson, Toronto, 1976.

Smiley, D.V., "Territorialism and Canadian Political Institutions," *Canadian Public Policy* 3, Autumn 1977, pp. 449-457.

Stein, Michael, "Federal Political Systems and Federal Societies," *World Politics* 20, July 1968, pp. 721-747.

Stevenson, Garth, "Federalism and the Political Economy of the Canadian State," in L. Panitch, Editor, *The Canadian State: Political Economy and Political Power*, University of Toronto Press, Toronto, 1977.

Strick, J., "Conditional Grants and Provincial Government Budgeting," *Canadian Public Administration* 14, Summer 1971.

Veilleux, Gerald, *Les Rélations Intergouvernmentales au Canada 1867-1967*, Presses de l'Université du Québec, Montréal, 1971.

Westmacott, Martin, "The National Transportation Act and Western Canada: A Case Study in Cooperative Federalism," *Canadian Public Administration* 16, Fall 1973, pp. 447-467.

Whalen, H., "Public Policy and Regional Development. The Experience of the Atlantic Provinces" in A. Rotstein, Editor, *The Prospect of Change: Proposals for Canada's Future*, McGraw-Hill, Toronto, 1965, pp. 102-148.

CHAPTER 6. SOCIAL DEVELOPMENT POLICIES.

1. Health and Welfare

Andreopoulos, S., Editor, *National Health Insurance: Can We Learn from Canada?*, John Wiley, New York, 1975.

Armitage, Andrew, *Social Welfare in Canada*, McClelland and Stewart, Toronto, 1976.

Aucoin, Peter, "Federal Health Care Policy," in G.B. Doern and V. S. Wilson, Editors, *Issues in Canadian Public Policy*, Macmillan of Canada, Toronto, 1974, pp. 55-84.

Bagley, R.F. and S. Wolfe, *Doctor's Strike: Medical Care and Conflict in Saskatchewan*, Macmillan of Canada, Toronto, 1967.

Bryden, Kenneth, *Old Age Pensions and Policy-Making in Canada*, McGill-Queen's University Press, Montreal, 1974.

Bryden, Kenneth, "How Public Medicare Came to Ontario," in Donald MacDonald (ed.), *Government and Politics of Ontario*, Macmillan, Toronto, 1975, pp. 34-46.

Canadian Council for Social Development, *Social Security for Canada*, Ottawa, 1973.

Cassidy, Henry, *Public Health and Welfare Reorganization*, Ryerson, Toronto, 1945.

Copp, Terry, *Anatomy of Poverty*, McClelland and Stewart, Toronto, 1974.

Department of National Health and Welfare, *Review of Health Services in Canada*, Queen's Printer, Ottawa, annual publication.

Evans, R.G.: "Health Services in Nova Scotia," *Canadian Public Policy* 1, Summer 1975.

Fry, Brian R. and Richard F. Winters, "The Politics of Redistribution," *American Political Science Review* 64, June 1970, pp. 508-522.

Government of British Columbia, *Health Security for British Columbians*, Victoria, 1973 (Folkes Report).

Government of Manitoba, *White Paper on Health Policy*, Winnipeg, 1972.

Government of Ontario, *Health Planning, Task Force Report*, Toronto, 1974 (Mustard Report).

Government of Quebec, *Report of the Commission of Inquiry on Health and Social Welfare*, Quebec, 1970 (Castonguay-Nepveu Report).

Heclo, Hugh, *Modern Social Politics in Britain and Sweden*, Yale University Press, New Haven, 1974.

Mishler, William and David Campbell, "The Healthy State, Legislative Responsiveness to Public Health Care Needs in Canada, 1920-1970," *Comparative Politics* 10, July 1978, pp. 461-478.

Manga, Pran, *The Income Distribution Effect of Medical Insurance in Ontario*, Ontario Economic Council, Toronto, 1978.

Marsh, Leonard, *Social Security for Canada*, King's Printer, Ottawa, 1943.

Ontario Economic Council, *Issue and Alternatives 1976: Health*, Toronto, 1976.

Reuber, Grant, "The Impact of Government Policy on the Distribution of Income in Canada: A Review," *Canadian Public Policy* 4, Autumn 78, pp. 505-529.

Rimlinger, Gaston, *Welfare Policy and Industrialization in Europe: America and Russia*, John Wiley, New York, 1971.

Royal Commission on Health Services, *Report*, Queen's Printer, Ottawa, 1964.

Shillington, C.H., *The Road to Medicare*, Del Graphics, Toronto, 1972.

Special Senate Committee on Poverty, *Poverty in Canada*, Information Canada, Ottawa, 1971.

Splane, Richard, *Social Welfare in Ontario 1791-1893*, University of Toronto Press, Toronto, 1965.

Swartz, D., "The Politics of Reform: Conflict and Accommodation in Canadian Health Policy," in L. Panitch, Editor, *The Canadian State: Political Power and Political Economy*, University of Toronto Press, Toronto, 1976, pp. 311-343.

Taylor, Malcolm, "The Role of the Medical Profession in the Formulation and Execution of Public Policy," *Canadian Journal of Economics and Political Science,* February 1960, pp. 233-255.

Taylor, Malcolm, "Quebec Medicare Policy Formulation in Crisis and Conflict," *Canadian Public Administration* 15, Summer 1972, pp. 211-250.

Titmuss, Richard, *Commitment to Welfare,* Allen and Unwin, London, 1968.

Tuohy, Carolyn, "Pluralism and Corporatism in Ontario Medical Politics," in K. Rea and J. McLeod, Editors, *Business and Government in Canada,* Methuen, Toronto, 1976, pp. 395-413.

Tuohy, Carolyn, "Medical Politics after Medicare: the Ontario Case," *Canadian Public Policy* 2, Spring 1976, pp. 192-208.

Weller, G., "From 'Pressure Group Politics' to Medical Industrial Complex," *Journal of Health Politics, Policy and Law* 1, Winter 1977, pp. 444-470.

Weller, G.R., "Health Care and Medicare Policy in Ontario," in G.B. Doern and V. S. Wilson, Editors, *Issues in Canadian Public Policy,* Macmillan of Canada, Toronto, 1974, pp. 85-114.

Wilensky, Harold, *The Welfare State and Equality,* University of California Press, Berkeley, 1975.

2. *Education*

Chalmers, John, *Schools for the Foothills Province,* University of Toronto Press, Toronto, 1967.

Cameron, David, *Schools for Ontario,* University of Toronto Press, Toronto, 1974.

Clark, Lovell, Editor, *The Manitoba School Question: Majority Rule or Minority Rights,* Copp Clark, Toronto, 1968.

Manzer, Ronald, "Public School Policies in Canada: A Comparative Developmental Perspective," paper presented to International Studies Association, Toronto, 1976.

Martin, W.B.W. and A.J. Macdonnel, *Canadian Education,* Prentice-Hall of Canada, Scarborough, 1978.

Mehmet, O., *Who Benefits from the Ontario University System?,* Ontario Economic Council, Toronto, 1978.

Munroe, David, *The Organization and Administration of Education,* Information Canada, Ottawa, 1974.

Organization for Economic Cooperation and Development, *Reviews of National Policies for Education, Canada,* Paris, 1976.

Rowe, F.W., *Education and Culture in Newfoundland,* McGraw-Hill Ryerson, Toronto, 1976.

Schmeiser, D.A., *Civil Liberties in Canada,* Oxford University Press, Oxford, 1964.

Sissons, C.B., *Church and State in Canadian Education*, Ryerson, Toronto, 1959.

Walker, Franklin,*Catholic Education and Politics in Ontario*, Thomas Nelson, Toronto, 1964.

Wilson, J. Donald, Robert Stamp and Louis-Phillippe Audet, Editors, *Canadian Education: A History*, Prentice-Hall of Canada, Scarborough, 1970.

CHAPTER 7. RESOURCE DEVELOPMENT POLICIES.

Atlantic Provinces Economic Council, *Aspects of Transportation in Atlantic Canada*, Halifax, 1976.

Atlantic Provinces Economic Council, *Energy: Its Sources, Production, Distribution and Financing in Atlantic Canada*, Halifax, 1976.

Baldwin, J., "The Evolution of Transportation Policy in Canada," *Canadian Public Administration* 20, Winter 1977, pp. 600-631.

Bercuson, David, Editor, *Canada and the Burden of Unity*, Macmillan of Canada, Toronto, 1977.

Black, Edwin, "British Columbia, the Politics of Exploitation," in W.E. Mann, Editor, *Social and Cultural Change in Canada*, Copp Clark, Toronto, 1970, pp. 112-129.

Bonsor, N.C., *Transportation Rates and Economic Development in Northern Ontario*, Ontario Economic Council, Toronto, 1976.

Copes, Parzival, "Canada's Atlantic Coast Fisheries: Policy Developments and the Impact of Extended Jurisdiction," *Canadian Public Policy* 4, Spring 1978, pp. 155-171.

Doern, G.B., "Science and Technology in the Nuclear Regulatory Process: The Case of Canadian Uranium Miners," *Canadian Public Administration* 21, Spring 1978, pp. 51-82.

Dwivedi, O.P., Editor, *Protecting the Environment*, Copp Clark, Toronto, 1974.

Economists Intelligence Unit, *Atlantic Provinces Transportation Study*, Ottawa, 1967.

Energy, Mines and Resources, *An Energy Strategy for Canada: Policies for Self-reliance*, Ottawa, 1976.

Fowke, V., *The National Policy and the Wheat Economy*, University of Toronto, Toronto, 1957.

Garland, S.W. and S.C. Hudson, *Government Involvement in Agriculture: A Study for the Federal Task Force in Agriculture*, Ottawa, 1968.

George, Roy, *The Life and Times of Industrial Estates Limited*, Institute of Public Affairs, Dalhousie, Halifax, 1974.

Irvine, William, *The Farmers in Politics*, McClelland and Stewart, Carleton Library, Toronto, 1976.

La Forest, Gerard, *Natural Resources and Public Property under the Canadian Constitution,* University of Toronto Press, Toronto, 1969.

Maxwell, Judith, *Policy Review and Outlook, 1976, Challenges to Complacency,* C.D. Howe Research Institute, Montreal, 1976.

Mathias, Philip, *Forced Growth,* McClelland and Stewart, Toronto, 1975.

McKillop, William and Walter Mead, Editors, *Timber Policy Issues in British Columbia,* University of British Columbia Press, Vancouver, 1974.

Mitchell, C.L., "The 200-Mile Limit: New Issues, Old Problems for Canada's East Coast Fisheries," *Canadian Public Policy* 4, Spring 1978, pp. 172-183.

Nelles, H.V., *The Politics of Development, Forests, Mines and Hydro-Electric Power in Ontario, 1849-1941,* Macmillan of Canada, Toronto, 1974.

Porter, Glenn and R. Cuff, Editors, *Enterprise and National Development,* Hakkert, Toronto, 1973.

Pratt, Larry, *The Tar Sands: Syncrude and the Politics of Oil,* Hurtig, Edmonton, 1976.

Purdy, H.L., *Transport Competition and Public Policy in Canada,* University of British Columbia Press, Vancouver, 1972.

Ruppenthal, K. and W. Stanbury, Editors, *Transportation Policy: Regulation, Competition and the Public Interest,* University of British Columbia Centre for Transportation Studies, Vancouver, 1976.

Schaffner, Richard, *New Risks in Resource Development: the Potash Case,* C.D. Howe Research Institute, Montreal, 1976.

Scott, Anthony, Editor, *Natural Resource Revenues: A Test of Federalism,* University of British Columbia Press, Vancouver, 1976.

Schultz, Richard, "Intergovernmental Cooperation, Regulatory Agencies and Transportation Regulation in Canada: The Case of Part III of the National Transportation Act," *Canadian Public Administration* 19, Summer 1976, pp. 183-207.

Smithies, W.R., *The Protection and Use of Natural Resources in Ontario,* Ontario Economic Council, Toronto, 1974.

Studnicki-Gizbert, K., Editor, *Issues in Canadian Transport Policy,* Macmillan of Canada, Toronto, 1974.

Thompson, A.R. and H.R. Eddy, "Jurisdictional Problems in Natural Resource Management in Canada," in W.D. Bennett *et al., Essays on Aspects of Resource Policy,* Science Council of Canada, Ottawa, 1973.

Veeman, M. and T. Veeman, "The Directions of Canadian Agricultural Policy," *Canadian Journal of Agricultural Economics* 24, July 1976, pp. 78-90.

Weller, G., "Hinterland Politics of Northwestern Ontario," *Canadian Journal of Political Science* 10, December 1977, pp. 727-754.

Whittington, Michael, "Environmental Policy," in G.B. Doern and V.S. Wilson, Editors, *Issues in Canadian Public Policy,* Macmillan of Canada, Toronto, 1974, pp. 203-227.

INDEX

Acadians, 235
Access, 71-72, 113, 275
Accountability, 133
  CTC, 275
Ad hoc committees, cabinet, 102
Advisory Council to the Government
  for Transportation Policy
  (Saskatchewan), 280
Age, voting and, 50-54
Agricultural and Rural Development
  Act (ARDA), 1961, 168, 270
Agricultural Products Marketing Act,
  1949, 270
Agricultural Stabilization Act, 269
Agriculture, 268-271
  jurisdiction over, 150
  problems of, 268-269
  production and marketing, 270
  promotion of, 253
  research extension and education,
  269
Aitkin, H.G.J., 21, 22
Anglophone, 30, 32
  attitudes of, 75
  (See also Language)
ARDA, 168, 270
Athabasca tar sands, 266
Atkinson, Michael, 117
Atlantic Provinces Economic Council,
  275
Attorney General, Department of, 100
Aucoin, Peter, 113
Autonomy, provincial, 165, 169
  in health policy, 214
  impact of Quiet Revolution, 156
  Quebec, 297
  in resource policy, 267

Backbencher:
  resources of, 114, 120
  role of, 118
"Battle of the balance sheets," 170
Beck, J. Murray, 65
Beliefs about provincial politics, 1
Benign neglect, 202, 204
Bennett government (1960s), 132

Bennett, W.A.C., 39, 56, 128, 132, 260
Bennett, William, 59, 128
Bertrand government, 236
Bilingualism, 234, 236
  (See also Language and Appendices)
Bill 1 (101): education and language,
  236
Bill 22: bilingualism, 236
Bill 63: language rights in education,
  1969, 236
Bill 65: welfare reform, 1971, 193
Bipartism, 55, 59
Black, Edwin, 163
Blakeney government, 264, 265, 293
Block financing, social welfare, 188
Blue Cross, 206, 207
B.N.A. Act, 13, 150, 262
  agriculture, 268
  amendments to, 186
  education, 231
  education: section 93, 228
  fiscal arrangements, 155
  health, 199
  provincial executive councils, 100
  social welfare, 181
  transfers, 157
Board of Transport Commissioners,
  273
Bonsor, N.C., 280
Bourassa Government: language and,
  236
Brokerage parties, 67
Bracken, John, 62
Bricklin, 261
Bryden, Kenneth, 74, 192
Bryne Commission, 122
Bucovetsky, M., 72
Budgetary data:
  as policy indicators, 68
Bureaucracy, 108-114
  discretionary power, 109, 112
  impact of, 5, 8, 108, 124, 293
  transportation policy, 275
  province building, 237
  selection, 38
Budget, 124, 128, 291
  (See also Expenditures)

Budgetary process:
  compared with regulatory, 135

Cabinet:
  budget, 136
  bureaucracy, 111-112
  growth, 98
  and legislature, 115
  policy impact, 293
  pressure groups, 72
  regulation, 134, 136-137
  secretariat, 98, 104
  selection, 38
Cabinet committees, 101-104, 136
Cabinet decision-making and natural
    resource policy, 268
Cabinet departments, 98, 99
  as regulators, 129
Cabinet overload, 98-108
Cabinet policy-making capability, 108
Cabinet reform, 98-108, 113
Cable television, 151
Cairns, Alan, 296
Canada Assistance Plan, 1966, 167,
    186-187, 194, 196
Canada Pension Plan, 162-163, 184
Canadian Consumer Council, 130, 134
Canadian Medical Association, 211
Canadian Pacific Railway (CPR), 278
Canadian Transport Commission,
    274-276
Canadian Trucking Association,
    273-274, 277
Cape Breton Development
    Corporation (DEVCO), 24
Careless, Anthony, 168
Carter Commission, 73
Cash payments:
  federal payments for social welfare,
    237
  health financing, 214, 215
Cassidy, Henry, 197
Castonguay-Nepveu Commission, 197
Catholic Permanent Committee,
    Quebec, 223
CCF-NDP:
  health insurance, 206
  government and bureaucracy, 114
  policy impact, 67-69, 103-104, 293
  support, 59, 61-63, 65
  (See also NDP)
Central Control Agencies, 125
  budget, 136
  regulation, 137

Central Board of Public Health, 198
Centralization:
  federal system, 296
  regulation, 136
  of school financing, 225
  Welfare State, 237
Centre-periphery: transportation
    policy, 275
"Chicken and egg war," 150
Chretien, Jean, 170
Church:
  and education, 223, 233
  and health, 203
  Quebec, 29-30
  and social welfare, 193
Churchill Falls, 261
Civil Service (See Bureaucracy)
Civil Service Commission, 110, 111
Civil Service, Department of (Quebec),
    110
Clarke, Harold, 75
Class, 17, 20, 54
  conflict, 17
  division of labour, 20
  health utilization, 212
  voting, 41-45, 54, 67
Clientele relationships, 254, 267, 293
Clientelism, 72
Coal, 266
Coalition government, 59, 62, 119
Collective bargaining, in public service,
    111
Colleges of Applied Arts and
    Technology, 227
Collèges classiques, 223
Collèges d'enseignement général et
    professionel (CEGEPs), 223, 227,
    233
College of Physicians and Surgeons,
    74, 204
Colonial tradition, 29
Commission of Inquiry on Health and
    Welfare Services in Quebec
    (Castonguay-Nepveu), 193
Committee on Government
    Administration and Productivity
    (Newfoundland), 102, 127
Committee on Government
    Productivity (Ontario), 101-103,
    106-107, 120, 127
Committee of Ministers of Finance
    and Provincial Treasurers, 152
Committee of Supply, 119
Committee of the Whole, 118

Common School Act, 1871 (New Brunswick), 235
Community Colleges, 227
Community Health Centres, 212-216
Community Resources Board Act, 1974 (British Columbia), 197
Compulsory education, 217
Concurrent power, 296
Conditional grants, 157-159, 186
    impact of federalism, 169
    revenue imbalance, 164
Conflict, patterns of:
  social welfare and resource development, 292
Conservation, 280, 293
Conservatives, 59
  bases of support, 42-54
  one-party dominance, 57
  (See also Progressive Conservative Party)
Consociation of school districts, 224-233
Constituency and legislative role, 120
Constitutional jurisdiction (See Jurisdiction)
Constitutional reform and decentralization, 297
Constraints, 121, 294
Consumer participation and regulation, 134
Consumer interests in transportation policy, 280
Continuing Committee on Fiscal and Economic Matters, 152
Cook, Ramsay, 193
Cooperation, federal-provincial, 136
Cooperative federalism, 151
Corporatism, 73-74, 293
Cost-sharing, and health financing, 214
Cottage Hospital and Medical Care Act, 1935 (Newfoundland), 206, 210
Counter-cyclical policies, 170
Courchene, Thomas, 264
Créditistes, bases of support, 42-45
  (See also Social Credit)
Crisis management, 294
Crop Insurance Act, 1959, 269
Crown corporation, 24
Crown ownership, and forest lands (British Columbia), 260
Crow's Nest Pass Agreement, 272, 274

Cultural autonomy and social welfare, 186
Cynicism, provincial differences in, 79

Darby, L., 280
Davis, William, 232
Decentralization:
    education, 230
    federal system, 296
    health policy, 203
    (See also Centralization)
Decision-making capacity, 295
Decision-making innovation, 107
Defensive expansion, 12
Delegated legislation, 109, 131
Demand management, 182
Democratically open model, 134
Denominational system, 224, 229, 233
Departmentalism, 113
Depletion of natural resources, 261
Deprivation, threat of, 67
Deterrent fees (copayment), 211
Development corporations, influence of, 131
Discretionary authority, in regulation, 129, 135
Distributive politics, 123, 267
Distributive policy, agriculture, 270-271
Doern, G. Bruce, 106, 134
Dominion-provincial premiers conferences, 152
Douglas, T.C., 114
Drew, George, 69
Duplessis, Maurice, 30, 162, 223
Duval Potash Company, 2
Dwivedi, O.P., 11, 100, 109
Dynamics, 121

Easterbrook, W.T., 21, 22
Economic Advisory and Planning Board, Saskatchewan, 103
Economic Council of Canada, 275-276
Economic development, 12-13, 20-24
  export staples, 21-22
  facilitation of private resource mobilization, 253
  industrial structure, provincial comparisons, 22-23
  industrialization, 20
  initiatives, 22-24
Economic effectiveness, 133

Economic growth, 255
  basis in resource wealth, 257
  Smallwood era, 261
Economic interests and federal-
    provincial relations, 171
Economic rents, 260
Economic and social cleavages, bases
    of, 17
Education, 216-237, 253
  bilingual, 121
  and equality, 216-217
  immigration, 216
  impetus for change, 228
  and industrialization, 216
  interested publics, 228
  linguistic-ethnic cleavages, 234
  objectives, 221
  policy innovations, 233
  religion, 228-234
    (See also Denominational systems)
  sectarian conflict, 32
  urbanization, 216
Education, Department of (Quebec),
    100
Education, finance, 224-225
  property tax, 231
  provincial grants, 231
Education, Superintendent of
    (Quebec), 100
Egg marketing board, Quebec
    (FEDCO), 149
Election Survey, 1974, 1, 42, 44, 76
Elections, provincial, 7, 39, 59-66, 69
Electoral competition, patterns of, 40,
    54-59
Elite accommodation, 73
Energy, Canada as per capita
    consumer of, 254
Energy crisis, 255, 265-267
Energy prices, 257
Energy sources, 22
English language schools, 236
Enrolment trends, 217-218, 227
Environment, Department of, 100
Environmental costs, resource
    exploitation and, 267
Environmental factors, as policy
    determinants, 7
    (See also Socio-economic
    determinants)
Equalization, 156, 158-159, 263-264
  based on fiscal capacity, 166-167
  in HIDS, 208

by national minimum standards, 184
  and provincial autonomy, 168
  of provincial resources, 165-168
  and resource policy, 257
  tax agreements, 1967 and 1972, 156
Established Programmes (Interim
    Arrangements), 156
Ethnicity and voting, 46-50, 54
Executive councils, 100
Executive dominance, 114, 122, 295
Exhortation, as a policy instrument,
    131
Expenditure:
  control by legislature, 119
  education, 217
  goods and services, 9
  health, 188-189, 199, 201
  natural resources, 179
  per capita, 9, 167
  as policy indicators, 3-4, 178
  as policy instruments, 131, 291
  transfers, 9
  transportation and communication,
    276
Exploitation, politics of, 260
Export staples, 21-22, 267

Family Benefits Act, 1966 (Ontario),
    194, 196
Farm Stabilization Board, 269
Farmers and Depression, 269
Federal impact, education policy, 228
Federal initiatives, social policy, 295
Federal-Provincial Fiscal Arrangements
    Act, 1967, education, 228
Federal-provincial arenas, 152-155
Federal-Provincial Conference on
    Reconstruction, 1945, 211
Federal-Provincial Conference of
    Welfare Ministers, 187
Federal-provincial conflict, resource
    policy, 263-265
Federal-provincial entanglement, 170
Federal-provincial interdependence,
    151
Federal-provincial relations, resource
    policy, 255
Federal Unemployment Assistance
    Act, 1956, 186
Federal Welfare programmes:
  family allowance, 179, 182, 185-186,
    194, 237

old-age security, 179, 182, 185-186, 194
unemployment insurance, 179, 182, 185, 194
Fifty-cent dollars, 169
health, 213
transportation, 276
Finance, Department of, 100, 125
Financial barriers to health service, 212
First ministers' conferences, 11
Fiscal Arrangements and Established Program Financing Act, 1977, 156 165, 214, 215, 264
Fiscal year, 124
Fishery policy, 261-262
Foreign investment, in resource industries, 260-261
Foreign ownership, 254
in resource industries, 261
Forest resources, 260
Foundation programmes, 225
Fractionalization, 56, 59, 61
Francophone, 30
(See also Language)
Franco-Ontarians, education, 235
French immersion programmes, 235
French language enrolments, 235
French language rights, 235
French language schools (Ontario), 234-235
Frost, Leslie, 206
Functions of the Legislature, 116, 117-119, 120-121

General Development Agreements (GDA's), 167
Government-industry clientele relationships, 254, 267, 293
General Welfare Assistance Act, 1958 (Ontario), 194
Glassco Commission, 125
Government-private industry partnership, forest resources, 260
Governments, growth of, 253
(See also Public sector)
Governor General, 115
Gow, Donald, 113
Guaranteed Annual Income System (GAINS), 196

"Hard frontier," 12
Hatfield, Richard, 65

"Have" and "have not" provinces, 28, 154, 260
Horowitz, Gad, 75
Heclo, Hugh, 180
Health care delivery system, 214-215
Health policy:
and agriculture, 202-203, 269
community disease control phase, 201-205
community health centres phase, 201, 212-216
costs, 212-213, 216
electoral support, 213
criteria of development, 202
ideas, 292
innovations, 202
public insurance phase, 201, 205-212
scope, 4, 199, 253
Hepburn, Mitch, 63
High School Act, 1871 (Ontario), 232
Hodgetts, J.E., 11, 100, 109, 110
Horizontal equity, 196
Horizontal portfolios, 105-106
Hospital insurance, 165
Hospital and medical insurance:
fiscal arrangements, 156
in Saskatchewan, 24
Hospital Insurance and Diagnostic Services Act (195), 4, 206, 207-208, 211-213
federal criteria, 208
methods of financing, 208-209
Hospital Construction Grants, 207
Hospital prepayment plans, 207
Hospitalization Act, 1946 (Saskatchewan), 206
House of Assembly, 115
(See also Legislature)
House of Commons, 116
House of Commons Advisory Committee on Post-War Reconstruction, 181
Hydro, 109, 266-267
Hydro-electric power, 260

Ideas, political, 74-83
(See also Ideology, Public opinion)
Ideas and values, as policy determinants, 292
Ideological convergence, 114
Ideology:
and party, 41, 65, 67
policy impact, 74, 75, 132

Immigration, 150, 192
Implementation, 122, 123
Income, per capita, 24, 29
Income distribution, and welfare state, 238
Income maintenance, 184
  farm, 264
  impact, 238
  and political ideas, 292
Income redistribution and transportation policy, 272
Income supplementation, 189, 197
Income transfers, welfare state, 238, 239
Incrementalism, 123
Industrial Estates Limited, 24, 261
Industrialization, 20-24
  (See also Economic development)
Industry, promotion of, 253
Innovation and CEGEPs, 233
Instability of party systems, 57, 66
Institutions, 97-121
  policy impact, 293
Intergovernmental Affairs, Department of, 100
Intergovernmental relations, 11, 12
  federal-provincial committees, 152
  federal-provincial conferences, 153
  First Ministers' Meetings, 153
  Intergovernmental Liaison on Fiscal and Economic Matters, 153
  Minister of State, 152
  (See also Federal-provincial relations)
Interest groups:
  resource industries, 261
  and resource policy, 254
  and resource wealth, 259-260
  scope of public sector, 71
  (See also Pressure Groups)
Interests, private economic and resource policy, 254
Interprovincial activity, 154
Irvine, William P., 50

Jackson, Robert, 117
James Bay project, 28, 268
Jenson, Jane, 75
Judicial Committee of the Privy Council, 150-151
Jurisdiction, 149-151
  autonomy and interdependence, 149
  federal regulation of trade and commerce, 151

federal-provincial conflict, 263, 296
  Local Prohibition Case, 150
  natural resource, 33, 255, 262-265
  transportation, 273-276

Kohn, Robert, 199

Lalonde, Marc, 188
Language, 29-33
  divisions, 30, 32
  and policy, 234
Language bills (Quebec), 219
Language rights, 234
Language of instruction, 224
Language policy, in public service, 234
Laurier-Greenway Compromise, 235
Law-making, 116, 117-119
LeDuc, Lawrence, 75
Left-Right continuum, 67, 75
Legislative Assembly (See Legislature)
Legislative committees, 117-120, 136-137
Legislative functions (See Law-making, representation and surveillance)
Legislature, 116
  and bureaucracy, 112
  committee (See Legislative committees)
  and expenditure-budget, 116, 124-125, 135-136
  professionalization, 116
  and regulation, 134
Legitimacy, 97
Lesage government, 163, 223
Lesage, Jean, 132
Levesque, Rene, 106
Liberal government (Manitoba), 278
Liberal Party:
  bases of support, 42-54, 57, 59, 62-65
  and cabinet reform, 103
  health policy, 210
  and ideology, 67, 190
  policy impact, 293
  provincial variations, 40
  and separate school support, 232
  (See also Parties)
Lowi, Theodore, 123
Lieutenant-Governor, 115, 129, 150
Lipset, Seymour M., 108, 114
Liquor control, 4
Local autonomy, 192
Low income families, 189

Lower Canada, 198
Lyon government, 293

Macdonald National Policy, 12, 21, 272
McMenemy, John, 67
MacPherson Royal Commission on
    Transportation, 1961, 274
Macro-policy goals, transportation,
    272
Mallory, J.R., 113
Management by objective, 107
Manitoba Development Corporation,
    24
Manitoba School Question, 219, 231
Management Board, 126
    (See also Treasury board)
Manning, E.C., 56
"Manufacturing Condition," 12
Manzer, Ronald, 74
Maritime Freight Rates Act, 1927,
    272, 274
Maritime Marshland Rehabilitation
    Act, 1948, 270
Marketing Boards, 130, 150, 270
Marsh Report, 181
Meanings of public policy, 2-3
Means test and pensions, 186-196
Medical Care Insurance Act, 1966,
    159, 164, 205, 211-213
Medical Insurance (See Medical Care
    Insurance Act)
Medical profession, 205, 212, 215
Medical resources, maldistribution of,
    238
Meisel, John, 50
Methods of policy, 178
Minister of Education:
    Ontario, 221
    Quebec, 233
Minority group autonomy and
    education, 232
Minority language rights, 223, 235
Mixed scanning, 123
MLA, 116, 118, 120
    (See also Backbencher, Legislature)
MPP (See MLA)
Mobility of disadvantaged groups, 272
Moncton, 235
Morin, Claude, 163
Mother's Allowance, 190, 192, 193
    (See also Federal welfare
        programmes)

Motor Vehicle Transport Act, 1954,
    273
Multipartism, 55, 64
Municipal affairs, 4
Municipal Doctor System, 203, 205
Municipal transit systems, 279
Municipalities:
    health policy, 199, 204
    social welfare, 181, 182, 189, 190,
        193, 196

National Adjustment Grants, 155, 166
National Assembly (Quebec), 64, 115
    (See also Legislatures)
National Energy Board, 263, 266
National Health Grants Prgramme,
    1948, 207, 213
National hospital insurance, 205
National minimum standards of
    service, 184, 237-239
    health, 208, 238
    education, 216
    welfare, 189-194
National policy, 12, 21, 272
National Transportation Act, 1967
    274-275
National Transportation Council, 275
National unity, and transportation,
    271-272
National Urban Transportation
    Development Corporation, 279
Nationalism, in Quebec, 75, 162
Native peoples and language, 234
Natural Products Marketing Act
    Amendment Act, 1936, 270
Natural resources, 28-29, 253, 254,
    255-262
    expenditure trends, 179
    and interest groups, 28, 254
    provincial comparisons, 28-29
    and redistribution, 268
    regulation, 179, 260
NDP:
    bases of support, 40, 42-54, 59,
        61-62, 63
    commitment to guaranteed income,
        188
    health policy, 206, 210
    innovation, 6
    and separate school support, 232
    (See also CCF-NDP, Parties)
Negative income tax plan, 197
Nelles, H.V., 72, 254

New Democratic Party (*See* CCF, NDP)
New France, 29
Non-sectarian school system, 229
Northern Affairs, Department of, 101
Northern Pacific Railroad, 278
Nuclear energy, 266, 268

Official Language Act (Bill 101,
    Quebec), 3, 31-32
Oil and Gas Conservation, Stabiliza-
    tion and Development Act, 1974
    (Saskatchewan), 264
Oil pricing and federal-provincial
    conflict, 263
Oil embargo, 255
Oil supply, 266
Old age pensions, 150, 237
    (*See also* federal welfare programmes)
Old Age Pensions Act, 1927, 186
Old Age Security Act, 1951, 186
Ombudsman, 131
One-crop economy, 21
One-party dominance, 56-57, 59, 61,
    64, 66, 114, 119
Ontario Committee on Government
    Productivity, 133
Ontario Economic Council, 167, 214
Ontario Hydro, 109
Ontario Medical Association, 204
Ontario Municipal Board, 4
Ontario Transportation Development
    Corporation, 1975, 279
OPEC, 255, 265
Operational policy committees in
    cabinet, 214
Opting-out, 121, 157, 193
    [*See also* Established Programmes
    (Interim Arrangements)]
Opposition in legislature, 114, 119
Organizational reform in health, 215
Olympic stadium, 2

Pammett, Jon, 75
Parent Commission, 223, 227
Parliament, provincial, 115
    (*See also* Legislatures)
Parliamentary parties, role of, 120
Participants, and natural resource
    policy, 268
Participation, provincial differences,
    79, 82-83
Partisan cleavage, and federal-
    provincial relations, 154

Parti Québécois:
    administrative, cabinet reform, 103,
        106
    bases of support, 42-54
    and constitutional issues, 151
    and language, 236-237
    policy objectives, 5, 57, 64, 67
Parties, 7, 38-69
    bases of support, 40-54
    electoral competition, 40, 54-66
    federal-provincial differences, 40
    functions, 38-39
    modernization, 41-42
    and natural resource policy, 268
    and policy impact, 66-69, 132, 293
    protest, 39, 40, 55
    recruitment, 39
Party in power and policy, 132
Party support:
    age, 50, 52-54
    ethnicity, 42, 46-50, 54
    occupational class, 42-45
    religion, 46-50, 54
    sex, 50-52
    subjective class, 42, 44-45
Party systems, 54-66
    three party competition, 62-63
    two party competition, 54, 56, 61,
        65-66
Patriation, 151
Patronage, 109, 110, 267
    in Atlantic provinces, 193
Patullo Government, 206
"Peace, order and good government,"
    150, 263
Peak organizations and policy impact,
    71
Personnel:
    growth of, 11
    management, patterns of, 111
    (*See also* Bureaucracy)
Penner, Norman, 69
Phillips, Paul, 277
Pluralism, 7, 8, 73
    (*See also* Interest groups, Pressure
    groups)
Pluralist conflict, 293
Planning Advisor to Cabinet (British
    Columbia), 128
Planning Board, Economic Advisory
    and (Saskatchewan), 107
Planning and Priorities Committee and
    budget, 127, 136

Planning, programming, budgeting system, 107-108,
  and change in budgetary process, 126
Poel, Dale, 68
Policy contagion, 69
Policy definitions, 2-3
Policy determinants, 5, 7, 66-69, 292, 294
Policy diffusion, 68
Policy disentanglement, 297
Policy flexibility, 6
Policy formation, and bureaucracy, 114
Policy goals:
  economic development, 132
  regional growth, 132
  social equity, 132
Policy impact:
  bureaucracy, 114
  socialism, 75
  study of, 4
  toryism, 75
Policy implementation, study of, 4
Policy innovation:
  and bureaucracy, 114
  and ideology, 193
  sources of, 68
Policy instrument, public ownership, 132-133
Policy legacy, 294
Policy machinery, 97-121
  growth of, 295
Policy ministers, 105
  (See also Policy secretaries)
Policy options and resource endowments, 259
Policy principles, 74
Policy priorities, interest groups, 260
Policy resources, limitations of, 5-6
Policy scope and institutional change, 97
  (See also Public sector)
Problem identification, 122
Policy types, 123
Policy-making capability and cabinet reform, 98
Political cleavages, 67, 76
  and pressure groups, 72
  and social class, 42-45, 97
Political forces, 38-96
  and federal system, 171
  as policy determinants, 292

Political interest, provincial differences, 76
Population characteristics:
  migration patterns, 17-19
  urbanization, 19-20
Post-secondary education, 225-228
  federal payments, 165
  funding of, 156
  impact, 238
  tax abatements, 162
Potash case (Saskatchewan), 132
Poverty line, 189
Prairie Farm Rehabilitation Act, 1935, 270
Premiers, 153
  and cabinet, 98, 102
Pressure groups, 7, 8, 69-74
  and bureaucracy, 111
  and federal-provincial relations, 154
  institutionalized groups, 70
  issue-oriented groups, 70
  models of influence, 73
  policy impact, 293
  producer groups and regulation, 129, 134
  provision of information, 122
Presthus, Robert, 72, 111
Principles of assistance:
  insurance, 185
  relief, 184
  universality, 185
Priorities and Planning, cabinet, 103
Professional model, regulation, 134
Professionalization (Legislative), 116
Programme Management Information Systems, 107
Progressive Conservative Party:
  bases of support, 42-54, 62, 64-67
  and cabinet reform, 103
  ideology, 40, 190
  policy impact (Ontario), 69
  and separate school support, 232
  (See also Conservatives, Parties)
Progressives, 62
"Project disentanglement," 296
Property taxes, source of revenue for education, 232
Prorationing, 265
Pross, A. Paul, 70
Protest movements, 55, 66-67
Protest Parties, and policy innovation, impact, 190

Protestant churches and education, 233
Protestant schools system (Quebec), 232
Protests, farmer, 271
Province-building, 8-13, 163, 294
  and bureaucracy, 109, 295
  executive dominance, 295
  and expenditures, 178
  federalism, impact of, 170
  and institutional change, 98
  and natural resources, 294-295
  and policy homogenization, 295
  socio-economic determinants, 32-33
Provincial development initiatives, 22
Provincial secretaries, 106
  (See also Policy ministers)
Provincial Secretary, Department of, 100
Public accountability and regulation, 134-135
Public Accounts Committee, 119, 120
Public Charities Act, 1921 (Quebec), 193
Public control, over resource mobilization, 253
Public Education Council, 233
Public health boards, 199
Public health insurance, 201, 205-212
  (See also Medical Care Insurance Act)
Public ignorance, regulatory agencies, 134
Public interest:
  activist state, 261
  conservation policies, 255
  regulation, 134
  representation of in transportation policy, 279-280
  resource policy, 254
Public Medical Care Act, 1946 (Saskatchewan), 205
Public opinion, 75-76
  beliefs about provincial politics, 1
  problem identification, 122
  and resource exploitation, 268
  (See also Ideas, political)
Public ownership, 262
  British Columbia Electric, 132
  CCF-NDP, 132
  Hydro-Quebec, 133
  Ontario Hydro, 132
  as policy instrument, 6, 278-279
  public utilities, 132

Sidbec, 132
Syncrude, 132
  transportation, 278-279
Public-private mix, transportation, 272, 276-277
Public protector, 131
  (See also Ombudsman)
Public sector, 162
  facilitative role for resource development, 255
  growth, 114, 178
  size and scope of, 8, 161
Public service, growth of, 11
  (See also Bureaucracy)
Public Welfare, Department of (Ontario), 192
Public works, 260
  Department of, 100

Quebec Industrial Development Corporation, 22
Quebec Pension Plan, 162-163, 184
Quebec School Allowance, 185
Question Period, 119
Quiet Revolution, 156
  denominational system, 233
  and education, 223
  educational conflict, 232
  and language rights, 32
  party support, 64
  social welfare, 193

Rae, Douglas, 55, 57
Railway Relocation and Crossing Act, 279
Ralliement Créditiste, 64
Rational policy-making, 107-108, 123
The Real Poverty Report, 197
Redistribution, 26, 182
  and welfare state, 238
Redistributive arena, 196
Redistributive policy, 123, 268
Reed Paper, 268
Regional development:
  impact of transportation policy, 280-281
  and resource policy, 257
Regional disparities, 24-26, 161, 165-168, 297
  and equalization, 159
  intraprovincial, 26
  and transportation policy, 272

Regional equity, and transportation, 271
Regional interests, 149, 154
  and province-building, 295
  and provincial consultation, 296
Regional Economic Expansion, Department of (DREE), 167-168
Regionalization of health, 214-216
Regina Manifesto, 1933, 206
Regulation, 17, 21, 191-192, 235
  agriculture, 291
  and cabinet, 136
  and federal-provincial relations, 161
  and legislature, 134, 136-137
  of medical profession, 205, 212, 215-216
  and policy, 3-4, 123, 131
  and producer groups, 134
  resource policy, 130, 179, 260, 267, 291
  transportation, 271-281, 291
  telecommunications, 130
Regulatory agencies, 133
  accountability, 135
  Canadian Transport Commission, 130
  Hydro Power Commissions, 130
  (See also Regulation)
Regulatory functions, 10-11
  (See also Regulation)
Regulatory issues, 133-135
Regulatory policy, 123, 133
  (See also Regulation)
Regulatory process, 128-132
Regulatory role and redistribution of income, 238
Religion, 29-33
  cleavages, 54
  and ethnic divisions, 64, 67
  impact on policy, 234
  and voting, 46-48, 64, 67
Religious and linguistic minorities, 236
Representative government, 116
Representation, 116, 120-121
  of public interest, 133-135
Reserve tax, 264
Resource bases, 255
Resource industries, 267
Resource mobilization and economic development, 253
Resource policies, 253-268
  compared with social policies, 292

Resource staples, export of, 254
Resource wealth, impact on provincial politics, 259-260
Responsible government, 7, 38, 98, 135
Revenues, 10, 32-33, 155-161
  equalization payments, 167
  and federal transfers, 164
  non-tax, 155, 160-161, 257
  per capita, 10
  and province-building, 33
  from resources (Alberta), 259
  resource taxes, royalties, 6, 264-265
  (See also Taxes and Transfers)
Robarts government, 211
Robin, Martin, 67
Rose, Richard, 5
Rowell-Sirois Commission, 152, 155, 166, 181
Royal Commissions, 113, 122, 260
  on Bilingualism and Biculturalism, 30
  on Consumer Prices and Inflation, 280
  on Dominion-Provincial Relations, 152, 155, 166, 181
    (See also Rowell-Sirois Commission)
  on Education and Youth, 233
  on Government Operations, 125
  on Health Services, 1961 (Hall), 210-211
  of Inquiry on Constitutional Problems (Tremblay), 163
Royalties, 264
Royalty surcharge (Saskatchewan), 264
"Rules of the game," 293
Ryerson, Egerton, 221

Schwartz, Mildred A., 75
Schools Act, 1850, 221
Schools Act, 1871, 221
School districts, 121, 232
  (See also Separate schools)
Schultz, Richard, 276
Scope of policy, 178, 294
Scope of public sector, 71, 109, 291
  (See also Public sector)
Secondary education and separate schools, 232
Select committees in legislature, 118
Selection, 122

Separatist sentiment and schools, 236
Separate Schools Act, 1863, 221, 231
Separate School System, 229-230, 232
  financial support for, 231-232
Service state, 291
Sex and voting, 50-52
Shared-cost programmes, 162, 163, 165, 182, 295
  (*See also* Conditional grants and transfers)
Simeon, Richard, 75
Smallwood, Joey, 56, 66, 102, 261
Smiley, Donald, 164
Social cleavages and education, 219
Social costs, of resource exploitation, 267
Social Credit Party, 6, 39, 57, 59, 61
  bases of support, 45
  ideology, 67
  policy impact, 104, 128
  (*See also* Political parties)
Social and economic conditions (*See* Socio-economic conditions)
Social development tax, 212
"Social learning" and bureaucracy, 293
Social policy:
  compared with resource policy, 292
  and transportation, 272-273
Social Security in Canada, 197
Social Security Review, 187
Social Services Bill (C-57), 188
Social welfare:
  and the Depression, 181
  reform, 198
  regulation and administration, 179
Social welfare policy:
  determinants, 190
Socialist ideologies, 132
Socio-economic conditions, 17-33, 171, 292
Socio-economic status and health utilization, 212
Solar, wind energy, 266
Special Senate Committee Report on Poverty, 1971, 187, 197-198
Stages of policy-making, 112
Stages of public sector growth, 291
  (*See also* Public sector)
Stanfield government, 261
Stanfield, Robert, 65
Staple economy, and transportation, 271
State intervention, tradition of, 254
State involvement, agriculture, 269

Stevenson, Garth, 73
Subsidies:
  natural resources, 260
  transportation, 271-272, 281
Supply and demand and energy crisis, 265
Support for aged, 121
Support for unemployed, 121
Surveillance, 116, 120
Swift Current Health Region, 205
Syncrude, 132, 259, 266
Szablowski, George, 105, 106

Task Forces, 113, 122, 260
  (*See also* Royal commissions)
Tax abatements, 156-157
  and health financing, 214-215
  as payment for social welfare, 237
  (*See also* Transfers)
Tax incentives, home ownership, 3
Tax room and health financing, 214
Tax system, impact, 238
Taxation:
  collection agreements, 151
  corporate tax, 155
  direct taxes, 155
  Federal-Provincial Tax Arrangements, 1952, 156
  impact of Depression, 155
  income, 259
  natural resources, 260
  personal income, 155
  property tax credits, 157
  rental agreements, 157, 161
  rental payments, 156
  resource income, federal revisions in, 263-265
  sales tax, 155
  tax burden, 164
  tax room, 165
  Tax-sharing Agreement, 1957, 166
  Tax-sharing Agreements, 1962, 156
  Wartime Tax Agreements, 1941, 156
Technical and Vocational Training Act (1960), 3, 217, 228
Tennant, Paul, 104
Terms of Union, 233
Territorial cleavage, impact of federalism, 169
Third parties, 57
  (*See also* Party systems)
Time limits on legislature, 117
Titmuss, Richard, 182

Trans Canada Highway Programme, 1950, 276
Transfers, 155-160, 165-170
  conditional grants, 24, 151, 165-166
  conversion from conditional to unconditional grants, 165
  impact on the scope of provincial policy, 169
  and provincial autonomy, 169-170
  statutory subsidies, 157
  tax abatement and shared-cost programmes, 151, 156-157, 168
  unconditional grants, 151, 165, 168
Transport Act, 1938, 273
Transportation, 271-281
  centre-periphery, 275
  Department of, 276
  development of trans-Canadian network, 21
  expenditure trends, 179
  federal-provincial relations, 275
  as federal responsibility, 149
  impact of regulation, 279-280
  in Atlantic provinces, 280-281
  infrastructure, 253
  and social policy, 272-273
Transportation and communication, 153
Treasury Board:
  and budget, 124-125, 127-128, 136
  and cabinet reform, 102-104
  and personnel management, 110-111
  rational policy formation, 107
  staff, 124
  (See also Management Board)
Treasury Board Secretariat, 136
Treasury, Economics and Intergovernmental Affairs (TEIGA), 102
  and policy reform, 106
Trebilcock, Michael, 135
Tremblay Commission, 163, 186
  and education, 223
Trudeau, Pierre Elliott, 101
Trucking industry, regulation, 273-274, 277
Tuohy, Carolyn, 74
Turner, John, 263
Two hundred mile zone, 262
Two-price system, 263-264

Unconditional grants, 157-159, 162
Uncontrollables, budget, 128
Unemployables, 197
Unemployment, 168

and fishery resource management, 262
and lack of exploitable resources, 261
Unemployment insurance, and federal power, 237
Union Hospital District, 203, 205
Union Nationale:
  abolition of Legislative Council, 115
  bases of support, 57, 64
  language and education, 236
  (See also Parties)
United Farmers, 62-63
University of Quebec, 223
Upper Canada, 198, 221
Upper Houses (former), 115
Urbanization, 19-20
  and public service growth, 33
  and taxation, 155
User costs, transportation, 281
User-pay formula, and social welfare, 188

Victoria Conference, 187
Vocational schools, 228

Wealth, 24-29
  income, 24
  natural resources, 28-29
Welfare state, 13, 21, 162, 180, 253, 276
  Canada compared to Europe, 237
  distribution of income, 238
  and economic development, 180, 182
  and education, 216
  and expenditures, 179
  health care, 199, 204
  and individual benefits, 291
  and provincial jurisdiction, 294
  and socio-economic determinants, 292
Weller, Geoffrey, 204-205
Western Economic Opportunities Conference, 1973, 275
Wheat, 21, 269
Wilson, G., 280
Winn, Conrad, 67
Winner case, 1951, 273
Working Party on Income Maintenance, 198
Working poor, 189, 197
Workmen's compensation, 4, 185, 192

Young Voyageur Programme, 152

5449